Secondary Progressions

TIME
TO
REMEMBER

Nancy Anne Hastings

SAMUEL WEISER, INC.

York Beach, Maine

First published in 1984 by
Samuel Weiser, Inc.
Box 612
York Beach, Maine 03910-0612

99 98 97 96 95 94
11 10 9 8 7 6 5 4

Library of Congress Catalog Card Number: 84-50243

ISBN 0-87728-599-3
BJ

About the cover: The progressions of life portrayed are from personal
photographs taken of statues that can be seen in Frogner Park in Oslo,
Norway. The artist, Gustav Vigelund, specialized in stone and bronze
sculpture. He was born in 1869 in Mandal, Norway, and died in 1943
in Oslo.

Typeset in 10 point Andover

Printed in the United States of America

The paper used in this publication meets the minimum requirements of
the American National Standard for Permanence of Paper for Printed
Library Materials Z39.48-1984.

CONTENTS

LIST OF CHARTS

FOREWORD

One of the most widely used predictive techniques in astrology is secondary directions, or progressions as they are also called. The basis of this technique is simple, although a bit mind-bending to those not used to the ways of astrology. One simply substitutes one day for each year of life after birth. If an individual is 30 years old, a chart is erected for 30 days after birth, examined both in its own right and compared to the natal chart as well.

As I have indicated, the rationale for this process is not immediately evident and I will go into a possible rationale below, but the important thing for the reader to grasp at this point is simply this: Secondaries are among the most widespread and useful predictive techniques in the astrologer's toolbox. Not only do most astrologers use basic secondaries, but also a number of related techniques such as tertiaries (day for a lunar month), minors (a lunar month for a year) and solar arc directions based on the motion of the secondary Sun. Yet despite the importance of the technique, there is relatively little in the astrological literature that deals comprehensively with secondaries. There are a number of books on the subject, although far fewer than one might suppose, but they tend to deal with the subject on a technical level—how to compute the charts, for example—or with technical refinements on the method. But most of the books, once they get to the point of giving you the chart, do not give you any decent idea of what to do with it. It is obvious from most of the books that one might want to look at aspects both within the progressed chart and also between the progressed and natal chart, but not much more is said. This leaves the student with a problem. How does one go from the details of the aspects forming in the secondary chart to an understanding of the evolution of the individual as a whole? There is very little aid for the student to answer this question.

Also, it is not at all obvious from the existing literature on the subject that there is a wide variety of tricks that astrologers actually use when dealing with secondary charts, tricks that enable the astrologer to separate the important from the trivial, or enable an astrologer to gain a perspective on an individual's entire life from combination of the birth chart with the progressed chart.

In this book, Nancy Hastings has begun to fill the gap, a gap which she will fill even more completely with a second book to follow up on this, one with more advanced techniques. In this book she concentrates on what I call the broad-brush techniques for using the secondary chart. Broad-brush techniques are ones that are used to get an overview of the entire picture, much the way an artist uses a broad paint brush to fill in the main elements of a portrait before using the finer brushes to fill in the details. Even though the broad aspects of a life must be understood before one can understand the details, previous authors have left out precisely the broad aspects from their studies of progressions. In the later book the author will fill out more of the detail work.

However, the techniques used in this book—the progressions of the Moon, the changing of element and quadruplicity emphasis, the changing of the chart's overall form, changing of hemisphere emphasis, and so forth—all enable the reader to look at a chart and its progressions and form a view of the overall pattern of the life. With each of the techniques that she explores, she gives comprehensive sample interpretations so that the student may compare the author's interpretations to real life observation and understand the usefulness of the methods from his or her own perspective. As Nancy, herself, has said in the beginning of the book, she and I do not always agree on methods. I would, personally, not always use the particular techniques that she has chosen to describe in this book. But that is not important. It is more important that competent astrologers set forth works like this one that enable the student to see what is actually done by practicing astrologers and evaluate the techniques for themselves. The methods set forth here are described in such a way that one *can* evaluate them. The writing and reasoning are both clear. One is not left confused about what the author is doing. This is the best that any astrologer can do in writing a book for students. If some persons following this book conclude that a particular technique does not work well for them, at least the technique was described clearly enough so that the student could make such a judgment. This may seem like damning with faint praise, but that is not the case at all. The kind of clarity that Nancy Hastings exhibits in this book is not at all common in astrological writing. She is to be commended.

However, lest I create a misimpression, this book is not limited to clear descriptions of methods, or to well-written descriptions of particular astrological indications. The case studies given in this book are also very important for several reasons. First of all, they show the methods in actual application. Examples always make an idea clearer.

Second, the examples show a counselling method in operation. The cases that the author gives are often persons with difficult problems, but no more difficult than most astrologers run into in a typical practice. Nancy Hastings is one of the few astrological writers who show how to deal with a problem head on, avoiding vague euphemisms and pollyanna slogans that one often finds in contemporary astrological literature. And yet she shows us this in a way that does not damage the spirit of the client, making it harder to cope with life than it already is. The message is to take control and to take responsibility, but not to give way to guilt and blame. One is not merely the product of one's parents' actions and misdeeds.

Third, and related to above, the examples are given with a warmth and humor that would strengthen one's ability to cope with life. Life is not always (or even usually?) easy, but somewhere at the heart of it there is the God within living in us and through us.

Fourth, the examples serve to point the way beyond the scope of the book, to more advanced techniques used with progressions and to integrating the progressed chart with the natal and transit charts. It is not possible to cover everything in a book of any size, but in the case studies one reads about methods and techniques which point the way for the student to do work on his or her own. They are presented sufficiently clearly so that it is not difficult for a student to learn from them.

At the beginning of this foreword I mentioned the inherent problem with secondaries, that they have no plausible rationale, at least none that is given in the astrological literature. The noted author and metaphysical theorist Arthur Young has commented in a private communication that secondaries, and in fact all systems of directions, are the most revolutionary techniques in astrology. Most of astrology could conceivably be given an explanation that would fit into the prevailing mechanistic, materialistic worldview held by most of modern science. But directions which imply a strong connection between one's first year of life and the first day defy conventional causal explanations.

Only a symbolic world-view in which symbolism has the same level of reality that science gives to energy and matter can serve to explain secondaries and other kinds of direction.

Secondaries and most other systems of direction involve substituting one kind of astronomical cycle for another. The day for a year system is the classic case. Primary directions in which the whole of life is encompassed in the first six hours or so after birth appear to be inconsistent with this idea, but they are not. As Charles Jayne has pointed out, they are simply double secondaries. Where secondaries substitute a day for a year once, primaries do it twice; that is, secondaries are a day for a year, primaries are a day for a year squared.*

It is as if the experience of one type of cycle, usually the day cycle, prepares for the experience of all other types of cycle. Something in us, as John McCormick once said in a lecture, counts, "One!" during the first day of life. On the second day it counts, "Two!" and so forth. As we experience our first year again there is a count, "One!" and the soul registers a parallelism between the first day and the first year, the second day and the second year, and so on. The only thing that matters is how important the cycles are, how powerfully we experience them. The day and year cycles are among the most powerful cycles that we experience. Therefore, substituting the day cycle for the year cycle is very plausible. The lunar month cycle (in which the Moon moves from 0° Aries to 0° Aries) is also important, so tertiaries which substitute days for months are also plausible. Minors which substitute months for years are plausible, but would not be as strong because the month cycle is not as powerful as the day cycle. So one would expect minors to be less important, which, as their name implies, is the case.

One important consequence of this idea is that it tends to reject certain systems of direction which have been in common use. One degree for a year measures, for example, have no astronomical or cyclical basis except that they are approximately the motion of the Sun in a single day, but that supports solar arc systems better than a degree for a year. Carter's symbolic directions suffer from the same weakness. In Ronald Davison's book, *The Technique of Prediction*, he proposes a day for a week and a day for a month progressions. Day for a week is approximately four times the rate of day for a lunar month, but not exactly. Insofar as the rate is not exactly a day for ¼ × lunar cycle, it should be inaccurate. Similarly, day for a month as he uses it is a day for 1/12 of a solar cycle, which is not quite the same as the day for lunar month used in tertiaries. It may work, but I would not expect it to be as powerful as tertiaries because 1/12 of the solar cycle is a much more abstract cycle than the lunar month. If one used a day for a calendar

---

*Secondaries are derived by multiplying the age of an individual in days by $1/365.2422$. Primaries come from multiplying the age in days by $1/(365.2422 \times 365.2422)$ or $1/13340.8647$.

month one would have a particularly worthless system because calendar months vary in length and do not represent any real astronomical cycle exactly.

Whether the theory that has been presented here is corrected or not will be shown by its ability to predict which systems of direction or progression work effectively. So far, it is working well. Secondaries and tertiaries should, according to this theory, be the most effective and they seem to be. Neither of Davison's systems seem to have caught on especially, although this may be due to conservatism as much as the techniques not having been found worthy. I have not found symbolic directions to be worth much of anything. Time will tell if there is anything to the idea presented here. I offer it only as a possibility.

In the meantime, enjoy seeing how at least one astrologer really uses secondaries. Astrology is too much a folk art handed down by oral tradition. We need more of it in writing like this.

Robert Hand
April 11, 1984
Orleans, Massachusetts

ACKNOWLEDGMENTS

The material I've written here isn't a new invention. It's the result of study from 1968-1982. It's from every class, workshop, convention I've attended as well as every book I've read. It's from my teachers, clients, and students. It's from the people who were overwhelmed by the first lectures I gave, when I was so defensive that I included at least five times as much information as anyone could absorb or use. It's from later lectures, in which I included less and explained it more. Although I can't possibly acknowledge everyone who helped write this book the following people were and are major influences on my astrological thought.

Oscar Weber was my first teacher and instilled in me a respect for correct arithmetic and logic. He also got me started using a separate progressed chart rather than simply writing the progressed positions around a natal wheel. He laid the foundation upon which the discussion of aspects is based.

Dorothea Lynde was my second teacher and I studied with her for a long time. She taught me the method of approach to a chart used in this book by convincing me to look at the forest first—noting chart shape, polarities of Sun, Moon, and Ascendant, the signature—before I got involved with aspects or houses. Dorothea also gave me invaluable human lessons about interacting with clients. If you've ever had your chart read by Dorothea, you have truly received a gift.

Although I've never taken any formal lessons from Frances Sakoian, I've attended her workshops, listened to her lectures, and read her books. Her energy level and knowledge are awe-inspiring. *The*

Astrologer's Handbook (Harper & Row, 1973) contains an incredible amount of coherent information for the beginner. If you haven't read it, you probably should.

Through A. Charles Emerson I met a new world of astrologers and astrology. He introduced me to midpoints, to a new symbology, and to countless other fine astrologers. He encouraged me to lecture by leading me to believe that I had something to say that other people might want to hear. Thank you, Charles.

I don't know how to thank Rob Hand. We've argued and shouted and agreed and disagreed ever since we met in 1974. We both privately think that some of each other's sacred cows are silly. Overriding all of this is a true respect and love for each other. He always assumed I'd finish this book. For that faith, I thank him.

Without Betty Lundsted, I'd have given up two years ago. She looked at the 1000+ pages of the original manuscript and promptly said "That's two books." Then she insisted on better writing. Then she yelled at me. Then she comforted me. Then she encouraged me for an entire year while I went through a painful separation and became nauseous every time I thought about the last chapter.

Without my two friends at opposite ends of the astrological spectrum—Betty and Rob—I could not have written this. I'd advise all of you to read the books written by both of these fine astrologers. They provide point and counterpoint to the understanding of the roots of astrological archetypes.

Finally, I'd like to thank all of the people in this book. They all gave me permission to use their charts in lectures, articles, books. Without them, I could not have written any of this. Almost all of them have had the opportunity to read over the material and approve it. All of the charts (with the exception of the arithmetic example, John Doe) are real people. The sources of their birth data are listed with their charts (mother's baby book, birth certificate, hospital records, oral tradition.) None of the charts used have been rectified.

Although it's not possible to acknowledge every person or author who has contributed to my background in astrology, I've included in the bibliography books which have helped me understand astrology as well as those which have directly contributed to the writing of this book. I hope that you can use this bibliography to round out your astrological library.

INTRODUCTION

I began my study of astrology in 1968. A teacher in a three-week introductory course said that an astrologer could tell if a person was handicapped, and what the handicap was, from the time and place of birth. Since one of my twin daughters (born eight minutes apart) was handicapped, I asked the teacher if she could tell me which daughter was handicapped and what the handicap was from the birth data. She said she could, and she did. Three years later I found out just how difficult that question had been to answer accurately.

During my first year of study, Oscar Weber taught me how to erect a secondary progessed chart, as well as how to interpret transits. In the secondary progressed chart, each day after birth represents a year of life.

Since I am a cardinal grand square on the angles person (six planets in cardinal signs), I had to see for myself. I looked at all the events of my life and the lives of my friends and relatives, which I shared with fellow students. Teachers, books, workshops, newspapers all gave us more birth information and dates of events. Accidents, hospitalizations, marriage, childbirth, rapes, robberies, illness, lottery winners—we students looked at them all. This kind of "hindsight astrology" (when you already know what occurred and when) is really an excellent way to learn the symbolism of various astrological techniques.

I've never believed that we're pawns of the universe, pulled here and there willy-nilly by an unseen force or fate. Pretty soon I wanted to be able to do something *before* difficult symbolism became exact in a chart. Thus I became more and more involved in predictive astrology, not to scare the wits out of people, or to impress them with my power to tell them what was going to happen, but to help them avoid being in the wrong place at the wrong time. I wanted to be able to help my clients go through their "major life lessons" (such as natal Pluto at 21°♋30′, progressed Mars 21°♑30′, progressed Sun 21°♎30′, transitting Mars 21°♈30′)without the help of a mugger. Good predictive astrology involves psychology, study of past cycles in the client's life (what did they do the last time something similar showed up?) and, hopefully, some suggestions about how to sidestep the worst manifestations of any particular combination of secondary and transiting aspects.

Before you can make any decision about what's likely to happen in a client's chart, you need to see whether anything at all is going to happen. This seems pretty basic, but I know quite a few astrologers who don't do this.

The two places to look for indications of events are the secondary progressed chart and the outer planet transits. Most folks who know any astrology at all look at the transits, so you're probably aware of the importance of transits of the outer planets. The combination of the transits with the secondary progression gives a pretty sure method of prediction. I can't say that this is a perfect method of prediction, for I've yet to find anything that can predict every event perfectly *ahead of time*. I've looked at and studied lots of techniques that have fine results in hindsight, but they are, by and large, simply too cumbersome to use in your daily astrological practice. Even if you were willing to devote ten or twelve hours to the work-up of each client's chart, you couldn't remember the details you'd uncovered well enough to make sense out of them. "Hindsight astrology" has its uses, and I don't want to throw out the dials and the harmonics and all the other intriguing techniques which the micro-computer has put within our grasp. However, for finding the target times for events, I've never found anything that could equal the combination of the secondary progressed chart and the outer planet transits.

This book is about secondary progressions. Since you really need to use the secondary progressed chart with both the natal chart and the transits to get anywhere in your predictive technique, just about all the examples include the pertinent transiting positions. You really shouldn't try to use any astrological predictive technique without reference to the natal chart. With the secondary progressed chart, you must have both the natal chart and the outer planet transits to predict accurately.

Now we come to the "why bother" part of the introduction. If you have to use the transits with the secondaries, why not just skip the secondaries and use the transits. After all, secondaries were invented when there weren't any ephemerides, and the poor court astrologer had to rely on his evening's observations for the positions of the five planets, the Moon, and his daily record of the Sun's motion. So it's pretty obvious why he liked to use a predictive technique which equated each day after birth to a year of life. The first two or two and one-half months (or maybe even three weeks) after birth could be recorded and used for all those years of the new baby's life. But now that we've got ephemerides and computers that will give us planetary positions ad infinitum, why would anyone want to revive the system of secondary progressions, which is so darn dependent on the correct birth time for accuracy?

If you wanted to drive from Boston to San Francisco, you'd probably write to the AAA or go to a store and get a map of the country through which you'd be travelling. This map wouldn't have too many details, just the major routes. What you would not do is write to each city and town that you'd be near and buy a street map. However, once you got to San Francisco, you'd go get a street map, so that you could figure out how to get around the city.

The secondary progressed chart will get you to San Francisco. You won't fiddle around investigating every week of your client's year; you'll hone in pretty quickly on the target weeks when events are more likely to happen. Once you've got the target weeks in your sights, you'll turn to your transit scan (computerese for drag out your ephemeris) and see what else is going on during these critical weeks. Now if your client has two trines from Pluto, Neptune miraculously doing nothing (not too likely, if Pluto is trining, but never mind that now), Jupiter is benignly sextile something and Saturn isn't even close to anything, the progressed Sun square natal Saturn probably won't amount to a big deal. (It'll be a great time to diet, though.) However, if the same progressed aspect occurs while Pluto, Uranus, Saturn or Mars is in the middle of squares (90°), semi-squares (45°), conjunctions (0°), or oppositions (180°) to the natal Sun or Saturn, you can be fairly sure something's going to give in this client's life. The forty-five degree and ninety degree aspects are all action-oriented, so you'll be right on target if you decide that yes, indeed, an event is likely.

So why wouldn't you do as well without the secondary? Well, first of all, most aspects of transiting Mars, for instance, don't signify big events. Some folks slide through Saturn aspects (except for hard aspects to the Sun) without much activity. Then they'll get to a little picky thing by transit and fall apart. You can be sure, if it's really a little picky thing by transit that one of two things is true. Either the secondary progressed chart is extremely active, with all kinds of aspects exact, or you don't have the right chart (wrong time given, wrong date copied, wrong year looked up, chart erected for outer Mongolia instead of Madison, Wisc. etc., etc.).

The second major reason for using secondary progressions involves understanding *what kind* of event is likely to occur. In the final chapter, the analysis of Marjorie Singer's chart demonstrates that although the transits indicate an event, only the secondary chart shows a high probability of marriage.

It's true that there are some years when practically nothing goes on in the secondary progressed chart. Maybe there are two aspects from the progressed Moon, and nothing else is active. That's fine. You'll know that twenty years from now, the client won't remember a whole lot about this year unless Pluto by transit is square his Sun, Saturn squares it, too, and everything else conjuncts somewhere opposing his Moon. But other than that happening, your client is probably going to have a pretty uneventful year. Years like this are years to build self-esteem, years to consolidate accomplishments, years to encourage your clients to explore the depth and breadth of their abilities and strengths.

The secondary progression can give you and your clients a fuller sense of the complete picture of a whole lifetime. There will be time to change and time to rest; there will be time that is forgotten and time that is remembered. As our lives follow the symbolism of our progressing Sun, we can learn through our own individual cardinal, fixed and mutable times that we can indeed share with others the tremendous gift of life and love.

1

FOUNDATION TRILOGY:

CHART ANALYSIS—THE FIRST STEPS

BEGIN AT THE BEGINNING

SUN, MOON, AND ASCENDANT

When astrologers meet for the first time, we tend to get around to the basic questions fairly quickly. Where is your Sun? Where is your Moon? What sign do you have rising? This information is the foundation trilogy, the three factors which give us the most information about another person. We may get to the more trivial factors of where you live, work, and play later, but first most of us like to find out who you are, how you feel, and how you approach the world. Analyzing a secondary progressed chart starts out just like the analysis of a natal chart, with the sign positions of the Sun, Moon, and Ascendant. Since everyone analyzes the foundation trilogy a little bit differently, I'm starting with a brief description of my view of these symbols. You will find it easier to understand my analysis of the effects of progressions if you know what I think about the basic symbols of astrology. Try it out; it may work for you, too.

WHO AM I?

The Sun symbolizes the basic life force and the physical body. If the Sun suddenly disappeared, so would all forms of life on Earth. Your natal Sun represents your basic life energy, and your progressed Sun represents the present manifestation of your energy. The Sun stands for your most basic, inside, underneath-it-all self. Sometimes this self is so protected and hidden that we don't really recognize it ourselves, and we insist that we are really nothing like the description of our Sun sign. Sometimes we recognize it all right, but see only the difficult parts of the symbolism, and spend our lives trying to be anything but the sign we are. Then sometimes we see that although we are jealous, possessive, stubborn, obsessive in love situations, righteous, materialistic and self-indulgent, we are also warm, nurturing, supportive, loyal and steadfast. Then we can own our Taurus Sun, accepting the beauty and the beast within.

HOW DO I FEEL?

The Moon symbolizes your emotional response nature, your feeling self. The Moon is no less important to life on Earth than the Sun, for if the Moon were to disappear, life on Earth would last a fraction of a second longer than it would if the Sun vanished. Earth and the Moon are more like a dual planet system than a planet and satellite, for the Moon is too large and close to Earth for Earth to exist without it. If the Moon somehow entered a time warp and left us, Earth would immediately leave its orbit around the Sun and break apart. Without our ability to respond on an immediate gut level we can't survive. If our Moon symbolism falls apart, so do we. We call this kind of falling apart a nervous breakdown. Some astrologers call the Moon the "soul" symbol, but that doesn't quite fit my definition of "soul." I think the Moon symbolizes the part of ourselves which somehow absorbs the inconsistencies of daily life, allowing us to stay on our path. When our natal and progressed Moon are in harmonious aspect, we deal with all kinds of problems with ease. When these two symbols are out of balance, even little difficulties can throw us into emotional turmoil.

HOW DO I SEE THE WORLD?

Our Ascendant (Asc), like the outside of our home or the front door of our apartment, is the portion we make visible to the outside. We can choose how we want this part of the self to appear. As we become adults, we choose where to live, and thus choose the environment within which we will function. Do we mow the grass, trim the hedges, paint the door? Do we let the paint rot, or the lawn grow weeds and brambles? Do we throw garbage in the hall? How happy are we with our front yard? Does it reflect our inner selves or is it an anachronism?

While the Sun symbolizes our inner self, the Ascendant symbolizes our outer self, our personality or persona. The Sun is the "me" inside, the Ascendant is the "me" that we let the world see. The Ascendant axis (which includes the Descendant) symbolizes our interaction on the Earth plane. The Ascendant part is the "me" we project into the world, how we act in our environment, while the

Descendant is the "not me" of the world, all the other people around us. Anything that aspects the Ascendant also aspects the Descendant, because this is an axis. We filter our view of the world through the Ascendant axis, and at the same time monitor what we put out into that world through the same Ascendant. The progressed Ascendant is the here and now environment and our current mode of interaction with and projection ito that environment.

OUR BALANCING ACT:

POLARITIES OF SUN, MOON, AND ASCENDANT

The combination of our natal Sun, Moon, and Ascendant symbolizes how well our front yard harmonizes with the inside of our houses. As our charts progress, we grow through stages of comfort and discomfort with our projection into the environment.

POLARITY

Each sign has a polarity. Aries is yang or masculine or positive, while Taurus is yin or feminine or negative. I prefer to use the terms yin or yang when describing polarity because these terms from Oriental philosophy accurately describe the energy involved without the bias inherent in the other two sets of adjectives. The terms masculine and feminine carry whatever sexual role imagery each of us has, and every human being has some ideas about sexual roles.

A predominance in one or the other polarity does not mean that you are dominated by the sexuality associated with that polarity. Women with the majority of their planets in masculine signs do not grow beards and smoke cigars. But men with the majority of their planets in masculine signs don't have to grow beards or smoke cigars either. The polarity which contains the majority of the planets has nothing whatever to do with the presence or absence of sexual apparatus, and apparently has very little to do with our choice of sexual partners (either same sex or opposite sex).

Masculinity or femininity is not decided according to whether you have seven planets in Aries or seven in Taurus. The man with seven planets in Taurus will be bullheaded, loyal, practical, and will still have a penis. The woman with seven planets in Aries will be impetuous, hot-tempered, and still have breasts and a vagina. The signs do not define sexual roles.

The terms positive and negative, also used to describe polarity, are, if anything, worse than the terms masculine and feminine. Positive and negative imply good and bad, qualities which are not described by sign. In our society, active and passive are also terms connoting good and bad, or strong and weak.

The definition of yin and yang does not involve good and bad. Yin, like Jung's term *anima*, is the receptive, responsive part of each person's psyche. Yang, like the Jungian *animus*, is the active, initiatory part of the human psyche. No human is without both parts, although we often try to suppress one or the other part of our being. If we can't utilize both male and female parts of our psyches, we are like a person with a broken foot. We must hop or use crutches to get around. Although we may cope with day-to-day life, coping is more difficult, for we can't use both legs for walking. Should a major life crisis occur, we are like a person with a broken foot in a fire. He has to use both legs to run, but one of them does not work well. If we cannot integrate our yin and yang internally, we are helpless when we most need to cope.

In chart analysis, polarity signifies the initiatory and response nature of the individual. Humans must both initiate action (or nothing can ever happen) and respond to action (or put up with chaos). Conflicts arise for us when polarities in the chart are mixed. Then we may try to initiate action and respond to action at the same time. Table 1.1 indicates the polarities associated with each sign.

In order to understand our own essential natures, we must understand the symbolism of the polarities of our Sun, Moon, and Ascendant. When your natal Sun and natal Ascendant are the same polarity, you find that you can easily express who you are. When your natal Sun and natal Ascendant are of different polarities, you have difficulty excusing your own social gaffes, as your projected ego (Ascendant) does not agree with your inner self (Sun). Thus, when you meet someone you haven't seen for twenty years, you remember that you spilled soda all over that person at the eigth grade dance. You still feel embarrassed, for you have not yet forgiven yourself for your clumsiness. Meanwhile, they've probably forgotten all about the incident.

As both your Ascendant and your Sun progress into different signs, your ability to accept yourself as a human being who is occasionally gauche or rude or maudlin varies depending on whether the polarities of the progressed Sun and progressed Ascendant agree or conflict. Whenever our progressed Sun is the same polarity as our natal and progressed Ascendant, we are quite confident in our approach to the world.

When both natal and progressed Ascendant differ in polarity from our progressed Sun (for instance, natal Asc 2° Leo, progressed Asc 25° Leo, progressed Sun 28° Cancer) we have quite a bit of difficulty overcoming a feeling of social unworthiness.

Table 1.1 Sign Polarities and Keywords.

	Polarity	Quadruplicity	Element	Keywords
♈	yang	cardinal	fire	Exuberant, fiery, impulsive, quick, initiates contact, self-starter
♉	yin	fixed	earth	practical, persistent, possessive, sensual, tenacious, retentive
♊	yang	mutable	air	verbal, mental, social, changeable, curious, versatile
♋	yin	cardinal	water	sensitive, emotional, clinging, protective, nurturing
♌	yang	fixed	fire	dominant, proud, regal, obstinate, generous, showy
♍	yin	mutable	earth	observant, disciminatory, logical, practical, flexible, critical
♎	yang	cardinal	air	companionable, diplomatic, conciliatory, indecisive
♏	yin	fixed	water	tenacious, deep, retentive, passionate, vengeful
♐	yang	mutable	fire	idealistic, expansive, optimistic, unrestrained, scattered
♑	yin	cardinal	earth	controlled, ambitious, cold, practical, cautious, responsible
♒	yang	fixed	air	reasoning intelligence, stubborn, anarchistic, unconventional, independent, humanitarian
♓	yin	mutable	water	emotional, intuitive, unclear, compassionate, sacrificing, fluctuating

When the polarity of our natal Moon is the same as the polarity of our natal Ascendant, we find that we can easily express how we feel. We recognize habitual response patterns and do not feel that these patterns are inappropriate in the environment. When our natal Moon is different in polarity from our natal Ascendant, we don't have as easy a flow of emotion.

If our natal Moon is yin and our natal Ascendant is yang, we may accuse ourselves of oversentimentality. A slightly different, but equally common, reaction to this combination is that we are quite sensitive and emotional, but try very hard to cover up this fact.

When the polarity of our natal Moon is yang and our Ascendant is yin, we may question our real emotional responses to situations. We may worry that we do not feel deeply enough about emotional situations. Whenever we respond to an emotional situation in our yin Ascendant manner, the yang nature of our natal Moon wants to do something about the situation. This is the dilemma of someone with the natal Moon in Leo and the Ascendant in Scorpio.

Since the progressed Moon changes signs every two years or so, the polarities of the Ascendant and the progressed Moon frequently change from compatible to uncomfortable. Of course, none of us goes through major emotional changes every two years.

Rather, the polarity of the progressed Moon signifies how we respond to current emotional issues. When the polarity of the progressed Moon and the natal Ascendant are the same, we tend to handle emotional periods through the symbolism of our natal approach. When the polarity of the progressed Moon is the same as the polarity of our progressed Ascendant, we tend to utilize the newer approach to the world in confronting present emotional issues.

When the polarity of the progressed Moon is the same as the polarity of our natal Moon, we feel more at ease with our response nature. When the polarity of the progressed Moon is the same as the polarity of our natal Sun, we feel more healthy because we feel an accord between our essential physical self (Sun) and our emotional nature.

Now that we've put the three basic components of the chart together, we need to take them apart again to examine each in greater detail. No part of a chart stands alone. Each relates to the whole. As you work with progressed charts, you will find that the importance of each individual symbol change varies. When a particular symbol is active by aspect or angularity (either to other progressed positions or to natal positions) that part of your life is more active. The progressed chart fills in the rest of the details of the natal chart. If the natal Sun is "Who am I?", the progressed Sun is "How do I grow?"

HOW DO I GROW?

THE PROGRESSED SUN

The sun progresses about 1° per day (which equals a year in secondary progressions), a little faster in the winter, a little slower in the summer.[1] Your progressed Sun shows your current manifestations of

---

[1] You can get a rough approximation of your progressed Sun position by adding your age to the degree of your natal Sun. (If your natal Sun is 15° Libra, and you are 25 years old, add 15 to 25, getting 40° Libra, which equals 10° Scorpio, the position of your progressed Sun. This method is pretty close for those born near the equinoxes (April/September) but not as accurate for those born near the solstices (December/June).

your basic life energy. By the time you are sixty years old, your progressed Sun has changed sign twice, because it has moved sixty degrees. Consequently, every initiator (cardinal person) goes through a period of finishing things as the Sun progressed through a fixed sign, and every changeable person (mutable) goes through a period of initiating activity as the Sun progressed through a cardinal sign. Given the current life expectancy in the United States, the majority of people will experience some form of all three manifestations of life energy (cardinal, fixed, and mutable) during their lives.

With this in mind, the prejudices of one sign for or against another sign assume significantly less importance. If you are a mutable Sun sign, (Gemini, Virgo, Sagittarius, Pisces) and can't seem to understand the fixed signs (Taurus, Leo, Scorpio, Aquarius) around you, wait a while. Sooner or later you will no doubt experience a certain stubbornness, a certain rigidity, a changed view of your opinion and your direction. Likewise, if you are a cardinal Sun sign (Aries, Cancer, Libra, Capricorn) and simply can't stand the constant changes of your Gemini acquaintances, wait. After your progressed Sun has spent thirty years in a fixed sign, it will progress to a mutable sign. If you spent those thirty years of fixed energy denouncing mutability, you may have a bit of a shock when you find yourself changing your mind more frequently!

The signs are not only separated into quadruplicities (cardinal, fixed, mutable) as mentioned above, they are also grouped by triplicity or element (fire, earth, air, water). The Sun takes about thirty years to progress through a sign. Half the people in the world have their natal Sun in the last fifteen degrees of their Sun sign. By the time these people reach sixty-five, the Sun by progression has entered the last of the four elements. These people have had the opportunity to experience their life energy in terms of fire, earth, air and water during one lifetime. Just think of the possible changes this makes in the natal chart! The differences between natal Sun signs become less distinct as each person matures.

If your natal Sun is in a fire sign, it will progress to an earth sign. Then your desire to express your nature by aggressive action becomes tempered by a recognition of your need to respond as well as by your growing need to assess the practical outcome of the action you take.

If your natal Sun is in an earth sign, it will progress to an air sign. By nature you are practical and well-grounded. The progression requires that you learn to express your ideas. You will be asserting your selfhood, allowing the yang side of your nature to appear.

When your natal Sun sign is air, the Sun will progress to water. You will begin to recognize your feelings as well as your ideas. The natal air Sun assures you of the ability to talk about what you think, and the progressed Sun in a water sign will bring you the opportunity to explore how you feel.

When your natal Sun is in a water sign, you are a feeling or emotionally-based person. As your Sun progresses into a fire sign, you can begin to see the need for action in your life. When you blend the symbolism of progessed fire and natal water, you realize that both aggression and receptivity are important in the expression of your life energy.

All people have a time for yin response and a time for yang action in their lives. In all people there is a time to begin things, a time to finish things, and a time to change approaches.

When your radical (or natal) Sun is in the first decanate (0-10 degrees) of any sign, you will manifest the energy of the natal sign for the first twenty to thirty years of life.[2] Obviously, a twenty to thirty year investment in being an Aries or a Pisces or an Aquarius is a significant contribuiton to the development of your self-image. When your Sun progresses into the next sign, you will not manifest a great change outwardly. As the progressed Sun moves through the first decanate of the next sign, the combination of the natal and progressed influences will gradually become more obvious.

In contrast, when your natal Sun falls in the last decanate (20-30 degrees) of any sign, your Sun progresses to the next sign during the first ten years of your life. Since you have not spent adolescence insisting on being true to the natal Sun-sign traits, it is usually easier for you to accept inner change and the eventual growth that can occur.

The last three degrees of any sign are special examples of the third decanate Sun. Some astrologers call anyone with the Sun in the last three degrees of a sign a "cuspal" birth. Although this may loosely explain the influence of the next Sun sign on that particular native's life, it is an incorrect usage of the word cuspal.

A cuspal birth really occurs while the Sun is moving from one sign to another. Since the Sun is 30′ of arc wide, and moves an average of 60′ per day, each year there are twelve different periods that last for twelve hours when the Sun is partly in each of two signs. An ephemeris will show the time when the center of the Sun crosses from one sign to the next. Therefore, for six hours before the time that the center of the Sun crosses the cusp and for six hours after the center of the Sun crosses the cusp, the Sun is actually in both signs. Anyone born during this period will have characteristics of both signs. Whichever sign has more of the Sun in it will be the predominant natal influence.

Regardless of the predominant natal influence, during the first year of life this Sun will progress into the next sign. For the next

---

[2] Decanates: Each sign can be divided into three groups of ten degrees, which are called decanates. The first ten degrees are the decanate of the sign itself. The second ten degrees are the decanate of the next sign in the same element, moving clockwise from the sign itself, while the third ten degrees are the decanate of the second sign in the same element as the sign itself. Thus 5° of Aries is in the Aries decanate, 15° of Aries is in the Leo decanate of Aries, and 25° of Aries is in the Sagittarius decanate of Aries. In the same manner, 5° of Scorpio is in the Scorpio decanate of Scorpio, 15° of Scorpio is in the Pisces decanate of Scorpio, and 25° of Scorpio is in the Cancer decanate of Scorpio.

thirty years, the influence of the progressed Sun will be that of the sign following the cusp.

For example, a person born with the Sun at 29°♈55′ is an Aries. Most of the Sun (20′ of the 30′ diameter) is in Aries. In true Arian fashion, this native will rush in "where all others fear to tread." However, once in a situation, this person will also display a practicality about how to finish the matter (or how to extricate himself from the matter!). This is the Taurus influence of both 10′ of natal Taurus and the whole progressed Sun.

In a similar vein, the person with natal Sun at 29°♏50′ is as persistent, deep, and secretive as someone with Sun at 1°♏. But the Sagittarius overtones of the late Scorpio chart will allow this person to poke fun at some of the overintensity which a Scorpio readily displays.

On the other side of the cuspal fence, someone with the Sun at 0°♎1′ has 14′ of arc still in Virgo. This little bit of Virgo can give an underlying practicality often missing in a Libra Sun sign. The hint of Virgo can sometimes lead to a desire for "fairness" which exasperates the most patient parent. When you have to weigh the pieces of cake in order to insure that each sibling got the same amount, "fairness" has gone too far!

Before we leave the discussion of the Sun sign, we need to look at the position of Mercury relative to the Sun. Mercury symbolizes how you think and act. The sign that Mercury is in thus defines the external manifestation of your conscious mind. Mercury can be in the sign before the Sun, the sign after the Sun, or the same sign as the Sun.

When Mercury is not in the same sign as your Sun, you may experience a type of identity crisis, because the way you think and act is not always in harmony with your essential inner nature. For example, if you have the Sun in Taurus and Mercury in Gemini, you may vow to have your mouth sewn shut, because the taciturn nature of your Taurus Sun is often at odds with the more verbal nature of Mercury in Gemini.

When Mercury and the Sun are more than twenty degrees apart (the maximum angular separation between these two is 28°), others find it hard to know you. You are likely to let others see only what you want them to see about you. Of course, this grows out of your difficulty reconciling the inner and outer manifestations of your nature.

If you have Mercury in the sign behind the Sun, it is either direct, or if retrograde, about to form a station and turn direct. By the time you are a young adult, Mercury will be moving quite rapidly in direct motion. You will be assimilating new ideas, trying out new modes of thought, and maturing mentally all at the same time. You may find that you wish you could slow down a bit, for often this terrific mental pace leaves you longing for the simpler time when you did not know who you were!

At the opposite extreme are those who have Mercury at maximum orb before the Sun. For you, Mercury will probably turn retrograde by progression, or may be retrograde at your birth. During your childhood, progressed Mercury and your progressed Sun are approaching each other very rapidly. Contrary to popular superstition, you probably don't stutter, nor are you incapable of communication because you have Mercury retrograde in either your natal or progressed chart. Rather, you are looking inward for the means to understand both your communication and the communication of others. As you mature, you begin to recognize your unique inner self. If your progressed Mercury retrogrades to the same sign as your natal Sun, you'll gain insight into why you are the way you are. Sometimes Mercury never retrogrades into your Sun sign. When this happens, you always have a hidden depth, a secret self, which few but the closest friends ever see.

Since Mercury and the Sun progress at different rates, all of us have at least one period during our lives when our progressed Sun is not in the same sign as our progressed Mercury. These periods are times of transition.

Transition periods are essential in our lives. We are all subject to a certain amount of habit formation. We get used to ourselves behaving in a certain manner, thinking in a certain manner, being in a certain manner. It would be quite disconcerting to go to bed on Tuesday, an Aquarius through and through, and wake up on Wednesday, a Pisces!

Whether it is before or behind the Sun, the progression of Mercury aids in the transition from one self-image to a new self-image. When Mercury progresses to the next sign before the Sun progresses to the next sign, we have time to become accustomed to thinking in a new manner. If the transition is from cardinal to fixed, we have time to explore persistence, time to decide how stubborn we want to be in certain matters, time to finish things. We can be reasonably comfortable with our cardinal side, for the Sun has not yet progressed into the fixed sign. By the time the progressed Sun joins the progressed Mercury in the fixed sign, we've thought about a change in self-image. We don't feel the change as a radical expunging of old concepts, but as a welcome recognition of a somewhat different self.

When our progressed Sun moves into the next sign before our progressed Mercury does, we are really getting ready for a change in ourselves before we are consciously aware of our growth. If, for example, our Sun has progressed from a fixed sign to a mutable sign, while our progressed Mercury remains in the fixed sign, we may insist that we still think exactly as we did a number of years earlier. Nonetheless, we find ourselves in situations which demand flexibility, situations which confound our logic and defy our conscious thinking process. Sometimes we back up and handle the matter in a fashion consistent with our natal positions. At other times we find ourselves settling the matter in an entirely new fashion. As Mercury joins the Sun in the mutable sign, we find that we are more comfortable with our ability to adapt to new situations.

As you compare a progressed chart to a natal chart, the sign positions of the Sun and Mercury, both progressed and natal, give you information about the combination of inner self and conscious manifestations of self. Who you are and what you think are not always the same. The differences between these ares of life are keys to self-awareness, and, consequently, keys to growth.

YOU CAN'T BLAME YOUR MOTHER

THE PROGRESSED MOON

The position of the progressed Moon is second in importance only to that of the progressed Sun. The Moon moves at an average of twelve degrees per year in the secondary progressed chart. Thus in two and a half years, the progressed Moon aspects every natal and progressed planet and angle as it moves through an entire sign. The Moon symbolizes our emotional gut level responses to our experiences. The progressed Moon mirrors our periods of stress and our periods of pleasure.

If you use nothing from secondary progressions but the positions of the progressed Sun and the progressed Moon, you can increase enormously the amount of information you can get from the natal chart.

The progressed Moon is almost always involved in major life changes. Cycles of emotional growth can be charted by the movement of the secondary progressed Moon.

The first half of the progressed Moon cycle seems to be the most difficult. After the first opposition, which occurs between ages thirteen and fifteen, you've been through all of the possible aspects between progressed and natal Moon, except for the conjunction. You tried most of these changes out on Mommy before you took your show on the road.

If for some reason, Mommy is not available for you, you try out these changes on the nearest nurturing female adult. Some of this learning spills over to your relationship with Daddy, although that relationship is more often characterized by a combination of the progressed Moon and transiting Saturn.

AGES AND STAGES:

CHILDHOOD

Between birth and adolescence, the progressed Moon traces your emotional response and your reaction to your own growth. The stages of growth indicated by the position of the progressed Moon clearly demonstrate the child's participation in the parent-child relationship. A careful study of the progressed Moon during childhood can show how the child elicits response from the parent as well as how the parent can best respond to stress from the child.

Yes, stress from the child. When we finally outgrow the effects of the first opposition (referred to as the "Adolescent Trauma" by many psychologists) we can recogize our own part in the struggle for emotional maturity.

Not only do all children have the ability to influence the adults around them, this interaction is essential for the growth of the child. Studies of children cared for in orphanages or hospitals where there is little or no interaction between the adults and the babies indicate that without close interaction with adults, many children stop eating, stop growing, and a disproportionate number of these children sicken and die in spite of the fact that they often have better medical care and a better diet than children not institutionalized.[3]

A newborn baby has a remarkable repertoire of behavior patterns which are used on the adults in its vicinity. At this point in the baby's life, the baby responds to emotion clearly and immediately. Is Mommy upset or harried? Baby will cry. Is this uncle really afraid to handle baby? No matter how uncle tries to soothe baby, baby fusses until safe in the hands of someone who is not apprehensive. If there are several newborns in the same room, they are either all peaceful or all crying, for as soon as one baby becomes distressed and starts to wail, the others alert to this emotion, and one-by-one join the chorus.

During the first two to two and one-half years of life, you experience aspects to every planet in your chart from your progressed Moon. You learn how Mommy responds to your actions. During the next two to two and a half years, you try out a whole different set of aspects as your progressed Moon is in the next cycle. Now the baby with the cardinal Moon tries out stubbornness, and the baby with the fixed Moon tries out whining. The baby with the mutable Moon tests the results of demanding action.

The difference between separating and approaching aspects from the Moon are immediately obvious during infancy.[4] Since the Moon

---

[3] See Bowlby, John, *Maternal Deprivation*, Basic Books, New York, 1969.

[4] A separating aspect is any aspect which was exact at some time before birth, e.g., ☽ 15° ♉ is separating from a square to ☉ 10° ♌ and approaching a square to ♀ 20° ♌. An approaching aspect is any aspect which has not become exact at the time of birth, e.g. ☽ 15° ♓ is approaching a sextile to ☉ 20° ♑ and separating from a sextile to ♀ 10° ♑.

progresses at roughly one degree per month, all of your approaching aspects will be perfected by the time you are a year old.[5] Most of us don't remember what happened during the first year of our lives, but sometimes we can get this information from our parents. Sometimes the first year was so traumatic for our mothers that they really don't remember much about it.

When a mother has been taught that she is the sole cause of her baby's behavior patterns, and then delivers a child with difficult approaching Moon aspects, the results are often emotionally devastating for the mother. Mothers of children with this type of chart (for example, ☽ 10°♑, ♂ 13°♈, ♅15°♋, ♄ 12°♎, ♆ 16°♎ should revive the use of the word "colic." "Colic" simply means crying for no apparent reason. Baby is fed, dry, been bubbled, and otherwise healthy. However, for a certain number of hours every day, baby cries. When Mommy gets extremely tense due to the crying, she may become angry with the baby. Since this is not an acceptable response to a new baby, Mommy feels guilty and inadequate. Then Mommy's behavior starts to mirror the difficult aspects in baby's chart. If this mother can realize that her baby needs to work out internal conflicts, and that these conflicts are not necessarily either her fault or her responsibility, then this mother can hire a babysitter during the baby's fussy times.

Of course, there are those who will argue that this, too, plays into the difficult aspects of the child's chart, for Mommy is not available during the daily times of stress. The people who argue this side the loudest are either men or people who had children with difficult separating aspects and approaching trines.

Those who have difficult separating aspects and easy approaching aspects from their natal Moons are more often described as "placid" or "calm" infants. Although mothers of these children often have just as many personal problems as the mothers of the children with difficult approaching aspects, mothers of babies with easier approaching aspects are more confident in their mothering role. After all, their babies do not spend large portions of their waking hours screaming.

Sometimes these two different types of children are siblings. The same person, Mother, will not behave in the same fashion to both children, because the two persons, the children, are not the same. Each infant elicits a response pattern more consistent with its own natal Moon position. In this section we will discuss the specific meaning of each stage of the first progressed Moon cycle.

---

[5] Some people use orbs of over 12° for the Moon approaching, which would mean that the approaching aspects could take more than a year to perfect. (The progressed Moon moves between 12 and 16 degrees a year.) I don't use orbs this big myself, because the effect of the larger orbs seems quite diffuse. If there are no close aspects in a chart, the larger orbs do work. When there are a large number of very close aspects in a chart, looking for the effect of the large orb aspect is a little like listening for the harp in a rock band. The close orb aspects will totally drown out the wider orb aspects.

In the process of becoming fully realized human beings, we have to let go of the "fix-the-blame" syndrome. Part of the process of maturing is realizing our own contribution to our childhood problems. We don't do this so that we can assume more guilt or wallow in self-pity. We did not make our parents alchoholic or abusive. Rather, the process of examining the first twenty-seven years through the progressed Moon cycle allows us to recognize the legitimacy of our own needs and how we go about satisfying those needs.

THE FIRST SEMI-SEXTILE

Between the ages two and two and one-half, the progressed Moon forms a semi-sextile (30°) to its natal position. The Moon has changed sign by this time, and some of the disruption of routine and emotional response has already become obvious. The baby who has his natal Moon in earth or water (yin polarity) sheds some of his sensitivity and begins to act out more aggressively, demanding his own way, as his Moon enters fire or air (yang polarity). The baby with her natal Moon in fire or air (yang polarity) withdraws from strangers and begins to whine. Then, just as Mommy started to understand what makes this baby tick, the progressed Moon aspects all of the natal planets from the next sign. All of the natal squares are now forming trines or sextiles. The fussy baby is starting to become more responsive! All of the natal sextiles (60°) are now forming squares (90°) or semi-sextiles (30°). The easygoing baby is starting to explore the "No-No's" of the world. Natal trines (120°) are forming squares (90°) or inconjuncts (150°), finding tension where none formerly existed. Natal oppositions still cause tension, for these aspects are forming inconjuncts to the natal positions.

The "terrible two's" are not too difficult to understand when the progressed Moon is analyzed, although understanding the two year old and living with him are often quite different proposals! Parents need to realize that they don't have to be drawn into the conflicts which the two year old sets up. In particular, mothers should recognize that 1) the behavior of the child is not always Mom's fault; 2) the behavior is temporary; and 3) Mom does not have to accept atrocious behavior. Somewhere between abuse by neglect and abuse by beating lies the middle path which parents must take to retain their own sanity while raising civilized human beings.

THE FIRST SEXTILE

Fortunately for the survival of the human race, the difficulties symbolized by the semi-sextile and changed aspects to natal positions yield to the ease of the sextile. Between ages three and six, the progressed Moon enters the second sign from the natal position. (See Table 1.2 on page 17.) The aspects now formed are more compatible

Table 1.2. Aspect Changes: Age Three to Six

Natal conjunction	→	Progressed sextile
Natal semi-sextile	→	Progressed square
Natal sextile	→	Progressed trine or conjunction
Natal square	→	Progressed inconjunct or semi-sextile
Natal trine	→	Progressed opposition or sextile
Natal inconjunct	→	Progressed inconjunct or square
Natal opposition	→	Progressed trine

with the natal aspects. The polarity (either yin or yang) of the sign that the progressed Moon is in during this time is the same as the natal Moon's polarity. Although there may be some residual conflict during this time, most children become quite nice for these few years. Both boys and girls try to imitate Mommy or whomever cares for them during the day. This age tries to sweep, tries to dust, tries to help pick up. If Mommy has gotten over the cross two year old stage, she can encourage the helping. The sextile is, after all, a working aspect.

The progressed Moon actually sextiles its natal position during the fifth year. As the sextile comes closer, boys start to concentrate on imitating Daddy, and they try to treat Mommy exactly the way Daddy treats Mommy. Girls also step up their imitative behavior, particularly in their responses to Daddy. The five year old girl wants to do whatever Mommy does to make Daddy happy.

THE FIRST SQUARE

Your Moon progressed to the first square (waxing)[6] to its natal sign when you were between five and seven and a half years old. This symbolized your first serious attempt to disengage emotionally from Mommy. Depending on the other aspects made by your progressed Moon while it was in the sign square its natal position and approach-

---

[6] Waxing and waning aspects: An aspect is *waxing* when the two planets are moving away from conjunction and towards opposition. An aspect is *waning* when the two planets are moving away from opposition and towards conjunctions. If you place the slower planet in the Ascendant position, the waxing aspects will occur below the horizon, between the first house and the seventh house, while the waning aspects will occur above the horizon, between the seventh house and the Ascendant. A waxing sextile is the same as a third house sextile; a waning sextile is the same as an eleventh house sextile. A waxing square is a fourth house square; a waning square is a tenth house square. The tone of the two types of aspect is slightly different. A third house sextile involves communication on a mundane or daily level, and siblings or neighbors; while an eleventh house sextile involves groups or long term goals. A fourth house square, connected symbolically to the roots of your being, is likely to indicate a tension

ing the square to its natal position, you may have started right away to separate your feelings from Mommy's feelings, or you may have waited until your progressed Moon made the exact square to its natal position. The actual square usually takes place between ages seven and eight and a half.

Hounding mother seems to be the principle activity we all pursue during the time of the first square from the progressed Moon to its natal position. Since we all respond with a combination of natal and progressed influences, during our first square we shift quickly from yin to yang, from receptive to active, in our response patterns. As confusing as this is for us as children, it is even more confusing for our mothers, who have to cope with us through both these expressions of emotion. How well your mother dealt with your inner turmoil depended on how well she handled her own emotions. If your first square occurred while your mother was in the middle of a crisis in her life, you probably did not get too much understanding from her. If your Mom was not under other stresses when your first square was exact, she may have realized that this was an obnoxious stage that you would probably outgrow. Then she could allow you to work out your own problems without assuming that your problems were all her fault.

The ways in which we created the tenison which allowed us to separate our feelings from Mommy's feelings were as varied as we are. Each of us combined the symbolism of our natal Moon, its aspects and position, with the symbolism of our progressed Moon, its aspects and position. Not only did we combine the aspects within our own charts, we interacted with our mothers in a manner symbolized by the synastry ties between our chart and our mother's chart.

Natal Cardinal Moon First Square: When your natal Moon is in a cardinal sign, you initiate most of the conflict situations with your mother. You are not always obvious about stirring up emotions, but you don't like to leave an unsatisfactory situation alone. You are posititve that dissatisfaction will not go away unless something is done about it. You will get the action you want whether it takes screaming or sulking. You are not particularly flexible, for you only like change when you have initiated it. When the result of your action is not exactly what

---

that will surface over and over again in your life. Dorothea Lynde called the fourth house square a "stumbling block." In contrast, the tenth house square often involves a problem which appears in childhood. Once you have recognized the tension area indicated by this square, you can use the energy productively in your life. When the tenth house square is activated in adulthood, you can learn from the problem and use your knowledge to further your own growth. Thus a tenth house square is a "building block." In the same manner, a fifth house trine involves your own personal pleasure, while a ninth house trine involves your philosophy of life. A sixth house inconjunct involves your tendency to put yourself at the service of another, and an eighth house inconjunct is usually connected to your beliefs about your own sexuality. In general, waxing aspects involve the self and personal interactions, while waning aspects involve the outer world.

you anticipated, you can become quite aggrieved and blame Mom for inconsistency.

Natal Fixed Moon First Square: You hate to let go of emotions. Although you rarely initiate conflict, you have great difficulty letting an emotional conflict die. As your mother is a human being, she will not always be fair, just, or reasonable. Since you latch onto your feelings so strongly, you may set up a cycle of brooding about how Mom really hates you. If you work at this hard enough, you may get the result that you expect. Then you can spend a lot of time and money when you are an adult trying to unravel your alienation from your mother.

Natal Mutable Moon First Square: Flexibility is your forte if your natal Moon is in a mutable sign. You swing from feeling absolutely awful to feeling buoyantly optimistic. During the first square, your moods change so rapidly that Mom may give up trying to keep up with you. You can set up a cycle of "Mommy doesn't understand me" which may result in quite a bit of resentment. If you can remember the happy feelings as well as the unhappy ones of this age, you can avoid the pitfall of blaming Mom for all your negative feelings (a phenomenon called transference).

PROBLEMS WITH THE FIRST MOON SQUARE: A CASE STUDY

Anthony Martin (Chart 1 on page 20) illustrates some of the issues which are often associated with the first square. The problems of the first square are somewhat exaggerated since Anthony's chart indicates a rather difficult personality.

Anthony's Sun and Ascendant in Libra are yang polarity, his Moon in Virgo, yin polarity. His nature is outgoing, he can express who he is more easily than he can recognize how he feels. The Mars-Pluto conjunction (within 1' of arc) indicates extremely strong passions, possibly rage, tremendous will and aggressive ability. The conjunction is in the twelfth house, so Anthony's parents will impose many strictures against any open display of this major energy pattern. As he grows, Anthony may not recognize his own desire to completely change the things around him. Because the conjunction is within 15° of the angle in a cadent house, the conjunction will be visible to the rest of the world whether or not Anthony ever acknowledges its

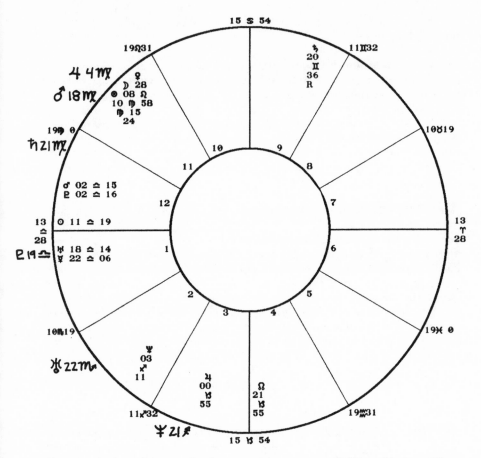

Chart 1. *Anthony Martin: October 4, 1972, 7:01 AM EDT, 42N17, 71W14; data from birth certificate; Placidus houses.*

energy.[7] The Sun-Ascendant conjunction shows that Anthony's inner ego and outer persona are the same. He has no mask to hide behind. Uranus conjunct this Sun-Ascendant from the first adds creative will, but also adds the expectation that the environment is subject to sudden change and disruption. If there is no chaos within the environment, Anthony will create it. This could lead to a rather brilliant ability to alter the world around him in adulthood, but in childhood this desire to rebel will be a source of irritation to all the others who have to share space with him. Uranus also confers a belief that he is unique (or odd) and that others won't understand him. Mercury in the first house conjunct Uranus points out the importance

[7] Gauquelin, Michel, *Planetary Heredity*, Paris Planete, Paris, France, 1966.

to Anthony of communication, an importance underlined by six planets and the Ascendant in air signs.

Anthony's Moon has only a separating square to Neptune (some confusion about feelings and about his relationship with his mother) and a separating trine to Jupiter (generosity—needed with Uranus pivotal on the Ascendant—and an ability to bounce back emotionally when difficulties hit.)

Parenting Anthony, with all of the assertive self-will indicated by his running conjunction in Libra across the Ascendant will not be easy. Because the Moon is not particularly afflicted, his main problems should not come from his mother, but his Moon-Neptune square shows that he may transfer the blame for his emotional upheavals to his mother.[8]

Anthony's early years were quite difficult. As his progressed Moon conjuncted his Libran planets, various physical difficulties surfaced. Anthony had tumors on his tongue and throat which were surgically removed when he was sixteen months old. The tumors made speech difficult. Although Anthony can now make himself understood, he has a speech defect. Anthony had twenty-two ear infections between the ages of fourteen months and three years. At three years of age, his mother took him off all dairy products, and the ear infections stopped. During this time he could not hear. At eighteen months, Anthony had to have root canal work done on his front teeth which were damaged when he was pushed down by a strange child in the park.

Because Anthony has six planets in air, communication is extremely important to him. For many years, his mother was the only person who could understand his speech. This created a dependency situation against which he raged furiously. In May 1979, Anthony's progressed Moon squared his natal Venus (28° Leo 58'). Anthony's parents separated, beginning what was to be a long, difficult divorce proceeding. Anthony had school-related problems, and problems with his peer group. As his progressed Moon entered Sagittarius, the sign square his natal Virgo placement, Anthony started to focus his anger on his mother. He demanded constant attention, interrupting her whenever she was involved with anyone other than him. He would disrupt telephone conversations, either by actually picking up an extension telephone and interrupting the conversation or by creating an emergency situation in the house (overflowing the sink, spilling things, fighting with his sisters) which forced his mother to abandon her own conversation and pay attention to him. Anthony did not care

---

[8] This analysis is not a complete analysis of Anthony's chart, nor is it in any way an indication of how he will choose to use the energies symbolized in his chart in the future. I don't know whether he will choose to use his strengths and talents to become a brilliant humanitarian, an anarchist, an unconventional businessman or a lawyer. He is from an upper middle class background, so his options probably include college. However, I've restricted this analysis to presently known behavior.

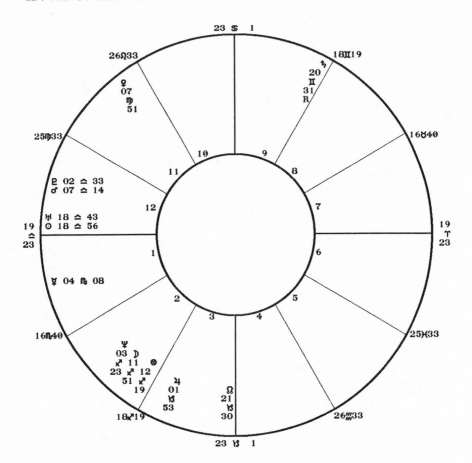

Chart 2. Anthony Martin: Chart 1 progressed to June 19, 1980 using the Sun's mean motion in RA for the MC.

that the attention was negative. In fact, he seemed to demand negative attention. While Anthony's progressed Moon was in the first degrees of Sagittarius, his progressed Sun conjuncted his natal, then his progressed Uranus (see Chart 2). He started to yell back at his father (a heretofore untried method of displaying anger). His relationship to his two older sisters deteriorated rapidly when he started to hit them, kick them, and throw things at them. Although his mother was taking him to a therapist, his behavior patterns did not improve. In many ways it seemed that the Martin family was under seige from an almost uncontrollably rageful little boy.

There was no definable "event" which marked the actual square from Anthony's progressed Moon to his natal Moon. Rather, this was a peak of his hateful behavior patterns. By June 1981, when Anthony's

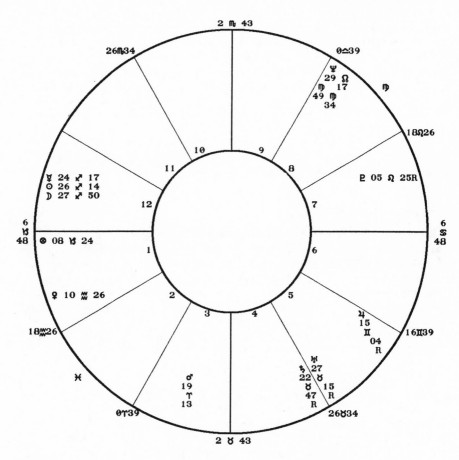

2 ♏ 43

26♏34

0♎39

♆
29 ♌
♍ 17
49 ♍
34

♍

18♌26

☿ 24 ♐ 17
☉ 26 ♐ 14
☽ 27 ♐ 50

♇ 05 ♌ 25R

6
♑
48

⊗ 08 ♑ 24

6
♋
48

♀ 10 ♒ 26

♃
15
♊
04
R

16♊39

18♒26

♅
27
♄ 22 ♉
♉ 15
47 R
R

26♉34

♓

♂
19
♈
13

0♈39

26♉34

2 ♉ 43

Chart 3. Beverly Martin (Anthony Martin's mother): December 18, 1941, 8:00 AM EST, 42N23, 71 W14; data from family records; Placidus houses.

progressed Moon started to conjunct his mother's Sagittarius conjunction of Mercury, Sun, and Moon (see Chart 3), the irritation between them was subsiding. Anthony's mother, Beverly, is quite patient and quite intelligent. However, it would have taken more than patience and intelligence to live through this period with an essentially wild child without some irrational response from his mother. Anthony may choose to remember these periods when he is an adult and parade them as proof that his mother was not perfect. As a fairly uninvolved bystander, I have the highest regard for Beverly, who handled this period with her son with amazing patience.

Because of his speech problems, Anthony had a greater than usual need to establish his independence from his mother. His mutable natal and progressed Moon symbolized rapid changes in behavior. Anthony's mood swings became a family legend. Aunts, uncles, cousins, and grandparents offered advice and sometimes offered help. Everyone had to live through the difficulties.

Although Anthony's behavior was extreme, his exaggerated patterns are basically typical of the patterns most of us go through during the first square. Most of us limit the tantrums to occasional outbursts; most of us limit the mouthing off to muttering. We all do feel some of the rage that Anthony expressed.

Despite the obvious differences in response from one person to another, during the first square there are certain similarities between people who have their natal Moons in the same quadruplicity.

THE FIRST TRINE

When you are between the ages of eight and twelve, your progressed Moon enters the sign trine its natal position.[9] This is a time for integrating emotional response patterns. All of your feelings flow more easily during the trine aspect. You get along better at school and at home because you tend to focus on the nicer aspects of all your emotional involvements. This time is similar to the sextile, and imitative behavior again becomes obvious.

By this time, there is a greater difference between the imitative behavior of boys and girls. Neither boys nor girls are ready to interact very much with peers of the opposite sex at this stage. So boys usually concentrate on learning how to make the most prominent female in their lives (Mommy) happy. Boys may try to treat Mom the way they see Daddy or other men treating her, particularly if these interactions seem to please her. If Mom is separated or divorced, boys at this age may become extremely protective and/or possessive of her.

Girls, on the other hand, are modelling their emotional responses on the patterns they think they see in their mothers. When mother and daughter have extremely different response patterns, the daughter's perception of mother's emotions may bear little resemblance to her mother's reality. Since the trine tends to idealize and smooth out friction, the concept of reality is relatively meaningless at this time.

---

[9] The energy of a trine aspect is expressed through the triplicities or elements (fire, earth, air and water) because these are third harmonic (120°) divisions of the chart. Thus, in any general description of trine aspects, astrologers use the elements, not the modes or quadruplicities (cardinal, fixed, and mutable) which are fourth harmonic (90°) divisions of the chart. When we look at the relationships between the Moon's trine aspects, we are looking at the Moon from a different perspective. Your natal Moon position shares some characteristics with other Moon signs in the same triplicity: fire sign Moons resemble each other in some ways, just as water sign Moons resemble each other. The shared characteristics are different in the elements from the characteristics shared by the quadruplicities. An Aries natal Moon shares cardinal attributes with Cancer, Libra, and Capricorn Moon positions, while the same Aries Moon shares fire attributes with Leo and Sagittarius Moons. For further information on modes and elements, see Lundsted, Betty, *Astrological Insights Into Personality*, Astro Computing Services, San Diego, California, 1980.

FIRE SIGN MOON

Your fire sign natal Moon indicates an active yang expression of emotion. Although some astrologers say that fire Moon people repress emotion (in the way men are taught to repress feelings), I don't agree with this analysis. You do something about your feelings, usually immediately. You admire people who can think about their responses, but since your Moon is fire, not air, you usually think about your responses after the whole thing is over. People around you may not notice this later-on thinking, because unless you have something else in your chart that indicates strong verbal ability (Mercury's position is a key here) you won't talk about your feelings. The common thread for all fire signs is expression, but each of the three does it a little differently. Aries flares up with emotion, then releases or forgets the issue. Leo displays feelings, then tends to hang on. Sagittarius idealizes response patterns, often changing expression during emotional times.

Natal Fire Moon First Trine: During the first trine from your progressed Moon to your natal Moon, boys adore and admire Mom, actively bringing gifts. Girls see Mom as active and warm. Both sexes base their emotional response patterns on an idealized initiatory role. These kids give praise lavishly, seeking the same in return.

EARTH SIGN MOON

Your earth sign Moon is yin, responsive, grounded. You are usually not emotionally volatile, for you absorb emotions before acting on them (hence your reputation for practicality). In spite of the inherent stability of your earth sign Moon, you can become obsessive about certain response patterns. The three earth signs usualy choose different areas of obsession. Taurus, where the Moon is exalted, is often described in such glowing terms that all other signs can only envy the Taurean Moon. But if you have a Taurus Moon and you can't satisfy your nurturing needs through relationships, you can become extremely possessive, jealous and quite materialistic. Your Virgo natal Moon can indicate a constant examining of motive which often leads to guilt. After you've got the guilt, you can decide whether to hang onto it or give it to someone else. If your natal Moon is in Capricorn, you have the dubious pleasure of finding mostly negative definitions of your Moon sign in astrology books. Because you have a huge sense of responsibility for your feelings, you tend to categorize them as "bad" or "good." Your particular obsession is control—you want to be in control of your feelings all the time, so that you can avoid "bad" feelings.

Natal Earth Moon First Trine: During the first trine from your progressed to natal Moon, boys become practical and nurturing. Girls try to internalize their perception of their mother's pattern of nurturing. This is a time for popsicle stick hot plates, decorated juice can pencil holders, potholders and paperweights. These kids give in order to gain physical strokes.

AIR SIGN MOON

Your air sign Moon is yang, initiatory, expressive. To other people it often seems as though you would rather think about feelings than actually feel the feelings. You admire people who can act on their feelings, but since you are air, not fire, you want to think and act all at the same time. You are most comfortable when you can analyze emotions, both your own and the emotions of others. Then you can compare your own response pattern to that of other people. The common thread between the air Moon position is a secret fear that you don't feel your feelings the way other people do. If you have an Aquarius Moon, you constantly weigh, sift, and compare so that you can decide that you really are weird, or decide that other people are not so very different from you. Gemini Moon people need verbal interchange to define your rapidly changing feelings. When you understand the "why" behind your response, you can accept your response. If your Moon is in Libra, you are looking for emotional equilibrium. You may alter your own responses to provide peace and quiet, for the whole point of your analysis of feeling is to find out how to balance emotions.

Natal Air Moon First Trine: During the first trine from your progressed to your natal Moon, boys try to intellectualize and thus solve all of the problems they think Mom faces. Girls recognize Mom's logic and attempt to duplicate this sensible approach to emotion. These kids make wall hangings, pictures, and poetry (if their scout leaders don't interfere!). Air sign Moons want to be appreciated for their intelligence.

WATER SIGN MOON

Your water sign Moon is yin, responsive, and very powerful. You feel emotion completely, and to other people you may seem to avoid thinking at all whenever you are emotionally involved. That's not quite true, for you tend to take in emotion and go over and over your own responses and the responses of those around you. Of all the triplicities, water Moon people have the strongest need to give and receive nurture. When you don't get enough physical stroking, you can turn your needs inward. Then the Cancer Moon can become the smothering mother (or father, or lover), the Scorpio can become the jealous fanatic, the Pisces can become the escape artist. When you develop relationships which allow you to physically display emotion, your water Moon shows up as intuitive, sensitive and sympathetic.

Natal Water Moon First Trine: During the first trine from your progressed to natal Moon position, boys develop extraordinary sensitivity, often exhibiting extreme protectiveness towards Mom. Girls adopt their own version of the flowing sensitivity they perceive in Mom. Often water sign Moon kids become cuddly or romantic. These kids want to be comforted and protected.

ADOLESCENCE

PROGRESSIONS AS INDICATORS OF GROWTH

Most of us would prefer to forget the details of our early adolescence. Astrologically, there are excellent reasons for our memory avoidance. Between the ages of ten and twelve, the progressed Moon makes its first inconjunct to its natal position. This inconjunct marks the beginning of our emotional transition from childhood to adulthood. Then between the ages of twelve and fifteen, the progressed Moon opposes its natal position. Finally, between ages fourteen and sixteen, the progressed Moon makes the second inconjunct to its natal position. All of us have had between four and six years of some inner turmoil.

Of course, not all of us have horrible experiences during early adolescence. The more favorable aspects the progressed Moon makes to both natal and progressed positions other than the natal Moon, the easier the transition time seems to be.

Nonetheless, all of us do go through similar stages of change between ages ten and sixteen. During the first inconjunct, we remove Mom from the pedestal we constructed while the progressed Moon trined its natal position. The opposition symbolizes both separation of our feelings from Mom's and comparison of our feelings with the feelings of others. The second inconjunct brings the tension between our own feelings and the feelings of others into sharper focus, adding a certain amount of sexual tension.

In this section, we'll divide the adolescent years into the three focal times symbolized by the progressed Moon. Each focus has different sources of and slightly different solutions to its problems.

THE FIRST INCONJUNCT

The first stage of adolescence begins between ages ten and thirteen when the progressed Moon is inconjunct its natal position. Since the natal Moon is stationary, this is a sixth house (or waxing) inconjunct. The sixth house overtones symbolize the tension between our resistance to the concept of service and our humble acceptance of an underlying position while our own distinct emotional personality emerges. Since the inconjunct aspect is associated with tension rather than action, our feelings alternate between yin and yang, between self-awareness and self-abasement. We are often emotionally touchy and vocal; the extent of this is determined more by the signs and other apsects involved than by the presence of the inconjunct alone. This aspect doesn't tell us what causes the stress, only that stress is likely. Causes are usually indicated by transits (particularly outer planet transits) or aspects formed between the progressed Moon and natal positions other than the Moon. (The example used for the first inconjunct, Derek, on pages 29-32, shows some of the kinds of aspects which can trigger off the tension of the progressed Moon inconjunct natal Moon.)

Most of us not only take out this tension on Mom, we accuse her of starting it. After all, she is the one who bosses us around. She is the one who will not believe that we are not infants any longer, and if she will not play our game, we agitate and aggravate until she has to holler and set limits. Then we are justified in our persecution complexes.

The higher and less realistically we built Mom's pedestal during the years that our progressed Moon was in the sign trine our natal position, the further Mom falls from glory during the inconjunct. We feel betrayed, as if it were Mom's fault that she does not live up to our own concept of the ideal mother. Now we notice all of the flaws in Mom's emotional patterns. Most of us determine that we will never, ever, behave in the manner we so dislike in mother.

Obviously, the tenison of the inconjunct is preparing us for our own independence. Unless we find something wrong with Mom's response patterns, we cannot justify adopting our own unique responses. Until we can see the differences between our feelings and Mom's feelings, we cannot freely choose our own emotional pathways.

Since the first inconjunct is within the inner-directed first half of the progressed Moon's cycle, you have little tolerance for Mom's needs. You cannot pay too much attention to the tensions and demands on your mother at this time without making yourself guilty over your growing need to be independent.

Guilt is a weapon chosen by countless generations of mothers to keep the tensions of adolescence from totally disrupting the fabric of daily family life. Whether you choose to internalize the guilt depends more on you as an individual than on the particular method your mother uses to generate guilt.

Natal Cardinal Moon First Inconjunct: Your first inconjunct involves a mutable progressed Moon. You face the problem of wishing to initiate action while your feelings about everything are rapidly changing. You often alternate between storming and sulking. Unless you have quite a bit of natal fixity elsewhere, you need limits from your parents. But you fight rules at every opportunity.

Natal Fixed Moon First Inconjunct: Your first inconjunct is from a cardinal sign. You want to initiate action while clinging to fixed natal response patterns. Unless your parents can develop quite a bit of flexibility, you can dig a hole of negativity, a huge bad mood, from which you will be extracted with great difficulty. You really want to be able to move into areas of independence without having to change any of your response patterns.

Natal Mutable Moon First Inconjunct: Your first inconjunct involves a fixed progressed Moon. Now you want to take a stand on how you feel. You want to be taken seriously and to take yourself seriously. You are tired of the inconsistency you perceive in your mother. You will use any capitulation as ammunition, bringing it up every time you disagree over any issue. She let you stay up until midnight last Tuesday. Why can't you stay up until midnight every night?

TENSIONS AND THE INCONJUNCT
A CASE STUDY

Chart 4 on page 30 (Derek Hadley), illustrates how the tensions of the first inconjunct can be exaggerated by other aspects from the progressed Moon and difficult transits from the outer planets.

Derek is an extremely bright boy who lives in an upper middle class suburb. He is the third of four children. His father and mother are both high-powered business executives. His father travels quite a bit, leaving the childrearing to Derek's mother.

While Derek's progressed Moon trined his natal Moon, the outer planets moved into very difficult aspect to Derek's natal Moon-Mercury opposition. Transiting Pluto conjuncted Derek's Mercury, opposing his natal Moon, and transiting Uranus inconjuncted Derek's natal Moon. In spite of these aspects, the trine period was quite calm, and in fact fairly happy for Derek. He was in the sixth grade, in a school system in which the sixth through eighth grade students attend the same school. Following a fairly common pattern for this suburb, Derek decided to "go with" one of the girls in his class. He carried her books around school and sat next to her in all the classes that they shared. She went to his house for dinner; he went to her house for dinner. All through this period, he did very well in school. His progressed Moon was effectively counteracting the negative symbolism of transiting Pluto and Uranus.

Although Derek and his mother argued, the disagreements were of the type common in most families. Even these arguments calmed down when Derek's progressed Moon conjuncted his natal Jupiter and his natal Venus.

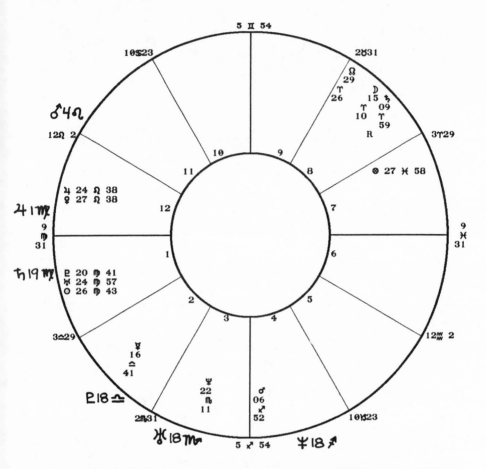

Chart 4. Derek Hadley: September 20, 1967, 5:14 AM EDT, 41N13, 73W04; data from birth certificate; Placidus houses.

The ease of the trine period came to an abrupt end when Derek's progressed Moon reached 7° Virgo and squared his natal Mars. At this time his girlfriend got tired of doing exactly what he told her to do. She decided to break up with him. Derek became more and more angry. He harrassed the girl on the phone and at school. Both Derek's mother and the girl's mother became infuriated. When Derek's progressed Moon was within one minute of arc to the square to his natal Mars, he accosted the girl in school. He slammed her against the wall and punched her a few times.

Derek would not let go. Although the girl by now refused to talk to him, he stepped up his verbal abuse, expanding it to include all of her friends. Soon none of the girls in school would speak to him. Derek further increased his verbal abuse, alienating most of the boys in the school. As his progressed Moon moved closer to the inconjunct

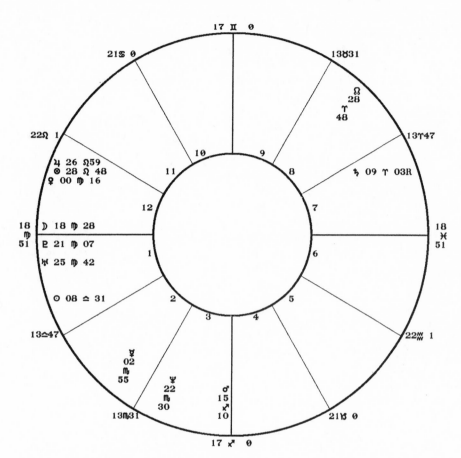

Chart 5. Derek Hadley: Chart 4 progressed to October 2, 1979 using the Sun's mean motion in RA for the MC.

with his natal Saturn, he was suspended for muttering vulgarities at the female teachers at school.

His situation at home had deteriorated to constant fighting with his mother (see Chart 6 on page 32). Pauline tried every possible approach. Mother and son went to a therapist. Although this helped define the power struggle between mother and son, no therapy can immediately remedy any situation. Pauline tried firmness, punishment, isolation, and any other approach which might work. Derek fought with everyone.

Derek's progressed Moon actually inconjuncted his natal Moon on July 13, 1979. In October (Chart 5) when his progressed Moon was 18° Virgo, transiting Saturn was 19° Virgo, transiting Pluto was 18° Libra, transiting Uranus was 18° Scorpio, and transiting Neptune was 18° Sagittarius. Derek was suspended for punching another girl who had

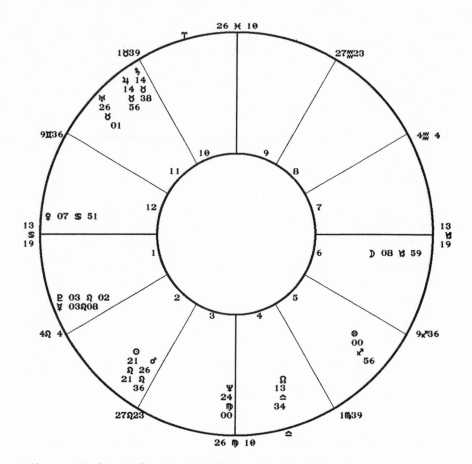

Chart 6. *Pauline Hadley (Derek Hadley's mother): August 14, 1940, 3:45 AM EDT, 36N19, 82W21; data from baby book; Placidus houses.*

laughed at him when he asked her to "go with" him. After this incident, Derek's hostility became more focussed on his mother, to her consternation and the relief of the school authorities. Derek's father finally become involved in the situation when Derek became physically abusive towards his mother. With the intervention of his father, Derek calmed down, at least externally.

THE FIRST OPPOSITION

As the inconjunct moves toward the opposition, your attention starts to shift from Mom to other people. If you chose to internalize massive doses of guilt during the inconjunct, you face the inevitable tension involved in interacting with others from a fearful or apologetic position. If you tempered your guilt with self-acceptance (a very rare condition among thirteen year olds) you tend to balance your needs against the needs of others you encounter. But if you totally rejected any guilt or responsibility for the tension of the inconjunct, you may be insensitive to the needs of others. In this last instance, you may blame everyone else for all the upheavals in your life and see other people as responsible for your happiness or misery.

The opposition is an action aspect, in contrast to the inconjunct, which usually symbolizes tension. The inconjunct prepared the way for the opposition by bringing to light the flaws in the emotional relationship between you and your mother. By the time your progressed Moon actually opposes its natal position, you should be asserting your independence from Mom. This does not have to involve shouting matches or other outward manifestations of rebellion. All too often, though, this is exactly what happens between you and your parents during the opposition year.

It is pointless to argue whether your mother was overly protective, for instance, or whether you subtly forced her into this position. If you can let go of the concept of blame, you will be able to forgive both your mother and yourself for the pain involved in leaving the relative safety of childhood.

The example for the opposition is Ann Martin (see Chart 7 on page 34), older sister of Anthony Martin whose chart was used for the first square. In contrast to both previous examples, Ann's opposition symbolizes a relatively easy transition through adolescence.

The synastry between Ann's chart and her mother's chart (see Chart 3, page 23) is complex. Although Ann's Sun opposes her mother's Sun-Moon-Mercury conjunction in Sagittarius, Ann's Moon sextiles this same conjunction. Ann's Mercury squares both her own Mars-Moon conjunction and her mother's Mars. While these powerful ties could symbolize friction, the aspects shared by mother and daughter indicate the understanding each has of the difficulties the other faces in daily life. Ann's trine from her Sun to her Mars-Moon conjunction reflects her mother's trine from the Mercury-Sun-Moon conjunction to Mars.

Ann has an easy flow of feeling and an ability to act on feelings, symbolized by this Sun trine the Moon-Mars conjunction. Fire and air signs in general get along well, since each of these triplicities admire the yang attributes of the other. Further, Beverly's Sun-Mercury conjunction amplifies the normal fire sign respect for intellect. Thus she enjoys her daughter's ability to intellectualize feelings.

When Ann's progressed Moon opposed her natal Moon (Chart 8 on page 35), it trined her mother's natal Mercury-Sun-Moon conjunction in Sagittarius as well as sextiling Ann's own natal Sun. This combination led to an unusual amount of understanding between mother and daughter. Ann does have her times of moodiness as well

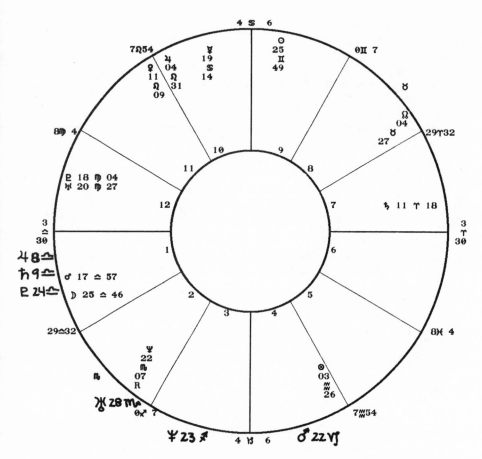

Chart 7. Ann Martin: June 17, 1967, 1:21 PM EDT, 42N22, 71W03; data from birth certificate; Placidus houses.

as her times of rebellion. However, Beverly did not find Ann's behavior during the opposition particularly difficult. Part of the ease Beverly perceived was undoubtedly due to the fact that Anthony, her son, was so terrible during the same period. Between the divorce and Anthony's atrocious behavior, Beverly simply did not have the time or energy to play into the usual adolescent games. Left without a sparring partner, Ann did not appear to be possessed of a need to increase the chaos.

Natal Cardinal Moon Opposition: You establish independence quickly during the opposition. The dictum of the cardinal Moon is "Do something!" The yang Aries-Libra axis tends towards fireworks, for you are bouncing back and forth between "do" and "think." In any

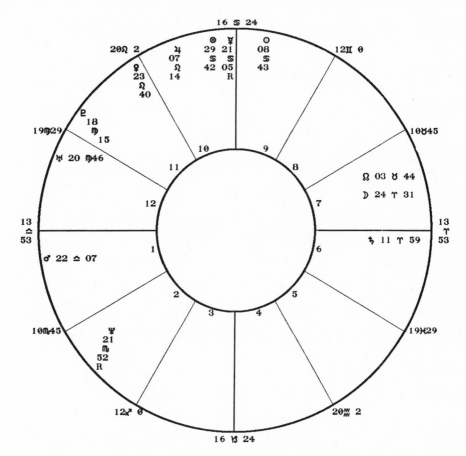

Chart 8. Ann Martin: Chart 7 progressed to December 20, 1980 using the Sun's mean motion in RA for the MC.

given situation you can choose to either shoot from the hip (expressing the Aries first) or vacillate without making any decision (expressing the Libra). If you choose the Libra, you can then explode with the Aries if the decisions made by others in the face of your vacillation do not please you. If you choose the Aries expression first, you can switch to Libra expression to smooth ruffled feathers. After you have acted, you can reason and even agree with the other point of view. Thus you can totally disarm the other side, achieving your aims along the way. The yin Cancer-Capricorn axis is usually involved in quieter assertions, because you are trying to decide what to do about guilt. If you choose to express the Capricorn side, you accept total responsibility for everything, becoming the greatest martyr in the world, but you don't tell anyone about this. Your silent suffering is partly due to a fear that you really are responsible for everything and partly due to a Capricorn desire to be in control of all your responses. If you choose the Cancer side, you let others know about your emotional trauma while you try to get them to feel guilty about hurting you. Of course, you refuse to let go of any of your hurt feelings.

Natal Fixed Moon Opposition: You move slowly but relentlessly towards your own independence. The fixed Moon says "Persist!" and you do. The yang Leo-Aquarius axis often rebels loudly and argumentatively. When you are in the Leo mode, you leap into the fray, defending your position with all the strength you have. When you choose to use the Aquarius response pattern you may be secretly afraid that you are a little weird, but, nonetheless, you are determined to have your own way and will argue with anyone who wishes to change your position. The yin Taurus-Scorpio axis simply seizes independence by doing and feeling exactly as it wishes to feel, regardless of what Mom (or anyone else) says about it. This axis holds to world's record for procrastination, silent rebellion and passive resistance. If you choose to respond with the Taurus side, you may say "Yes, Mom" while you go on about whatever you were going to do anyway. Later on, if you are still in the Taurus mode, you'll try to get out of any difficulties by giving Mom a hug. If you decide to express the Scorpio side, the most you will say is "in a moment." Of course, the moment never comes. Then when Mom gets angry, you unleash the full fury you've stored up from every single hurt you can remember. Scorpio can remember hurts going back to birth. In this way, you can remind Mom of her own less-than-perfect parts. After you have levelled a volley against Mom, you retreat to your room, exuding such a black cloud of hurt feelings that no one in their right mind would dare intrude. Should Mom by now be out of her mind with anger, you will greet any more words from her with total silence.

Natal Mutable Moon Opposition: You dart one way then another, discovering independence by surprise during your journeys. Your mutable Moon says "Try it!" The yang Gemini-Sagittarius explores unceasingly and vocally. While you are in the Gemini mode, you have something to say about all your feelings and your feelings are likely to change in the middle of your explanations. Further, as you swing back and forth between Gemini and Sagittarius, you can change the topic so quickly that your Mom may not even notice that you've done it. Then the scolding turns into a discussion of the relative merits of various kinds of discipline. While you are in the Sagittarius expression, you'll get in a few licks about totally irrelevant but much larger emotional concerns. Thus you can completely stop the conversation with the assertion that "they'll probably nuke the world anyway, so all this is stupid." If that works, you have a whole new ball game, and by the time Mom remembers what it was she wanted to say, you've been gone for at least an hour. The yin Virgo-Pisces axis examines each feeling in minute detail. You are more critical of yourselves than any other sign combination. Although you have the mutable trait of changing the subject, you personalize this change of subject. If Mom says "Your shirt is dirty" you hear "You are dirty." Then if you choose to express the Pisces side of this axis, you rush off to your room or out the door, leaving Mom to wonder what set you off. If you choose to use the Virgo expression, you immediately tell Mom that she always picks on you, while you worry about why she said you are dirty.

THE SECOND INCONJUNCT

The last aspect in the adolescent group is the second inconjunct. Just as you start to reach an equilibrium in your ability to interact on an emotional level with others, a new source of tension—sex—enters your life. The second inconjunct is an eighth house, or waning inconjunct. An eighth house inconjunct is no more of an action aspect than the sixth house inconjunct was. Thus it merely symbolizes a growing awareness of your own sexuality. Whether or not you choose to become sexually active during this period (between ages fourteen and sixteen), sex will become part of your emotional life.

If you've become insecure about your own worth as a human being, you may find that during the second inconjunct you are more likely to be involved in self-destructive behavior patterns. For many people this is an actively rebellious stage. Fast cars, various drugs (alchohol, marijuana, etc.), cigarettes, and sex all can add up to an extremely confusing and difficult time. Of course, not everyone experiments with all or even any of these things during the second inconjunct. But nearly every one of us at least wonders about this forbidden world, for we see our peers trying out these things.

The general description of the quadruplicites that follows may not seem to be accurate for you. Many of you work through the second inconjunct from your progressed Moon by dating someone who strongly projects the qualities of the quadruplicity of your progressed Moon. Very often, this is your first love. This is an extremely important part of the maturing process, for through this relationship you can learn about your own response patterns, tensions, and conflicts.

Natal Cardinal Moon Second Inconjunct: Your second inconjunct involves a fixed progressed Moon. Your habit of initiating emotional responses runs into a block here, as you deal with the conflicting desire to maintain the status quo. The progressed position shows that you want to hang onto your response patterns, at least long enough to be sure about how you feel. At the same time, your cardinal natal

Moon wants to get on with things. You may become quite fixed in your emotional responses to sex.

Natal Fixed Moon Second Inconjunct: While your progressed Moon is in the mutable sign inconjunct your natal position, the only absolute in your emotional life is that your feelings will change. The harder you try to hang onto old habit patterns, the more the situations around you will demand flexibility. When you depend on Mom to say you can't go to a party, she'll turn around and say you can go, ruining your excuse. When you really do want to go somewhere, you can bet she'll say no.

Natal Mutable Moon Second Inconjunct: Your Moon has progressed to the cardinal sign inconjunct its natal sign. While part of you is still "going with the flow," another part wants to start on new ventures. Further, your cardinal progressed Moon wants to decide between good and bad, right and wrong feelings. Meanwhile, deep in your heart, your natal mutable Moon knows that this black and white division of feelings is ridiculous.

REBELLIOUSNESS AND THE SECOND INCONJUNCT
A CASE STUDY

The example for the inconjunct, Billie Carpenter (Chart 9 on page 39), is a woman who was one of the actively rebellious teenagers. Her outer planet transits were not particularly difficult during the second inconjunct, but transiting Saturn was afflicting her chart, squaring her natal Moon and North Node, inconjunct natal Mercury and natal Saturn. The progressed chart indicates her life's turmoil.

In the secondary progressed chart (Chart 10 on page 40) we see that Billie's progressed Moon had just conjuncted her progressed Jupiter, opposed her progressed Mars and squared her progressed Uranus. Billie's progressed Sun was approaching an inconjunct to her progressed Mars. Comparing progressed and natal positions, we find that Billie's progressed Moon inconjuncts her natal Moon, opposes her natal Mars, semi-sextiles her natal Mercury, and semi-sextiles her natal North Node. Billie's progressed Sun trines her natal Uranus.

Billie had been experimenting with any type of drug that she could get since she was thirteen. She is very vague about the actual time she first started using drugs; thus this cannot be traced astrologically. By sixteen, she had run away several times, although never for more than a few days, as she is extremely dependent on her mother. Her drug dependency and running away increased during 1974. She was never

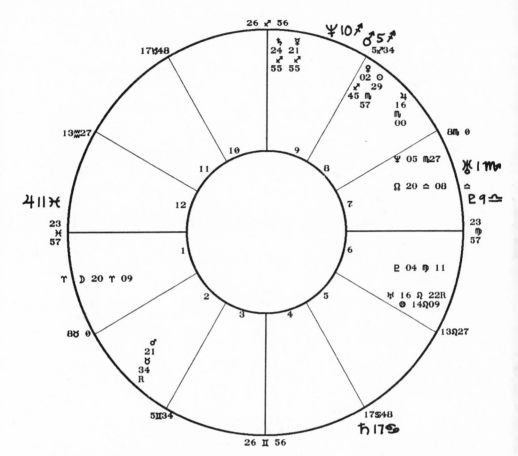

Chart 9. Billie Carpenter: November 22, 1958, 1:27 PM EST, 42N38, 71W19; data from birth certificate; Placidus houses.

destructive to anyone other than herself and never expressed anger at her mother, although she readily expressed frustration and rage over her relationship with her father.

The synastry between Billie's chart and her mother's chart (Chart 11 on page 41) is not as clear or as easy as the synastry between Ann Martin and her mother. Billie's Moon forms a T-square with her mother's Moon-Pluto conjunction opposing Mars. Billie's Jupiter-Mars opposition is in sextile/trine relationship to the Moon-Pluto-Mars configuration in Martha's chart. Billie's Moon-Uranus-Mercury grand trine ties into Martha's Saturn (conjunct Billie's Mercury). Since Martha's birth time is simply family tradition or memory, they may have the Ascendants conjunct. The synastry suggests that the dependency may be mutual, as Billie expressed Martha's own desires. Since

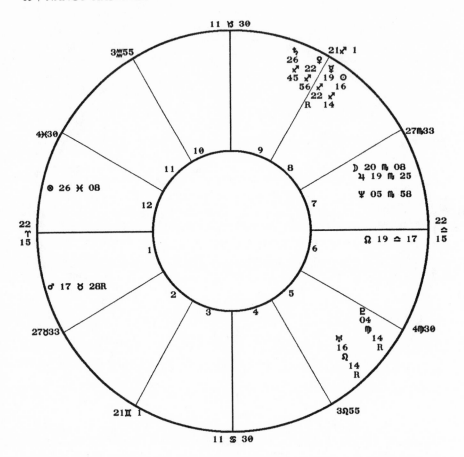

Chart 10. Billie Carpenter: Chart 9 progressed to December 18, 1974 using the Sun's mean motion in RA for the MC.

Martha has probably got both Sun and Mercury in the twelfth house, she has difficulty expressing herself well. Billie's Sun-Venus conjunction trines her mother's Uranus-Jupiter conjunction. Through each other, the energies of these combinations can be expressed in the world.

During the time of the second inconjunct from her progressed to natal Moon, the grand trine in Billie's chart was quite operative. Three ministers, two youth advisors, and a social worker (all ninth house people) consistently rescued her, took her to the hospital, dried her out and tried to help her see that the person she was harming was herself.

Billie quit high school during Christmas vacation (just after her progressed Moon actually inconjuncted her natal Moon). She began dating a man who was physically and emotionally abusive. In 1975, Billie briefly tried to return to high school, but when her progressed

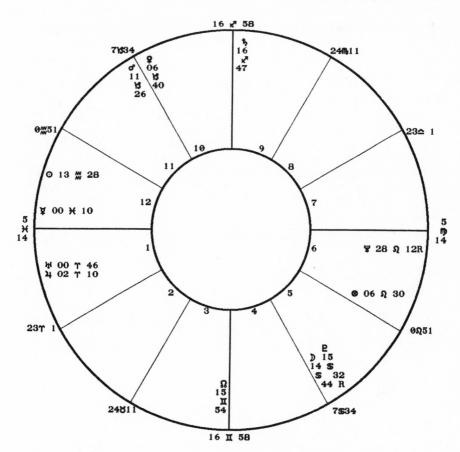

Chart 11. Martha Carpenter (Billie Carpenter's mother): February 3, 1928, 8:00 AM EST, 42N05, 71W38; data from family records (oral); Placidus houses.

Sun inconjuncted her progressed Mars, she quit high school for good. Since then she has had several factory jobs, usually falling into the "last hired, first fired" category. She has never made much more than minimum wage. She has never moved away from home. She cannot bear to be away from her mother for more than a few days at a time. She has not been involved with drugs other than alcohol and marijuana since 1975. She has failed the high school equivalency test three times.

THE SECOND TRINE

The idealization and ease of the trine aspect now influences your interactions with other people. The ninth house influence of the waning trine introduces you to new concepts and new ideas. The world moves more easily for you. Although you are aware of the flaws in your parents and the flaws in their relationships with each other, you are positive that you will not repeat these mistakes.

Very few of us have completely resolved our personal problems when we are eighteen. However, many of us really feel that we have gotten to a point where we can understand ourselves better. Even the very troubled Billie, of the example above, reached a kind of equilibrium when her progressed Moon trined its natal position. At that time she got her first slightly rewarding factory job. She did not fight as constantly with her father; she felt better about herself. She was able to contribute financially to her family and often bought things for the house or her mother. The boyfriend who had treated her so miserably while the inconjunct was present got sent to jail. Thus he was out of her life for the two years that her progressed Moon was in the sign trine her natal Moon.

Natal Fire Moon Second Trine: You're bursting with energy and confidence while your progressed Moon is in the sign trine your natal Moon. You're positive that you can do something about most of the problems you face, and you are usually right. As long as you don't attempt to solve everyone else's problems as well, you should do well. You may overidealize emotional resiliency, expect instant results, or provide solutions which others see as simplistic.

Natal Earth Moon Second Trine: You've developed a pattern of response which seems to work for you. You are content to cope with daily stress in a grounded realistic manner. You need to watch for a tendency to believe that your pattern of response is the only sane, normal pattern which exists. Other people may find this belief somewhat condescending!

Natal Air Moon Second Trine: You've reached an equilibrium in your analysis of emotions. Your personal responses don't dismay you and you are not as quick to compare your responses to the responses of other people. Because you've thought about your response patterns you do tend to analyze the reactions of others. Be careful, for unless another person actually asks you for help with an emotional issue, they may resent your input. Not everyone wants to think about why they do what they do.

Natal Water Moon Second Trine: During the two and a half years that your progressed Moon is in the sign trine its natal position, you flow positively in most relationships. You've gained the ability to trust your basic response nature. Thus this is the time to rely on your strong intuitive side. You may find that you are picking up the feelings of other people in the room with you, or you may actually start to pick up psychic inputs from others. At the very least, you can tell immediately how another person feels about you, and whether or not you wish to pursue a friendship with that particular person.

TRADITIONAL USE OF THE SECOND TRINE
A CASE STUDY

The example for the waning (second) trine, Carolyn Diamond (Chart 12), represents another completely valid expression of the energy of the trine. Again, it's not exactly how each of us would choose to express the energy, but it is internally consistent.

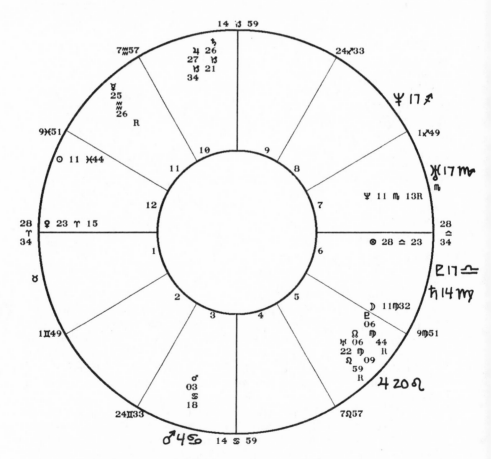

Chart 12. Carolyn Diamond: March 2, 1961, 8:10 AM EST, 42N38, 71W19; data from birth certificate; Placidus houses.

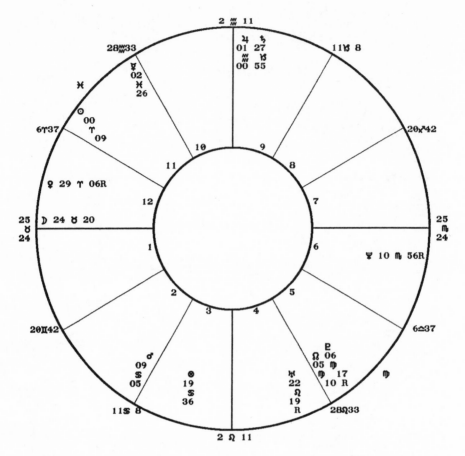

Chart 13. Carolyn Diamond: Chart 12 progressed to August 15, 1979 using the Sun's mean motion in RA for the MC.

Carolyn did not exhibit any of the outward signs of rebellion shown by Billie during the inconjuncts and the first opposition from the progressed to natal Moon. Rather, Carolyn seemed to handle all of these tensions with minimum disturbance to herself or to others in her life.

In the early summer of 1978, when her progressed Moon trined her natal Moon, Carolyn became engaged. She was married on August 15, 1979 (Chart 13). Although the marriage indicators hop out all over this chart, the marriage time was not chosen astrologically (at least consciously!). Progressed Jupiter was 1° 11' past conjunct the progressed Midheaven, progressed Venus 32' past her natal Ascendant. Progressed Moon approached the progressed Ascendant, 1° 4', and approached the trine to natal Saturn, 2° 1'. Progressed Venus approached the square to progressed Jupiter, 54', approached the square to progressed Jupiter/Saturn midpoint, 22', approached the square progressed Jupiter/natal Jupiter midpoint, 11'. The squares from Venus to Saturn are particularly good indicators of a long-lasting marriage, for they indicate stability and an ability to accept responsibility.

Does this indicate that the marriage will last forever? Nothing in a chart can indicate this, no matter how much we hope. However, their marriage does seem to be off to an excellent start. Both Carolyn and her husband have jobs, he as a salesman and she as a waitress. They seem to be quite happy and are saving towards the time that they will start their family.

Interestingly, this example has upset more students than Billie's example. It seems that many of us are thoroughly imbued with a work ethic which demands that we postpone marriage until we have achieved something. The concept of a couple who have no particular materialistic ambitions and do not seek out high pressure work situations is apparently an anathema. Many students working with Carolyn's example go out of their way to find flaws in the relationship, as they wish all teenage weddings to fail.

THE SECOND SQUARE

As we enter the time of the second (or waning) square from our progressed Moon to its natal position, we separate more fully from Daddy as well as Mommy. We are now legal adults, as the square occurs about age twenty-one. We are either in college or out on our own, finding jobs, meeting new people, setting up our own lives. Those of us who have not let go of Mommy often find that this time recapitulates all of the problems of our relationship with our mothers. We may go from this to another form of rebellion, trying to make ourselves as different as possible from our mothers. Or we may suddenly seem to give in and become much more like the person our mother wanted. Either response usually involves considerable anger, although the anger is often hidden from ourselves as well as from our mothers. Thus we feel tense, upset, aggressive, but cannot quite grasp the reasons for this uncomfortable feeling. If we can direct the aggression towards career aims, we can indeed devote considerable energy to our own advancement.

When I've questioned people who were in college at the time of the first waning (second) square, I've often found that this was the time that they changed their college major, rejected or suddenly accepted a path chosen either overtly or subtly by their parents.

Natal Cardinal Moon Second Square: This square allows you to manifest the most dearly held desire of your cardinal Moon— independence. Even if your natal Moon is in Cancer, and you need lots of nurturing, you want to express emotion in your own way. If you can't let go of your adolescent anger with Mom, you may rebel against anyone in a position of authority or emotional prominence in your life. Since you initiate most of the emotional exchanges in your life, you need to look at your own inner situation if you find yourself continually involved in stressful situations.

Natal Fixed Moon Second Square: During this second square, you are likely to confront situations which demand some change in your emotional response nature. But you will resist change vigorously, for the square emphasizes your natal fixity. You need to back away a bit so that you can determine why you are upset by situations around you. Are you afraid that any change in your feelings will result in a loss of security or a loss of your ability to depend on your own responses? Although you may not want to change your gut level responses to events, you need to understand these resonses before you can fully accept them.

Natal Mutable Moon Second Sqaure: You may have the feeling that your whole emotional life is going to pieces because you have so many shifts in your responses. One moment you are very up, and the next moment you are in the pits. Sometimes merely recognizing that this is normal for you helps you calm down. During the second square it is very important that you get enough sleep, for you use up enormous amounts of energy just worrying about the fluctuations in your emotions. If your situation becomes difficult enough, you may let go of guilt and blame, the two major causes of your own stress.

THE SECOND PROGRESSED MOON SQUARE
A CASE STUDY

Jayne Fredrickson (Chart 14) is an extremely bright and attractive woman. When her progressed Moon squared its natal position, she was an undergraduate at an Ivy League college, majoring in business. Jayne is also a dancer. In February 1972 (see Chart 15 on page 48), she implemented a change which she had been actively considering for about a year (from approximately the time that her progressed Moon actually squared its natal position) and began to work as an exotic dancer in clubs. At first she was dancing to earn money for her college expenses. Soon, however, Jayne was earning more money than her professors at college. She loved the danger and the excitement of the clubs. She was very attracted to the clubs' owners, an attraction which was returned. The men who owned the clubs in which Jayne danced all had powerful mob connections. Jayne

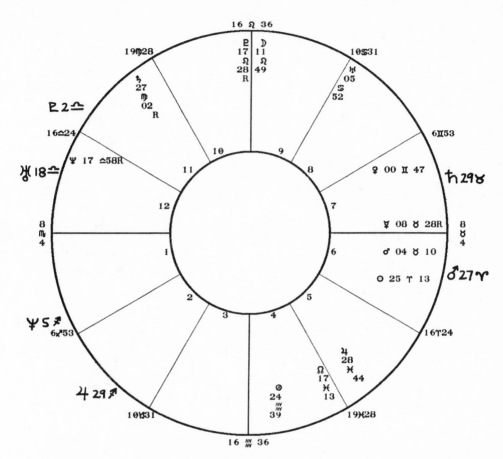

Chart 14. Jayne Fredrickson: April 15, 1951, 7:27 PM EST, 42N22, 71W03; data from birth certificate; Placidus houses.

did not drop out of college, for she realized that she would not be able to dance for the rest of her life, but it did become difficult to keep the two sides of her life separate. She did not dare tell her parents where she was working and did not want any of her college associates to know about her work. In spite of all these tensions, Jayne graduated with high honors.

Jayne's natal Moon-Midheaven-Pluto conjunction symbolizes her attraction to power and danger. Just after the second square from her progressed Moon to its natal position, Jayne's progressed Sun squared the point exactly between her natal Moon and her natal Pluto. This square showed that the natal tenison of the Moon-Midheaven-Pluto conjunction would be at a peak while Jayne's progressed Moon was in the sign square its own natal position. The midpoint of Jayne's progressed Sun and progressed Mars exactly squared Jayne's pro-

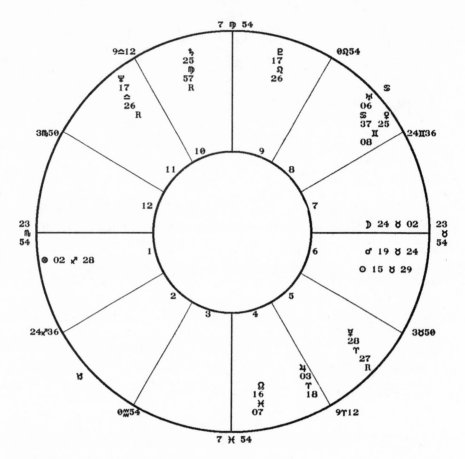

Chart 15. Jayne Fredrickson: Chart 14 progressed to February 6, 1972 using the Sun's mean motion in RA for the MC.

gressed Pluto. This configuration indicates danger, possible violence and strong physical exertion. Further, transiting Uranus began opposing Jayne's natal Sun during this period. This aspect often manifests as a radical change in self-concept, usually brought about by sudden exposure to physical stress or danger. Because transiting Uranus was conjunct Jayne's natal Neptune, and in her natal twelfth house, the full effect of the changes in her self-image were not obvious to Jayne. All the aspect patterns which indicate danger manifested externally through Jayne's dancing job. During 1972, Jayne's progressed Saturn squared her progressed Venus, and transiting Saturn conjuncted her natal Venus. Any relationships with club owners revolved around the issue of control. Of course, all of the owners were quite a bit older than Jayne, another consequence of Saturn aspects to Venus. She formed no strong love relationships during this period. The Saturn aspects actually stabilized her emotional conflicts by providing a clear path of self-control in love situations.

THE SECOND SEXTILE

This is another time of integration with our emotions. We usually take advantage of the working symbolism of the sextile aspect by smoothing out our relationships both at work and at home. This is often a time when we are involved with marriage, children, and/or career pursuits. The only real difficulty with the sextile aspect from the progressed Moon is that usually nothing actually happens. Unless there are aspects from outer planet transits or other progressions, we have a gloriously uneventful time while the progressed Moon sextiles its natal position. Our relationships move along easily. Our jobs don't make us scream with frustration. We even start to understand some of the reasons our mothers are the way they are. If we have not been able to deal with our relationship with our mothers, we have probably moved out, and we proceed through the sextile to ignore that piece of unfinished business.

If the outer planet transits are terrible, or other progressed aspects are difficult during this time, the sextile makes us more able to withstand the emotional drain. We can, and do, make it through all kinds of problems without going berserk.

THE SECOND SEMI-SEXTILE

Semi-sextiles are not action aspects.[10] Thus, there are rarely events associated with this position of the progressed Moon. However, it is a time in which we start to reevaluate our own feelings about nearly every aspect of our lives. The Moon is in the sign behind its natal position, and tends to remind us of all the possible drawbacks in our habitual response patterns. During the first semi-sextile, in our infancy, we tried our new patterns of emotional response on our mothers. Now we seem to try different patterns of response on ourselves, in a particularly twelfth house and hidden manner. Although we may not outwardly manifest any tension or anxiety, we are preparing ourselves for the time of the conjunction. If the progressed Moon is making strong aspects to other natal positions, we may be quite confused by our own reactions to the events of our lives.

---

[10] I find the semi-sextile a slightly difficult aspect, for it unites two planets in the same fashion that an inconjunct unites them. Planets which are 30° apart differ in triplicity, quadruplicity and polarity. Thus the energies cannot blend in a harmonious fashion. The semi-sextile indicates tension rather than action.

FACING THE SECOND SEMI-SEXTILE
A CASE STUDY

The following example (Chart 16) illustrated this type of difficulty with the waning (second) semi-sextile. The twelfth house influence is heightened in this case, because Marjorie's natal Moon is in her first house. During the year that the semi-sextile aspect from the progressed Moon became exact, Marjorie's progressed Mars squared her progressed Jupiter, and Marjorie's progressed Sun inconjuncted her progressed Uranus. When we compare the progressed (Chart 17 on page 51) and natal charts, the following aspects are also apparent. Marjorie's progressed node squared her natal Mars and her progressed Sun approached the opposition to her progressed Pluto. The progressed Moon squared Mercury, conjuncted the twelfth house cusp,

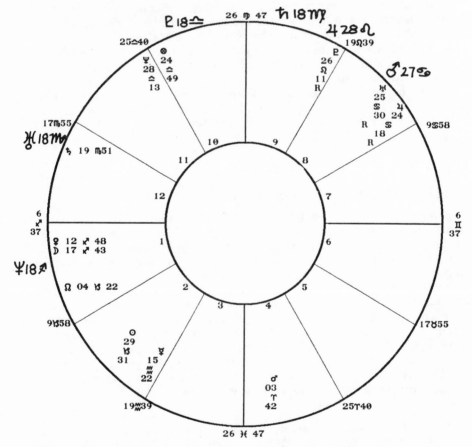

Chart 16. Marjorie Singer: January 20, 1955, 3:45 AM EST, 44N01, 73W10; data from hospital records; Placidus houses.

conjuncted Saturn and semi-sextiled natal Venus as well as natal Moon.

Marjorie gave birth to her second child on November 7, 1979. Her older child was nineteen months old at the time. Marjorie, her husband and two children went on an extremely hectic visiting tour over Christmas 1979. Meanwhile, Marjorie's emotional world was falling apart. By turns she was extremely manic, doing enough for three people, and then she would not be able to get anything done at all. She could not keep track of her own emotions or feelings and described this time as if she were sometimes watching someone else respond to situations in a manner completely different from her own. Transiting Saturn was moving back and forth over Marjorie's Midheaven, transiting Uranus was trining her natal Jupiter and Uranus from the twelfth house; transiting Neptune conjuncted her natal Moon. Although the transits of the outer planets are not all that difficult, the

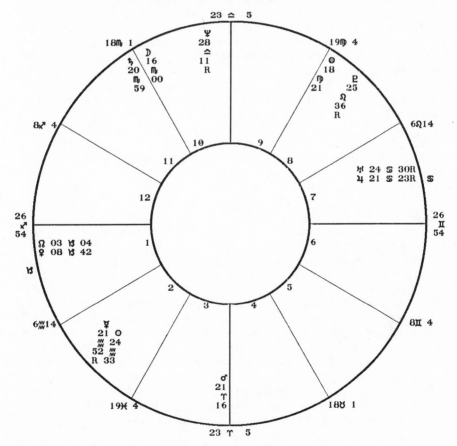

Chart 17. Marjorie Singer: Chart 16 progressed to September 20, 1979 using the Sun's mean motion in RA for the MC.

combination of transits and progressions was quite a problem. The inconjunct between the progressed Sun and progressed Uranus symbolizes tension or conflict between the self-will and the basic self of a person. Mars square Jupiter symbolizes energy expressed in large or possibly uncontrolled ways. When transiting Neptune conjuncted Marjorie's natal Moon, she started to have hallucinations. As the progressed aspects became more exact, it became more and more difficult for her to distinguish the hallucinations from reality. On March 17, 1980, Marjorie was hospitalized with a nervous breakdown.[11]

THE CONJUNCTION OF PROGRESSED AND NATAL MOON

Many books on astrology define the conjunction as a variable aspect, indicating that it is neither favorable nor difficult. This is particularly true when the conjunction is the conjunction of the natal and progressed Moon. Here the sign position and the natal aspects to and from the Moon determine the probable ease or difficulty of the conjunction year.

If your natal Moon is in Taurus, for example, where it is exalted, and has a trine and two sextiles as its only aspects, your conjunction time is likely to be quite easy. In fact, you may have a truly joyful year. On the other hand, you may have your natal Moon in Aries square Saturn, Mars, Mercury, and the Midheaven, opposing Neptune and the Ascendant, trine Pluto and sextile Uranus (as I do). In that case, the year of the conjunction could well be a year of emotional estrangement, colored by rather specific events.

Given these two extremes, and the continuum between, the problem of delineating the quality of the conjunction year becomes enormous. For every difficult example, there is an equally valid easy one. For every one of us who encounters specific events, there is another one who has a peaceful, uneventful year.

There is, however, a thread which ties us all together during the conjunction year. This is a year of reassessment. We can look back and look ahead, evaluating our past feelings and projecting our future responses. Our natal response nature is intensified, because every natal Moon aspect will be exact during the year of the conjunction. Remember that Moon-Mars square in your natal chart? You will have to cope with conflict with the women in your life. If you have developed some insight into your own response nature, you may discover your own contribution to the tensions around you. Do you have a natal Moon-Saturn opposition? You have to work on your tendency to assume responsibility too quickly. Perhaps you wander

---

[11] For an in-depth analysis of this chart, see Chapter 5.

around apologizing for every negative event, whether or not you had anything to do with it. You may be able to find out why you feel so guilty about the things that you did not cause.

While our progressed Moon is in the same sign as our natal Moon, we can figuratively return home to discover the responses we like and the responses which make us unhappy within ourselves. We can find out some reasons why we behave the way we do and decide whether we wish to continue behavior patterns which do not bring us peace. If we retreat, and continue to blame some other person for our own responses, we have chosen to ignore the potential for growth within ourselves.

You can't blame your mother. Whether she loved you, hated you, smothered you with affection (often a thinly disguised control situation), or totally rejected you, you are not your mother. You are the only one who can determine your responses to any situation. When you forgive Mom for being a human being with faults, you can forgive yourself for your own inconsistencies.

The conjunction is the beginning of the adult cycle of your life. You alone can make the choice to enter this cycle as a free and whole human being.

HOW DO I SEE THE WORLD?

THE PROGRESSED ASCENDANT

The Ascendant axis, the last member of our foundation trilogy, symbolizes the face we show to the world, the persona we project out to others, the window through which we filter information about what is in the world around us. The sign and degree on the eastern horizon when we are born is the Ascendant, the first house cusp. It's opposite, 180° away, is the Descendant, or seventh house cusp. Anything that aspects the Ascendant also aspects the Descendant. Because the Ascendant-Descendant is an axis, it is sometimes difficult to completely separate the meaning of the two sides.

The traditional concept of the Ascendant indicates that the eastern side of the axis shows how you face the world. This is the interaction between you and the immediate environment. It is the personality you display. The Descendant deals with everything that is not you, with all the other people in the world and with your partners. We have seen that the Sun and the Moon define your physical and emotional self. When these two parts are combined with the Ascendant, we can paint some details into the picture, and the combination tells us about that elusive spark we call the personality. As the Ascendant progresses to a different sign, your outlook or perspective

Figure 1.1 Sign progression through the triplicities and quadruplicities.

on the world changes. In this section, we will investigate some of the change indicated by the changing Ascendant.

Let's imagine the differences between two people born on the same day, same hospital, but a few hours apart in time, to clarify the significance of the natal Ascendant. Jim and Joan both have the Sun in Pisces and Moon in Scorpio. Jim has Cancer rising, while Joan has Leo rising.

Joan, with Leo rising, will have more difficulty reconciling her approach to the outside world with her basic nature and emotional response patterns. Her Pisces Sun does not wish to brag or show off, and her Scorpio Moon certainly does not wish to carry her heart on her sleeve. Yet the Leo Ascendant symbolizes a desire to be noticed and praised, a desire to be seen within the environment.

Meanwhile, Jim, with Cancer rising, is quite comfortable with the projection of sensitivity which goes along with the Cancer Ascendant. While Joan may hate the tears common to the Pisces Sun, Jim will utilize the tears and/or moodiness to his own best advantage.

For all of us, as the chart progresses, the Ascendant moves onto the next sign, and we mature to the next stage in our personal growth. Whether the next sign is more compatible or less compatible with our natal positions, we will change our outlook and approach to the environment. In order to visualize the pattern of the progressed movement, see Figure 1.1, which shows how the signs progress in terms of the triplicities and quadruplicities.

The rate of ascent of the signs is not constant, but depends on the latitude of birth and upon the sign itself. Table 1.3 on page 56 gives the differences in rate of ascent in either Placidus or Koch for northern latitude. As you go over the times shown in Table 1.3, you can see that if you have 0° Leo or Scorpio rising, and were born in the northern hemisphere, you would be forty years old before your Ascendant changes sign. This certainly contributes to the reputation these two signs have as extremely powerful influences on the Ascendant. In contrast, if you had 0° Taurus or 0° Aquarius rising, you would be two-thirds of the way through Gemini or Pisces as a progressed Ascendant by the time you were forty!

Cardinal to Fixed Ascendant by Progression: Your cardinal Ascendant symbolizes your desire to move within your environment. You have an initiatory urge, and don't like to leave the surroundings untouched. As your Ascendant progresses into a fixed sign, you tend to solidify your gains. You become more consistent in your interactions with the world. Often this combination yields self-assurance, for your natal cardinal sign begins things while your progressed fixed sign finishes them up.

Fixed to Mutable Ascendant by Progression: Your fixed natal Ascendant symbolizes your tendency towards stable, "tried and true" kinds of interactions with your environment. The progression of your Ascendant to a mutable sign opens the door to flexibility. You can now loosen up your approach to the world, thereby gaining an ability to adapt to new situations.

Mutable to Cardinal Ascendant by Progression: Your mutable natal Ascendant symbolizes your ability to adapt quickly to whatever the outer situation demands. This flexibility carries its own dilemma, for you may have inner confusion concerning your position in a multitude of situations. As your Ascendant progresses to a cardinal sign, you will notice a growing ability to make decisions concerning how you want others to see you.

Fire to Earth Ascendant by Progression: When you have a fire sign as your natal Ascendant, you approach the environment with dash and enthusiasm. As your Ascendant progresses to earth, you can add circumspection and practicality to your approach. Earth is responsive, and you now can respond to cues from the environment instead of always rushing into immediate action.

Earth to Air Ascendant by Progression: When you have an earth sign rising, you tend to be quite concerned with the practical outcome of your impact on the environment. You wait until you have collected information before you respond to stimuli. The air sign progression brings not only intellectual patterns of behavior, but also a growing awareness of your need to act rather than respond in some situations.

Air to Water Ascendant by Progression: When you have an air sign rising, you think and act on whatever presents itself. Communication is your most vital link to the world around you. The progression of your Ascendant to a water sign introduces a need to be responsive to the environment. Furthermore, the water sign underlines your growing ability to accept emotional cues in understanding your impact on others and theirs on you.

Water to Fire Ascendant by Progression: When you have a water sign rising, you tend to respond to the environment in a rather emotional manner. As your Ascendant progresses to fire, you want to initiate activity. You want to be seen and appreciated for what you are. The combination can be difficult if both your natal Sun and natal Moon are in either earth or water. However, if either natal Sun or natal

*Table 1.3 Table of Ascensional Arcs of Zodiacal Signs in the Northern Hemisphere*12

Lat.	♈	♉	♊	♋	♌	♍	♎	♏	♐	♑	♒	♓
0	27 55	29 54	32 11	32 11	29 54	27 55	27 55	29 54	32 11	32 11	29 54	27 55
5	26 54	29 5	31 51	32 31	30 44	28 56	28 56	30 44	32 31	31 51	29 5	26 54
10	25 51	28 15	31 30	32 51	31 34	29 58	29 58	31 34	32 51	31 30	28 15	25 51
15	24 47	27 23	31 9	33 13	32 26	31 2	31 2	32 26	33 13	31 9	27 23	24 47
20	23 40	26 28	30 47	33 35	33 21	32 9	32 9	33 21	33 35	30 47	26 28	23 40
21	23 26	26 17	30 42	33 40	33 32	32 23	32 23	33 32	33 40	30 42	26 17	23 26
22	23 12	26 5	30 37	33 45	33 44	32 37	32 37	33 44	33 45	30 37	26 5	23 12
23	22 58	25 53	30 32	33 50	33 56	32 51	32 51	33 56	33 50	30 32	25 53	22 58
24	22 43	25 41	30 27	33 55	34 8	33 6	33 6	34 8	33 55	30 27	25 41	22 43
25	22 29	25 29	30 22	34 0	34 20	33 20	33 20	34 20	34 0	30 22	25 29	22 29
26	22 14	25 17	30 17	34 5	34 32	33 35	33 35	34 32	34 5	30 17	25 17	22 14
27	21 58	25 4	30 12	34 10	34 45	33 51	33 51	34 45	34 10	30 12	25 4	21 58
28	21 43	24 51	30 6	34 16	34 58	34 6	34 6	34 58	34 16	30 6	24 51	21 43
29	21 27	24 38	30 1	34 21	35 11	34 22	34 22	35 11	34 21	30 1	24 38	21 27
30	21 11	24 24	29 55	34 27	35 25	34 38	34 38	35 25	34 27	29 55	24 24	21 11
31	20 54	24 10	29 49	34 33	35 39	34 55	34 55	35 39	34 33	29 49	24 10	20 54
32	20 37	23 56	29 43	34 39	35 53	35 12	35 12	35 53	34 39	29 43	23 56	20 37
33	20 20	23 42	29 37	34 45	36 7	35 29	35 29	36 7	34 45	29 37	23 42	20 20
34	20 2	23 27	29 30	34 51	36 22	35 47	35 47	36 22	34 51	29 30	23 27	20 2
35	19 44	23 11	29 24	34 58	36 38	36 5	36 5	36 38	34 58	29 24	23 11	19 44
36	19 26	22 55	29 17	35 5	36 54	36 23	36 23	36 54	35 5	29 17	22 55	19 26
37	19 7	22 39	29 10	35 12	37 10	36 43	36 43	37 10	35 12	29 10	22 39	19 7
38	18 47	22 22	29 2	35 19	37 27	37 2	37 2	37 27	35 19	29 2	22 22	18 47
39	18 27	22 5	28 55	35 27	37 44	37 22	37 22	37 44	35 27	28 55	22 5	18 27
40	18 6	21 47	28 47	35 35	38 2	37 43	37 43	38 2	35 35	28 47	21 47	18 6
41	17 45	21 28	28 38	35 43	38 21	38 4	38 4	38 21	35 43	28 38	21 28	17 45
42	17 23	21 8	28 30	35 52	38 41	38 26	38 26	38 41	35 52	28 30	21 8	17 23
43	17 0	20 48	28 21	36 1	39 1	38 49	38 49	39 1	36 1	28 21	20 48	17 0
44	16 36	20 27	28 11	36 11	39 22	39 13	39 13	39 22	36 11	28 11	20 27	16 36

Table 1.3 Table of Ascensional Arcs of Zodiacal Signs in the Northern Hemisphere (Continued)

Lat.	♈	♉	♊	♋	♌	♍	♎	♏	♐	♑	♒	♓
45	16 12	20 5	28 1	36 21	39 44	39 37	39 37	39 44	36 21	28 1	20 5	16 12
46	15 46	19 42	27 50	36 32	40 7	40 3	40 3	40 7	36 32	27 50	19 42	15 46
47	15 20	19 18	27 39	36 43	40 31	40 29	40 29	40 31	36 43	27 39	19 18	15 20
48	14 53	18 53	27 27	36 55	40 56	40 56	40 56	40 56	36 55	27 27	18 53	14 53
49	14 24	18 26	27 14	37 8	41 23	41 25	41 25	41 23	37 8	27 14	18 26	14 24
50	13 55	17 58	27 0	37 22	41 51	41 55	41 55	41 51	37 22	27 0	17 58	13 55
51	13 23	17 28	26 45	37 37	42 21	42 26	42 26	42 21	37 37	26 45	17 28	13 23
52	12 51	16 57	26 29	37 53	42 52	42 58	42 58	42 52	37 53	26 29	16 57	12 51
53	12 17	16 23	26 12	38 10	43 26	43 32	43 32	43 26	38 10	26 12	16 23	12 17
54	11 41	15 47	25 53	38 29	44 2	44 8	44 8	44 2	38 29	25 53	15 47	11 41
55	11 3	15 9	25 32	38 50	44 40	44 46	44 46	44 40	38 50	25 32	15 9	11 3
56	10 24	14 27	25 8	39 14	45 22	45 25	45 25	45 22	39 14	25 8	14 27	10 24
57	9 42	13 42	24 42	39 40	46 7	46 7	46 7	46 7	39 40	24 42	13 42	9 42
58	8 57	12 54	24 12	40 10	46 55	46 52	46 52	46 55	40 10	24 12	12 54	8 57
59	8 10	12 0	23 38	40 44	47 49	47 39	47 39	47 49	40 44	23 38	12 0	8 10
60	7 19	11 1	22 58	41 24	48 48	48 30	48 30	48 48	41 24	22 58	11 1	7 19
61	6 26	9 55	22 10	42 12	49 54	49 24	49 24	49 54	42 12	22 10	9 55	6 26
62	5 28	8 42	21 11	43 11	51 7	50 21	50 21	51 7	43 11	21 11	8 42	5 28
63	4 26	7 18	19 56	44 26	52 31	51 23	51 23	52 31	44 26	19 56	7 18	4 26
64	3 19	5 41	18 13	46 8	54 8	52 30	52 30	54 8	46 8	18 13	5 41	3 19
65	2 6	3 48	15 40	48 42	56 1	53 43	53 43	56 1	48 42	15 40	3 48	2 6
66	0 47	1 30	10 47	53 35	58 19	55 2	55 2	58 19	53 35	10 47	1 30	0 47

*Find the latitude column on the left (Lat.), go across the table to the appropriate sign. These values (in years) are the length of time it takes for each sign to cross the Ascendant if you are using Placidus or Koch houses. Copyright © Robert Hand. Used by permission.

12 In the southern hemisphere, exchange times with the sign opposite each sign. Aries changes with Libra, Taurus with Scorpio, etc.

Moon are in fire or air, this progression will feel as if you are finally coming into your own, able to show the world your true nature.

CHANGING COMBINATIONS
CASE STUDIES

The following examples show the polarity shifts of Sun, Moon, and Ascendant in two different people. The analysis gives an idea of how a comparison of natal and progressed charts would begin.

Sandra's natal chart (Chart 18) has Sun in Libra (yang), Moon in Gemini (yang), and Ascendant in Capricorn (yin). This combination

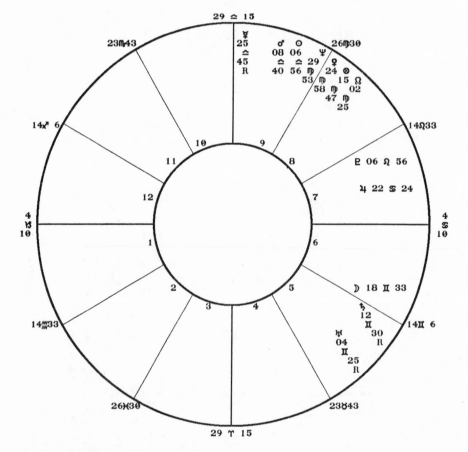

Chart 18. *Sandra: September 30, 1942, 1:58 PM EWT, 41N42, 71W09; data from hospital records; Placidus houses.*

symbolizes a difficulty in expressing who she is (Sun) or how she feels (Moon). Both her Sun and Moon are in air; an intellectual approach is her basic personality force and her emotional response pattern.

But Sandra's Capricorn Ascendant projects a practical, responsive approach to the outside world. Although the cardinal nature of Capricorn allows some expression of the initiatory impulses of Libra, the yin nature of the earth sign urges a foresight which is at times very difficult for her to maintain.

When Sandra was in her late twenties (Chart 19), her Sun and Ascendant had both progressed to the next sign, changing polarities. Sandra then found it easier to project her essential self (natal Sun) and her habitual response nature (natal Moon) through her progressed Aquarius Ascendant. Her strong intellectual nature easily adapted to this air sign. Meanwhile, her progressed Sun, in Scorpio, uses the natal

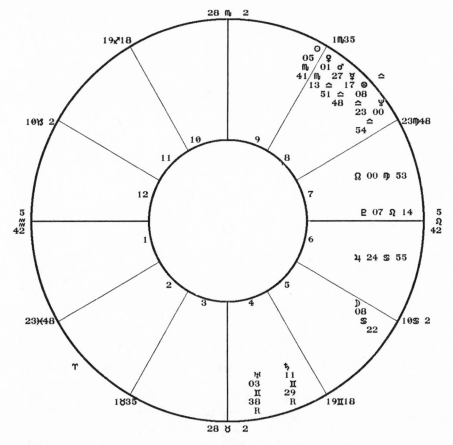

Chart 19. Sandra: Chart 18 progressed to September 30, 1971 using the Sun's mean motion in RA for the MC.

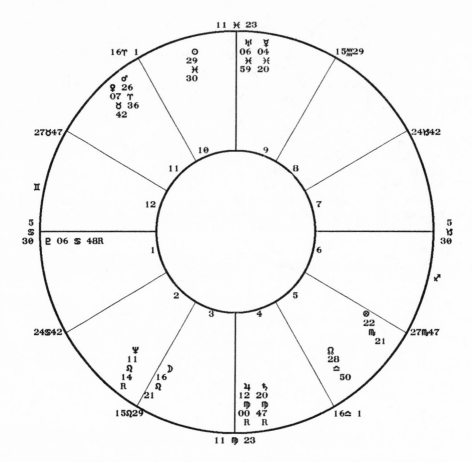

Chart 20. David: March 20, 1921, 10:45 AM EST, 42N21, 71W03; data from baby book; Placidus houses.

Capricorn Ascendant symbolism as a means of expression. In spite of the air triplicity present with the progressed Ascendant, natal Sun, and natal Moon, the progressed Sun combines with the natal Ascendant to provide an undeniable yin component for Sandra's personality for twenty-eight years. During this twenty-eight year period, Sandra's progressed Moon completely circled the signs. Its position tells us which of the crossovers is predominant for the two year periods that the Moon is in each of the signs. When the progressed Moon was in earth or water, Sandra had full use of both yin and yang as means of self-expression. When the progressed Moon was in fire or air, Sandra tended towards a more aggressive projection of her personality.

The next example (Charts 20, 21, and 22) is more complicated and does not indicate as easy a combination of natal and progressed influences. This is due to the fact that David's Sun is very late in Pisces, while his Ascendant is in early degrees of Cancer.

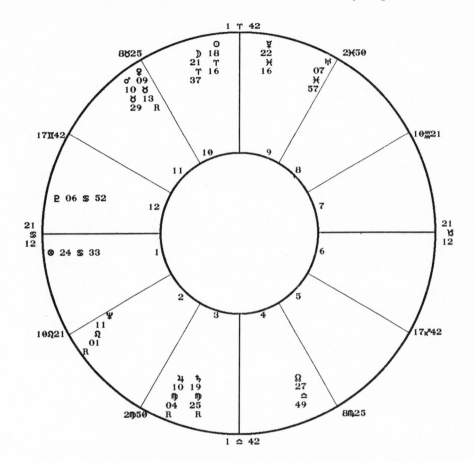

Chart 21. David: Chart 20 progressed to March 20, 1940 using the Sun's mean motion in RA for the MC.

David's natal combination shows that while he is emotional and sensitive, he has difficulty expressing his feelings. At times he worries about whether or not he actually has any deep feelings as he finds himself using emotion to manipulate others.

David's Sun progressed into Aries when he was two years old, but his Ascendant did not enter Leo until he was twenty-five. Thus he had no means of effectively projecting his progressed Sun during his childhood. The aggressive undercurrents of the Aries progression only surfaced through skillful manipulation of parents, teachers, and siblings with the emotion of water.

Until age 32, David's progressed Sun was in Fire. During this time, he was more willing to show the yang side of his personality in his interactions with the world. He returned to college (interrupted by WW2), got a degree, started teaching, got married. Although he was able to project more self-confidence, he is not in retrospect sure that

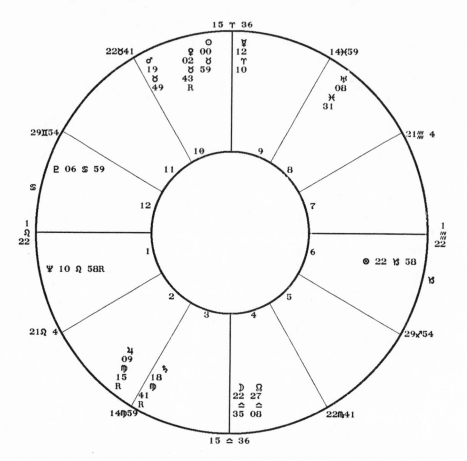

Chart 22. David: Chart 20 progressed to March 20, 1953 using the Sun's mean motion in RA for the MC.

he was actually any more confident of himself during this period. (Progressed Ascendant is still in Cancer.) Once David's Sun progressed into Taurus, he seemed to completely abandon the Leo mode of interaction except in emotional exchanges. Both natal and progressed Sun had an easier expression through the natal Cancer Ascendant. When David reacts on a purely emotional level, the Leo parts of his personality become more obvious. If the event is negative, he yells and stamps quite actively. If the event is positive, he takes charge and immediately becomes active in some physical fashion. David's main problem is his inability to integrate the yin and yang sides of his nature, for he has these rather rigidly compartmentalized. He does not let go of past hurts and has difficulty recognizing his strong manipulative tendencies.

2

BASIC ANATOMY:

THE CHART AS A WHOLE

GIVING AND TAKING

HEMISPHERE DIVISION

Every circle can be divided into hemispheres, or halves, by drawing a line through the center of the circle. When we divide a chart into hemispheres, the division lines customarily run along the Ascendant-Descendant (horizontal) axis or along the Midheaven-Nadir (vertical) axis. (See Figure 2.1 on page 66.)

Let's look at the horizontal division of the chart first. Planets above the Ascendant axis are in the southern hemisphere, while planets below the axis are in the northern hemisphere. When the majority of your planets fall in the northern half of your chart (below the horizon) you tend to be introspective, seeking and finding strength within yourself for the solutions to the problems of everyday life. Conversely, if you have the majority of your planets in the southern half of your chart (above the horizon), you look outside yourself for both solutions to daily problems and the strength to cope with difficulty. Often the terms "introvert" (majority below the horizon) and "extrovert" (majority above the horizon) are applied to this division. These labels are highly charged and deceiving. Most of us tend to believe that introverts are unfriendly and extroverts lack depth. That is not the real meaning of these words nor is it the meaning of this hemisphere division.

As we'll see when we analyze Toby's chart (Chart 23 on page 68) and Tina's chart (Chart 25 on page 70), not all of us with a majority of planets below the horizon are hermits, nor are all of us with a majority above the horizon social butterflies.

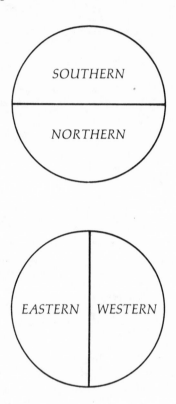

Figure 2.1 Hemispheres.

The other major hemisphere division is along the vertical or Midheaven-Nadir axis. When you have the majority of your planets on the eastern, or Ascendant, side of the chart, you are accustomed to making decisions based on your own wants and needs at the time of the decision. When the majority of your planets is on the western, or Descendant, side of the chart, you usually base your decisions on the wants and needs of the people around you. Neither hemisphere is intrinsically "better" or "more spiritual" than the other.

Simplistic terms such as "self-centered," "self-sufficient" or "ruggedly individualistic" for the eastern hemisphere and "self-sacrificing" or "martyr-like" for the western hemisphere reflect the astrologer's bias more than the true meaning of a heavy emphasis in either of these hemispheres. As with the northern and southern hemispheres, the inherent tendencies of the sign positions of the Sun, Moon, and Ascendant will be emphasized or muted by the east-west division of the planets in the chart.

Hemisphere emphasis shifts very slowly as the chart progresses. Often, your natal emphasis will remain for your entire lifetime. Figure 2.2 demonstrates why hemisphere division changes so slowly.

When the chart progresses, the cusps move in a clockwise direction, while the planets move in a counterclockwise direction. The Sun, Mercury, Venus and Mars often move at a rate that is the same or faster than the cusps, while the planets from Jupiter on out always move much slower than the cusps. Due to these differences in rate of progression, the inner planets often stay in or near the same house as natally, while the outer planets change houses as the cusps progress in the secondary chart.

Because of the relative motion of the planets, it is uncommon to have a chart in which a heavy emphasis in one hemisphere is reversed by the progression of the chart. The planets from Jupiter outward move so slowly that the motion of the angles carries them in a clockwise direction, while the faster planets stay in the same position relative to the angles. This means that most charts having a strong natal hemisphere emphasis will become more balanced as the chart progresses.

As with every rule or generality in astrology, this, too, has exceptions. The importance of understanding hemisphere emphasis in the analysis of a secondary progression is in the exceptional charts, in those few charts in which the hemisphere emphasis does change radically within the lifetime of the individual.

The examples in this section demonstrate the four extremes of hemisphere division. The first two examples do not change hemisphere emphasis during the progression. The second two examples

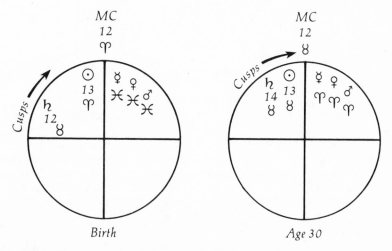

Figure 2.2 Changes in hemisphere emphasis by progression.

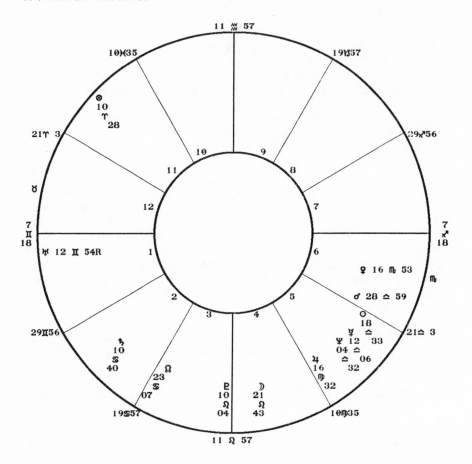

Chart 23. Toby: October 11, 1944, 8:20 PM EWT, 42N21, 71W03; data from hospital records; Placidus houses.

become more balanced as the charts progress. The last example is a woman's chart that completely reversed hemisphere emphasis by the time she was twenty-nine.

The first example, Toby (Charts 23 and 24), with Gemini rising, Sun in Libra, and Moon in Leo, has all ten planets below the horizon. But the triple yang nature of Toby's Sun, Moon, and Ascendant is certainly not symbolic of a recluse! (Of course, Uranus in the first house also indicates a rather outgoing nature, and I'm sure you can find at least nine other astrological reasons for Toby's effervescence.)

But Toby does gain a certain stability from this hemisphere division. Toby can, and does, use her inner strength to deal with the problems which are inevitable in her life. Although she enjoys other

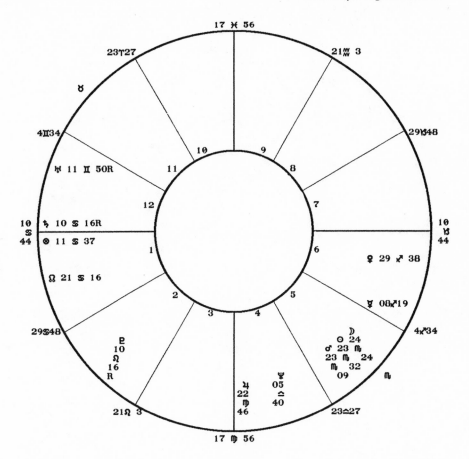

Chart 24. Toby: Chart 23 progressed to October 11, 1979 using the Sun's mean motion in RA for the MC.

people and is often the "life of the party," Toby is also able to be alone without excessive anxiety. Had she been born twelve hours earlier or later, she might have great problems with living alone. As it is, Toby is quite self-sufficient.

The progressed chart for Toby shows that the hemisphere emphasis had not shifted by the time she was thirty-five. In her life, she will never have more than three planets above the horizon in her progressed chart. Her hemisphere emphasis will always play counter-point to her triple yang natal Sun, Moon, and Ascendant. Toby will always be able to draw on her own reserves to accomplish her aims.

Tina's charts (25 and 26 on pages 70-71) are an interesting contrast, for Tina is a triple yin personality, with Sun in Virgo, Moon in Cancer, and Scorpio rising. Despite the fact that all ten planets are above the

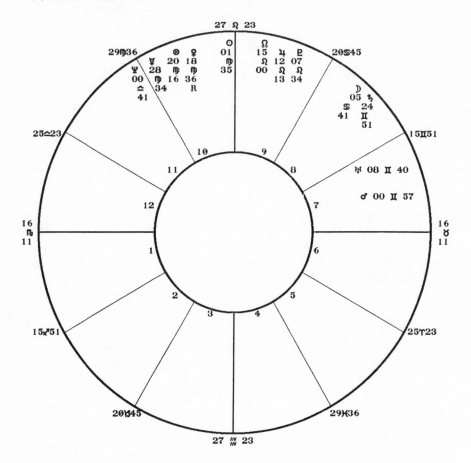

Chart 25. Tina: August 25, 1943, 12:30 PM EWT, 42N22, 70W59; data from hospital records; Placidus houses.

horizon, Tina was terribly shy as a child and had to work consciously at building up self-confidence. Tina accepted the teasing of her parents and her peers as confirmation of her own poor self-image. She did not break out of the self-imposed isolation her shyness conferred on her until after graduation from high school.

The southern hemisphere emphasis here indicates that Tina is not happy in solitude. In fact, Tina has never lived by herself, for she moved straight from her parents' house into a marriage.

As her Ascendant progressed into a yang sign, Sagittarius, Tina found it easier to venture into the world, and she got her first job. When her Sun progressed into Libra, Tina became more active in a volunteer group and ran for a rather demanding board position. She won the election easily and performed her duties quite well. At this

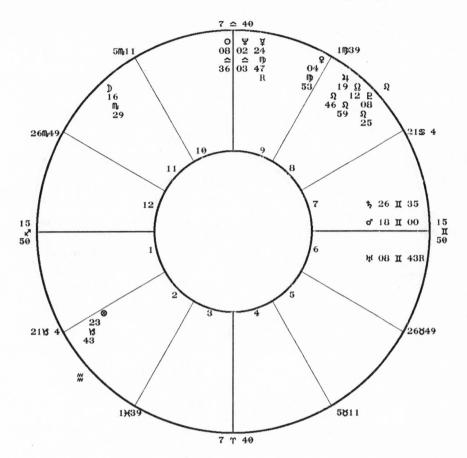

Chart 26. Tina: Chart 25 progressed to August 25, 1981 using the Sun's mean motion in RA for the MC.

time, she feels quite assured of her own competence and ability to cope with the difficulties which have arisen in her life.

Our next example, Sophie (Charts 27 and 28 on pages 72-73), has eight planets on the western side of the chart, Sun in Gemini, Moon in Libra, and Sagittarius rising. The general description of a triple yang personality indicates that Sophie should be outgoing, active, initiatory. Because Sophie has a western hemisphere emphasis, however, with Mercury in Cancer and Saturn rising (and forming the handle of this bucket-shaped chart), very little of the yang aggression in her personality is obvious to the outside world.

Sophie is quite shy, usually soft-spoken, and a bit of a recluse. However, behind this approach, Sophie is actually quite strong, given to analyzing situations and eventually getting her own way. In

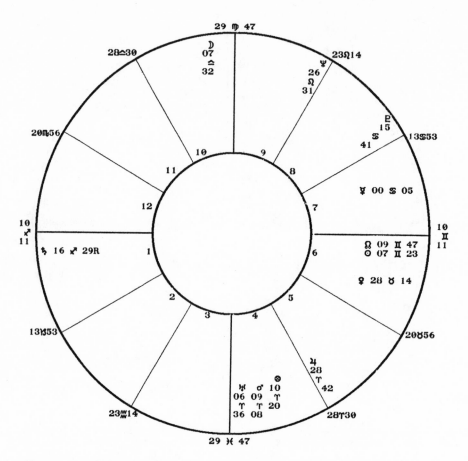

Chart 27. Sophie: May 28, 1928, 8:30 PM EDT, 41N55, 73W59; data from family records; Placidus houses.

Sophie's words, she tends to "pour out herself for others," at times over-sacrificing to her own ultimate loss.

As Sophie's chart progressed, the hemisphere balance between east and west evened out. By age fifty-three, as shown, she had four planets in the east and six in the west. By then, Sophie had learned to say "No" to some of the requests of others.

Steve (Charts 29 and 30 on pages 74-75) has a heavy eastern hemisphere emphasis, with nine planets on the eastern side of his chart. His Sun in Libra is yang, Moon and Ascendant in Scorpio are yin. Although the first house Moon in a yin sign could indicate a sensitivity to the environment, in this case it manifests as a strongly suspicious and secretive attitude towards others. Since the ruler of

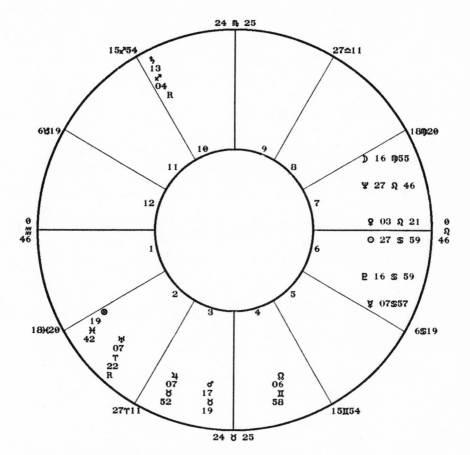

Chart 28. Sophie: Chart 27 progressed to May 28, 1981 using the Sun's mean motion in RA for the MC.

Scorpio (Pluto) is conjunct the Midheaven, Steve's Scorpio traits are intensified. He uses emotion to manipulate his environment, and particularly to manipulate the women in his life. During childhood, he constantly changed his relationships to his parents, his sister and his teachers in an attempt to dominate his mother. (Sophie, Charts 27 and 28, is Steve's mother.)

As Steve's chart progressed, the hemispheres became more evenly balanced. The extreme self-centeredness of his childhood began to lessen, although he still has difficulty with dominance-control issues. However, he is relating to others in a more balanced fashion.

The preceding examples have shown the typical effect of secondary progressions on hemisphere emphasis. The majority of charts will

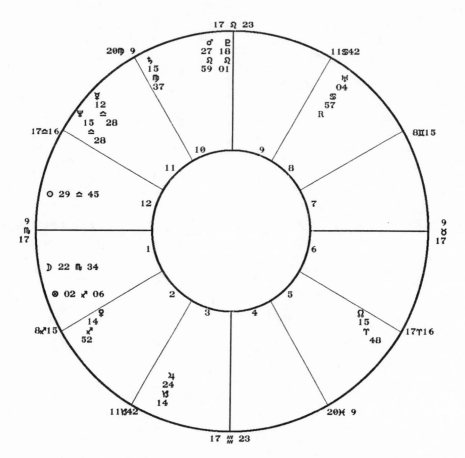

Chart 29. Steve: October 23, 1949, 7:09 AM EST, 40N42, 74W00; data from hospital records; Placidus houses.

either remain the same or tend towards balancing the hemisphere emphasis.

Josi's charts (Charts 31 and 32 on pages 76-77) show that her hemisphere emphasis changed radically by the time she was twenty-nine.

When Josi came for a consultation, she was seeking direction in her life. She had always been extremely dependent, first on her family, then on her husband. Because of the relatively weak position of Saturn in both natal and progressed charts, she did not want to accept responsibility for her own actions. Her husband was balking at being required to make all the decisions in the marriage, for if anything went wrong, Josi's Virgo responded with heavy criticism of his decisions.

Initially, in keeping with her natal set-up, Josi sought to have me make all her decisions for her. Josi called me several times a week to

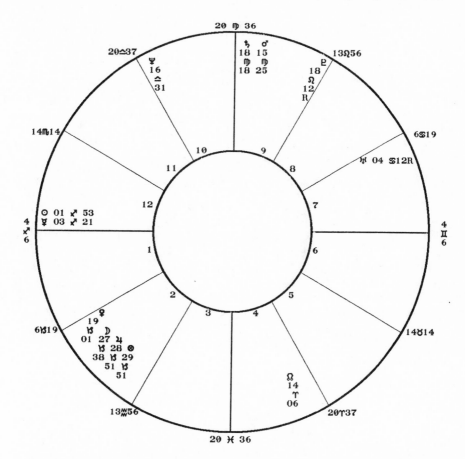

Chart 30. Steve: Chart 29 progressed to October 23, 1981 using the Sun's mean motion in RA for the MC.

ask what she should do in even the most trivial situations. In effect, she tried to place the responsibility for her life on me.

I suggested, without avail, that Josi seek psychiatric aid. Josi could not understand or accept that her problems were connected to her desire to have someone else direct her life.

Because Josi so obviously needed a sense of community and sharing, I suggested that Josi (brought up Roman Catholic) investigate a group of Charismatic Catholics in her area. Since she was totally unwilling to undertake therapy to help uncover the roots of her dilemma, and since I am not a psychotherapist, I felt that such a religious group might be able to provide the constant feedback and approval which she sought.

As Josi's Mars-Venus conjunction became exact in her secondary chart and moved on to square her progressed Saturn and sextile her

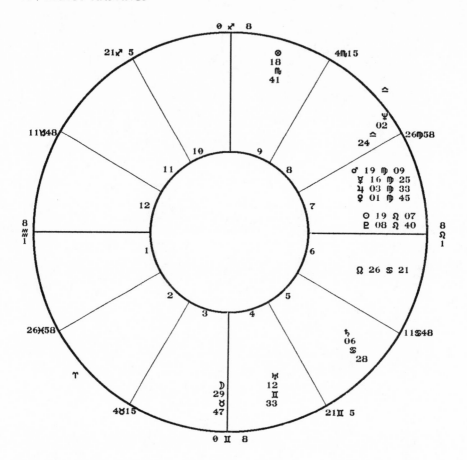

Chart 31. Josi: August 11, 1944, 7:15 PM EDT, 42N22, 71W05; data from baby book; Placidus houses.

progressed Pluto, Josi became a born-again Christian. As a member of this religious sect, Josi was able to cope with the problems of day-to-day life more easily. Her dependency needs, projected on other people through the natal positions, became projected upon an internal "other," or a religious belief system. Within this system, choices are proscribed and restricted.

Has the extrovert become the introvert with the hemisphere shift? Not exactly. Within the framework of her church involvement, Josi sought and received approval from others. At this point, Josi restricted most of her friendships and social exchanges to the church group. Within this group, her natal division was still the most obvious, as she sought advice and direction from the other members of the group. In the world as a whole, however, the secondary progressed chart more accurately described Josi's interactions.

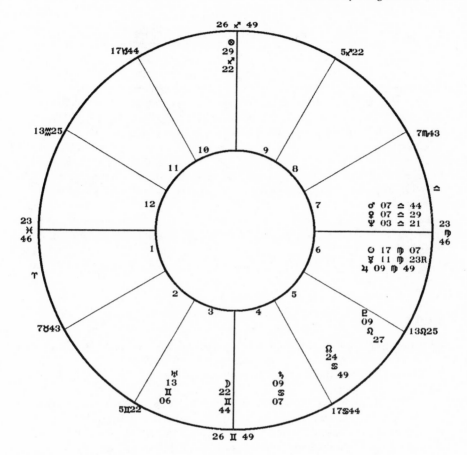

Chart 32. Josi: Chart 31 progressed to August 11, 1973 using the Sun's mean motion in RA for the MC.

Josi slowly stopped asking permission from her husband or other people before she made any decisions. She started to control daily realities (sixth house) in a slightly less compulsive manner. Although her house was still spotless, she began to relax a little about perfect cleanliness. That meant that she could invite people over occasionally, in spite of the fact that other people would use the house and probably get things dirty.

Josi did finally get some therapy (during the year that her progressed Saturn and progressed Mars-Venus squared each other). By this time she was not seeing me (as astrology was the mark of the devil, according to her current belief system). Information on this period of her life is therefore hearsay. However, according to relatives, she is now functioning quite well, holding down a job, and making daily decisions with little outward difficulty.

FOCUS ON THE WORLD:

CHART SHAPE

After determining the hemisphere emphasis in a chart, I look at the overall shape of the chart to determine the general framework or pattern from which the person is operating. Mark Edmund Jones wrote extensively about chart shape,[13] but that type of exhaustive analysis is beyond the scope of this book. We will limit the discussion here to the six simplest shapes. These are the bowl, the bundle, the bucket, the seesaw, the locomotive, and the splash/splay.

The shape of a chart changes slowly as planets progress around the wheel. A bundle chart will change to a bowl or locomotive (or vice versa) and with the progression of the Moon will change to a bucket at times. A seesaw changes to a splash or a locomotive as the planets progress. The differences between the shape of your natal chart and the shape of your progressed chart symbolize a different pattern in your overall approach to life.

BOWL

The bowl chart has every planet within an 180° span, or within one opposition. The hemisphere containing the planets will not necessarily correspond to the hemispheres created by dividing the chart along the MC or Asc axes.

If you have a bowl chart, you are faced with constant and demanding choices in your life. The choices always involve issues of self-interest versus self-sacrifice. There seldom seems to be an in-between area where both of these extremes can mingle.

Should you choose to keep your talents for yourself, you might become very bitter. Having always guarded your possessions and abilities, you may find at the end of your life that the closely-guarded bowl is nearly empty, and the residue gall and wormwood. In contrast, if you choose to pour out your talents and abilities for the betterment of those around you, you will never have an empty bowl. At the end of such a life, your bowl will brim with the achievement of your unselfish life.

The reality of life with the bowl chart falls somewhere between these two extremes. If your personality is completely devoid of selfish interests, you probably didn't need to incarnate, so you are not reading this from a physical body. Those of you who are here trying to manage unselfish sharing are manifesting the best of this type of chart. (Chart 23 on page 68 is a bowl.)

---

[13]Jones, Marc Edmund, *The Guide to Horoscopic Interpretation*, David McKay, Philadelphia, Pennsylvania, 1972.

BUNDLE

In the bundle chart, all of the planets are within the space of a trine, or 120°. If you have this type of chart, your life is characterized by an intense interest in one area. The bundle will always emphasize one of the hemisphere divisions. If the bundle crosses the Asc/Dsc axis (as in Chart 31 on page 76), it emphasizes either the eastern or western hemisphere. If the bundle crosses the MC/IC axis (as in Chart 25 on page 70), it emphasizes either the northern or southern hemisphere. Occasionally, a bundle chart will have seven or more planets in one quadrant (see Chart 31). In this case, the affairs of that quadrant will be of utmost importance in your life.

The concentration of planets in the bundle chart underscores your need to move out of yourself and consider using your talents and abilities for the good of others. This may be more obvious to the people around you than it is to you. People with bundle charts are often brilliant in particular areas of life. However, if you do not choose to develop the other areas of your life, the narrow area of your expertise may become more of a prison than a true means of self-expression.

BUCKET

The bucket shape has nine of the planets within the space of an opposition (180°) with one planet opposing the center of the opposition (the handle of the bucket). The planet in the opposition position does not have another planet in sextile or closer relationship. Some astrologers insist that a true bucket has no planet closer than a square to the handle. (Chart 7 on page 34 and Chart 27 on page 72 are bucket charts.)

The Sun, Mercury, and Venus will never be the handle of a bucket, for these planets never exceed a sextile relationship to each other.

In the bucket chart, the planet in the handle position is in high focus. When this planet has close oppositions, the entire symbolism of the chart can center on it. You'll tend to express your energy through the lens of this planet.

SEESAW

The seesaw chart has two groups of planets, each group within about 90° of arc, which oppose each other. (Chart 4 on page 30 is a seesaw.) When you have a seesaw chart, you tend to flip back and forth between two modes of behavior. The more oppositions there are in the seesaw, the more extreme your behavior changes are. There is always an inner tension driving you towards action. Whether you can resolve the tensions inherent in this chart depends primarily on how honest you are about your own tendency to create tension in any given situation.

LOCOMOTIVE

In a locomotive chart the planets are spaced around the chart so that there is one empty space equal to a trine, or 120°. (Chart 14 on page 47 and Chart 16 on page 50 are locomotive charts.) The planet next to the empty trine in a clockwise direction is the planet in high focus or in the lead. You will channel your energies along the direction of the lead planet, according to the house and sign occupied. You have a single-minded determination akin to a train which only runs on "one track." Every planet has positive and negative possibilities as the lead planet of a locomotive. For instance, Neptune in the lead could mean a musical or artistic track or simply a foggy and very obscure track!

SPLASH/SPLAY

The splash or the splay chart has all of the planets evenly distributed around the chart. There is no empty space greater than 90°. The splay chart has several planets in angular positions, while the splash may or may not have many angular planets. It is often quite difficult to distinguish the splash from the splay chart, which is why I've combined them here. Mark Edmund Jones in one workshop classified my chart as a splash, and then in another conversation classified it as a splay. After that I stopped worrying about which was which. (Chart 3 on page 23 and Chart 12 on page 43 are splash charts.)

If you have a splash or a splay chart, it is difficult for you to excel in any one specific area, for you tend to scatter your abilities and talents over a broad spectrum. You are the "renaissance man/woman." Nonetheless, you are often in the public eye, for when this type of chart is combined with high intelligence you cannot only master several fields, you can transfer information from one area to another with relative ease. Thus the baby doctor is also a political activist, the violinist a political scientist.

PROGRESSED CHART SHAPE

Chart shape changes slowly as the chart progresses. There is no practical way to say, "Today this is a bowl. Tomorrow it will be a locomotive." Difference in life-styles don't change overnight, either. The simplest and most direct method of understanding the changes indicated by progression in chart shape is the use of key words for each shape.

Thus the bowl (self-sacrifice vs. self-interest) goes to the bundle (concentration in one area of life), to the locomotive (tremendous energy along a single track) or, with the progressed Moon, to the bucket (handle planet—Moon in high focus). The bundle (concentration in one area of life) goes to the bucket (handle planet in high focus) or the bowl (self-interest vs. self-sacrifice), etc. The splash chart (energy scattered in many areas) usually goes toward the locomotive (energy along a single track), while the locomotive may go towards the splash.

MIXED REVIEWS:

INTERCEPTED SIGNS AND MIXED ANGLES

Every sign which is intercepted in your natal chart will sooner or later show up on the cusp of that house as your chart progresses. It is as if the expression of the intercepted sign is delayed until you have gained the experience to utilize the strength of the intercepted sign in the area of life symbolized by that house.

Charts with intercepted signs have different quadruplicities on the angles. Thus, if you have Capricorn rising (cardinal) and were born in the northern hemisphere, you are very likely to have Scorpio (fixed) on your Midheaven. If you were born in the southern hemisphere, you probably have Virgo (mutable) on the Midheaven with Capricorn rising. If you have Cancer rising (cardinal), you may have a Pisces (mutable) Midheaven in the northern hemisphere, or a Taurus (fixed) Midheaven in the southern hemisphere.

Although there are surface benefits to having a mundane trine or sextile between angles, this relationship more often poses problems. First, you do not integrate your approach to the world with your career or life direction very well. Although both will be the same polarity, the Ascendant will urge you to action, or to stay put, or be flexible, while the Midheaven indicates that your needs are not satisfied by your projection through the Ascendant. The second difficulty is that you are not always able to recognize and utilize both yin and yang sides of yourself. When the Ascendant and Midheaven are in mundane trine or sextile, you may project one polarity onto the other people in your life, forcing them to provide this expression for you.

Thus, if you have Cancer rising and a Pisces Midheaven, you may require your marriage partner and your family to perform all of the yang functions for you, while you project your yin side. In contrast, if you have Aquarius rising and a Sagittarius Midheaven, you may project yourself in a completely yang fashion, relying on family members to supply the yin needs in your life.

This doesn't always work in the wonderfully clear manner just outlined. Josi (Chart 31 on page 76) has Aquarius rising, Sagittarius Midheaven, Leo Sun and Taurus Moon. She has a yang predominance, yet demanded that others in her life perform the yang functions for her.

The progression of the chart straightens out the mixture of quadruplicities, or at least helps out a bit. For instance, if you've got a Sagittarius MC and an Aquarius Ascendant, your Ascendant will progress to Pisces—mutable like your natal MC—although your MC will progress to Capricorn, a cardinal sign. If you have a Pisces MC and a Cancer Ascendant, your Ascendant progresses to fixed (not much help to your mutable natal MC), but your MC progresses to cardinal, which agrees with your natal Ascendant. This still leaves you coping with a mixture, for you have to combine your habitual, or natal, projection with your right now, or progressed, projection. You do have a unique ability to understand all of the quadruplicities, for they'll all be appearing on your angles through natal and progressed charts fairly often in your life.

Regardless of what's going on with the angles in your chart, if you have mixed quadruplicities on the angles, you have two signs intercepted in opposite houses. Whenever a house has a sign intercepted in it, you'll experience two different modes of action in the affairs of that house. The houses that contain the intercepted sign need to be expanded upon, while the houses that are very small, having the same sign on the cusp as the sign on the cusp of the following house, indicate areas of your life which should be less emphasized.

Houses one through six involve the self, while houses seven to twelve involve the outside world. Each house interacts with the house opposite it on the wheel. Thus, the meaning of the first house cannot be completely understood without considering the meaning of the seventh, the meaning of the second is involved with the eighth, and so on. When we discuss signs intercepted in houses, we must consider this interaction, for it is the key to the integration of the inner and outer person.

In the following analysis of interceptions, the houses are treated as pairs since all interceptions occur that way.

FIRST HOUSE—SEVENTH HOUSE:
ME AND OTHERS

Cardinal Signs on the Cusps—Fixed Signs Intercepted: Cardinal signs jump into relating to the environment and to others, for cardinal signs prefer to initiate action in these areas. When the intercepted fixed signs progress to the cusps of the first and seventh houses, you solidify these patterns of relating.

Fixed Signs on the Cusps—Mutable Signs Intercepted: Fixed signs on the first and seventh houses like to categorize the environment and other people, then relate to both in a preconceived, planned manner. When mutable signs progress to these cusps, you begin to vary your approach to relating. Clichés and prejudices will not do for you any more. It's as if you've let go of a huge weight which kept you from being able to enjoy the spontaneity of the mutable sign while it was locked into the interception.

Mutable Signs on the Cusps—Cardinal Signs Intercepted: You are changeable in your interactions with the environment and other people. As the cardinal interception progresses to the cusps, you can make decisions more easily, initiate action more often. You can decide whether you want to project a flexible, accommodating image or a more decisive, action-oriented image.

SECOND HOUSE—EIGHTH HOUSE:
MINE AND YOURS

Cardinal Signs on the Cusps—Fixed Signs Intercepted: Cardinal signs conceptualize the notion of "mine" and "yours" and then initiate action concerning these ideas. When the intercepted fixed signs progress to the second-eighth axis, you add the concept of "I keep mine, you keep yours" to your value system.

Fixed Signs on the Cusps—Mutable Signs Intercepted: Fixed signs on the second-eighth axis are notorious for the possessive "I keep mine, you keep yours" value system. When your mutable interception progresses to the cusps, you can release this, for the mutable signs indicate that what's mine and what's yours may depend on the circumstances.

Mutable Signs on the Cusps—Cardinal Signs Intercepted: Here you go from the mutable belief that what's mine and what's yours may be relative to a sense that sometimes you have to make clear decisions about possessions and values. The cardinal sign isn't necessarily any more possessive than the mutable sign, but when your cardinal interception progresses to the cusp, you'll recognize your growing need to know what's yours, and what isn't.

THIRD HOUSE—NINTH HOUSE:
I THINK AND THEY THINK

Cardinal Signs on the Cusps—Fixed Signs Intercepted: Cardinal signs on the third and ninth houses rush into new concepts, initiate new ideas. When your fixed interception progresses to these cusps, you'll start to hang onto some of your old philosophies. You may begin to recognize that you only like to change your way of thinking when you initiate the change. Cardinal signs aren't flexible—they just like to start new things!

Fixed Signs on the Cusps—Mutable Signs Intercepted: You hold onto ideas and philosophies, for you like to test them before you change anything. When your mutable interception progresses to these cusps, you're likely to hate it at first. Too many changes make you revert to the natal expression instantly. After you've had time to get used to it, though, you'll start to enjoy the ability to consider different viewpoints and philosophies.

Mutable Signs on the Cusps—Cardinal Signs Intercepted: This change will probably sneak up on you when you aren't looking. Your natal signs indicate a flexible approach to philosophy and thinking. The change to cardinal signs may result in some soapbox stands that you don't realize you're making, because cardinal signs really tend to believe that there is some "right" way to do things.

FOURTH HOUSE—TENTH HOUSE:
WHERE I COME FROM AND WHERE I'M GOING

Cardinal Signs on the Cusps—Fixed Signs Intercepted: When you have a cardinal MC-IC axis, you tend to initiate action concerning your career as well as your home. If you have the yang Aries-Libra axis, you rush into changing things, while if you have the yin Capricorn-Cancer axis, you are a bit more conservative. The cardinal trait that all four share is the belief that first, there is a correct way to approach things, the second, the correct way is your way. When your fixed interception progresses to these angles, you may become positively hidebound about the "right" way to look at your ancestry, to look at your career, to decorate your house, or to go about reaching spiritual goals. Alternately, you may start to believe that you can no more change where you're going than you can change where you came from. The secret that you may want to think about is that you *can* change how you feel about where you came from, and you *do* choose where you want to go.

Fixed Signs on the Cusps—Mutable Signs Intercepted: Once you've made up your mind about either your family background or your career direction, you can be very stubborn and stuck. However, your particular ace in the hole is your mutable interception. Once the mutable signs progress to your MC/IC axis, you can loosen much of the rigidity that may have plagued your childhood. You might even take on second career!

Mutable Signs on the Cusps—Cardinal Signs Intercepted: When you have mutable signs on the MC-IC axis, you don't tend to have a single career goal. There are so many things that are so interesting—both in what you want to do and how and where you'd like to live—that you don't like to settle down. Soon after your intercepted cardinal signs progress to these angles, you'll find that you can choose directions much more easily. It will begin to occur to you that there are some approaches that work better than others. Although you'll never be very dogmatic about your choices, you will settle down somewhat.

FIFTH HOUSE—ELEVENTH HOUSE:
MY PLEASURES AND GROUP ACTIVITIES

Cardinal Signs on the Cusps—Fixed Signs Intercepted: When you have cardinal signs on the fifth and eleventh houses, you like to initiate group activities and you like to decide where to go and what to do in your leisure time. Moreover, you want to do things your way in both cases. When your fixed interception progresses to the cusps, you'll find that you're much more determined to finish the projects you start, both in groups and singly. You'll either throw away or finish that afghan, and you'll either change friends or take on more responsibility for carrying out plans with a group.

Fixed Signs on the Cusps—Mutable Signs Intercepted: You really enjoy familiar leisure activities and old friends. You aren't comfortable in a group of strangers and don't particularly want to embark on new escapades, particularly if you don't know the people in the group very well. As your mutable interception progresses to the cusps of these houses, you'll relax more with groups, and you'll enjoy spontaneous events more. You'll finally be able to let go of some things you really don't like doing. You'll always have a tendency to finish your projects, but now you'll be able to change course in the middle when it seems sensible to do so.

Mutable Signs on the Cusps—Cardinal Signs Intercepted: When you have mutable signs on the fifth-eleventh axis, you'll try nearly anything with a group and you'll take most risks with your many talents and abilities. What you are not particularly good at is finishing any of these things. The cardinal interception won't help you finish things, but will give you the impetus to keep on trying new experiences.

SIXTH HOUSE—TWELFTH HOUSE:

DAILY RESPONSIBILITIES AND PERSONAL IRRESPONSIBILITY

Cardinal Signs on the Cusps—Fixed Signs Intercepted: When you have cardinal signs on this axis, you prefer to start right in dealing with the daily grind while trying very hard to appear unaggressive in order to pass off your irresponsible twelfth house side (onto someone else, if possible). As your fixed interception progresses over the cusps, you'll solidify a daily routine, preferring not to change one you've found works for you. You'll need to watch out for stonewalling your subconscious needs, an easy thing to do with this combination.

Fixed Signs on the Cusps—Mutable Signs Intercepted: With fixed signs on this axis, you set up a routine and stick to it even though you have an unconscious fear of rigidity. The progression of your mutable interception to your sixth-twelfth axis often provides a relief valve for you, because as you become less tied to the daily grind, you can begin to recognize and forgive some of your own personal irresponsibility.

Mutable Signs on the Cusps—Cardinal Signs Intercepted: You may be a great list-maker, but terrible at following routines. Subconscious fear of vacillation ties you down. You feel very guilty about not following your lists of things to do. When your cardinal interception progresses to these cusps, you'll have an easier time prioritizing the lists. Once you figure out that you've done the important things, the fact that you irresponsibly ignored the dirty laundry for a few days won't bother you as much. After you stop being so guilty about the dirty laundry, it will be much easier to get it done before you run out of clothes to wear.

ITCHY UNDERWEAR:

THE VOID OF COURSE PLANET

The planet highest in degree in any sign is the void of course planet in your chart. When you sort out the planets by degree (a thiry-degree sort), you start the list with any planets at 0° of any sign, then 1°, 2°, and so on up to 29°. In this kind of sorting, the void of course planet comes last. Major transits and progressions aspect every other planet before they aspect the void of course planet. If there are two planets at the same highest degree, the one with the higher minutes is the void of course planet. If there are two planets at exactly the same highest degree and minute, the faster planet takes precedent and is the void of course planet. Right now, Pluto is moving faster than Neptune and takes precedence over Neptune if the two of them are at the same degree and minute in your chart (e.g., both were at 29° 7'—Pluto in Libra, Neptune in Sagittarius—on March 12, 1983). Other than that exception, the rest of the planets behave fairly regularly: Jupiter is always faster than Saturn, Mars is always faster than any planet from Jupiter outward, and so on. In this context only the relative rate of the orbit matters, not whether the planet is direct or retrograde. As you can see in Figure 2.3, determining the void of course planet is usually very easy.

When either the Sun or Moon is void of course, the position takes on added significance in your life, for the lights symbolize your physical and emotional self. When your Sun is the void of course planet, as in the second example in Figure 2.3, you tend to put yourself and your own physical needs last. You may be careless of your physical safety or health. You may wear your clothes until they literally fall off you because you simply don't think about buying things for your body. Keeping a jacket for twenty years probably won't hurt you, but ignoring your body's care can. You need to view yourself in a more positive light, to be a little more selfish in your actions.

When your Moon is the void of course planet, you put your emotions last. This is unfortunate, for you may put off response

☉ 9°♋01'	♃ 10°♒39'	☉ 29°♋03'	♃ 18°♒18'
☽ 16°♋18'	♄ 26°♊09'	☽ 14°♈25'	♄ 28°♊45'
☿ 2°♌05'	♅ 18°♎56'	☿ 26°♋13'	♅ 19°♎13'
♀ 0°♌46'	♆ 5°♐12'	♀ 26°♌16'	♆ 4°♐50'
♂ 6°♈33'	♇ 1°♎46'	♂ 19°♈08'	♇ 2°♎06'
♄ is the void of course planet at 26°.		The ☉ is the void of course planet at 29°.	

Figure 2.3 Void of course planets

habitually so that when you finally do react emotionally, it is not a clear response to a single input. Your eventual emotional response, complicated by all the things you put off, may have very little to do with whatever triggered it. You need encouragement to explore your feelings in order to recognize emotional stresses before they build up to difficult levels.

The void of course planet indicates some frustration in the house ruled by that planet. This is not an overt or crippling type of frustration, but rather more like a pair of itchy underpants. They were not uncomfortable enough for you to notice when you first put them on, but they color the activities of your day because after a while you are constantly aware of those itchy underpants. Whatever house (or houses) the void of course planet rules indicates an area of life in which you are never completely comfortable. If the void of course planet rules a sign which is intercepted, and thus does not appear on any house cusp, then no area of frustration is symbolized. But if the void of course planet is Venus or Mercury which each rule two signs, and one of the signs ruled covers two houses, you could have up to three houses involved in this symbolism.

VOID OF COURSE PLANETS AND THE PROGRESSED CHART

Dorothea Lynde taught me the meaning of the void of course planet in the natal chart. I then tried using it in the progressed chart and have found the results quite interesting. Often the progressed house ruled by the progressed void of course planet will be a source of minor irritation not easily explained through any other symbolism in the chart. The irritation is always minor, and could be avoided if you consider the matters of the house involved before everything gets into a mess.

Although the void of course planet in your natal chart remains the same for life, the planet which is void of course in your progressed chart changes. Every two and a half years, your progressed Moon changes sign. After your progressed Moon has made its last aspect and before it changes sign, it is the void of course planet. Whatever house has Cancer on the cusp in your progressed chart will indicate where the frustration is until the Moon enters the next sign. If your progressed Jupiter is 29°50′ of a sign and your progressed Moon is about to change sign, the progressed Moon (which moves roughly 2′ per day) will only be the void of course planet for five days. You may not have time to notice the slight frustration of the void of course Moon in this case. You are more likely to be aware of irritation in whatever house Jupiter rules in your progressed chart.

The following delineations work equally well with the natal and the progessed void of course placement. The only difference is that the natal lasts a lifetime, the progressed only until the ruling planet changes sign. I've not been able to confirm any effect on the natal houses from the progressed void of course planet unless the sign on the natal and the progressed houses is the same.

Void of Course Planet Rules the First House: You are dissatisfied with your personality or with the face you show the world. You can always think of what you should have said or done when it is too late to say or do it. You won't accept anything other than perfection from yourself. You resurrect adolescent worries about your face and figure. Relax. Nobody is looking.

Void of Course Planet Rules the Second House: You are uneasy about money or finances. This worry rarely has anything to do with your actual financial situation. You may sail through periods of poverty when your void of course planet does not rule the second house and become itchy during times of relative affluence when it does. One interesting alternative is to squirrel away lots of food, just in case, during this period. Some of my clients kept cases of tuna fish, canned soup, and other foodstuffs and then ate them up after the period ended.

Void of Course Planet Rules the Third House: Siblings or communications may become a source of frustration. You may have difficulty understanding others or may find that others misunderstand you. However, in the secondary progressed chart, this house more often indicates minor mechanical problems. Your car seems to need more care and attention now, regardless of how well you look after it. Your telephone answering device develops a mind of its own and randomly deletes messages or adds mysterious noises to recorded sounds.

Void of Course Planet Rules the Fourth House: You have a little difficulty finishing things, for when you decide they are done, you discover something you forgot. Little things go wrong at home. Stock up on light bulbs; they all burn out. When you are out you worry about whether or not you shut off the stove before you left home. It's easier to make a habit of checking everything before you leave than to worry about it after the fact.

Void of Course Planet Rules the Fifth House: You are tired of hearts and flowers (or the lack of them) on the dating front. Dating games become boring. If you are married, your talents or hobbies may become sources of aggravation more than sources of relaxation. Your children, particularly the oldest, may start to sass you. The movie you want to see is the one that is always sold out, so you wind up paying four dollars to see *The Revenge of the Grade B Producer*. Your TV makes green people and red snow.

Void of Course Planet Rules the Sixth House: Your day-to-day routine falls apart or becomes unwieldy. Your pets start chewing up your furniture. Someone starts running a jackhammer outside your workplace. Repairmen show up at random, regardless of when they said they would come. Your washing machine walks off across the room into a wall and the laundromat closes down.

Void of Course Planet Rules the Seventh House: Other people in general bother you. Your spouse leaves stuff in the sink whenever you want to use it. Your partner's habit of (fill in the blank...anything from throat-clearing noises to being late) becomes infuriating. You are able to see the faults of others with great clarity, and you know that Mark Twain was right when he said "Nothing so needs reforming as other people's habits."

Void of Course Planet Rules the Eighth House: Sometimes this reflects sexual tension. You may read some article or other and wonder whether your current relationship is normal or screwy. Your partner may wear socks to bed and this drives you to distraction. You may become concerned about joint finances or tax returns. This is a terrible time to try to shave your tax bill, for you will worry so much about the darn thing that it won't be worth the few dollars saved.

Void of Course Planet Rules the Ninth House: Your in-laws start to behave just like all the jokes about in-laws, but you have difficulty laughing about it. Dumb little things go wrong when you travel. You need some safety pins and don't know how to ask for them in Greek. If you are in college, you get up at six a.m. to be first in line to register for the fabulous course taught by the most illustrious professor at the entire school, the one you came to this college to study under. When registration opens at ten a.m., you find out that he is on sabbatical, and the course is being taught this semester by D. Idiot, graduate student.

Void of Course Planet Rules the Tenth House: You begin to wonder if you chose the right career. All bosses (including yourself, if you are self-employed) expect utter perfection. Your own inner critical parent goes on overtime, reminding you of every career decision you could have made or done differently. You are not satisfied with your public image, but are not too sure of what you would rather be. You think longingly of a career as a beach bum.

Void of Course Planet Rules the Eleventh House: You decide that all of your goals stink, but you don't have any alternatives. The groups of people with whom you are associated never do what they say they are going to do. So you wind up at the bowling alley (or the library, or the museum, or the...) when everyone else knows that the group decided to go over to Melvin's house to play volleyball.

Void of Course Planet Rules the Twelfth House: You tend to bury subconscious thoughts or motivations as far away from consciousness as possible. You resent being told that there might be reasons for your illogical actions. (You may resent the implication that your actions are illogical.) Restraint, such as hospitalization, is particularly hard to bear during this time. You know that Robert Lovelace had rocks in his head when he said: "Stone walls do not a prison make, nor iron bars a cage."

OUR IDEAL PERSON

SIGNATURE

The signature in your chart is the sign indicated by the combination of the quadruplicity with the most planets and the triplicity with the most planets. In order to determine the signature, count the number of planets in cardinal signs, the number in fixed signs, and the number in mutable signs. Then count the number of planets in fire, earth, air and water. The two with the largest number tell you the signature. You can add the Ascendant in case of a tie, but you must add the Ascendant to both the quadruplicity and the triplicity.

The signature in any chart is symbolic of an ideal personality which we try to become. To get a quick handle on what this means specifically, take the positive attributes for the sign of your signature and add "I would like to be more..." in front of each trait. In other words, if you have an Aries signature, you want to be more aggressive, forthright, initiatory. If you have a Taurus signature, you want to be more patient, persistent, loyal and dependable. If you have a Gemini signature, you want to be more verbal, curious, flexible. No one aspires to negative personality traits, so you don't want to be a motor-mouth if you have a Gemini signature, or a nag if you have a Cancer signature.

When your signature is the same as your Sun sign (which happens a little over 25 percent of the time because Mercury and Venus are frequently in the same sign as your Sun) you want to be exactly what you already are. The woman indicated in Figure 2.4 on page 92 has a Capricorn Sun and a Capricorn signature. She is quite content with her Capricornian traits.

If your natal Sun is in the same sign as your progressed signature, you are becoming more aware of the strengths inherent in your

☉ 28°♑	♃ 27°♍			Fire: 2	
☽ 4°♈	♄ 5°♋	Cardinal: 6		Earth: 4	
☿ 5°♑	♅ 9°♊	= Fixed: 1	and	Air: 2	
♀ 15°♓	♆ 6°♎	Mutable: 3		Water: 2	
♂ 10°♑	♇ 9°♌				

Figure 2.4 The signature is Capricorn for the majorities are cardinal/earth. (Birth data for a female born 1/18/1945, 11:20 PM, EWT, 71W17, 41N57, data from family records.)

internal "I" in your basic self. If your progressed Sun is in the same sign as your natal signature, you are becoming more like your ideal person. When your natal Sun is in the same sign as your natal signature, and your progressed Sun is in the same sign as your progressed signature (Figure 2.5 in the examples), you continue to work at manifesting the best attributes of both natal and progressed symbolism. When your progressed signature is in a sign different from both natal and progressed Sun, you have begun to see areas in your life which could be improved, particularly if your natal signature was the same sign as your natal Sun.

But what do we do with a chart which has no signature, and what about the times when your progressed signature agrees with neither your progressed Sun sign nor your natal Sun sign? If your natal chart has no clear signature (as in the example in Figure 2.6 on page 93), you do not have a clear concept of what you want to be like. This does not imply that you have no goals, for the signature has nothing to do with goals. Rather, your ideal personality is not really like any single sign. The lack of a signature won't cause any problems except to the astrologer who must define your majority in either a quadruplicity or a triplicity rather than simply telling you the positive traits of a single sign. You will always have a majority in either a quadruplicity or a triplicity because when you add the Ascendant to the planets, you have

☉ 28°♒	♃ 25°♍			Fire: 2	
☽ ♉	♄ 4°♋	Cardinal: 3		Earth: 2	
☿ 20°♒	♅ 9°♊	= Fixed: 5	and	Air: 5	
♀ 14°♈	♆ 6°♎	Mutable: 3		Water: 1	
♂ 2°♒	♇ 9°♌				

Figure 2.5 The signature is Aquarius for the majorities are fixed/air. This is the progressed signature for the data used in figure 2.4.

☉ 5°♓	♃ 25°♍	⎫		Fire: 3
☽ ♌	♄ 4°♋	⎬ = Cardinal: 3 and	Earth: 1
☿ 1°♓	♅ 9°♊		Fixed: 3	Air: 3
♀ 20°♈	♆ 6°♎	⎭ Mutable: 4	Water: 3
♂ 7°♑	♇ 9°♌			

Figure 2.6 This is the same example used in figure 2.4, but the chart has been progressed to age thirty-six. There is now no signature at all. If you add the Ascendant (fixed water), it creates a tie in quadruplicites between fixed and mutable while giving a majority in water.

eleven points to divide into either three or four groups. You will try to increase your use of the symbolism of whichever element or quality contains the majority.

The chart data used for Figures 2.4, 2.5, and 2.6, is just one example of how the signature can change during your life. Because this woman's natal Sun is at 28° Capricorn, it progressed into Aquarius long before her signature changed to Aquarius. For most of her first thirty years, her signature remained Capricorn in spite of her Aquarius progressed Sun. The combination of Aquarius progressed Sun and Capricorn progressed signature produced a rather linear, or black and white, approach to her choices about almost everything. Once the progressed signature agreed with the progressed Sun, and her natal signature agreed with her natal Sun, she began to assert (and like) the more mental and yang (Aquarius) side of her personality, which up to then she had supressed somewhat under the Capricorn signature.

As her progressed planets moved into mutable signs, she began to recognize the rigid patterns which were stifling her creativity. The combination of cardinal and fixed did not allow flexibility in approach. The new emphasis on mutability, while encouraging change, is not yet pronounced enough to overcome her inherent natal cardinality, i.e., she likes change only when she initiates it. The years in which her progressed Moon is in Sagittarius, Gemini, or Pisces will be the years that are actually the most flexible for her in this period of her life, for then she will have five planets in mutable signs and a majority in fire, air, or water.

When your signature differs from your Sun sign, it may differ in element or quality or both. The following descriptions of the differences are applicable to natal and progressed analysis, although the natal will be a constant background or lifelong lesson, while the progressed will be specific to the time span of the progression.

QUADRUPLICITY DIFFERENCES

Cardinal Sun—Fixed Signature: You want to finish things. If Mercury is in a cardinal sign along with your Sun, you may not be consciously aware of this desire. If your Mercury is in a fixed sign, you truly think that you are more comfortable with the tried and true. However, you will have an inner desire to initiate action due to the position of your Sun. So you may start new things and then never deviate from your original decision about how to finish them. You may wish that you did not get yourself into so many new projects, for your ideal person finishes absolutely everything.

Cardinal Sun—Mutable Signature: You really want to be more flexible. Thus you listen carefully to all the opinions of others, then go off and do exactly what you were going to do in the first place. You only really like change when it was your own idea.

Fixed Sun—Cardinal Signature: You want to be more innovative, but inside you are scared stiff. So you try to be inventive in proven ways. You may dabble in various areas, but you are determined to finish whatever you begin. Even if an ideal is really silly or unworkable, you won't let go of it until you have completely exhausted yourself and everyone around you.

Fixed Sun—Mutable Signature: You like Emerson's observation that "A foolish consistency is the hobgoblin of little minds." In fact, you like that quote so much that you say it all the time, particularly if your Mercury is in the fixed sign along with your Sun. You don't like to change your mind, no matter what your ideal person is like. You want everyone else to be flexible so that you can be more accommodating.

Mutable Sun—Cardinal Signature: You want to be more deliberate in decision making, but you find yourself listening to the opinions of others. You want to jump into new things with true cardinal abandon, but you vacillate about where to jump. You may find that Churchill spoke about this combination when he said "Decided only to be undecided, resolved to be irresolute..."

Mutable Sun—Fixed Signature: You want to be more stubborn. You accuse yourself of spinelessness whenever you vacillate. You may swing from listening to everyone to listening to no one. You want to finish everything you begin. Thus, you may not start anything rather than leave it half done.

TRIPLICITY DIFFERENCES

Fire Sun—Earth Signature: There is a yin-yang difference here, indicating you have a basic struggle with either your masculine or feminine projection. Since your Sun is yang, and your signature is yin, you want to be more receptive, more responsive. You choose to show your yin side through groundedness or practicality. If you are a woman, you may try to be so good at handling things that no one can fault your performance. If you are a man, you try to act in careful, logical ways to offset your tendency to impetuous decisions.

Fire Sun—Air Signature: Actually, this combination works quite easily, for your Sun and signature are the same polarity. You want to be more intellectual, but this desire compliments rather than conflicts with your fire Sun commitment to action. You are capable of considerable success, for you try to think and act on all input.

Fire Sun, Water Signature: The combination of fire and water tends to bring out the most intense yin-yang conflict, for in our society the stereotype of the "macho male" is fire and the "total woman" is water. You want to be emotional, sensitive and flowing, while your Sun sign indicates a personality which is abrupt, forthright, and action-oriented. If you are a woman, you may try to hide or deny your yang Sun. Although you may be quite intelligent, you might try to be the ingenue in social situations. If you are a man, you want to develop more sensitivity and feeling, and indeed may do exactly this. However, you are quite uncomfortable with the projection and unwilling to admit your discomfort.

Earth Sun—Air Signature: The yin-yang difference here indicates conflict between the masculine and feminine sides of your personality. Your Sun is yin, indicating a receptive, practical nature. The signature shows that you want to be more assertive, particularly in intellectual areas. If you are a woman, you may accept criticism of your cooking, but you cannot abide being called an idiot. You may, in fact, do all of the traditionally "feminine" jobs very well, but you prefer to be considered for your yang intelligence. If you are a man with this combination, you may not like to admit your competence in domestic matters. You can usually rationalize this skill as necessary for survival, while your mind is, of course, the area you choose to develop and show.

Earth Sun—Water Signature: This is an easy combination, since earth and water are both yin. You try to be more emotional and flowing, and your yin Sun indicates that you are not worried about appearing nurturing or sensitive. You may choose to live with or associate with people who express emotion easily. Alternately, you may choose to live with someone who cannot express emotion well at all, for then you can function gloriously as the emotional barometer of the entire relationship.

Earth Sun—Fire Signature: There is a yin-yang polarity difference here, as well as a penchant for action contrasted with a concern for practicality. You may try to be more spontaneous, but may actually plan your acts of apparent spontaneity well in advance. This can lead to quite forced behavior. If you are a man, the yang signature indicates that you keep trying to be more masculine. You may become quite obnoxious about male supremacy, for you are insecure about your own masculinity. If you are a woman, you want to be more assertive. You take umbrage at any sign of male dominance, yet feel ambivalent about your own position. You go to feminist meetings after you have cooked supper, cleaned up a bit, and made sure there are clean clothes for everyone for tomorrow.

Air Sun—Water Signature: The yin-yang polarity difference here indicates that you may try to be more sensitive and less intellectual in your dealings with others. You idealize emotion or receptivity. If you are a woman, this combination may indicate that you try to be the "total woman" following in the shadow of the nearest male. Your air Sun, however, reveals that you are anything but helpless. You may be stronger than most men, particularly in any intellectual areas. If you are a man, you regard sensitivity and caring as your highest ideals. You may write poetry about the wonders of feeling while expecting your wife or girlfriend to handle all the details of the house. You may claim that men should be liberated enough to cry, but find that you cannot bear to break down in front of anyone.

Air Sun—Fire Signature: The yang elements work well together, so this combination is usually quite easy. Your fire signature pushes your air Sun into action. You love tales of courage, but, of course, you really want to think before acting. For some of you, the solution is an endless attempt to think faster. You wish you had instant reflexes as long as the reflex action is the correct action. You are usually strong thinkers and doers, accomplishing many things.

Air Sun—Earth Signature: Your Sun is yang and your signature yin. You are trying to combine the two symbolisms into some sort of practical intellect. You try to bend all things into useful tools and want to be good at everything. If you are a woman, you try to run everything perfectly. This combination can lead to the "superwoman" syndrome, for you want to be good at your job, have perfect kids, and run a perfect house. You may drive yourself to nervous exhaustion before you realize the yin-yang conflict at the root of this behavior. If you are a man, you also want to be androgynously perfect. You want to be responsive and responsible as well as aggressive and intellectual. You may work yourself into a corner by placing impossible demands upon yourself. Both men and women with this combination find it very difficult to admit that they themselves are the cause of their own overwork.

Water Sun—Fire Signature: The combination of water and fire brings out the most intense yin-yang conflict within you. When your Sun is in water, and your signature is fire, you want to be more aggressive and less emotional. Whether you are male or female, you may try to stamp out "overemotional" responses, perhaps to the extent of trying to completely deny or hide them. This is protective behavior, designed to hide what you consider your weakness—your sensitivity. If you are a woman, you want to stand alone. You may be a strident feminist. However, you can drag out your water Sun whenever you need it to manipulate others. If you are a man, you also idealize rugged individualism. However, you don't have the luxury of dragging out your yin side when it suits you, for you fear your feminine, since you really don't understand it. You try to maintain a stiff upper lip no matter what is going on, for society reinforces your fear that your emotionalism indicates weakness. It takes enormous courage and honesty for you to deal with and display your Sun.

Water Sun—Earth Signature: Since water and earth are both yin, this is an easy combination. You want to become more practical, but do not in the process disdain the sensitivity or emotion which are part of your water sign Sun. You wish you were more hardheaded about life in general. Since your inner self responds quickly and completely to emotional input, you may spend time after the fact justifying your emotional responses. Your ideal self thinks about the outcome (in good earth fashion) before doing anything, but you are usually satisfied as long as you can ground your sensitivity with logic. The worst effect of this combination is the possibility of boring other people with your need to rationalize your emotional side. If you can realize your ideal self, you can become like watered earth which yields abundantly.

Water Sun—Air Signature: The polarity difference here, with yin Sun and yang signature, symbolizes a conflict between your feminine nature and your desired masculine projection. You may try to intellectualize emotion. Through your constant attempts to make your yin into a yang, you may become very good at "analysis" games. Although you can explain all your emotional hangups in great detail and with complicated psychological jargon, you may not have any gut level understanding of your own feeling nature. If you are a woman, you are very likely to use your yin Sun to manipulate others, for you can rationalize this easily if you notice that you are doing it. You prefer to regard yourself as intellectual, rational, and self-sufficient and will retreat into psychological language to explain away any inconsistencies in this view of yourself. Men with this combination are comfortable in analyzing intimate situations. You love show and tell types of group therapy sessions, for you are very good at ostensibly revealing your yin water side while actually indulging in a yang aggressive intellectual game.

EXPRESSING ENERGIES

RULERSHIP, DETRIMENT, EXALTATION, AND FALL

Rulership, detriment, exaltation and fall are terms which have fallen into disuse in many astrological circles as they often conjure up images of crystal ball type astrology. This really need not be the case, for if we understand the meaning of these ancient terms, the application of their principles needn't be negative or confining.

Rulership: Planets rule the signs through which the energy of the planet is most clearly and easily expressed. The major problem with the word "rule" is that it implies some sort of control, authority, or government. Planets don't control us or control signs. If I replace the word "rule" with a word like "affinity," though, very few astrologers will have any idea what I mean. Thus, I'm keeping the traditional word, with a newer meaning.

Detriment: The sign opposite the sign that a planet rules is called the sign of its detriment. This simply means that the energy of the planet is difficult to express through this sign. You still have the energy of the planet, but you don't get that energy into gear as easily as someone might who has that planet in a more compatible sign.

Exaltation: Planets are exalted in signs through which they are expressed readily, but not quite as easily as in the signs they rule. A planet's energy is altered somewhat in the sign of its exaltation, but this change does not interfere in any way with your ability to express that planet's energy.

Fall: The sign opposite the sign in which a planet is exalted is called its fall. You won't express the energy of a planet in its fall as easily as you would if the same planet were in the sign it rules or in its exaltation, but it won't be quite as difficult to bring out as a planet in its detriment.

The exaltations of the three outer planets are still debated. The sign associations with the outer planets given in Table 2.1 show my opinion. Since the outer planets stay so long in each sign, the sign position seems to have a generational rather than a personal meaning. Thus the assignation of exaltation to each outer planet may have dubious value. You should examine the times in history when the outer planets were in the sign of their rulership, detriment, exaltation and fall; then decide for yourself what these positions should be.

The traditonal rulerships of Mars (Scorpio), Saturn (Aquarius), and Jupiter (Pisces) are listed in parentheses in the table. Although in the text (and in practice) I call them traditional rulers, I treat them as

Table 2.1. Planetary Expressions

Planet	Exaltation	Fall	Rulership	Detriment
Sun	Aries	Libra	Leo	Aquarius
Moon	Taurus	Scorpio	Cancer	Capricorn
Mercury	Aquarius	Leo	Virgo or Gemini	Pisces or Sagittarius
Venus	Pisces	Virgo	Taurus or Libra	Scorpio or Aries
Mars	Capricorn	Cancer	Aries or Scorpio	Libra or Taurus
Jupiter	Cancer	Capricorn	Sagittarius or Pisces	Gemini or Virgo
Saturn	Libra	Aries	Capricorn or Aquarius	Cancer or Leo
Uranus	Scorpio	Taurus	Aquarius	Leo
Neptune	Cancer	Capricorn	Pisces	Virgo
Pluto	Leo	Aquarius	Scorpio	Taurus

exaltations in determining their strength in these signs because although they are not as strong in these signs as in the signs they rule, they are at least as strong in these positions as in the signs in which they are exalted.[14]

When a planet rules a sign, it takes precedence over any other planet in that sign. In other words, Mars is stronger in Aries than any other planet placed in Aries. The energy symbolized by Mars is clearest and most easily expressed when Mars is in the sign of its rulership. When Mars is in Capricorn, where Mars is exalted, the energy is still strong, albeit somewhat controlled. The energy symbolized by the planet Mars is expressed in a Capricornian fashion, which tends to direct and organize this behavior. The energy is not diminished by placement in Capricorn, merely channeled. In a similar fashion, Mars is strong in Scorpio, where the energy is expressed with depth and intensity, often along a single fixed line or path. Mars in Capricorn organizes and controls in order to bring things into reality. Mars in Scorpio is willfully directed towards either total change or transformation of whatever it touches. In Capricorn, Saturn influences the expression of Mars. In Scorpio, Pluto has an analogous influence over the expression of Mars.

---

[14] For an in-depth discussion of the concept of rulership, detriment, exaltation and fall, see Hand, Robert, *Horoscope Symbols,* Para Research, Gloucester, Massachusetts, 1981, pp. 200-210 (In general he disagrees with what I've said.) Also Sakoian, Frances, and Acker, Louis, *The Astrologer's Handbook*, Harper and Row, New York, 1973, pages. 242-250. (In general, they agree with what I've said.)

In a similar manner, Saturn rules Capricorn. Saturn is the symbol of crystallization. It is the strongest planet in Capricorn, where Saturn is clearly and easily expressed as discipline and order. In the sign of its exaltation, Libra, Saturn is the lawmaker, because through Libra Saturn extends the weight of discipline and order to include the "other." Then the symbol of reality becomes the symbol of the law. Saturn in Aquarius is equally strong, for through fixed air Saturn brings ideas to reality. Practical inventiveness occurs with Saturn in Aquarius.

Jupiter rules Sagittarius. Jupiter is the symbol of expansion, growth, and ethics. For some, this means that Jupiter, not Saturn, is connected with law. However, the body of law which controls and disciplines is Saturn. The body of ethics which uplifts and directs is Jupiter. Jupiter is exalted in Cancer. It is in the home, with the nurturing mother symbol, that the child first develops a sense of ethics as well as the ability to expand and grow in body and in mind. In Cancer, the symbol of the idealistic centaur is focussed on individual caring. When Jupiter is in Pisces, its traditional rulership, there is a similar emphasis on caring, but in Pisces this caring is directed towards empathy with the larger world.

These concepts of exaltation and fall are relevant in the progressed chart when a planet changes sign. Any natal planet which falls in the sign of its rulership or exaltation will be expressed through its natal sign strongly during your life. Althought the expression of the energy of a planet alters when the planet changes sign through progression, you will not note a major change if the natal position is stronger through rulership or exaltation.

For example, if you have Mercury in Aquarius natally, and in direct motion, it will progress into Pisces. Mercury is exalted in Aquarius and in its detriment in Pisces. Since your natal Mercury is considerably stronger than your progressed Mercury, you will not express the Pisces progression unless your progressed Mercury conjuncts an angle or makes major aspects. You will continue to think and act like a person with Mercury in Aquarius.

When a planet is in a sign to which it is not connected by exaltation, fall, rulership, or detriment, and it progresses to another sign to which it is equally unrelated, the progressed and natal signs have roughly equal strength. For example, Mars is not elevated or weakened in Aquarius, nor is it distinguished in Pisces. Venus is not connected to Gemini, Cancer, or Leo by exaltation, rulership, or their opposites. When you have these planets in any of the above positions, you must look at the house placement and aspects to determine whether the natal or the progressed symbolism will be expressed.

With Jupiter it is often very difficult to distinguish any effect of a progression from Aries to Taurus or from Libra to Scorpio (or the reverse by retrograde motion) because none of these signs strengthens or weakens the expression of Jupiter. In like manner, Saturn's expression probably won't change much when it progresses from Taurus to Gemini or from Scorpio to Sagittarius. Although the decanate position can add or subtract a little bit, these changes of Jupiter or Saturn are not visible unless the planet is angular or heavily aspected.

It is even more difficult to assign specific changes in response to the time that the three outer planets change sign. We don't have Pluto's position precisely in any of our ephemeride's yet, for Pluto has not been observed through a complete orbit around the Sun. We can't even pinpoint the time that Pluto changes sign unless we have access to extremely sophisticated astronomical measurements. The sign changes of the three outer planets really reflect generational change rather than personal change. Consequently, the sections in the analysis of planets changing sign are shorter for the outer planets than for the inner planets.

Each of us is the combination of our progressed and natal charts. The use of the concepts of rulership, detriment, exaltation and fall, particularly with the inner planets, helps us to understand how the energies combine to give us the present expression of our life energies.

3

COMING ON STRONG:

ANGULARITY

THE ANGLES:

THE CROSS OF LIFE

Any planet postioned in the first, fourth, seventh or tenth house in our natal chart is an angular planet, for these are the angular houses. However, this general definition has two serious drawbacks. First, this definition does not account for the strength of a planet in a cadent house within five degrees of the angle. Second, this definition accords equal strength to a planet fifteen or more degrees from the angle, which does not bear up under examination of actual client data.

In all subsequent discussions, we will refer to any planet within five degrees of a natal angle as an angular planet, while any planet in an angular house positioned more than five degrees from the angle will be referred to simply as a planet in an angular house.

When any planet conjuncts a natal angle, your interaction in that particular quadrant of your life will be colored by the symbolism of the planet. We can only discuss the general effects of these conjunction here, because the precise effect of the conjunction involves the symbolism of the sign involved and the aspects made by the planet.

There are three types of conjunctions to angles. First, and most influential, is a natal planet conjunct a natal angle. After this, two types of conjunction formed by the secondary chart are most important, i.e., progressed angles can conjunct natal and progressed positions, and progressed planets can conjunct natal angles.

All of us have one or another of these types of angularity at some time in our lives. Inner planets in direct motion in cadent houses will progress to conjunct natal angles. Progressed angles will conjunct natal planets in our angular or succedent houses.

WHERE AM I GOING?

PLANETS CONJUNCT THE MIDHEAVEN

The Midheaven (MC) symbolizes your life direction, your career, the path you choose to follow. If you were to extend both arms sideways, your left arm would symbolize your Ascendant, your right arm your descendant. Both of these would be at the edges of your peripheral vision. The direction straight ahead symbolizes your Midheaven. Just as you see whatever is directly ahead with the most clarity, whatever is on or near the MC is a highly visible influence on your life. The closer in longitude a planet is to your MC, the stronger the influence of that planet will be.

There is a special designation for the planet closest to the MC, which does not follow the five degrees from the angle rule. Whichever planet is closest to the MC in your chart is called "Accidentally Dignified." In order to be accidentally dignified, a planet must be within sixty degrees of the Midheaven. If there is no planet within sixty degrees of the Midheaven, there is no planet accidentally dignified.

As your angles progress, different planets will become accidentally dignified. You will have a year of transition while your progressed Midheaven is exactly between two planets. During that year you have a powerful midpoint configuration, and you will find yourself in a state of flux concerning career or life goals. Then you will have a number of years characterized by the new planet in accidental dignity. The influence of a planet accidentally dignified but not conjunct the Midheaven, while not as strong as the conjunction, is nonetheless significant enough to alter your ideas about what things are important in career choices as well as your ideas of how you want to go about getting or making career changes.

From the time that the progressed Midheaven is within a degree of the natal or progressed position of any planet until it is a degree past the natal or progressed position, the influence of the planet is extremely marked in your life. Any aspects to or from that position will affect your career or life direction. Thus, if your progressed Midheaven was 28° Aries conjuncting your natal Jupiter at 29° Aries during January 1983, you would have transiting Pluto opposing this conjunction. You could see the transiting Pluto opposition to your natal Jupiter without the progressed chart, but you would not necessarily see it in terms of a change in career or life direction if you had not looked at the position of the progressed Midheaven.[15]

---

[15] If you work with the ninety degree dial at all, the position of the progressed MC (at least if you progress it the way I suggest on page 305) shows up regularly in events. The progressed MC is quite useful for rectification of charts.

When a progressed planet conjuncts your natal Midheaven, you are very likely to make radical changes in your life direction. All the planets (except for the progressed Moon) progress so slowly that a planet will be within minutes of the MC for a year. Everytime your natal MC is aspected by a transiting planet or the progressed Moon, you'll find the symbolism of the progressed planet manifesting in the events.

Each of the planets has a different significance when in the position of accidental dignity or actual conjunction to either the natal or progressed Midheaven. In the following delineations, I'll explain the symbolism of each.

SUN—MIDHEAVEN PROGRESSIONS

Depending on the method you choose to direct the secondary progressed Midheaven, the Sun changes position not at all or only slightly in relation to the progressed Midheaven.[16] Thus, unless you were born at solar noon, you won't have your progressed Sun conjunct your progressed Midheaven.

Since both the Sun and the Midheaven progress at approximately one degree a year, your Sun will progress to conjunct your natal Midheaven if your natal Sun is in the seventh, eighth, or ninth house and within sixty or seventy degrees of your natual Midheaven. Your Midheaven will progress to conjunct your natal Sun if your natal Sun is in the tenth, eleventh, or twelfth houses and within sixty or seventy degrees of your natal Midheaven.

When your Sun is in the eighth or ninth house natally, the conjunction to your natal Midheaven involves the motion of your progressed Sun from the ninth to the tenth house. The month that the conjunction is exact will signify a particular reward or recognition for your achievements, especially in areas of higher learning or mass communication. For some of you, it means extensive travel. If your progressed Sun is heavily afflicted, this recognition may not be pleasant. (You might become #1 on the FBI's most wanted list!) Whether the conjunction signifies fame or infamy is up to you: your choices while the Sun was in the ninth house will now bear fruit.

When your natal Sun is in your tenth or eleventh house, your Midheaven will progress to conjunct your natal Sun. You're not very likely to be surprised by the events which occur when your progressed Midheaven conjuncts your natal Sun, for you've been creating these events all the time that your natal Sun was in the tenth house of your progressed chart. While your natal Sun is in the tenth house of your

---

[16] The only exception to this rule is the Quotidian method of progression, which is not addressed in this book. The other methods of directing the secondary progressed Midheaven all move it at approximately the same speed that the Sun progresses.

progressed chart, you tend to align your physical and spiritual direction in life. This means that you won't be able to work at a defense plant if you have decided that your spiritual goals involve working for world disarmament. You will make choices that really integrate your inner sense of self with your spiritual and physical direction in life. Thus, by the time that your progressed Midheaven conjuncts your natal Sun, you know where the recognition will come from, and what it will involve.

MOON—MIDHEAVEN PROGRESSIONS

When the Moon is accidentally dignified in your natal chart, you show your emotions fairly readily. If your Moon is squaring your Ascendant, or aspecting your natal Saturn, you may be quite unaware of your emotional impact upon other people. One of the key words associated with the Moon is sensitivity. When the Moon is the planet closest to your MC, you are indeed sensitive, but you may choose to be sensitive to yourself rather than to the needs of others. If you choose the path of self-sensitivity, you'll always be vulnerable to hurt by the authority figures in your life. You may weep and retreat from such figures, unwilling to acknowledge that your own responses contribute to what occurs.

You can choose to use your highly placed Moon in a much more positive fashion. You do have an immediate instinctive response to the stimulus of career or authority figures. You can grow through emotional involvement in your career or life path. You have a tremendous investment in nurturing or mothering others. Whether or not you decide to have children of your own, you can grow by helping other people grow. Foster parenting, being a "Big Brother" or "Big Sister," coaching sports teams, as well as the many careers involved with nurturing others, all offer possibilities for growth through this placement of the Moon.

Your progressed Midheaven will conjunct your natal Moon if your natal Moon falls within sixty degrees after the Midheaven. During the year that the progressed Midheaven conjuncts your natal Moon, you will experience the culmination of the symbolism of the Moon in the tenth house. You will need to watch your tendency to take everything that happens in your career very personally. Unless you have strong aspects from other progressed planets or from the outer planets by transit, you aren't as likely to change careers as change your response to the whole concept of career/life direction.

All of us have the progressed Moon conjunct our natal Midheaven and our progressed Midheaven during the first twenty-eight years of our life, and every twenty-eight years thereafter. If you back up and look at what happened on the first conjunction, you will have an idea of what to expect during subsequent conjunctions.

Unlike the conjunctions of the other progressed planets to the natal or progressed Midheaven, the progressed Moon takes only six months to come into orb (I use a 3° orb), conjunct the angle, and leave the orb of conjunction. During this six months, you'll find yourself more sensitive to anything going on in your career or life path. This is one of the most common positions of the progressed Moon when people get married.

If your progressed Moon is aspecting any natal planets at the time that it conjuncts the natal or progressed MC, you'll find yourself reworking any leftover emotional problems associated with that planet. Not only will you go over these issues, you'll incorporate them into your immediate life in one way or another. If the aspects are soft (trine or sextile), you'll draw on the strength of the other planet to stabilize your emotional responses to career or life-direction changes. If the aspects are hard (squares or oppositions), you'll work on unravelling the problem, or you'll simply include the problem in whatever career changes you make. In the latter case, you may feel emotionally low (rather than the usual emotional high) when your progressed Moon conjuncts your natal or progressed Midheaven. If that happens, it's a good clue that you're carrying some emotional baggage which you need to throw away.

MERCURY—MIDHEAVEN PROGRESSIONS

When Mercury is the planet closest to the Midheaven in your natal chart, you are known for intelligence, talkativeness, dexterity, or all three. You may be the salesman who communicates easily, or the honored scholar who publishes regularly. Mercury may also symbolize the inveterate gossip who knows all and tells all.

The mere presence of Mercury closest to the Midheaven in your chart does not guarantee a high IQ (or high scores on any other standard measure of intelligence). A highly psychic person or a person with extraordinary small motor control could have Mercury accidentally dignified and not be successful in school.

When the progressed Midheaven conjuncts your natal Mercury, the conjunction culminates many years of Mercury in the tenth house of your progressed chart. As your progressed Midheaven moved closer to your natal Mercury, you began to think more about your direction in life. The conjunction of your progressed Midheaven to your natal Mercury will not automatically confer a desire for spiritual direction or goals. Each of us freely chooses to develop or ignore the spiritual side of life. For those of us who prefer to function on a mundane level, the conjunction signifies considerable thought (and possibly worry) about career and job situations. We may seek a job which requires more communication skills, or we may place ourselves in a position where communication with authority figures is essential. Alternately, we may bore our friends to death by talking incessantly about our job, our boss, our last operation and the doctor's opinion. (The tenth house cusp also signifies medical treatment.)

Of course, in an ideal world we would all take up philosophy and begin to learn the ultimate spiritual goals of this incarnation when the progressed Midheaven conjuncted our natal Mercury and carried Mercury into the ninth house of the progressed chart. Those who have developed some spiritual insight often find this a time of heightened curiosity and learning about our ultimate goals. For most of us, the conjunction combines spiritual enlightenment and thought or worry concerning the earning of our daily bread.

If you check the two months following your birthday in an ephemeris, you can see whether or not Mercury will progress to conjunct your natal Midheaven, and how often. If Mercury goes retrograde after your birth, you could have up to three conjunctions of progressed Mercury to your natal Midheaven. Distinct career changes often occur while progressed Mercury is conjunct the natal Mid-heaven. Most people are consciously involved in the direction and content of career changes which occur while progressed Mercury is conjunct the natal Midheaven. Take advantage of this knowledge to create a life direction which leads you towards your goals!

VENUS—MIDHEAVEN PROGRESSIONS

When Venus is the planet accidentally dignified in your chart, you are often known for your love of beauty and artistic appreciation. Kindness and a sense of freely given affection and support often accompany the placement of Venus closest to the MC. While this position does not guarantee a beautiful body or countenance, those of you with Venus accidentally dignified will have an aura of grace and proportion in your career, no matter what you pursue.

There are, of course, a few drawbacks to Venus accidentally dignified, as even the benefic planet has a darker side.[17] One possible difficulty has been exacerbated by the currently popular belief that if you think only loving, harmonious thoughts, only loving, harmonious things can happen in your life. Although this philosophy has merit (for we do create our own realities to a large extent), this belief can lead to an overwhelming guilt if negative things happen. If, for example, you are an artist, or would prefer to earn a living as an artist, thinking

---

[17] Benefic and Malefic planets: The benefic planets are Venus and Jupiter. Aspects from either of these planets are considered easy to integrate. The malefic planets are Mars and Saturn. Aspects from these planets are considered difficult to integrate. Some people include Uranus, Neptune, and Pluto as malefics, but I think this is going a bit far. Then we have five rotten planets and only two nice ones, because you don't count the Sun or Moon as they are lights, and most people agree that Mercury is neutral. We may not have learned how to integrate the energy of the outer planets, but I don't think their energy is always difficult.

good thoughts will not sell paintings. Perhaps painting better pictures will sell paintings, but this is a function of Saturn, not Venus.

The other potential pitfall of Venus accidentally dignified involves self-indulgence. When you have Venus closest to your Midheaven, and choose to focus on the mundane rather than the spiritual, you may become completely involved in the pleasure principle. Because the Venus energy is so appealing, others may allow you to be the outrageous little girl or boy. One day you may bring your whole world crashing down about your own shoulders through overindulgence in food, drink, drugs or other pleasure mechanisms.

When your progressed MC conjuncts your natal Venus, you will start to sort through your feelings about the things and people you love. At this time, you will be better able to discern the obstacles to harmony that you create. If you can accept responsibility for some of the disharmony without going to the extreme of assuming total blame for all difficulties, you can start to alter nonproductive behavior patterns. You'll probably have to try out both ends of the continuum from complete irresponsibility to complete responsibility before you come to the middle ground of self-love and self-acceptance.

When your progressed Venus conjuncts your natal MC, you take another look at the importance of harmony and peace in your career and life direction. You are no longer willing to put up with chaos (or dirt) in careers, nor will you continue to work for a boss who is bellicose. Unless there are such difficulties in your life, the conjunction does not signify a job change. Once you are in a career in which your Venus can show, you will find that as far as this year goes, you can do no wrong in the eyes of the boss. However wonderful this sounds, you need some kind of hard aspects to use the energy well. If this is the only major aspect to your Midheaven, and you don't get married (this is a powerful marriage position), you may just bask in glory, do nothing, and come down to a painful reality later.

MARS—MIDHEAVEN PROGRESSIONS

When Mars is accidentally dignified in your natal chart, you prefer action to any other way of life. Mars often falls within five degrees of the MC in the charts of athletes, surgeons, and military men.[18]

If you don't choose to develop the positive side of Mars through your career and life path, you may simply be known for a vile temper. You can't hide your light under a bushel, for the energy of Mars will ignite the bushel and create a bonfire for the world to see.

When you do not have Mars accidentally dignified in your natal chart, but it becomes accidentally dignified by progression, you'll find that during the time that Mars is closest to your MC you will be much more assertive.

---

[18] Gauquelin, Michel, *Planetary Heredity*, Paris Planete, Paris, France, 1966.

If Mars itself is progressing towards your natal MC, your energy can be channelled through higher learning (college, apprenticeship, internship) or through experiences involving travel (military service, jobs which require considerable moving around, or actually moving to a different locality). All of this energy can be directed toward the eventual achievement of some career (or life direction) goal. At the same time, the closer progressed Mars gets to your natal MC, the more you need to address your own aggressive tendencies. In our society anger, the most repressed emotion, is not allowed in polite company. A good person never gets angry with anything. This unrealistic attitude fosters terrible guilt and perverts a perfectly sane and sound response. Without the energy of Mars, we would not be able to function because we would lack the strength to become self-determining.

While we pay lip service to the use of physical exertion to release Mars energy (you can chop wood or beat carpets, neither of which are easily accomplished if you live in an apartment), we try to lock up someone who yells obscentities while chopping wood or beating carpets. Perhaps the need for such a release contributed to the growth of the study of Oriental martial arts. You have to holler as well as jump around when you're practicing some types of martial arts.

If you can develop some way to discharge excess energy, you'll be able to direct your energy while Mars conjuncts your natal MC. Then you can expect a major advance or event in your career during the year that the conjunction is exact. If you haven't developed release mechanisms for yourself, the event associated with this conjunction may be quite negative. The sign position and the aspects indicate the best outlets for energy. For example, Mars in Pisces conjuncting the natal MC might seek swimming competition, sailing, surf sailing or some similar activity to release energy, while Mars in Taurus conjuncting the MC might do better with breaking ground for a new garden.

When your progressed Midheaven conjuncts your natal Mars, Mars has been in the tenth house of the progressed chart for quite a few years. With Mars in the tenth house, you direct energy towards career options. You really prefer to be your own boss. If this is at all possible, it's a good choice for you. You won't do very well in a career which doesn't demand action, or in which you must obey a dictator-like superior. If you are stuck in a low profile job or career, the Mars can sometimes surface in street brawls. Once you understand the connection between your aggressive feelings and the lack of advancement at work, you may be able to direct your efforts towards more productive areas. If you try, you can probably develop your own career while you continue at a job which feeds you. What you've done then is to remove the tedium from the tenth, place it in the sixth house of daily grind, and release the tenth house energy for future gains.

JUPITER—MIDHEAVEN PROGRESSIONS

Jupiter moves an average of six degrees per month when it is in direct motion, and much less when it is retrograde or approaching a station. Thus natal and progressed Jupiter won't get more than eighteen degrees apart during your life. Furthermore, unless your natal Jupiter is less than eighteen degrees from your natal MC, it won't progress to conjunct your natal MC during your life. If your natal Jupiter is in your tenth, eleventh, or twelfth house, your progressed Midheaven may progress to conjunct both natal and progressed Jupiter.

When Jupiter is the planet highest in your natal chart, you are known for far-reaching plans, optimism, a great sense of humor, and a tremendous amount of charisma. If Jupiter aspects your natal Neptune, you may be a renowned storyteller or, less fortunately, a renowned liar. Jupiter is often within five degrees of the MC in charts of politicians, lawyers, and humorists.

As explained above, Jupiter will only progress to conjunct your natal MC if it is within eighteen degrees of your MC at birth. When the conjunction occurs, you're at a peak of personal charisma. It may signify a major campaign won, a major book published, a major advancement in career. Even if your progressed Jupiter is not well aspected, it rarely symbolizes any difficult or negative events. The worst problem of this conjunction is usually weight. You'll have an awful time dieting, regardless of all the other benefits associated with Jupiter.

When your progressed Midheaven conjuncts natal or progressed Jupiter, you will make a larger impression on the world around you. If your career aims have been completely thwarted, you may have problems with overindulgence in food or alchohol. Jupiter itself only symbolizes possible excess. If you have developed avenues for expansion in career or life direction, the conjunction of your progressed Midheaven to your natal or progressed Jupiter shows tremendous success. The years between the two conjunctions (to natal and progressed positions) are years of nearly unlimited growth. Do use this time to reach for major goals. Your own vision is the only limitation to the achievements you can expect.

SATURN—MIDHEAVEN PROGRESSIONS

When Saturn is the planet accidentally dignified in your natal chart, you tend to have an exaggerated sense of responsibility. As natural ruler of the tenth house, Saturn is most powerful at the MC position. Saturn accidentally dignified assures neither success nor failure of your career aims. Rather, Saturn indicates that you will take your career quite seriously, whatever that career might be. Saturn on the

Midheaven is the Puritan work ethic personified. You believe that if a thing is worth doing, it is worth doing well. Saturn here is at once the janitor who cleans all the corners and the bank president who checks the corners for dirt.

If you are conscientious about the details of your career, you will be successful. However, Saturn symbolizes the need for strict honesty in the pursuit of career. Without this honesty, the Saturnine influence will assure that you will sooner or later pay for dishonesty. You will either be caught and disgraced or you will suffer so much from the strain of trying to appear honest and upright that whatever material gains you have made will not overcome the pessimism you feel about your career.

If Saturn is not accidentally dignified in your natal chart, but becomes accidentally dignified as your chart progresses, the years in which Saturn is closest to your progressed Midheaven are years in which you seriously pursue your career. These years will be years of hard work and possible pessimism about your own abilities. As your progressed Midheaven comes closer to your natal and progressed Saturn, you may find yourself working for an extremely demanding boss. The relationship you have with your superiors relates directly to the relationship you had with your father (or whomever was the disciplining parent in your life). If you haven't worked out the relationship with your critical parent, you will transfer this to your critical superior. Changing jobs won't help, for you must develop your own sense of self-worth during this time. If you can separate Daddy from boss, you can use Saturn's accidental dignity to build a career foundation which paves the way for enormous success after the progressed Midheaven conjuncts natal and progressed Saturn. Unfortunately, you may not recognize your own success. Saturn can so fill you with a need to be perfect that all you see are the flaws. Back away for a moment, ask some other people, or actually make a list of your accomplishments. You may be the only one who does not think you are an astounding success story.

THE OUTER PLANETS CONJUNCT THE MIDHEAVEN

The outer planets—Uranus, Neptune, and Pluto—move so slowly that they cannot progress to an exact conjunction to the Midheaven unless they are within a few degrees of the Midheaven in the natal chart. Furthermore, if they do, they may be within a few minutes of conjunction for many years. Considering that we don't know the birth time to any more than a minute's accuracy and we don't really know Pluto's position to more than ten minutes of arc accuracy, we really cannot pinpoint a date on which Pluto will make an exact conjunction to a natal Midheaven.

We do know that whenever any of the outer planets is within thirty minutes of the Midheaven, we've got an extremely intense manifestation of the energy of that planet in our lives. Rather than try to time events through this conjunction, use the transiting aspects (or aspects to the MC/planet conjunction from other progressed positions) for timing. The outer planet conjunction to your natal MC serves as a background rather than an event indicator.

Thus the only type of truly significant accidental dignity other than natal accidental dignity is the conjunction of the progressed Midheaven to the natal and progressed positions of the outer planets.

URANUS—MIDHEAVEN PROGRESSIONS

If you have Uranus accidentally dignified in your natal chart, you tend to be unconventional. Often you have problems with authority figures. Although you may not recognize this as a problem, your parents did while you were growing up. Uranus symbolizes the inventor, the changer, the anarchist. The closer Uranus falls to your natal MC, the more obvious your unconventionality.

As with all astrological generalities, this, too, must be understood within the context of your environment. You must behave more strangely in some areas of the world to be considered uncoventional. For example, a strong desire to become a movie producer or a cameraman would not be considered unusual for a child brought up in Hollywood, California, while this same desire would be quite outside the norm in Ava, Missouri. At the same time, the child in Ava, Missouri, who wants to be a hunting guide would have the understanding (and probably the support) of the community, while the child from Hollywood would doubtless face many obstacles in the pursuit of the same career.

Everyone who has Uranus in the tenth or eleventh house natally will have Uranus accidentally dignified at some time in your progressed chart. During the time that Uranus is closest to your progressed Midheaven, you will explore different careers, different philosophies, different life directions. You'll be drawn to the newest, the least staid, the most challenging in any of these areas. When your progressed MC actually conjuncts your natal and progressed Uranus, you'll have a year of flux as you break out of any ruts you are in. Two areas of enormous interest to many people with Uranus accidentally dignified in their progressed chart are astrology (ruled by Uranus) and electronics. This is a wonderful position for Uranus in the high-technology eighties, for working with computers, communication and inventive change fits in beautifully. Uranus won't guarantee anything except that you'll change your ideas about your goals and your life direction. It's up to you to take charge of the change so that after it's done you can reap some rewards.

NEPTUNE—MIDHEAVEN PROGRESSIONS

When Neptune is accidentally dignified in your natal chart, you may have a gift for music or art. Neptune is also involved with psychic ability, lying, and general vagueness. Imagination, inspiration and drug abuse also fall under the influence of Neptune. Beethoven, Tchaikovsky, and Johannes Brahms all had Neptune accidentally dignified, as did Max Heindel, a well-known occultist; Joanne Woodward, the actress, also has the same configuration.

When your progressed Midheaven conjuncts your natal and progressed Neptune (it will probably conjunct both within the same year), the imaginative, creative parts of your career are strengthened. If you don't have Neptune accidentally dignified in your natal chart, but it becomes accidentally dignified in your progressed chart, the years that Neptune is closest to your progressed Midheaven will be years of creativity or vagueness or both. If you've never chosen to develop the artistic side of your personality, you may be vaguely discontented with yourself and your career while Neptune is closest to your progressed Midheaven. When you have no outlet for the energy symbolized by Neptune, the negative side involving drugs or alcohol may surface. This may lead to a drop in your ability to concentrate on career goals. Unless you can direct this energy into an area of service to others or into spiritual growth and self-development, you may lose your ambition and drive while Neptune is conjunct your progressed Midheaven. This can be a most difficult conjunction for someone mired in mundane purpose, for without some Neptunian outlet in the arts or helping professions, Neptune conjunct your progressed Midheaven can be disastrous.

PLUTO—MIDHEAVEN PROGRESSIONS

When the outermost planet, Pluto, is accidentally dignified in your natal chart, your personality is strong and dominant. Although what little has been written about Pluto in this position seems to indicate that the profession of soldier or surgeon should be amplified, Pluto appears to have much wider influence. Schubert and Berlioz both had Pluto accidentally dignified; Helena Blavatsky, Ernest Hemingway, and Richard Nixon had Pluto closest to the MC in their charts. The thread which connects these prominent personalities is depth and strength. Since Pluto symbolizes the deepest will of a person, it is not surprising to find Pluto on the MC in particularly dominant individuals.

Unlike Neptune, Pluto does not impart any vagueness whatsoever to your personality. During the years that Pluto is accidentally dignified in your progressed chart, you become singleminded, at times nearly fanatical, in the pursuit of your objectives.

Since Pluto moves so slowly, your progressed MC will conjunct both natal and progressed Pluto within the space of one year. That year will be characterized as a time in which you are able to work extremely hard towards a particular goal.

If you've had previous difficulty with authority figures, or if natal configurations suggest potential problems with such persons, you may be intensly uncomfortable around these figures during the time that your progressed MC conjuncts Pluto. It is glib advice to suggest that you work alone or in your own business during this time. Of course, if you can do this, it is a wonderful way to use the dominant symbolism. However, not all of us have either the means or the ability to be our own boss. If you have to work for someone else during this period, you must look at your own internal conflicts with authority in order to understand what is manifesting in your career. You will have a strong urge to make major,permanent changes in your career. Be sure you think through these changes carefully, for with Pluto here you won't be able to put back anything you destroy. This configuration has the potential to be the most powerful influence you will have in your life in terms of career and life path.

WHAT WILL I SHOW YOU?

PLANETS CONJUNCT THE ASCENDANT

The Ascendant in your chart symbolizes your projected ego, your interface with the environment, and thus your personality. Through the Ascendant, you act or react to the issues and events in the world around you. This interaction is altered in specific ways when planets are conjunct your Ascendant.

The orb of influence in a conjunction depends to a certain extent on the planet involved in the conjunction. If we think in terms of time instead of degrees, this variability in aspect size becomes logical. Aspects which can never be exact are less influential in general than those which will become exact by progression during a person's lifetime.

For example, planets conjunct the Ascendant from the twelfth house may or may not ever progress to conjunct the natal Ascendant. If you have Pluto five degrees from the Ascendant, but in the twelfth house, it won't conjunct your Ascendant. This does not mean that it has no influence, but Saturn or Jupiter or any of the inner planets (when in direct motion) will progress to the Ascendant and on into the natal first house. Their influence will be more visible in your life, for they will come out of the closet, so to speak, and for much of your life will act from your natal first house.

Your Ascendant will progress to conjunct any planet in your first house. When any planet is within five degrees of the Ascendant on the first house side, you will openly approach the environment with the energy of the planet rather than the energy of the sign. Your progressed Ascendant will conjunct this planet within your first seven years, moving the energy of the planet to your twelfth house of habit and ingrained subconscious action. You won't even notice that your approach to the world is thoroughly colored by the planet you have conjunct your natal Ascendant.

SUN—ASCENDANT PROGRESSIONS

When you are born at dawn, with the Sun on your Ascendant, you truly put yourself on the line in all of your interactions with the environment. You project your basic self, greeting the world with your entire being. You do best when you can lead others, for you need recognition from the immediate environment. Don't scorn little ponds, for you will be happier as the biggest fish in a puddle than as a medium-sized fish in the ocean.

When your Sun and Ascendant are conjunct by progression, you have a year of major recognition. It's best to prepare for this year, because if you do, you can get positive types of recognition. This conjunction often signifies a major life event, an achievement of one sort or another which brings you to the attention of everyone around you. If you haven't done anything to merit reward, the conjunction year may be filled with temper tantrums or some kind of adverse notoriety. You will manage to become either famous or infamous this year.

MOON—ASCENDANT PROGRESSIONS

When your Moon is conjunct your natal Ascendant, you project an emotional, nurturing, fluctuating and responsive personality. You may have difficulty initiating action in the environment because you're constantly responding to its inputs. When the conjunction is in a yang sign, you may be quite frustrated by your responsiveness and may actually respond and act so quickly that it seems that you actually initiate action. You will be heard with this combination. You're very sensitive, particularly to any slights, hurts, or innuendoes, both real or imagined. You may hang onto others emotionally, sometimes to the extent that you drive away the support you so desperately need.

Unlike the other planets, the progressed Moon moves around the chart every twenty-eight years. Thus, the conjunction of the progressed Ascendant to the natal Moon position is quite different in effect from the conjunction of the progressed Moon to either natal or progressed Ascendant. When the progressed Ascendant conjuncts your natal Moon, the conjunction stays in effect for the year that the Ascendant is within a degree of the position of your natal Moon. During this year you will experience intense emotional reactions to the events occurring in the world around you. Should the natal Moon be within five degrees of your natal Ascendant and in the first house, this will occur during childhood. You should investigate the events of this year in order to understand emotional reactions or blockages which show up later in adulthood.

This year is also a key to later health, for your natal Moon immediately moves into the twelfth house by progression where the events occurring during the conjunction to the Ascendant are buried in the subconscious. If this does signify a major blockage in emotional response, you may need to work with a therapist to unravel this year's internal significance.

In contrast, the conjunction of your progressed Moon to your natal and/or progressed Ascendant is rather quick, for there is a six month period (three degrees approaching, three degrees separating) in which there is a slight effect, and only a one month period (thirty minutes approaching, thirty minutes separating) in which the effect is quite strong. These conjunctions symbolize a new emotional beginning, a new phase in your life. For approximately two years before the progressed Moon conjuncts your Ascendant, it has been moving through the twelfth house in your chart. During this time, you probably won't notice any emotional upheavals or reactions because your growth is occurring internally, on the subconscious level. When your progressed Moon moves out into the first house, your internal changes become visible, both to you and to those around you. People often get married or have children when their progressed Moon conjuncts their natal or progressed Ascendant. Whatever the event, there is heightened emotional response for about two years, or the length of time the progressed Moon will be in your first house.

MERCURY—ASCENDANT PROGRESSIONS

When you have Mercury conjunct your natal Ascendant, you tend to think and/or worry about your projection into the world. If the conjunction is from the twelfth house, you may not talk a lot, and you may have a very soft voice. On the other hand, when the conjunction is from the first house, you may talk in bursts so that you either dominate the conversation or don't enter it. In a positive sense, you are very adaptable to changing situations, but this very adaptability may lead to indecisiveness. You are restless and may find it very hard to sit still. You have the Sun somewhere close by, and the real meaning of Mercury conjunct your Ascendant depends on the house position of your Sun. If your Sun is in the twelfth, you vacillate between incessant talking and complete silence, as you are not too sure whether you want to be seen (and heard) or whether you want to be invisible. When your Sun is in the first and Mercury is conjunct your Ascendant, you know that you want to be both seen and heard.

You have to consider the position of the natal and progressed Sun in order to analyze a progressed conjunction of Mercury and the Ascendant. If your natal and progressed Sun indicate twelfth house reticence, the characteristics discussed below will be muted. If the position of the Sun indicates first house outgoing action, the following traits will be stronger.

You will experience both a heightened verbal ability and a desire to keep moving while Mercury is conjunct your Ascendant. As you become more aware of your environment, you may vacillate between thinking about action and acting to change your personal projection. When progressed Mercury crosses your natal Ascendant, you are symbolically taking conscious thought out of the hidden twelfth house and expressing it in the outside world. Now you are becoming more assertive and are better able to verbalize your ideas. When your progressed Ascendant conjuncts your natal Mercury, you are moving from a highly verbal framework (Mercury in the first house) in which listening is not a strongly developed skill towards a projection which includes paying attention to the thoughts of others. The conjunction by progression always indicates a change in your conscious projection into the environment, but the direction of change is indicated by the direction of the planet's motion.

VENUS—ASCENDANT PROGRESSIONS

When Venus is conjunct your Ascendant you project the pleasure principle. You are usually quite agreeable, and others in your environment find you delightful—unless your desires are thwarted. Then you may become quite manipulative. If charm does not work, you'll resort to other tactics, for with Venus conjunct the Ascendant, you want your own way. Since you project a loving, soft face to the world, you usually get what you want without a battle.

During the year that Venus is conjunct your Ascendant by progression, you'll use both charm and manipulation to achieve whatever goals you have set. This is traditionally considered a marriage aspect, although curiously I don't have any marriages in my files which occurred with Venus conjunct the progressed or natal Ascendant. You may want to follow this up yourself with your own client data.

I have found that this is a year for social climbing, for acquisition of nice things, for noticing the beauty around you. You may become more aware of personal looks, trying to improve your physical shape or at least display your body to best advantage. At the same time, you will find it difficult to deny yourself in any way. Thus, you experience problems with weight during this year.

When your progressed Ascendant conjuncts your natal Venus, Venus is moving into the twelfth house of your progressed chart. If your natal Venus is within seven or eight degrees of your natal Ascendant, this occurs during childhood. In this case, you may be totally oblivious to the ways you manipulate others to get what you want in life. You have internalized the charming child until it is part of your unconscious mind set. This charming child is not necessarily negative, for unless your demands are completely self-centered it may simply signify an easy manner that endears you to all those around you.

When your progressed Venus conjuncts your natal Ascendant, your Venus is coming out of the hidden twelfth house and into the first house of your natal chart. Now you can release the romantic, soft side of yourself. You can openly enjoy the nice things that you are now likely to notice around you; you can express love and delight. You are much more likely to fall in love with people who are available (not married, not ten million miles away, not priests or nuns).

The most noticeable thing about the Ascendant-Venus conjunction by progression is an almost complete absence of major life events. Since most of the things that we call "major life events" are negative, I could conclude that Venus confers some sort of protection from negativity. However, none of my clients have achieved any major awards during the year that Venus was conjunct the Ascendant. Perhaps a better conclusion might be that Venus conjunct the Ascendant indicates a peaceful, non-strenuous enjoyment of the objects and people around you.

If you give in to the negative side of Venus, the self-indulgent, selfish, sensual side, the years after the conjunction has separated are the event years. That's when the things you did (or avoided doing) during the conjunction year become obvious to you and to everyone else. By that time, no one is interested in the spoiled, sweet kid who charmed them while Venus conjuncted the Ascendant.

MARS—ASCENDANT PROGRESSIONS

Everyone notices you if you have Mars conjunct your Ascendant. You have a very high energy level in all your interactions with the environment. Many of you were very difficult children, and your temper tantrums caused amazement and fury in the adults around you. If your Mars is well aspected, you were merely an active, aggressive youngster. If your Mars is not so happily aspected you may have been abused, although this can get into the sticky area of who abused whom, for with this position you can irritate everyone when you feel cross. You will not express anger so visibly if Mars is conjunct your Ascendant from the twelfth house, but you will still want to rearrange your environment to suit your own particular needs.

When Mars conjuncts your Ascendant by progression, you must deal with your aggressive tendencies. Sometimes this does not seem to be at all the issue, as there may be events occurring in your life which absolutely require that you pour all of your energy into restructuring, in a most active sense, the environment around you. If someone wants to site a nuclear waste facility in your backyard, or if Mars conjuncted your Ascendant when Mt. St. Helens erupted and you live in Washington, you don't need to read any further. You won't have any subconscious issues to face because you'll be too busy dealing with the here and now. This should not force you into a complete panic, for most of us don't experience major disasters when Mars conjuncts the Ascendant. But some of us choose to move out to Mt. St. Helens after the explosion in order to help with the rebuilding. This is a very appropriate and useful Mars conjunct the Ascendant response. Others will decide to be on the front line repairing other natural catastrophies. If that occurs, you're not running away from your Mars; you are using it well.

The rest of us may want to go and do something similar, but really have other responsibilities which keep us in the same environment we've been in for years. For us, the Mars conjunct the Ascendant by progression means we have to take a long hard look at our own aggressive tendencies. If your progressed Ascendant is conjuncting your natal Mars, you will internalize the events of this year, hopefully learning the results of action taken in the environment. If progressed Mars is conjuncting your natal Ascendant, you are moving the energy from the hidden twelfth house to the first house. You'll surprise yourself with the amount of change you can actually create within your environment. You may not really recognize this as an emergence of energy, for you may just feel that it is a necessary part of growing up.

If you find that everyone else is being totally obnoxious during the year that Mars conjuncts your Ascendant, you should look at your own behavior. It's easy to project this energy, making it someone else's fault. All too often, this symbolizes difficulty in personal relationships (divorce, arguments, fighting) because you won't acknowledge your own part in what's happening.

JUPITER—ASCENDANT PROGRESSIONS

The natural effervescence, charisma, and attraction of Jupiter conjunct the Ascendant natally make you the perfect politician. You are open, optimistic, and enthusiastic. You may brag or exaggerate, but others usually take this with good humor for you have a wonderful sense of the ridiculous. At times this conjuction signifies argumentative behavior, primarily because you love to interact with the environment in a big way. If other factors in your chart indicate that your action is frustrated or contained, you may have problems with weight.

Although Jupiter conjunct the natal Ascendant is very often associated with varying degrees of obesity, not everyone with this position has this problem. Those who are not overweight have all become involved in a project or "cause" which can uplift the lives of the people around them. It seems that in order to release the full faith and optimism of this Jupiter position, you have to get out of selfish or self-centered activities and take a look at the wider world. Once your attention encompasses more than your immediate family, you can throw away the diets, for your weight will normalize quickly.

When Jupiter conjuncts your Ascendant by progression, you will experience a year in which it seems that all things are possible. While this may be quite positive, for the energy is very buoyant, you may seriously overextend, leaving a wake of unfulfilled promises.

It's not too likely that you can time events by the conjunction of progressed Jupiter to your natal Ascendant, for Jupiter does not move quickly and the Ascendant is probably not exact to the minute. During the year(s) that Jupiter is within a few minutes of arc of your natal Ascendant, you can achieve some marvelous recognition.

On the other hand, the conjunction of your progressed Ascendant to your natal Jupiter is not quite so difficult to time. It can be thrown off considerably by an error of a few minutes in birth time, but can be used to rectify a close birth time because the natal Jupiter will be exact. Both conjunctions often occur during a major change (almost always favorable) in your approach to the environment. You'll really have to work at being negative and unresponsive to have anything difficult occur with either type of Jupiter/Ascendant progressed conjunction. (It can be done; you can sink into a bottle of gin and expand all your rotten habits, but most of us don't put that much effort into making sure we fail.)

SATURN—ASCENDANT PROGRESSIONS

If you have Saturn conjunct your natal Ascendant, you are shy, conservative, and lack self-confidence. You may feel unloved or unwanted. If you pursue this to its roots, you may find out that your parents did not expect you and did not really want a child at the time you made your appearance. Although your parents probably became reconciled fairly quickly to your presence, babies can sense rejection. You can carry this sense of rejection to adulthood, never understanding the underlying cause. In order to compensate for this sense of personal inadequacy, many of you become experts, or at least very highly educated people. You need to be right and need to be revered within your environment. Sometimes Saturn conjunct the natal

Ascendant becomes over-responsible, legalistic, even quite rigid about "rules" of behavior.

During the years that Saturn conjuncts your Ascendant by progression, you may feel quite alienated from your environment. You are at a psychological low point, given to worrying about your choices and your impact upon others. You tend to assume responsibility automatically and to apologize for events that are entirely out of your control. You may choose to use this time to become the world's expert in a particular field. In this case, you won't actually get any reward for your study until Saturn finishes the conjunction, but then you will be recognized.

When the progressed Ascendant conjuncts your natal Saturn, you can dig down and find some of the causes for your insecurities. You will decide to take charge of your interactions, for Saturn symbolizes control. This conjunction also indicates a release because Saturn is moving into the twelfth house from the first. You will be able to decide exactly where your personal responsibility starts and ends. Then you can stop trying to carry the whole world on your back and get on with the process of living your own life.

In spite of all the difficulties outlined above, Saturn conjunct the Ascendant is a strong success indicator because it implies ambition, persistence, and hard work. Those of us who do not have this aspect tend to say "how awful" while those of us who do have it simply get on with the business at hand, namely, succeeding in this lifetime.

THE OUTER PLANETS AND THE ASCENDANT

The three outer planets can stay within a degree of their natal position for thirty years in a progressed chart. Since we usually only have fifteen minutes of orb accuracy (at most) at the angles, we can't time much of anything by the conjunction of the progressed position of the three outer planets to the natal angles. The following discussion only considers the conjunction of the progressed angle to the natal (and progressed) position of the outer planets. The angle will usually conjunct both natal and progressed position the same year, spreading out the effect of the conjunction by the distance between the natal and progressed planet.

URANUS—ASCENDANT PROGRESSIONS

If you have Uranus conjunct your natal Ascendant, you are highly individualistic and prepare the way for the new by breaking up and sweeping away the old. Your parents probably did not find Uranus conjunct the Ascendant a blessing, for when the old includes bedtime, toilet use, doors, windows, and mother's favorite antique vase, parents find it difficult to sweep away the fragments without wishing to sweep away the fragmenter.

Unconcerned with social niceties, you delight in the unconventional, seizing whatever opportunities arise to mold the environment to your views. Unless you develop the socially aware, humanitarian side of your natal Uranus, you may become stuck in a never-ending temper tantrum against the world around you. Then the more you look at what is going on around you, the more upset it makes you, and the more erratic your behavior becomes. If you can separate a little, you can determine what bothers you the most about your interactions and then set about to change specific situations. When you can't or won't go after the things you are able to change, you can become quite frustrated with your life.

When your progressed Ascendant conjuncts your natal and progressed Uranus, you may experience a total change in your world. Some of the changes which can occur include moving to a totally different and unusual environment (like the Moon), having people suddenly appear (or disappear) in your life, receiving completely unexpected recognition, for good or ill. Whatever happens is very likely to surprise you, even though the conjunction culminates the years you've had Uranus in the first house of your progressed chart. You've really been getting ready for change for a long, long time. During the year that your progressed Ascendant makes the conjunctions, you will complete your break with past behavior. If your natal Uranus is being aspected by transits during this year, the transits will trigger far more change than is usually associated with the transits alone.

NEPTUNE—ASCENDANT PROGRESSIONS

With Neptune conjunct your natal Ascendant, your ladder of life is based on a mashmallow, resting on a cloud. Amazingly, you often complete the climb to your higher self, rung by rung, heedless of the soft and sinking ladder base.

Neptune conjunct the Ascendant symbolizes your sensitive, possibly psychic personality, which is easily upset by disruptive conditions within the environment, and is often completely out of touch with reality. The dreamer, the schemer, the artist and the escapist are the Neptunian ones among us. Emily Dickinson, in poem #214, stanza 2, captures the elusive spirit of Neptune conjunct the Ascendant:

Inebriate of Air am I
And Debauchee of Dew
Reeling—through endless summer days—
From inns of Molten Blue

When your progressed Ascendant conjuncts your natal Neptune, you find that your carefully constructed reality starts to fragment, dissolving into the smoke of in-betweens and uncertainties. This period can be one of great psychic growth, but can also be one of entanglement in a web of self-deception—escape from any difficult reality in your life. You may simply refuse to see unpleasant things that are right in front of you. So while everyone else is telling you that you must be having difficulty coping with whatever is going on, you blithely insist that all is well.

You must ascertain how you respond to Neptune in general before you decide how you are dealing with the conjunction. Transits to Neptune will trigger events that involve the way that you project yourself into the world during the year that your progressed Ascendant conjuncts Neptune. It will be nearly impossible to clearly define the events of the year, for you can't see them clearly. Hence, this conjunction can usually only be analyzed in retrospect, for it is too nebulous to pin down while it is occurring.

PLUTO—ASCENDANT PROGRESSIONS

When you have Pluto conjunct your natal Ascendant, you are a powerhouse, determined to change the environment in a very complete manner. You may not act immediately, but when you do act, everyone in the environment notices the transformation you are effecting. You either integrate or disintegrate all around you. Power, force, and dominance are usually issues throughout your life. As a child you constantly pushed and tested the pressures to conform, and as an adult you frequently exert pressure on those around you. You may be totally unaware of the impact you have on others, particularly if your natal Pluto is within six or seven degrees of your natal Ascendant and moved into the twelfth house of your progressed chart during your childhood.

When your progressed Ascendant conjuncts your natal and progressed Pluto, you feel and project tremendous force for permanent change in the world around you. You may be quite antagonistic towards others at this time, particularly if there are transiting aspects to your natal Pluto which trigger the potential for change inherent in this aspect. In the absence of transiting influences on your natal Pluto, you experience the conjunction as a time of confrontation with the people and things around you. This confrontation defines the limits of your personal power over these things and people. Do not be deceived by the fact that Pluto often works under the surface, for in spite of the fact that you may not be overtly acting towards change, you are very busy manipulating the environment to make it move in your direction.

WHERE DO I COME FROM?

PLANETS CONJUNCT THE NADIR

The Nadir, or fourth house cusp (the IC—Imum Coeli or "bottom of the sky" in Latin), symbolizes your inner self, in contrast to the MC which symbolizes your direction in both professional and spiritual life. The IC is where you come from, what you hold dearest, and how you conduct your private, personal life. The Nadir symbolizes the "I" without its projections to the outer world. It symbolizes your all-alone internal self.

The fourth house also stands for several mundane parts of life, just as the tenth house signifies your boss, your Dad, and your reputation. The fourth house shows how you finish things (the sign on the IC and any planets in the fourth house will color this). Your home (real estate) is connected to your fourth house, your view of your Mom is filtered through the fourth house, as are your connections to your past and your ancestors (whether through the possession of antiques or through tradition.) The IC connects you to your roots, both psychological and physical. I believe that the IC is also associated with past lives and past life ties, but this is not easily proven.

The tension between the concepts of "where I'm going to" and "where I'm coming from" are inherent in the opposition of the Nadir and the Midheaven. Aspects to one must include aspects to the other. Thus, part of any analysis of a conjunction to the Nadir is the analysis of the opposition to the Midheaven, just as part of the conjunction to the Midheaven is the opposition to the Nadir.

Although the conjunction to the MC is one of the most powerful aspects in the chart, it does not follow that the conjunction to the IC is therefore weak. The conjunction to the IC must move through your entire being in order to surface, but this very need indicates that you will feel conjunctions to the IC from the totality of your experience.

SUN—NADIR PROGRESSIONS

When you are born at midnight and have your Sun conjunct your natal IC, you often put on a great show of bravado to hide the timidity which you really feel. This bravado is more obvious if you are a man, for our society frowns on the fearful man. Thus you may appear more egotistical than your brother with his Sun conjunct his MC. When your Sun is conjunct your Nadir, you must overcome obstacles in order to be recognized. However, you have a strength of purpose and inner identity which serves you well whenever outer life becomes difficult. Your aim and direction in life stem directly from your own sense of self and ego identity. Since the IC and the Sun progress at nearly the same rate (depending on the method used to progress the angles) a natal conjunction will be a lifelong conjunction in your progressed chart.

When your progressed Sun conjuncts your natal IC or your progressed IC conjuncts your natal Sun, you will experience a sense of rootedness or connection to past events, or even to your ancestral heritage. You will be increasingly sensitive to the events at home, for you may completely identify with what is going on in your home. Are the kids disruptive? Does the roof leak? You may feel that peace (or comfort) at home is entirely dependent on what you do. Conversely, you may become obsessed with how you finish matters. If you identify yourself with the end products of your efforts, you may develop many reasons to feel inadequate. No one can finish everything perfectly or in a blaze of glory. On the positive side, this conjunction often occurs when you *do* finish some major project in your life.

When your progressed IC conjuncts your natal Sun, moving the Sun to the third house in your progressed chart, you are more willing to communicate your basic needs to others.[19] You are also more likely to get to know your neighbors or become more involved with your siblings (third house people).

When your progressed Sun conjuncts your natal IC, it is moving from your natal third house to your natal fourth house. If you've never paid too much attention to your own background or to where you set up housekeeping, you're in for a change of habit. Even the most confirmed Sagittarian-type rolling stone can decide to put down roots when his progressed Sun conjuncts his natal IC. If you've already settled down, you'll be making your own home more compatible with your view of yourself. Whether your taste runs to brass and glass modern or to Victoriana, you will want to develop your home as an extension of yourself.

MOON—NADIR PROGRESSIONS

When you have the Moon conjunct the IC in your natal chart, you are at once very emotionally attached to the idea of home, roots, and family and sensitive to all kinds of hurts from these same sources. You may find that your mother smothered you in an emotional blanket,

---

[19]Although Mercury rules the conscious mind, the third house is also connected to communication. The way you communicate with others is really a combination of the position, sign, and aspects of Mercury and the third houses. Both the sign on the third and any planets in the third house affect how you communicate with others. Most of the third house communication is on a mundane or daily level, involving telephone conversations, daily interchanges with others and short letters. Oscar Weber called Venus in the third house a "merry mind" and Jupiter in the third house can offset a twelfth house Mercury, indicating that you will not be as silent as the Mercury position might indicate. You communicate readily and clearly if your Mercury in Scorpio is in the third house.

thus making it very difficult to separate from her. At the same time, many with this position find that mother provides an anchor against the vagaries of the outside world. Either way it's difficult to be as emotionally complete as you consider your mother to be, and it's hard to let go of this idea of mother and mothering. You need an emotional base, a home, and will go to all kinds of extremes to make sure that you have one.

Unlike the other planets, the progressed Moon moves completely around your chart every twenty-eight years. Thus a conjunction of your progressed IC to your natal Moon lasts twice as long as the conjunction of your Progressed Moon to either the natal or progressed IC. The conjunction of the progressed IC to your natal Moon will last for about a year (giving a thirty minute orb to the conjunction). During this year you are very sensitive to home-related or mother-related matters. You may be very attached to your mother or your home, or you may try to be the supreme nurturing person within your home. When conditions in the outer world get difficult, you'll retreat to your home to lick your wounds and recover.

When your progressed Moon conjuncts either natal or progressed Nadir, you begin a two year connection to the emotional under-pinnings of your reality structures. This conjunction may accompany an event such as marriage, childbirth, or a time when you have to care for a parent. This conjunction symbolizes both emotional giving at home and emotional strength gained through the people in your home. Whatever occurs at home during this time, you will experience it with unusual depth of emotion, and you will respond quickly and completely to each event.

MERCURY—NADIR PROGRESSIONS

When Mercury is conjunct your IC natally, you worry about your home, your mother, and how to finish things. You prefer an intellectual environment in your home, and even if your childhood home was not geared to intellectual pursuits, you will set this up in your own home. You may be something of an intellectual snob, at least within the confines of your own house. On the other hand, Mercury here may indicate that you have great manual dexterity and have a home hobby shop or studio where you tinker or create contentedly.

When your Nadir and Mercury are conjunct by progression, you reach a crisis point concerning communication and your home life. Often this communication crisis involves your career (Mercury op-posing the MC). If you have support at home, you can iron out the communication difficulties at work. If you don't have support at home, you may be bringing home the problems of the tenth house, further alienating those at home.

When your progressed Mercury is conjunct your natal IC, Mercury is moving from the third house of communication to the fourth house of home. This implies that the changes in communication involve increased attempts to communicate within the family. Even though the Nadir usually involves Mom (or through the opposition to the MC, Dad), most of us really talk more to our spouses when progressed Mercury conjuncts to our natal IC. The most common *topic*, however, is our parents, or our concept of parenting. If we don't have a spouse to talk to, we talk to our friends or our therapist about these things.

In contrast, when the progressed Nadir conjuncts your natal Mercury, the motion is from the fourth house to the third house. This indicates that you can take whatever communications skills you have developed while Mercury was in your fourth house to the world outside through the third house of conscious communications. During the conjunction year you'll be very likely to address all of the same issues that your friend with progressed Mercury conjunct the natal IC is thinking about. However, due to the direction of your progression, you'll be finding support from neighbors and siblings, and you'll find that the worries associated with the Mercury conjunction to the IC color all of your daily communication patterns.

VENUS—NADIR PROGRESSIONS

When Venus is conjunct the IC in your natal chart, you seek and find harmony in your home. You surround yourself with beauty, softness, comfort. You are an incurable romantic, particularly within the privacy of your own home. This hidden romanticism may cause you some difficulties in your career, for you dislike the harsh realities of the outer world. As long as you can set up your home as a refuge against the jangling clashes of personality you find outside, you can retreat to your personal oasis for renewal. You need to be able to have soft colors and soft fabrics, for you are quite aware that the soothing quality of pleasure (even in small things) is what allows you to cope with everything else in life.

Abrupt change is not the hallmark of Venus conjuncting any of the angles by progression. Rather, you become aware that you need to soften the shape and contour of your own life, that you need to recognize your love of beauty and sensuality. Venus conjunct any of the angles signifies marriage, because it symbolizes a change in your view of yourself in relation to the things and people you love. But marriage is not the only possibility, for you may simply be getting to a point where you can accept the secret romantic in you. When the progression takes Venus from the fourth house to the third, you'll find more pleasure in communications, in siblings, in neighbors. When the conjunction moves from the third to the fourth, you'll soften all of the things in your house, adding pillows, rugs, anything that feels nice.

The only way you can encounter negative repercussions from Venus conjunct the Nadir is to become so greedy that you negate all the positive benefits. If you sit at home nibbling chocolate and insisting that everyone else serve you, you'll come down to earth with a bit of a thump after Venus is done with the conjunction. Not only will you look like a house (fourth or not), others will get tired of living with a prima donna.

MARS—NADIR PROGRESSIONS

Mars conjunct the Nadir (either natally or by progression) is like a fire in the cellar. If you have a furnace housing around the fire and the duct work to take the heat all through the house, a fire in the cellar is a truly marvelous thing. But every so often you need to go look at the fire in the cellar to make sure it is still working correctly.

When Mars conjuncts the IC natally, you have endless energy to expend at home. Often this means just plain too much energy and this results in irritation. To put it bluntly, there's often discord in your home. When you were little you probably drove your mother up a wall. Now as an adult you still bring all your problems home with you. It's a wonderful position for anyone who wants to work out of their home, because then there's a legitimate outlet for the energy that gets created on the domestic front.

When your IC and Mars are conjunct by progression, you will have to learn about dealing with your own anger, aggression, and energy. You may feel that your fury is invisible to the world at large, but this is usually untrue. Although you may only express your feelings at home, the tension caused by this conjunction cannot be hidden. Every so often someone comes up with a perfect use for the Mars-IC conjunction and proceeds to build a house, remodel an existing structure, make a workshop in the garage or spare room. I have one client who spent that year being a "house father" in a group home for problem adolescents. Those kids did their Mars trip around him all the time. His Mars gave him the energy to deal with them.

Fortunately, a progression is not a sudden thing. You have time to figure out what you want to do with the energy of this conjunction. It's only when you won't check the fire in the cellar, even though the furnace light is flashing, that you get into real problems with Mars conjunct your IC by progression. Transits to this conjunction (or to natal Mars or your natal IC) can trigger all kinds of change at home. You are the one who determines the final outcome of that change.

JUPITER—NADIR PROGRESSIONS

When you have this conjunction in your natal chart, you finish things with a flourish. You prefer to have a large, open home, filled with graciousness and taste. You probably grew up in a home that had these qualities. You may be a bit of a windbag, especially at home, but your almost extravagant generosity towards family members usually makes up for this. This position usually indicates you have a good relationship with your parents, particularly your mother.

When the Nadir and Jupiter are conjunct by progression, you will feel optimistic and successful at home. It often looks like Santa has arrived during this conjunction, for you may tend to spend very freely for anything you can use at home. If you are using your generosity to cover up worry about your career (the opposition to the MC) you can get yourself deeply into debt before you realize what's going on. You may move to larger quarters, or expand the living space you currently have. You do need to watch out for overoptimism (remember that houses and their additions have to be paid for). Although the major pitfall of the Jupiter-IC conjunction is bankruptcy, there are usually few other problems.

I realize that some people will somehow manage to avoid pleasant experiences while Jupiter is on their Nadir by progression. Jupiter basically expands everything it touches. Thus, you can expand in negative ways at home if you want to while Jupiter conjuncts your Nadir. This means that if you've had a difficult time at home, or setting up a home for yourself, Jupiter's presence on the Nadir may allow you to enlarge those pre-existing problems to positively gargantuan size. Most of us have Saturn somewhere in our chart, preventing us from abandoning all responsibility while Jupiter, the incredible optimist, conjoins our Nadir. But if you manage to ignore Saturn, you can get into a great deal of trouble taking chances during this conjunction. (Jupiter is also connected to gambling.) This is *not* the appropriate time to quit your job and move to Las Vegas, unless you have some good aspects to Saturn. Even then, I'd suggest you wait a year, until the conjunction is done.

SATURN—NADIR PROGRESSIONS

When you have Saturn conjunct your IC natally, your parents may have required perfection from you as a child. Then as an adult you demand the same perfection from yourself. The resulting fear of imperfection may make if difficult for you to decide when a task is finally done. (You could always redo a little part of it, making it better!)

You may literally live out of a closet, for you discount any need for space or comfort in your surroundings. Alternately, and particularly if you are a woman, you may feel inadequate if everything is not spotless at home even though you are holding down a full-time job outside the home. If this sets up a large conflict between home and career, you will decide to spend more energy on whichever of these is less pleasing (or on whichever seems to be the one "duty" requires you to do).

If you are a man with Saturn conjunct the Nadir, you may get involved with a house that always seems to need repairs, a "handyman's special," particularly if you are not really handy and hate fixing things. Then home matters will chew up your leisure time until you are constantly tired at work. Both men and women with Saturn conjunct the IC need to take the home situation a little less seriously.

The year that your Saturn and your Nadir are conjunct by progression, you need to take stock of all those little guilt buttons you've developed concerning things at home. If at all possible, hire someone else to paint and paper or to scrub the floors. Throw away all those things that clutter up the place and make your dual jobs that much harder. Quit trying to strip the ornate Victorian molding. Paint it. Stop playing critical, guilt games with your spouse. You are forcing your spouse into the role of critical parent. That's the bottom line the year that Saturn and your Nadir conjunct by progression. You have to deal with the internalized version of your critical parent.

THE OUTER PLANETS AND THE NADIR

The three outer planets move so slowly that the only conjunctions that will occur are the natal conjunction and the conjunction of the progressed Nadir to the natal and progressed position of the planet.

URANUS—NADIR PROGRESSIONS

When you have this conjunction natally, your mother was probably positive that you incarnated expressly to drive her crazy. Of course, you may have chosen a crazy lady for a mother, too. But if your mother wasn't crazy when you were born, and didn't become crazy while you grew up, it was not your fault. Between your abrupt changes in behavior and your completely indomitable will, your parents may have despaired of ever civilizing you.

If your childhood home was truly chaotic, yours may have been the only voice of sanity therein. However, if your childhood home tended towards normal, you had to stir things up. When your progressed Nadir conjuncts your natal and progressed Uranus (the two conjunctions usually occur within the same year), your home, your attitudes towards your career, and/or your relationship to both parents will undergo a major change. If major transits to your natal Uranus occur during this year as well, you may have to reevaluate all of these areas. You may not recognize the part that your will plays in these changes, for it's often easier to view them as accidents of fate. In reality, you've been building towards these changes for the five years that Uranus was within five degrees of your progressed IC.

NEPTUNE—NADIR PROGRESSIONS

If you have Neptune conjunct the IC in your natal chart, you probably constructed a dream world in your childhood home, a world replete with unseen people and pets. Elusive as a moonbeam, you may not have established a firm relationship with your mother, preferring the idealized person you have created to the reality of the mother you had. There may have been situations within your home which reinforced your sense of unreality or your desire to escape into a world of imagination. You are, as a consequence, uncertain about ending things, preferring to let matters wander along until they appear to resolve themselves or at least go away.

When your progressed Nadir conjuncts your natal and progressed Neptune, you rarely feel the conjunction directly. There will have to be many other transiting aspects for you to be literally carried away by a flood. Instead, you see the conjunction after it is done, for then you will notice an increased ability to articulate your dreams, a better ability to see the reality of your home, and a sense that you've come out of a rather dense fog. You may be more aware of and more receptive to psychic influences during the year of the conjunction. However, the sense of unreality which accompanies this conjunction often confuses the psychic events so that you can't quite sort them out until after the whole thing is over.

PLUTO—NADIR PROGRESSIONS

When you have Pluto conjunct the Nadir in your natal chart, you have to cope with an extremely dominant mother figure. The results of this early dominance are either an internalization of dominance patterns so that you become the dominant figure, or an outward abdication of the dominant role so that you attempt to get your way through subtle manipulation. Regardless of how meekly and unassumingly you approach life, this natal conjunction indicates a rather deep-seated, iron will. You may choose to reveal the dominant part of yourself only at home, but at home you will not be crossed.

When your progressed Nadir conjuncts your natal and progressed Pluto, formerly hidden problems of self-determination and power come to light. You may undergo a complete transformation as the conjunction occurs, demanding far more prominence in the decision-making process at home or at work. The opposition of your progressed MC to Pluto often symbolizes a determination to set your own career goals independently of what the boss at work may want. This will only create problems if you won't admit that you are really doing this. If you insist on maintaining an internal charade, where the boss is the one who makes all of the decisions and you are the poor put-upon peon, you may find that the year of the conjunction of Pluto to your progressed Nadir is a year of tremendous pressure from career directions. Any changes in home or career that you initiate during this year will be permanent, so think before you change things.

WHAT WILL YOU SHOW ME?

PLANETS CONJUNCT THE DESCENDANT

The descendant, or the seventh house cusp, symbolizes the "other" in your life. Just as the Ascendant is how you project yourself into the environment, the Descendant is how you act or react with all the other people in the world. Since this is an axis, any planet which aspects your Descendant also aspects your Ascendant. This axis signifies the confrontation with the world outside yourself which began at the moment of your birth. The Ascendant side signifies your projection of yourself, your persona, while the Descendant signifies all that is not you, all the other people out there who are not specifically addressed by other houses. The seventh house thus deals with all relationships in general.

The seventh house cusp reflects both intimate relationships (marriage) and distant relationships (other people in general), harmonious relationships (partnerships) and disagreeable relationships (open enemies). Except for grandparents, the seventh house does not deal directly with members of your family, for these are indicated by the fourth house (Mom), tenth house (Dad), third house (siblings), and fifth house (children), nor does it deal with neighborhood groups (third house) or friends (eleventh house). The seventh house signifies partnerships of any kind, marriage or business. Your interactions involving the seventh house cusp take you into relationships where you do not have a specific role model to follow. Except for extremely traditional marriages in which each partner adheres to specific cultural roles, seventh house relationships are not automatic. We have specific roles to play as child, parent, brother or sister, and even pretty well-defined roles as neighbor and friend (though this may vary from region to region). Relating to superiors or authority figures (tenth house) is also well-defined behavior. In contrast, your seventh house relating is much more independent. You decide how to cope with marriage, with partnerships, with the people at the market or on the street, at cocktail parties or business meetings where there are others who don't like you.

How you choose to relate to the other people depends on the persona you choose to display in the world. The persona you show to the world around you depends on your relationships to the people in that world. This is the interaction of the Ascendant/Descendant axis; the Ascendant is the "me" I'm going to show you, and the Descendant is the "you" that I see.

SUN—DESCENDANT PROGRESSIONS

When your natal Sun and Descendant are conjunct, you see others in terms of yourself. Easily impressed by others, you may try to be all things to all people. Unless you have a strong internal identity, you may experience periods of self-doubt. This is, in part, due to a tendency to seek confirmation of your own identity from other people. All too often, Sun conjunct the Descendant people seek others to tell them who they are and how they should act. If you are stuck in this mode, you need to think about your own right to exist as an independent person. Although you developed the social graces of tact and cooperation early in life, there are times that both of these must be abandoned if you are to avoid the position of doormat to the world.

As a result of this reliance on cues from others, you do not function well alone. You allow yourself to be forever subject to the whims and vagaries of your spouse, your partner, the people around you. You may find it very difficult to withstand peer pressure. If your natal Sun is well aspected, these difficulties will be minimal, but regardless of the aspects to your natal Sun, you can learn to differentiate yourself from other people as you grow.

When your Sun and Descendant are conjunct by progression, you experience a year in which the needs of others supercede your own. This can symbolizes a major love, partnership, or marriage.

When your progressed Sun conjuncts your natal Descendant, your progressed Sun is moving from the sixth house of your natal chart to the seventh house of your natal chart. You are in the process of changing your self-image from service, or daily routine in the work-related world, to a closer identification of your internal self (Sun) with other people. When the motion is the other direction, and your progressed Descendant conjuncts your natal Sun, your natal Sun is moving from the seventh house in the progressed chart to the sixth house. You are moving from a close identification with other people towards an identification with the idea of service or daily work routine.

The third type of conjunction, when the progressed Sun conjuncts the progressed Descendant, only occurs when you have a sign of fast or very slow ascent rising. Furthermore, this last type of conjunction is spread out over several years because the Descendant and the Sun progress at nearly the same speed. You need to look at the positions of natal Sun in the progressed chart and progressed Sun in the natal chart to get an idea of how you can use the energy of this conjunction.

MOON—DESCENDANT PROGRESSIONS

Unlike the other planets, the progressed Moon moves completely around the chart every twenty-eight years. Thus the meaning of the progressed Moon conjunct the seventh house cusp is quite different from the meaning of the progressed Descendant conjunct the natal Moon. The progressed Moon symbolizes cyclic emotional phenomona and is frequently connected to major life events when conjunct any angle in your chart. Your natal Moon symbolizes your internal response nature. Changes in your entire emotional attitude are likely when your progressed angles conjunct your natal Moon's position.

When your natal Moon is conjunct your Descendant, you seek emotional reassurance from others. You are likely to get involved in the personal lives of others in order to guarantee the emotional exchange you need to validate your own feelings. You will sit up all night with another during a crisis time, but you need the support of others constantly and may resort to manipulation in order to have the reassurance that you are loved. You need to separate love from dependence. Otherwise, you may set up a marriage in which you are either completely dependent on your partner for emotional support or you are the complete source of emotional support for your spouse.

The year that your progressed Descendant conjuncts your natal Moon, you will experience many of the feelings associated with the natal conjunction. You will need to assess your ability to give and receive emotional support. You need to distinguish between the feelings that are yours and the feelings that are, in reality, a reflection of someone else's moods.

When your progressed Moon conjuncts your natal Descendant, the conjunction symbolizes a shift in the focus of your emotional responses. During the fourteen years that your progressed Moon was below the horizon, you internalized your response patterns. The conjunction with the seventh house cusp initiates a fourteen year cycle above the horizon where you learn to externalize your emotional responses, beginning with the expression of your feelings in relationships. The two years following the conjunction are years in which you will be concerned with the responses and needs of your spouse, second child, or other people in general. This conjunction often symbolizes marriage, childbirth, or marks the time you move out of Mom and Dad's house to set up your own space.

MERCURY—DESCENDANT PROGRESSIONS

When you have Mercury conjunct the Descendant in your natal chart, you constantly think about others and worry about your contacts with them. Because you are ever conscious of public scrutiny, you may try too hard to be liked. Curiosity is characteristic of Mercury, and you are endlessly curious about other people. You may be so intent on discovering what makes other people tick that you completely disregard your own motivations. Although this can lead to terrific investigative reporting, it may make more mundane interactions with others somewhat difficult. Your penchant for analysis may be taken for criticism, or worse, for just plain nosiness, and you will alienate the very people you are trying to understand.

When Mercury conjuncts your Descendant by progression, you experience a year in which others' concerns dominate your consciousness. When the progressed Descendant conjuncts your natal Mercury, you will concentrate on making contacts that can enliven your day-to-day routine, because your natal Mercury is moving from the seventh house to the sixth house in the progressed chart. When your progressed Mercury conjuncts your natal seventh house cusp, you are changing from a concentration on the details of daily life to a much larger world view. Here your progressed Mercury, moving into the seventh house of your natal chart, is moving above the horizon. Not only does this motion involve relating, it gets Mercury into the outer-directed southern hemisphere. The conjunction in either direction is more often connected to an event that opens intellectual doors than to events such as marriage or childbirth. Other people appear who stimulate you intellectually during this time.

VENUS—DESCENDANT PROGRESSIONS

When you have Venus conjunct the Descendant natally, you may indeed be called "a child of God," for you are a peacemaker. Preferring harmony in all your contacts with others, you tend to smooth over all disagreements. A few flaws do accompany this position of Venus, however. You prefer people of status and may be a bit of a snob. The great lengths you go to in order to be loveable may disguise an inner insecurity about your own desirability. You may feel that everyone else in the world is more worthy of love than you are. You do tend to attract gentle, generous people in relationships. As wonderful as this can be, if you decide that you are the only person in the world who is selfish, self-indulgent, or lazy, this natal conjunction can undermine your self-confidence.

When Venus is conjunct your Descendant by progression, you attract harmonious relationships. During the year that this conjunction is exact, you will have a strong desire to please the other people (particularly partners) in your life. This is a wonderful position for marriage, and very often accompanies a decision to marry. Any marriage begun with this conjunction will gain strength from your determination to provide the Venusian qualities of love and comfort for your spouse. Moreover, the conjunction indicates that you are likely to choose a person who can return your affection.

When progressed Venus conjuncts your natal seventh house cusp, Venus is moving from your natal sixth house of work and service into your seventh house of relationships. Furthermore, Venus is moving from the inner-directed northern hemisphere (below the horizon) to the outer-directed southern hemisphere (above the horizon). You will find that you have more ease in relationships after the conjunction. You will attract gentleness, because you are better able to show your own gentle side to the rest of the world.

When the secondary progressed Descendant conjuncts your natal Venus, the motion of the secondary cusps carries your Venus from the seventh house of the progressed chart to the sixth house of your progressed chart. This usually accompanies an easing of conditions in your working life, for the sixth house involves the daily grind. The sixth house Venus doesn't change anything in your career, but it makes the rat race easier to run.

MARS—DESCENDANT PROGRESSIONS

When you have Mars conjunct your Descendant natally, others probably think that the only reason you would consider marriage is to have a built-in sparring partner. Other people irritate you. Because of your impatience with the world in general, you are perhaps the world's worst salesperson. You are extremely competitive and need to develop self-control. Because you do not always recognize your own aggressive tendencies, you may feel that other people always pick fights with you. If you can integrate your competitive instincts in a positive fashion, Mars can provide endless energy for achievement. One of the most successful ways to integrate your highly competitive nature is to choose a highly energetic, interactive career. If your tenth house indicates a capacity for a strong career direction, you can use your seventh house Mars with all the people you meet in the business world. Arguments which would devastate someone with Venus on the Descendant stimulate you.

When Mars is conjunct the seventh house cusp by progression, you'll experience at the very least a year of intensely directed energy. This particular conjunction is very often associated with events, for even an inner planet transit can trigger this energy. Whether the events are positive or difficult depends on how well you have mastered the art of self-control.

Watch transiting aspects closely during this year, for you will certainly remember the things that happen now. Marriages contracted during the year of the conjunction are often hasty, leaving you (and your spouse) many years to repent. If you are already married, the conjunction year may accompany tremendous difficulties within your marriage. Mars here does not automatically indicate divorce, but it does reveal a need to reassess your own temper and your use of competition within a partnership.

When your progressed Mars is conjuncting your natal seventh house cusp, it is moving from your natal sixth house (below the horizon) to your natal seventh house (above the horizon). Your initiative, drive, and energy are now openly directed toward relationships. What you attract in relationships is directly connected to how well you understand and use your own initiatory energy.

When your progressed Descendant conjuncts your natal Mars (or when your progressed Mars is retrograde when conjuncting your natal Descendant), the direction of change is different, for Mars is moving from the seventh house into the sixth house. In this case, you are directing your energy towards your daily routine, and more towards your own inner needs. If you can incorporate an energy intensive activity into your daily grind, Mars in the sixth house can improve your general health. If you refuse to engage in physical activity on a daily basis, you may find that co-workers are a constant source of irritation.

JUPITER—DESCENDANT PROGRESSIONS

When you have Jupiter conjunct your Descendant natally, you are open and expansive with others. Much of this openness may be at your own expense, for you are given to making jokes about your own foibles. (All the Capricorns and Scorpios reading this just cringed.) You are idealistic about others, but, at the same time, you are not adverse to using others for personal gain. You seek successful people for associates, admiring wealth and power in others. If your tenth house career indicators show strong interactive potential, you may be very good at public work (law, social work, mediation) or in public office, for you love to give advice.

Jupiter progresses very slowly (14′ to 15′ a year, when it is moving quickly in direct motion). Thus the conjunction of progressed Jupiter to your natal Descendant could take quite a few years, even if you knew the birth time to the second. While your progressed Jupiter is within 15′ of arc of your Descendant (about the most accuracy you'll realistically be able to achieve on the Ascendant position) all of the characteristics of the natal conjunction will be heightened. Although you could marry a millionaire and live happily ever after, Jupiter is worth more than that in terms of potential personal growth. You will attract larger-than-life persons and relationships. All of these relationships can help you to expand and grow. When your progressed Descendant conjuncts your natal and/or progressed Jupiter, you usually experience a wonderful year of success by association. Your partner or spouse may be tremendously successful, allowing you to bask in reflected glory. Don't deceive yourself—you put a lot of hard work into the glory achieved whether or not you are the one receiving the praise.

If you have just been through a few years of difficult Saturn aspects, the conjunction may indicate that you can now reap the rewards and gain recognition for past work-related effort. Unless you have some sort of Saturn influence, the conjunction may not bring lasting success, for Jupiter talks big but does not necessarily perform well.

The one area in which this conjunction is almost always an unqualified success is marriage. When you begin a marriage with this conjunction, you will expand, grow, and have a lot of fun in it.

SATURN—DESCENDANT PROGRESSIONS

When you have Saturn conjunct your Descendant in your natal chart, you may be considered rather cold, for you have difficulty interacting with other people. The opposition of Saturn to your Ascendant indicates that you are preoccupied with yourself, because you are never pleased with your interaction with the environment. Fear of rejection may cause you to retreat from interactions with others. Your careful consideration of each move may make you appear extremely calculating. In fact, you are afraid of making a mistake.

You have good reasons for being circumspect in alliances, for with Saturn here, you often end up assuming responsibility for other people. Because you are never sure you can control your own impact on the environment, you find taking responsibility for others difficult. This is the rather classic bind of Saturn conjunct the natal Descendant. You hate having responsibility for anyone other than yourself, yet you are usually the one who gets saddled with that kind of responsibility. You get the responsibility because Saturn angular really makes you aware of duty in life. Often others think you are only accepting responsibility in order to control everyone else, but when Saturn is conjunct the Descendant, you accept it because you are supposed to accept it. Thus you will either delay marriage until later in life, when you are sure that you can financially provide for your spouse and family regardless of whatever happens, or you will choose to marry a much older person who can provide the stability and security you desperately need. If you choose the second option, you may allow (or require) your much older spouse to completely take over your Saturn. In that case, you can be a kid as long as you do everything that your surrogate parent demands.

The fastest that Saturn can move in secondary progression is 7' a year. Obviously, a conjunction of progressed Saturn to your natal Descendant is going to take a few years to complete, even if you allow only 10' approaching and separating. We don't usually know the Ascendant to that accuracy. If you live to be ninety, and Saturn was in fast direct motion at your birth, Saturn will progress about ten degrees. Thus, most of you who have progressed Saturn conjunct your natal Descendant already have a conjunction of natal Saturn and natal Descendant. During the years that progressed Saturn is closest to your natal Descendant, the natal symbolism discussed above will be strongest. Transits to this position can trigger acceptance of extremely limiting responsibilities. Try to spread around the duties a little. If you are one of ten children, insist that your siblings also contribute to the support of Mom or Dad. Don't assume so much of the burden that you become bitter.

When the progressed Descendant conjuncts natal and/or progressed Saturn, the most common event is marriage, and, in fact, this is an excellent marriage indicator. However, if no other aspects are being made to or from your Moon (progressed or natal) and/or Venus (progressed or natal), then Saturn conjunct the Descendant won't mean marriage. In the presence of other marriage indicators, the Saturn-Descendant conjunction brings a reality, a form, and most of all a long term commitment to the marriage. I have never found these negative in a marriage.

If Saturn and your Descendant are conjunct and you are not getting married, and you don't initiate a business partnership (this carries all of the positive long term allegiance that the marriage does), you will go through a year of serious introspection, self-doubt, and questioning of purpose, particularly in relationships. You may let go of any partnership which does not include responsibility and purpose.

THE OUTER PLANETS AND THE DESCENDANT

The three outer planets progress so slowly that the only conjunction not present in the natal chart is the conjunction of the progressed angle to their natal and progressed positions. The angle will usually conjunct both natal and progressed positions within the same year.

URANUS—DESCENDANT PROGRESSIONS

When you have this conjunction in your natal chart, there may have been many disruptive events during your childhood which lead to your extreme desire for freedom. You may have been very difficult to parent, for you seemed determined to break every rule your parents made, breaking some of them before your parents even considered that a rule was necessary. As you reached adulthood, you gravitated towards original and/or unusual people. Although this leads to rather exciting attachments, the magnetism can wear off, leaving you with relationships that end as abruptly as they begin. You are likely to marry someone because they are unusual in some way. Then as the marriage continues, the very behavior which attracted you in the first place starts to drive you crazy. If you chose someone who refuses to be tied down, you may find that your partner's freedom needs severely curtail your own. In spite of this desire for change and excitement, Uranus conjunct the Descendant is not competitive. Rather, this position symbolizes that you truly love living as close to the edge as you can get.

When your progressed Descendant conjuncts your natal and progressed Uranus, you undergo a change in existing relationships. Although it is difficult, it is not impossible to sustain a relationship during the year that your progressed Descendant conjuncts Uranus. If your partner allows you freedom, you can sort out the confusion generated by this conjunction. Your whole concept of interaction with the outside world is changing. Aspects from transits or other progressed planets to your natal Uranus during this year will indicate the direction the change is likely to take. It's not a wonderful aspect for marriage because you have not formed any clear idea of what relating is all about, but if you are determined to get married during this year, no astrologer will ever be able to change your mind.

NEPTUNE—DESCENDANT PROGRESSIONS

With Neptune on the Descendant natally, you tend to romanticize your view of the world. Christopher Marlowe captures this in his poem "The Passionate Shepherd to His Love," which begins

> Come live with me and be my love
> And we will all the pleasures prove,
> That valleys, groves, hills and fields,
> Woods or steepy mountains yields.

In spite of the actual nature of the people around you, you prefer to idealize your contact with them. Because you steadfastly refuse to see others as human, with human flaws, you are often lied to, gypped, or otherwise deceived. Of course, you are not entirely without blame for this dishonesty, as the opposition of Neptune to your Ascendant indicates that you have rose-colored glasses on whenever you consider your own behavior. Neptune conjunct the Descendant can indicate that you need to revere others in order to feel wanted. You may be the willing martyr. It is difficult and often exasperating to associate with someone who continually ascribes lofty motivations to another's actions. ("He must have been in a great deal of inner turmoil to rob three stores and kill four people. I really pity the poor fellow. WHAT? YOU WANT TO LOCK HIM UP?")

When you get that far out on the Neptune limb, you've removed the concept of personal responsibility from your mind. Fortunately, all of us also have Saturn somewhere, balancing the Neptune with a dose of reality.

When your progressed Descendant conjuncts your natal and progressed Neptune, you have a year of idealistic relationships, confusion, service to others. During this year it will be very difficult to ascertain why you do or anyone else does anything. Relationships seem to be enveloped in a shining haze of ideals, which dissolve as the conjunction separates. After the conjunction has moved Neptune to the sixth house, you are likely to join Sir Walter Raleigh in his rueful poem "The Nymph's Reply to the Shepherd" (verses 1, 2, 3):

> If all the world and love were young
> And truth in every shepherd's tongue,
> These pretty pleasures might me move
> To live with thee and be thy love.

> Time drives the flocks from field to fold
> When rivers rage and rocks grow cold,
> And Philomen becometh dumb;
> The rest complain of cares to come.

> The flowers do fade, and wanton fields
> To wayward winter reckoning yields;
> A honey tongue, a heart of gall
> Is fancy's spring, but sorrow's fall.

PLUTO—DESCENDANT PROGRESSIONS

When two male dogs meet for the first time, they go through a series of maneuvers which in dog language determines who will dominate in the relationship which has just begun. Should the two dogs not be able to establish a clear dominance quickly, they will fight. If you have Pluto conjunct the Descendant in your natal chart, you go through similar verbal maneuvers whenever you meet a new person. Dominance and submission in relationships are key factors in your life. Unlike the dogs, however, you are not attracted to people who do not respond to your signals. Relationships mean change. You will change the other person or be changed by that other person, but no strong relationship for you can leave either party unaltered. Those of you who choose to grow spiritually in this lifetime find that each deep relationship involves transformation towards a higher expression of self. However, when you do not choose to transcend the material, the changes can become notches on your tally stick, each notch signifying another person under your sway.

When your progressed Descendant conjuncts your natal and progressed Pluto, you encounter all these issues of dominance in your personal relationships. Any changes made in relationships during this year will be permanent. Aspects to your natal Pluto from transits and other progressed planets will symbolize the areas of your life affected by this transforming influence.

4

CHANGING EXPRESSIONS:

PLANETS IN PROGRESSION

HOW DO WE GROW?

SIGN CHANGES

As your natal chart progresses, many of your planets will change sign. This chapter delineates the basic meaning of each planet in each sign and the meaning of the progression to the following sign.

The influence of any progressed sign depends on the strength of the planet in that sign. When a planet has progressed to a sign in which the energy of the planet is easily expressed, we tend to readily incorporate the symbolism of the progression into our life-style.

Although each progressed position exerts some influence on our total projection, we will not permanently adopt a progressed symbolism which is counterproductive. Should a planet progress into the sign of its detriment or fall, we only express the symbolism of the planet through that sign when the planet is angular or heavily aspected. After the apsect(s) has passed, we will revert to the stronger natal expression of the planet.

When planets make a station, turning either direct or retrograde in your progressed chart, the zodiacal position (degree, sign, minute) of the station lingers as a sensitive point in your chart. Thus, even after the planet has moved away from that position you will find that transits or other progressions to that position can trigger events. The planets from Jupiter on out won't move very far from that station during your life, making it nearly impossible to differentiate the station from the progressed position of the planet, but the inner planets do move far enough to notice the effect of the position of the station.

Mercury goes retrograde three times a year, for a three week period each time. Three weeks translates to twenty-one years when we are counting a day for a year in secondary progressions. Thus even if Mercury is retrograde during part of your life, you will have many years that it is in direct motion. Venus turns retrograde approximately every year and a half, remaining retrograde for about six weeks (or forty-two years by progression). Most of us will have Venus direct during at least part of our lives. In contrast, Mars goes retrograde every two years, staying retrograde for ten to eleven weeks (seventy to eighty years). If you were born just as Mars turned retrograde, you may have it retrograde for all your life. Jupiter and Saturn are retrograde every year for periods of four to five months. Over one-third of us have one or both of these planets retrograde. The outer planets go retrograde every year for periods of about five months. Nearly half of us have outer planets retrograde.

Table 4.1 shows the average motion of the planets (when direct) each year and after sixty-five years. When the planets are retrograde, they move much more slowly. If Jupiter makes a station, turning retrograde or direct during your life, it may only move two or three degrees in sixty-five years. If Saturn makes a station, it may move one or two degrees in sixty-five years. The three outer planets may move *less than a degree* in sixty-five years.

Not too many of us will have any planet beyond Mars change sign during our lives. Furthermore, the effect of Jupiter or Saturn changing sign won't be very pronounced unless they are progressing into a sign

Table 4.1. The Average Maximum Motion of Planets When Direct†

Planet's Personal Significance	Planet or Midheaven	Maximum Motion Per Year*	Maximum Motion by Age 65*
Inner	Midheaven	1°	65° (2 signs + 5)
Inner	Sun	1°	65° (2 signs + 5)
Inner	Moon	13°	2½ Complete cycles
Inner	Mercury	1°20′	80°-90° (2-3 signs)
Inner	Venus	1°10′	70°-80° (2-3 signs)
Inner	Mars	40′-50′	44°-55° (1-2 signs)
Transition	Jupiter	14′	15°
Transition	Saturn	7′	8°
Outer	Uranus	2′-3′	3°
Outer	Neptune	1′-2′	2°
Outer	Pluto	1′-2′	2°

†For Ascendant information, see Table 1.3 on page 56.
*Maximum motion is much less when the planet is making a station. Consult an ephemeris of each person.

of rulership or exaltation, or during a time that they are aspected by other progressed planets or angles. The effect of the three outer planets changing sign by progression is usually generational rather than personal. This really means that those of us who are born just as one of the three outer planets is about to change sign are born during times of cultural change. We are the ones who bridge the gap between the old cultural values and the new outlook.

In order to use this section of your analysis of a progressed chart, look up each planet under its natal sign. You'll find a very brief, key word delineation of the natal position first, then the meaning of each possible progression.[20] At the end of this section, we will also discuss the north and south nodes.

PROGRESSIONS FOR ARIES NATAL POSITIONS

ARIES: YANG—CARDINAL—FIRE

NATAL SUN IN ARIES

Sun in exaltation in Aries
Sun keywords: basic life force, the physical body, internal "I"

Natal Sun Progressed to Taurus: The progressed Sun enters Taurus between age one week (natal ☉29°♈59') and age thirty (natal ☉0°♈00'). Your natal Sun is exalted, thus the Aries initiatory energy will always be the strongest expression of your basic energy. Nonetheless, Taurus can add staying power. This particular combination yields the ability to start over when faced with problems rather than relying on the fixed tendency to continue on the same track in spite of difficulties. During the thirty years that your progressed Sun is in Taurus, you learn to temper much of the brashness associated with your natal Aries. Although you will never have the patience of someone with natal Sun in Taurus, your life experience will teach you to appreciate the loyalty and perseverance of your progressed Taurus Sun.

Not everyone will use the combination of Taurus and Aries to steady their impulsive natures. If you choose to combine the negative

---

[20] For more complete natal sign delineations, I recommend: Hone, Margaret, *Modern Textbook of Astrology*, L. N. Fowler & Co., London, England, 1970; Sakoian, Frances, and Acker, Louis, *The Astrologer's Handbook*, Harper & Row, New York, 1973.

sides of both these signs, you can be bombastic as you make instant decisions then refuse to change your opinion regardless of circumstances. Neither Aries nor Taurus is particularly good at listening to the opinions of others (although a Taurus will appear to do so, then go ahead and do exactly what was planned before.) Unless you put forth some effort to pay attention to the needs of the others around you, you can isolate yourself. Then your basic Aries desire to be the first one into things will be quite frustrated, for it is hard to lead when no one wants to follow.

Natal Aries Progressed to Gemini: The progressed Sun enters Gemini between age thirty (natal ☉29°♈59′) and age sixty (natal ☉0°♈00′). After thirty years of Taurus progression, your Sun moves into Gemini. You will find that the Gemini progressed Sun combines with your Aries natal position much more easily. The yang qualities of Gemini, the curiosity and outgoing style, blend well with your natal yang Aries. You retain an ability to determine the practical outcome of your actions from your Taurus progression, while your ego drive finds more freedom of expression once your progressed Sun enters Gemini.

Gemini adds flexibility to the expression of your internal self. You are more comfortable with your internal inconsistencies. If you have worked towards cooperating with and understanding the needs of others, you will find it much easier to accept changes initiated by another. If you have gotten stuck in a negative expression of the Aries/Taurus combination, you may now begin to seek alternate means of self-expression. Just how you'll change yourself really depends on the position of the rest of the planets in your chart. The Gemini influence gives you both the desire and the ability to change, if change can bring positive results.

Natal Aries Sun Progressed to Cancer: The progressed Sun enters Cancer between age sixty (natal ☉29°♈59′) and age ninety (natal ☉0°♈00′). This progression returns your Sun to the cardinal quadruplicity. Thus the initiating energy of your natal Aries may surface again. However, the difference in polarity between Aries and Cancer symbolize your last attempt to balance yin and yang. If you have chosen to develop your higher self during your lifetime, you will not have a great deal of trouble integrating your masculine and feminine sides. If you have never paid much attention to spiritual matters, the Cancer influence provides the perfect opportunity for nagging and whining about how others, particularly family members, have no gratitude.

If you spent the thirty years of the Gemini progressed Sun thinking about how you could change your outlook without actually implementing any changes, you may find the Cancer progression reinforcing prejudices developed during childhood. Now, however, you can add emotion to your arguments. As your progressed Sun enters the last of the four elements, you have had the opportunity to learn all four kinds of self-expression (fire, your natal; earth, through Taurus; air, through Gemini, and now water, through Cancer). Unless you have absolutely refused to look outside yourself during your life, you now have an internal means to identify with all the others you meet. The emotional impact of the sign Cancer gives you a unique ability to empathize with others while developing your own capacity for responsiveness to the events now occurring in your life.

NATAL MOON IN ARIES

Moon keywords: emotions, responses to life, habit patterns

Natal Aries Moon Progressed to Aries: Every twenty-eight years the progressed Moon conjuncts its natal position. When your progressed Moon is in the same sign as your natal Moon, you again face the problems and joys inherent in your natal position. When your progressed Moon returns to Aries, you need to deal with your high level of emotional energy, your tendency to initiate emotional contacts, your desire to do something about any emotional discomfort, and your fabled emotional explosiveness. Your emotions can flare and die down as quickly as firecrackers at Chinese New Year. You need to make sure that other people are not igniting your firecrackers just to watch you jump. While your Moon progressed through earth and water signs, you had the chance to discover the advantages of absorbing the emotional impact of an event before you responded to it. Now you need to decide just how patient you want to be with emotional responses.

Natal Aries Moon Progressed to Taurus: The Moon is exalted in Taurus; thus this position of the progressed Moon is very strong. There is a yin-yang imbalance when your natal Moon is in Aries and your progressed Moon is in Taurus. You may try to act and respond at the same time. So you're busy doing something about whatever triggered your emotions before you completely understand what is actually going on. You know you should wait, but your natal Aries position makes waiting difficult. Sometimes the Taurus position increases your nurturing tendencies but does not change your yang projection of emotion. You are likely to take in stray animals and/or people while your progressed Moon is in Taurus. The combination of impulsiveness and protectiveness makes you particularly vulnerable to sob stories.

Natal Aries Moon Progressed to Gemini: Both Aries and Gemini are yang. You are comfortable with the combination of action-orientation and intellectual analysis of emotion. You may find it difficult to settle down with this combination as the Gemini influence scatters you emotionally. However, the sextile relationship of the two signs actually works very favorably. While there may be many different situations which demand response or involvement, you feel confident of your ability to cope with each situation. Further, you gain an ability to detach from situations so that you can analyze what is really going on. This detachment can allow you to see how others push your emotional buttons. Then you can decide whether or not you want to respond with your natal Aries habit of exploding, or whether you want to abandon some of your old responses. Any difficult transits or progressions will be easier to handle while your progressed Moon is in Gemini.

Natal Aries Moon Progressed to Cancer: Your progressed Moon, ruler of Cancer, is extremely powerful in this sign. This is also the square position to your natal Moon, part of your seven year emotional growth cycle. (See Chapter 1, "You Can't Blame Your Mother," page 13, for further discussion of this cycle.) This position highlights the inherent difficulties of the cardinal Moon, the conflict between action and reaction, because the yin-yang difference between the natal and progressed position increases the conflict. Your emotions are very intense during the Cancer progression. You alternate between explosive action and heightened emotional sensitivity. You may accuse yourself of lack of feeling, becoming quite maudlin about your supposed lack of compassion.

Of all the sign positions, this square will be the most difficult for you, because the intensity of emotion indicated by the sign Cancer may overwhelm your natal position. Your initial separation from Mom, at about age seven, is likely to be turbulent, and the second waxing square, which occurs around age thirty-five, will involve you in an examination of how you meet your needs for nurture. When your natal Moon is in Aries, you are more likely to think of nurture in terms of giving rather than in terms of receiving. While your progressed Moon is in Cancer you may have to accept the idea that you, too, have a need to be nurtured. This means accepting your own vulnerability and not using your natal Aries to compensate for or deny weakness. When you are sixty-three the cycle repeats again. This time you must deal with the vulnerability of your emotional response from the perspective of your own mortality. If you can integrate the needing, sensitive, Cancer parts with your outgoing Aries natal nature, the last waxing square needn't be difficult.

Natal Aries Moon Progressed to Leo: Whenever your progressed Moon is in the same element as your natal Moon, response flows easily. Here the yang nature of both natal and progressed positions encourages you to initiate responses, while the fixity of the progressed sign steadies your emotions. You may be more argumentative and more determined to retain habits while your progressed Moon is in Leo.

You will get through difficult life situations with a minimum of emotional upheaval while your progressed Moon is in Leo, for the trine to your natal sign confers a stability of response. This position does not indicate events, but softens any difficult symbolism from other positions. This is the time for you to rest and recuperate from the emotional upheavals of the two and a half years that your progressed Moon was in Cancer.

Natal Aries Moon Progressed to Virgo: This position is basically incompatible with your natal Aries Moon. The yin-yang problem increases during this two and a half years as you may get lost in little problems, responding to them in a yin receptive manner, while your natal position is itching to get on with bigger things. You may feel that others are picking away at you, draining off your energy a little at a time until you have none left for yourself. At this point your natal Aries Moon comes through with unsettling force, sweeping away petty annoyances.

The tension of this waxing inconjunct involves you in the issue of emotional bondage to others, and in the experience of serving or being subservient to the needs of others. Your natal Aries Moon is not particularly comfortable with basing responses on the needs of others, for this involves fully understanding emotional inputs before doing anything about them. Furthermore, you don't like to pay attention to the ways that you actually do serve others, for you prefer to think of yourself as emotionally independent.

Natal Aries Moon Progressed to Libra: This is the fourteen year half-cycle of your progressed Moon. The position is yang like your natal Aries. Overreaction may be a difficulty. The opposition sign brings out all the problems of cardinality in your Moon. Your response patterns fluctuate, and you alternate between concern for yourself (Aries) and concern for others (Libra). You have a desire for peace, but your Aries natal position indicates that you really prefer peace on your own terms. You may attempt to distance yourself from disagreeable situations rather than fight about them while your progressed Moon is in Libra.

The waxing square (when your progressed Moon is in Cancer) is actually a much more difficult part of the progressed Moon cycle for your Aries Moon than the opposition, for the natal and progressed Moon do not differ in strength during the opposition. The problems of the opposition are likely to be obvious only during the actual time of the opposition, rather than for the entire two and a half years that the progressed Moon is in Libra.

Natal Aries Moon Progressed to Scorpio: The Moon is in its fall in Scorpio, and this sign is basically incompatible with your Aries natal position. The yin nature of your progressed Moon makes you responsive, and the Scorpio influence suggests that you are more likely to hold onto your response patterns (or your grievances) during this two and a half year period. You will try to be quiet and receptive, particularly in relationships, but your natal Aries eventually explodes under the stress of trying to be a deep, retentive Scorpio. Then you are likely to utilize the combination to sweep away old habits and attempt a new start.

The waning inconjunct often involves sexual tension. The first cycle, occurring when you are about fifteen, is an expected part of maturing, but the second cycle may catch you by surprise when you are approximately forty-three. Then you need to reevaluate your view of your sexuality and the roles you've assumed or rejected because of your sex. Since the waning inconjunct comes from the sign Scorpio, you may never get the underlying tension out into the open. You need to ask yourself whether your emotional tension is really due to the partner you have or due to the role you've accepted.

Natal Aries Moon Progressed to Sagittarius: Whenever your progressed Moon is in the same element as your natal Moon, response flows easily. You are most comfortable with your natal and progressed combination. Initiating action again appears to be the proper course for you. You are more flexible in your response patterns. If you did get rid of some old habit patterns while your progressed Moon was in Scorpio, the Sagittarius position, willing to take a chance on new things, allows you to develop new patterns which are consistent with your Aries natal position.

When your natal Moon is in Aries, the drawbacks of the Sagittarius position (a tendency to hop from one emotional response to another, exaggeration, a tendency to trivialize or ignore major events, a tendency to separate from feelings) are not difficulties at all. You want a little distance, for you are very intense by nature. You will use the advantages of the Sagittarius Moon (idealization, the ability to take risks with emotional issues, the ability to see the larger picture) to balance your own fire. You will be able to slide through emotional issues with equanimity while your progressed Moon is in Sagittarius.

Natal Aries Moon Progressed to Capricorn: The Moon is in its detriment in Capricorn. This is also another part of your seven year emotional growth cycle. You will have difficulties with the yin-yang conflict between Capricorn and Aries as well as problems associated with cardinality. You may attempt to control all of your emotional responses. You may decide that the unbridled fire nature of your natal Aries is quite unbecoming, and, worse, actually interferes with your ambitions. You are trying to resolve the conflicts of cardinality while incorporating both yin and yang in your response patterns. Because the Moon is in its detriment, you're likely to see all that's wrong with your response nature and ignore all that's good and useful about your Aries energy.

You are particularly vulnerable to criticism from people whom you consider authorities during this time. The Capricorn progressed position indicates that you listen to the criticism, while your natal Aries position insures that you immediately jump to the conclusion that your responses are inappropriate and somehow "wrong." Before you dig yourself into a pit of emotional unhappiness, consider how well (or poorly) the person giving the advice handles emotion. Your Aries Moon isn't inherently better or worse than any other Moon position, but it *is* yours. You can choose to express it positively.

Natal Aries Moon Progressed to Aquarius: Yang air is compatible with yang fire, and this combination is easier for you than the Capricorn progression was. You may try to intellectualize emotional responses. You have a tendency to break off relationships which do not reflect the yang nature of your progressed and natal Moon. You may be more stubborn about your feelings during this progression.

Nonetheless, this is an excellent progressed position for you. You need to separate a little from your feelings, which the air sign encourages. After all the self-doubt of the Capricorn years, you need some stubbornness, some ability to stake out your ground, to say to yourself and others that your feelings are yours and are okay. The intellectualization allows you to sort out your dependent and your independent sides, and lets you release some of the fear that you are "wrong" in certain responses. Aquarius provides a good balance for your emotions, allowing you to cope with events during this period with little internal turmoil.

Natal Aries Moon Progressed to Pisces: The sign behind the natal position is always difficult, for it brings out hidden or weak areas in your response patterns. There is always a yin-yang conflict which suggests the necessity for integrating both sides of your emotional nature. Pisces brings out the variability in your emotional responses. You feel pulled in different directions, responding when you want to act, acting when response would be more appropriate. This is the classic position of second-guessing. Whichever way you respond, you think later of a better way that you might have handled the situation. You feel that you should be more sympathetic to the needs of others, yet when confronted with those needs, you attempt to change them. When action is impossible you feel quite frustrated, for all the energy you spend in being sympathetic may not produce immediate results and your natal Aries can't stand stagnation.

The other point of weakness underscored by your progressed Pisces Moon is your natal Aries dislike for openly expressed emotion. Now that may sound like a contradiction, for aren't you known for your temper outbursts? Those outbursts express Mars all right, but they don't express the Moon very well. What you are uncomfortable with is public crying. If something nasty happens, you want to do something about it, you don't want to sit and cry over it. While your progressed Moon is in Pisces, you may be in a position of either having to cope with someone else who cries or having to cope with your own tears. Either way, you have to recognize your aversion to showing vulnerability.

NATAL MERCURY IN ARIES

Mercury keywords: the conscious mind, thought and speech patterns, manual dexterity

Natal Aries Mercury Progressed to Taurus: Since Mercury does not gain or loose strength immediately through this progression (Mercury is not exalted or debilitated in either sign), you may not really notice the progression until Mercury has been in Taurus for quite a few years. Unless your progressed Mercury is angular or heavily aspected as it changes sign, it won't be until it gets past the first ten degrees that you see any Taurean traits in your conscious thought patterns and/or communications.

As your Mercury progresses into the second (Virgo) decanate of Taurus, you will find that you have somehow incorporated a more practical ability to organize your thoughts and your speech patterns. Other people may actually notice this before you do, for others will find it easier to communicate with you. You'll tend to think ahead more easily, considering the outcome in advance of a train of thought (or action). Even better, you may think about what you are going to say before you say it. This will help ease your natal penchant for sticking your foot in your mouth.

Natal Aries Mercury Progressed to Gemini: When Mercury progresses to Gemini, a sign that Mercury rules, you'll notice this position quite quickly. In a positive growth pattern this is a wonderful transition, for you can become more verbal, expressing the anxieties and excitements of your daily life more easily. If you have not chosen to develop the positive sides of your personality, the Gemini progression still increases verbal abilities, but you may utilize this to express the aggressive tendencies of your natal Aries position. In this case, you may argue louder and longer without regard for the other person's point of view.

Natal Aries Mercury Progressed to Cancer: After progressing through Gemini, Mercury may move into Cancer. (Mercury moves a maximum of 80-90° by age sixty-five. If Mercury is in the first half of Aries natally, or is moving slowly due to a retrograde position just before your birth or at any time during your life, it will not progress to this sign.) Because Mercury is so strong in Gemini, you will have incorporated many Gemini traits into your personality, and the transition to Cancer may be nearly impossible to detect. Intimate friends may notice that you now express emotion or feelings more easily. They may also notice an increase in your sensitivity (or perhaps an increase in your ability to nag!). Cancer will underscore your natal cardinality, helping you to focus your thoughts.

Natal Aries Mercury Retrograde by Progression to Pisces: You won't notice an outward change as Mercury moves from an essentially neutral sign (Aries) to the sign of its detriment (Pisces) because your natal Mercury is stronger. If, however, your natal Sun is in Pisces, you may embrace the Piscean quality of thought as this is in harmony with your Sun's position. Your natal Aries position is forthright, hasty, and aggressive, while the progressed position symbolizes a somewhat fluctuating empathy with others. If your natal Sun is in Aries, the Pisces progression of Mercury increases your self-doubt without altering your outward expression of thought. Put simply, you'll have more second thoughts about whatever you said or did.

NATAL VENUS IN ARIES

Venus in detriment in Aries
Venus keywords: loving, being loved, pleasure, self-indulgence

Natal Aries Venus Progressed to Taurus: When your Venus progresses to Taurus, a sign Venus rules, the fire of your natal Aries position can ignite a steady flame of love. The progression of Venus through Taurus symbolizes stabilization of your love relationships and stabilization of your feelings towards possessions. You will become more aware of the things that bring you pleasure and physical comfort. A positive combination of natal Venus in Aries and progressed Venus in Taurus can yield an impulsive, warm, affectionate manner in love. If you do not choose to develop the higher side of these positions, you may combine the possessiveness of Taurus with the headstrong aspect of Aries and get compulsiveness in love situations. In this case, you may scare away potential partners by your instant, permanent attachment. This kind of loving may work in romance stories, but isn't quite so viable in daily life. When you are thwarted in romantic situations you may turn to the refrigerator, for Venus in Taurus loves food.

You will retain the Taurean expression of Venus (sensual, possessive, nurturing, pleasure-oriented) for the rest of your life because your Venus will not progress to any sign which allows its expression more easily than its rulership. Whether you choose to develop the self-indulgent, acquisitive, materialistic side or the caring, loyal, compassionate side of this Venus, you will recognize the Taurus influence.

Natal Aries Venus Progressed to Gemini: When Venus progresses from Taurus to Gemini, the strength of the Taurus progression will still dominate. You may become slightly more flexible in attitude towards the things and people you love during this progression. The Gemini progression may prompt you to talk a little more freely about love situations and you might flirt a little more easily, but you probably won't be any more likely to change relationships than you were while progressed Venus was in Taurus. If your love relationships are difficult, you can get into the "ain't it awful" game in which you complain about all the problems your loved ones cause. You really don't want to change your situation if change will mean a loss of social status, possessions, or money (here's the Taurus influence).

Natal Aries Venus Progressed to Cancer: The years that your progressed Venus was in Taurus are still the dominant symbolism, even after your Venus progresses to Cancer. Thus, this position is more likely to reinforce Taurean traits than natal Aries characteristics. The yin nature of Cancer fits rather nicely with Taurus, and you can develop your responsiveness in love situations. You may become very possessive of both things and people during the years that your progressed Venus is in Cancer.

Venus progresses at most 70° to 80° in sixty-five years, so if your natal Venus is at 29° Aries and moving quickly, you will be in your fifties before Venus progresses to Cancer. You will be able to release the Gemini tendency to worry about love situations, never really a major part of your expression unless you have Gemini strong in your natal chart. That's about all you will let go of after your Venus progresses to Cancer, for the influence of water indicates you'll want to retain everything, or at least keep anything of possible sentimental value. Changes in love relationships will be very difficult to bear after Venus enters Cancer. You need to remember that love grows best when unconfined, for you're afraid of losing affection.

Natal Aries Venus Retrograde by Progression to Pisces: Venus is exalted in Pisces, where the softer, more romantic side of you comes to light. Pisces is the most idealistic position for Venus. You'll dream of knights in shining armor and maidens in distress. When Venus makes its station, turning direct, you will incorporate art, music, and appreciation of the beautiful into your life. Since the Pisces position is much stronger than your natal Aries, you are more likely to project and protect the Pisces quality of your love nature throughout your life.

The only drawback of the Pisces/Aries combination is your determination to put loved ones on a pedestal. If you absolutely refuse to allow your loved ones to be human and fallible, you may have many disappointments in love. Contrary to popular myth, it is very difficult to be the one adored. Your idealistic love may smother (and terrify) the very people you want to have in your life.

NATAL MARS IN ARIES

Mars is in rulership in Aries
Mars keywords: energy, initiative, aggression, anger

Natal Aries Mars Progressed to Taurus: As ruler of Aries, Mars is extremely powerful in this natal position. It is doubtful whether any progression will significantly alter your natal expression of energy, except when progressed Mars is angular or heavily aspected. The transition to Taurus might add a bit of stability when it comes to finishing things that you've started, or you may simply become a bit more stubborn about doing everything your way. A more difficult combination of Aries natal and Taurus progressed Mars energy is refusing to let go of past angers. Unless you are determined to live on the edge of rage all the time, you needn't fall into this particular difficulty. If this is actually happening, you are somehow thwarting your natal expression, either because you don't dare tell the person who angers you about your anger, or because you don't want to let yourself know what you are angry about. Use your natal Mars through active physical expression (play squash or run or take karate) in order to get back to a clear understanding of your own aggressive drives.

Natal Aries Mars Progressed to Gemini: When your Mars progresses to Gemini, the yang nature of the progressed sign may heighten your natal Aries initiative. At best, the mutable air sign will increase your ability to express your aggressive instincts; at worst, it will scatter your energy slightly so that you have more unfinished projects than ever before.

Interestingly, the most noticeable part of the progression to Gemini is the absence of Taurus. You let go of Taurus almost immediately after your Mars enters Gemini. Thus this progression appears to return you to your natal inclinations. Part of this is due to an increased ability to talk about your aggressive energy. The basic compatibility of Aries and Gemini accounts for the rest of the nearly invisible influence of Gemini on your progressed Mars.

Natal Aries Mars Retrograde by Progression to Pisces: Your expression of energy is stronger and clearer in your natal Aries position than it is in the Pisces progression. If you haven't developed any honesty in your life, you'll find it easier to rationalize your aggressive actions while Mars is in Pisces. You may misdirect your energy, shouting at the dog when you're really irritated with your boss. Your natal position indicates that you are usually very clear about who and what caused irritation. Thus the Pisces progression won't affect you much unless you really need to hide the causes of your aggression from yourself.

NATAL JUPITER IN ARIES

Jupiter keywords: expansion, growth, faith, optimism

Natal Aries Jupiter Progressed to Taurus: Jupiter progresses a maximum of 15° in sixty-five years. Unless your natal Jupiter is in the last half of Aries and in quick direct motion, it will not progress into Taurus during your life. When Jupiter progresses into Taurus, you can channel some of your enthusiasm into specific activities. You will still have difficulty saying "no" to any project that seems exciting. If you notice the Taurus influence at all, it will simply seem to temper your desire to take risks while expanding your horizons. Most of you will consider this a normal part of maturing rather than a specific change which could be attached to the position of progressed Jupiter.

Natal Aries Jupiter Retrograde by Progression to Pisces: When Jupiter is retrograde, it moves only about 6° in sixty-five years. Thus, unless your natal Jupiter is between 0° and 5° Aries and retrograde, it won't retrograde by progression into Pisces. Jupiter is stronger in Pisces (its traditional rulership) than it is in Aries. The energy gained during this progression usually tends towards service to others, increased empathy and an ability to expand with grace and humility. If you have not chosen to develop your life in a positive fashion, the progression may symbolize a growing ability to dissemble. In this case, you'll be able to charm everyone, becoming a pretty good con artist in the process.

NATAL SATURN IN ARIES

Saturn in fall in Aries
Saturn keywords: duty, responsibility, reality, restraint

Natal Aries Saturn Progressed to Taurus: Saturn progresses a maximum of 8° in sixty-five years. Unless your natal Saturn is between 24° and 30° Aries and in quick direct motion, it will not progress to Taurus during your life. When Saturn progresses into Taurus, you may become rather hidebound about your ideas of duty and responsibility. The Taurean fixity intensifies the natal dilemma about duty restricting action. It is, however, easier to accommodate to present conditions in your life after Saturn progresses into Taurus because you are not as likely to be frustrated by conflicting impulses toward action and restraint.

Natal Aries Saturn Retrograde by Progression to Pisces: Saturn only moves about 3° in sixty-five years by progression when it is retrograde. Thus, unless your natal Saturn is in the first three degrees of Aries and retrograde, it will not retrograde to Pisces during your life. When Saturn retrogrades into Pisces, you may make service to others a duty. Although you are more likely to recognize social responsibilities when your progressed Saturn is in Pisces, you may offer your sympathy so grudgingly that others hate to accept it. The year that Saturn crosses into Pisces will be an extremely important year for you. During this time you will reap whatever you've sown while Saturn was in Aries. You are often publicly recognized, for good or ill, when Saturn crosses into Pisces.

NATAL URANUS IN ARIES

Uranus keywords: self-will, change, creativity, inventiveness

Natal Aries Uranus Progressed to Taurus: If you were born during March, April, May, or early June in 1934 you may have Uranus progress from Aries to Taurus during your lifetime. Uranus in Aries symbolizes the resourceful reformer who may have an explosive temper. When the progression adds the Taurus energy, you either add practical considerations to the changes you initiate or you become unyielding about your methods for change.

NATAL NEPTUNE IN ARIES

This position will not occur during this century.

NATAL PLUTO IN ARIES

This position will not occur during this century.

PROGRESSIONS FOR TAURUS NATAL POSITIONS

TAURUS: YIN—FIXED—EARTH

NATAL SUN IN TAURUS

Sun keywords: basic life force, the physical body, internal "I"

Natal Taurus Sun Progressed to Gemini: The progressed Sun enters Gemini between age one week (natal ☉29° ♉ 59′) and age thirty (natal ☉0° ♉ 00′). Some of the stubbornness associated with the sign Taurus will be eased as your Sun progresses into Gemini. You will become aware of different ways to approach both things and people and you'll be more likely to consider altering your behavior. There is a yin-yang conflict between your progressed and natal positions which can produce internal tension, particularly if you have not integrated both male and female sides of your personality. Your progressed yang Sun symbolizes a growing need to initiate action, while your natal Taurus position symbolizes your desire to respond rather than act.

As your Sun progresses through Gemini, you will have many opportunities to release some of the rigidity of your natal Sun sign. You may choose to complain about external events rather than actually let go of your preconceived notions about how they should happen. If you decide to follow this particular path, others may see the Gemini influence as an increased ability to notice what's wrong without any increased desire to do something about the things that bother you. You can, however, choose to think about the things that need change, and then actually go about changing them. If you decide to follow this path, you are combining the flexibility of the Gemini with the forethought of the Taurus in what can be a wonderfully practical, effective blend.

Natal Taurus Sun Progressed to Cancer: The progressed Sun enters Cancer between age thirty (natal ☉29° ♉ 59′) and age sixty (natal ☉0° ♉ 00′). When your Sun progresses into Cancer, the polarity conflict is eliminated, for Cancer reinforces the yin nature of your natal Taurus Sun. Cancer adds sensitivity and emotion to your already nurturing natal Taurus position. If you have not chosen to develop the positive sides of your personality, the Cancer progression can be quite self-pitying.

Both Taurus and Cancer are known for keeping things: If you are not careful, you may fill your house from cellar to roof with old and ancient possessions that you can't bear to throw away. You may try collecting people rather than things. If anything, this can be more difficult, for people really don't like to be owned. The fewer strings you attach to the people you care about, the more likely they are to stay near you.

Natal Taurus Sun Progressed to Leo. The progressed Sun enters Leo between age sixty (natal ☉29° ♉ 59′) and age ninety (natal ☉0° ♉ 00′). Leo is the strongest position for the Sun. Your self-expression increases dramatically when the Sun progresses to the sign it rules. Qualities of leadership, generosity, and self-assurance surface quickly once your Sun has progressed to Leo. If you have developed the best attributes of your natal Taurus Sun, you can now add a wonderful warmth and excitement to your own self-image as well as your projection of yourself to others. If you have not developed any spiritual insight into how or why you are who you are, the Leo qualities which predominate will be pride, arrogance, and a desire to show off or dominate others.

NATAL MOON IN TAURUS

Moon in exaltation in Taurus
Moon keywords: emotions, responses to life, habit patterns

Natal Taurus Moon Progressed to Taurus: The Moon is exalted in Taurus; thus, your natal position will show throughout the Moon's progressions. Every twenty-eight years your Moon returns to its natal position. The conjunction amplifies both the problems and strengths of your natal sign position. The joys of this position are sensuality, practicality and an appreciation of beauty. You may need to address your extremely nurturing emotional response pattern, which while helpful, may at times be obsessive, tenacious, and jealous. You really can't take in every stray kitten, puppy, and person, you can't mother everyone you meet, nor should you follow loved ones around to "protect" them. If you feel this much concern about your loved ones, you need to look at your own insecurities, for what you are displaying is not protectiveness or love but jealousy.

Natal Taurus Moon Progressed to Gemini: When your progressed Moon is in Gemini, you have a yin-yang conflict. Your emotional patterns become scattered whenever you try to initiate activity on an emotional level, or whenever you try to think about your feelings. Since your natal Taurus position is so much stronger, you'll probably abandon Gemini intellectualization rather quickly as counterproductive, although you may feel a twinge of guilt about your refusal to analyze your feelings. If you find yourself in a state of near-panic whenever you must question your response nature, your rigidity indicates some sort of internal dishonesty about your emotional ties. You probably need to take some time to explore some of these painful areas.

Natal Taurus Moon Progressed to Cancer: Since the Moon rules Cancer, this is the most powerful position of the progressed Moon. Fortunately, the energy of Cancer blends well with your natal Taurus Moon. You feel comfortable with your sympathetic, nurturing responses. During this two year period, you may glory in an "earth mother" projection; if you are male, the male version of this is "savior of all in distress." You'll be willing to rescue the unfortunate and give help to the needy, especially if those needy are within your own family.

Although you'll sail through any emotional upheavals easily while your progressed Moon is in the sign sextile its natal position, the people around you may not find this combination as easy to deal with. You may be very possessive and rather smothering. All of those jokes about the ethnic mother (Jewish, Italian, Irish, etc.) could apply to you during this progression.

Natal Taurus Moon Progressed to Leo: This is a quarter cycle of the emotional growth cycle symbolized by the progressed Moon. (See Chapter 1, "You Can't Blame Your Mother," page 13, for further discussion of this cycle.) The Leo position amplifies problems of fixity in your emotional nature. Leo is yang polarity but since your natal position is so powerful, you won't develop a yang projection easily. For you, the major issues won't center around yin-yang response, but around your tendency to hang onto emotional issues long after you should have let them rest. You can forgive a hurt with extraordinary effort, but it is almost impossible for you to forget one. You form habit patterns quickly, patterns that you don't even notice until they are practically cast in concrete. You may have to get out a jackhammer when your progressed Moon actually squares its natal position.

Natal Taurus Moon Progressed to Virgo: Whenever your progressed Moon is in the same triplicity as your natal Moon, your response patterns flow more easily. If you managed to break up some of your emotional log jams when your progressed Moon squared your natal Moon, you can now use the mutable earth energy to explore some different response patterns.

The tendency of the Virgo Moon to separate from emotional involvement balances your natal Taurus inclination to be so involved in feelings that you can't see the issues themselves. You have such an intensity of response that some scattering helps put things into perspective. Furthermore, you can be wonderfully practical about how you feel while your progressed Moon is in another earth sign. All other progressions and transits will be eased while your progressed Moon is in Virgo, for you'll handle the events of this two and a half year period with emotional stability.

Natal Taurus Moon Progressed to Libra: This position is basically incompatible with your natal Taurus response patterns. The yin-yang difficulty between natal and progressed signs indicates that you may try to initiate and respond at the same time. You have an immediate desire for peace and harmony, but you are not comfortable making cardinal yang overtures (actually initiating contact) in the interest of that peace and harmony. The inherent strength of your natal Taurus position means that although the Libran energy may show in day-to-day activities (you'll pay lip service to thinking about why other people respond the way they do; you'll consider the possibility of thinking about why you respond the way you do), your deeper emotional response will follow your inner Taurean bent, and you're likely to refuse to analyze your deeper emotional make-up.

Natal Taurus Moon Progressed to Scorpio: The Moon is in its fall in Scorpio, and this position is the halfway point of the emotional growth cycle symbolized by your progressed Moon. Thus, for you, the Scorpio position emphasizes both problems of polarity and fixity. Jealousy, a sign of insecurity in a yin response pattern, may become an obvious issue for you while your progressed Moon is in Scorpio. You may have difficulty with overemotionalism and with habitual response patterns. The dynamic of the opposition represents a desire to change and grow. When the energy of Scorpio activates the more powerful natal Taurus, you may try to completely overhaul your emotional life. Scorpio represents energy for complete and permanent change, but doesn't really provide any notion of how to go about doing this. Because both natal and progressed Moon are in fixed signs, you'll have difficulty letting go of habits, in spite of your real desire to change. If you can tie into one of your other planets, such as the Sun or Mercury, through aspects from your progressed Moon, you can get through this particular part of the problem (the how). Then you can actually alter of habit patterns which block your ability to grow.

Natal Taurus Moon Progressed to Sagittarius: This sign is basically incompatible with your natal Taurus energy. The yin-yang difference suggests that you may be tired of responding to the projections of others. However, the strength of your natal Taurus position resists the dilution and scattering of responses characteristic of a Sagittarius Moon. Unless your progressed Moon is making some fairly strong aspects while it is in Sagittarius, you'll only notice this position as slightly uncomfortable.

The discomfort of the waning inconjunct relates directly to your emotional understanding of your sexuality. If you've absorbed the "role" definitions of sexuality given in our society, you may experience more than slight discomfort while your progressed Moon is in Sagittarius. In this case, you'll be restless, seeking some other way to express your feelings but not at all sure of what you don't like about your habitual patterns. You may choose to relate to someone who does not fit traditional "role" patterns in order to explore the differences in feelings without risking analysis of your own responses.

Natal Taurus Moon Progressed to Capricorn: The Moon is in its detriment in Capricorn. Thus the energy of this position is easily obliterated by the strength of your natal Taurus projection. Furthermore, Capricorn is in the same triplicity, symbolizing an easy flow of emotional response. The combination of weakness in the progressed sign and ease of action through the combination of two earth signs gives you the ability to pick and choose which attributes of the Capricorn projection you want to use. Do you want to control your emotions more closely? You'll be able to develop this ability. Do you want to distance a little bit from the involvements you have? Capricorn is wonderful at distance. Do you want to manipulate the rest of the world through you expression of emotion? Again, Capricorn energy helps show you how. The major drawback of this combination is not obvious to you, but rather to the people around you. You'll march right through any and all problems during this two and a half years with almost complete emotional stability. However, the people around you may start to complain that you are actually controlling them through your expression of emotion. It may be very difficult for you to pay much attention to these other people, for you are being completely practical and, besides, your responses seem to work very well for you. As long as you remember that what works for you only works for you, and you refrain from imposing your response nature on others, you should have no problems with this progressed position.

Natal Taurus Moon Progressed to Aquarius: This is the third quarter of your emotional growth cycle. You'll again experience problems with fixity, as well as friction from the yin-yang difference between your natal and your progressed position. You may feel that you should at least try to intellectualize emotional responses, although you may be quite unwilling to change habit patterns. If there are no other difficult aspects by progression or transit during this two and a half year period, you may be able to avoid thinking about why you feel the way you do. Any difficult aspects that occur now will trigger your need to examine your response nature. Then the events you could have ignored just last year, when your progressed Moon was in Capricorn, turn into the first cracks in the dam of fixity which your natal Taurus Moon doesn't want to think about. If little things are really getting you down emotionally, consider the possibility of talking about your old emotional issues with a therapist or a friend. By airing your feelings you have a chance to decide what to do about them.

Since your natal position is stronger, any Aquarius desire to initiate activity in emotional areas will be muted. You may want to appear outgoing, but you have little desire to be outgoing.

Natal Taurus Moon Progressed to Pisces: This position is quite compatible with your natal Taurus Moon. The energy of the progressed Moon in Pisces softens some of the stubbornness of your natal position. More importantly, this sign allows you to work easily with emotional issues, perhaps resolving some of the conflicts symbolized by the Aquarius progression. If you did start to examine some of your emotional "sacred cows" while your progressed Moon was in Aquarius, it will be much easier to get rid of them now. If you struggled along without examining past habit patterns, you'll be able to put the whole mess back on the shelf and shut the closet door after your Moon progresses into Pisces. None of the little things that bothered you while your Moon was in Aquarius will seem too important now. You'll either deal with events in a practical, straightforward manner, or wait. They'll go away eventually, whichever path you choose.

Natal Taurus Moon Progressed to Aries: The sign behind the natal position is always difficult, for it brings out hidden or weak areas in your response patterns. You have difficulty initiating change in emotional response patterns. You may feel quite ineffective when you respond in your natal Taurean manner. Nonetheless, the Aries position alone is not strong enough to cause more than irritation with your Taurean habits. If the progressed Moon is angular or making strong aspects to natal or progressed positions, the irritation will become acute. At that time, you can choose to do something (Aries energy) about the things that bother you. This choice will surprise you, for you are not accustomed to changing your habits, and it will astonish the people who think they know you.

NATAL MERCURY IN TAURUS

Mercury keywords: conscious mind, thought, actions, manual dexterity

Natal Taurus Mercury Progressed to Gemini: When your Mercury progresses into Gemini, a sign which it rules, Mercury gains considerable strength. You will easily incorporate the verbal abilities of Gemini into your life-style. Although you aren't likely to change from taciturn to verbose the moment Mercury progresses into Gemini, you will become more adept at expressing your thoughts. Unless your natal position is strong through house or aspect, the Gemini style of conscious thought will become more and more obvious during the years of this progression. You will at least entertain ideas of change, although your natal fixity may interfere with your ultimate ability to make such changes.

Natal Taurus Mercury Progressed to Cancer: When your Mercury progresses from Gemini to Cancer, you probably won't see any change at all, for the strength of the Gemini progression will dominate your conscious expression. Since Cancer is quite compatible with your natal Taurus position, this progression may seem to facilitate a better combination of Taurus and Gemini rather than bring out any new (Cancer) traits. If Mercury is angular or heavily aspected while in Cancer, you will add the one hallmark of Mercury in Cancer—more worry about emotional issues.

Natal Taurus Mercury Progressed to Leo: Mercury is in its fall in Leo, so this progression has even less effect on your conscious thought patterns than the Cancer progression did. Furthermore, Mercury only moves 80 to 90° in sixty-five years, so even if your natal Mercury is at 29° Taurus and in direct motion, you'll be nearly sixty before it can possibly get to Leo. (If Mercury is the first half of Taurus natally or moving slowly due to a retrograde position just before your birth or at any time during your life, it will not progress to Leo at all.) You may fall back into some fixity as it can reinforce that part of your natal Taurus Mercury. While Mercury is angular or heavily aspected you may notice some Leo pride and dash in the way you talk about the people and events of your life.

Natal Taurus Mercury Retrograde by Progression to Aries: Your solid, fixed thought patterns, symbolic of Mercury in Taurus, can combine with the action-orientation of Mercury in Aries to yield more aggressive verbal tactics and a greater willingness to initiate activity. You may actually start an argument, particularly if you believe that you are right. Your Taurus energy will continue to insure that you finish any argument. You are not likely to accept another's opinion after Mercury enters Aries, for this cardinal sign accepts change only when it's your own idea.

NATAL VENUS IN TAURUS

Venus in rulership in Taurus
Venus keywords: loving, being loved, pleasure, self-indulgence

Natal Taurus Venus Progressed to Gemini: Since Venus rules Taurus, your natal position will always dominate your ability to give and receive love. When your Venus progresses to Gemini, the only change may be a better ability to express your love nature. During the time that your progressed Venus in Gemini is angular or heavily aspected, you may be a bit more flirtatious or changeable in love. Love situations will seem to require more flexibility of response. After the aspects pass, you will settle back into your much more comfortable Taurus expression of love.

Natal Taurus Venus Progressed to Cancer: The Cancer progression reinforces your natal yin love expression. Thus, if you notice any change during this progression, it will seem to be towards an even more nurturing and possessive projection of love, for Cancer adds only a bit of emotionalism and an increased tendency to cling to love situaitons. (Taurus, a fixed sign, hangs on from stubbornness, while Cancer hangs on from fear of emotional loss.)

Natal Taurus Venus Progressed to Leo: Venus progresses about 1°10′ per year when direct. Thus, if your natal Venus is at 29° Taurus and in direct motion, you will be at least fifty-two years old before your Venus enters Leo. If your progressed Venus is heavily aspected or angular when it progresses to Leo, you may discover a desire to show off your beautiful things. Alternately, you may want loved ones to shower you with praise and glory (or at least presents!). You won't notice the Leo influence very much when it isn't aspected for your natal position is still much stronger.

Natal Taurus Venus Retrograde by Progession to Aries: Your Venus is progressing from a sign that it rules to a sign of its detriment. If your natal Venus is heavily afflicted, you may use the time of the Aries progression to work out your squares and oppositions, for the retrograde motion indicates your Venus energy is functioning on an internal level. If Venus becomes angular or makes strong aspects while it is in Aries, you may work even harder to understand how you give and receive love, using the initiatory impulse of Aries to clarify your understanding of your responses. On the other hand, you may find that love situations either demand more active interaction from you or involve fire sign people.

NATAL MARS IN TAURUS

Mars in detriment in Taurus
Mars keywords: energy, initiative, aggression, anger

Natal Taurus Mars Progressed to Gemini: After your Mars progresses into Gemini, you can develop an ability to vent your irritation verbally. Once you discover that you can talk about the things that make you angry, you'll find that fewer things infuriate you. The Gemini influence may also encourage you to do more than one thing at a time. If you've developed an overintensity in your drives (common with a Taurus natal Mars), you'll be able to take on projects without pressuring yourself quite so much. You won't change from total involvement to complete disinterest, but you'll be able to pause occasionally in the midst of a project and do something else, like go out on a date or go fishing.

Natal Taurus Mars Progressed to Cancer: The influence of the progression of Mars to Cancer really depends on whether or not you internalized any of the Gemini experience while Mars was in that sign. If you chose to manifest the Gemini energy through shouting matches, the Cancer position (where Mars is in its fall) may increase the negative use of energy. You may find it even harder to let go of hurts. You may brood and hang onto aggression. On the other hand, if through the Gemini years you learned to talk about what bothers you and to express your energy through many different outlets, the Cancer progression adds emotion to your energy patterns. This may indicate that you'll be able to direct your drives towards resolving emotional issues.

Natal Taurus Mars Retrograde by Progression to Aries: When Mars progresses from Taurus to Aries, even though it is in retrograde motion, you gain tremendous strength because Mars rules Aries. You'll find that you can direct your energies and express them in a far more forthright manner. Because your natal position is Taurus, this combination often results in hard work applied towards specific goals. Until Mars turns direct, the energy is expressed more internally, but all this usually means is that you may not tell people what your are up to until the project is done. Others may not realize how much effort lies behind your accomplishments during this period. After Mars turns direct in Aries, you'll be able to actually enjoy using your keen competitive nature to accomplish whatever tasks are at hand.

NATAL JUPITER IN TAURUS

Jupiter keywords: expansion, growth, faith, optimism

Natal Taurus Jupiter Progressed to Gemini: Since Jupiter only progresses at most 14' per year, it moves about 15° in sixty-five years. Unless your natal Jupiter is in the last half of Taurus and in direct motion, it won't progress to Gemini. When Jupiter progresses into Gemini, sign of its detriment, some of your steadiness may be dissipated. However, since Jupiter is stronger in your natal position, you won't notice this unless Jupiter is angular or heavily aspected. During these times, your progressed Jupiter is activated and you may feel some desire to change your opinions about faith, religion, or philosophy. Other people are likely to confront you with very different life philosophies when this Jupiter is triggered by aspects from other progressed positions or transits.

Natal Taurus Jupiter Retrograde by Progression to Aries: Jupiter only progresses about 6° in sixty-five years when it is retrograde. Thus, unless your natal Jupiter is in the first 6° of Taurus and retrograde at your birth, it won't progress into Aries.

Jupiter is slightly stronger in the last ten degrees of Aries (the Sagittarius decanate) than it is in Taurus. While it is in retrograde motion, you will internalize the expansion or visionary influence of Jupiter. In other words, only you will know that you've started to dream bigger dreams and plan for wider horizons. Your increased ability to project a bigger future for yourself can result in higher achievement if you can bring yourself to try to implement some of these schemes. Instead of saying "If only," ask "Why not?"

NATAL SATURN IN TAURUS

Saturn keywords: duty, responsibility, reality, restraint

Natal Taurus Saturn Progressed to Gemini: Since Saturn only progresses about 7' per year (a maximum of 8° in sixty-five years), your Saturn will not progress into Gemini unless its natal position is between 22° and 30° Taurus, the Capricorn decanate. Thus your natal position is stronger than the progressed position. Unless Saturn is angular or heavily aspected in Gemini, you won't notice any change at all. While it is aspected in Gemini, you may adopt some semblance of tolerance for other ideas about duty and responsibility. As soon as the aspects end, you'll go right back to your natal projection and your original opinions, which you know in your heart are right.

Natal Taurus Saturn Retrograde by Progression to Aries: Saturn only progresses about 3° in sixty-five years when it is in retrograde motion. Unless your natal Saturn is in the first few degrees of Taurus, it won't retrograde into Aries during your life.

Even though Saturn isn't elevated in Taurus, it's in its fall in Aries. Thus your natal position is stronger. The retrograde motion further inhibits any outward change from this progression. If Saturn is angular or heavily aspected while in Aries, you may have some internal doubts about your own opinions concerning duty and responsibility.

NATAL URANUS IN TAURUS

Uranus in fall in Taurus
Uranus keywords: self-will, change, creativity, inventiveness

Natal Taurus Uranus Progressed to Gemini: If you were born in March, April, or the beginning of May in 1942, you may have Uranus progress from Taurus to Gemini during your life. Uranus is in its fall in Taurus, where it symbolizes a tendency to be innovative in practical matters. After Uranus progresses into Gemini, you may be able to let go of some of your resistance to change. You may be able to use the newly freed energy to generate new ideas or original ways of thinking about the issues in your life.

NATAL NEPTUNE IN TAURUS

This position will not occur during this century.

NATAL PLUTO IN TAURUS

This position will not occur during this century.

PROGRESSIONS FOR GEMINI NATAL POSITIONS

GEMINI: YANG—MUTABLE—AIR

NATAL SUN IN GEMINI

Sun keywords: basic life force, the physical body, internal "I"

Natal Gemini Sun Progressed to Cancer: The progressed Sun enters Cancer between age one week (natal ☉ 29° ♊ 59′) and age thirty (natal ☉ 0° ♊ 00′). After your Sun progresses into Cancer, you add sensitivity and emotion to your basic sense of who you are. The yin nature of your progressed Sun will mute some of the yang eagerness of your natal Gemini position. Now you can develop the ability to listen as well as talk. Your natal curiosity and sociability aren't likely to change, but you'll have a growing ability to sense when you really should stop talking. Sometimes this combination manifests as finding double meanings in whatever another says. If you're doing that, you may want to examine your own motivations in communication, for you may be projecting onto others your double entendres.

Natal Gemini Sun Progressed to Leo: The progressed Sun enters Leo between age thirty (natal ☉ 29° ♊ 59′) and age sixty (natal ☉ 0° ♊ 00′). The Sun rules Leo, and after your Sun progresses into Leo, you'll develop a stronger sense of identity. If you've established any sort of self-esteem, you'll be able to express yourself more readily and much more positively. If you are really stuck in a negative self-image, the Leo progression may bring pride and braggadoccio to the forefront, alienating others. However, you have the ability to change this projection at any time while your progressed Sun is in Leo. Leo enhances rather than overshadows your natal Gemini intellectual approach to life.

Natal Gemini Sun Progressed to Virgo: The progressed Sun enters Virgo between age sixty (natal ☉ 29° ♊ 59′) and age ninety (natal ☉ 0° ♊ 00′). Because the Sun is strongest in Leo, you may not notice the transition to Virgo unless your progressed Sun is angular or heavily aspected. While your progressed Sun is being aspected, you may discover the critical, demanding side of Virgo. This may be helpful if you've been looking at the larger picture so long that you've neglected the details in your life. It isn't helpful when you turn this against yourself and develop a giant guilt about what you should have said or done after the time you could have said or done it.

NATAL MOON IN GEMINI

Moon keywords: emotions, responses to life, habit patterns

Natal Gemini Moon Progressed to Gemini: Every twenty-eight years, your progressed Moon returns to its natal sign as your cycle of emotional growth culminates and starts anew. At this point, you must face and deal with any problems inherent in your natal Moon position. Your Moon in Gemini symbolizes the intellectualization of emotional response patterns. This is more often a problem for others than a problem for you, because you are used to thinking about how you feel. Others have difficulty with this whenever you try to get them to analyze their own feelings. If these others have earth or water Moons, they really don't have the vaguest idea what you mean.

Gemini's yang polarity indicates that you may initiate emotional activity, sometimes to the point of precluding responses. You may scatter emotionally so that you lose effectiveness and have a hard time defining how you feel. On the positive side, you'll get back into the swing of analyzing what's happening in your emotional life when your progressed Moon enters its natal sign. You'll find that you've regained some of your humor about your response patterns.

Natal Gemini Moon Progressed to Cancer: The Moon rules Cancer, thus is quite powerful whenever in the sign Cancer. You will feel the yin-yang polarity conflict quite keenly, for your progressed Moon is nearly as powerful as your natal Moon. You may try to act and react at the same time, which inevitably leads to wide mood swings. You may desperately try to analyze why you are experiencing emotion in this fashion, further widening the gap between your head and your feelings. This is an impulsive, emotional time, and your natal position indicates that you prefer to know what's going on, rather than simply respond to it. Things may happen so quickly during this period that you simply have to allow gut level habit or response to take over now and then. Trust yourself. Even though you may not be able to reason through all your reactions, you probably won't disgrace yourself.

Natal Gemini Moon Progressed to Leo: The return to yang polarity symbolizes an easing of difficulties internally. You can again be comfortable with your natal desire to take the emotional initiative, and you can happily analyze all of your feelings. You may hang onto your emotions a bit longer, but you won't have the problem with unexpected mood swings. This sign position indicates stability. Any difficulties or crises which occur during this period will be easier to cope with, for you have emotional strength while your progressed Moon is in Leo.

Natal Gemini Moon Progressed to Virgo: This sign position is the first quarter of your twenty-eight year emotional growth cycle. (See Chapter 1, "You Can't Blame Your Mother," page 13, for further discussion of this cycle.) You'll be dealing with the problems of mutability (changing your mind about how you feel) and the yin-yang polarity difference between your natal and your progressed Moon.

Since both Virgo and Gemini are ruled by Mercury, this square is nowhere near as difficult for you as some of the other progressed positions. You may react too strongly to little things, leaving little emotional energy for the larger issues in your life. Then a medium-sized problem can turn into a giant headache because you ignored it while taking care of all those little loose ends.

Natal Gemini Moon Progressed to Libra: Whenever your progressed Moon is in the same triplicity as your natal Moon, your emotional response patterns flow more easily. This position reinforces your natal proclivity for intellectualizing emotion, as well as your natal desire to initiate emotional response. You'll find it easy to bring about peace on an emotional level, because if the issue is worth consideration, you'll analyze it completely. You'll be able to figure out the "why" behind most of the things going on in your emotional life. That means that none of the things happening can really bother you, for as long as you know why they are happening, you know you can handle them.

Natal Gemini Moon Progressed to Scorpio: The Moon is in its fall in Scorpio, and this sign is basically incompatible with your natal Gemini position. You don't like the depth of response which occurs while your progressed Moon is in Scorpio, because the intensity and depth mean you can't completely understand what's going on. You are not comfortable with the water sign emotionalism. You don't want to admit that you are sometimes jealous and sometimes irrational about your feelings. You may actually have to cope with someone else who has these Scorpio Moon tendencies while your progressed Moon is in Scorpio.

Natal Gemini Moon Progressed to Sagittarius: Although this is the half-cycle of your Moon's complete progression and it does emphasize problems of mutability and yang projection of emotion, it's actually easier for many Gemini Moon people than the Scorpio period just past. You'll recognize your tendency to scatter your emotional responses. You may find bigger and better things upon which to expend emotional energy. However, the basic problem in this opposition is not one of bigness or smallness of issues, but rather one of discriminating between major and minor emotional occurrences in your life.

Natal Gemini Moon Progressed to Capricorn: The Moon is in its detriment in Capricorn, and this position is basically incompatible with your natal Gemini Moon. You may try to control your own response nature, becoming rather cold in the process. If you decide to use emotion to control other people, your natal analytic nature won't let you forget that you are using emotion and using other people. Thus, your attempts to control others probably will bring you a lot of internal conflict. If you are trying to use the Capricorn energy to control your own responses, you'll hate the amount of forethought (which you'll feel is cold-blooded, materialistic manipulation) necessary to actually accomplish this end.

Natal Gemini Moon Progressed to Aquarius: Whenever your progressed Moon is in the same triplicity as your natal Moon, you find that your emotional responses flow easily. While your progressed Moon is in Aquarius, you can happily return to some intellectual understanding of your feelings. Not only will you think about your own feelings, but while your progressed Moon is in Aquarius, you'll offer free analysis to everyone who crosses your path, for you'll be absolutely positive that you've finally figured out what makes everyone tick. You may be right on target with your insights during this period. You won't have much difficulty with events occurring now, for you will be able to see the reasons behind habitual behavior patterns.

Natal Gemini Moon Progressed to Pisces: This position, the third quarter of your progressed Moon cycle, is more difficult for you than either the first square or the opposition. Not only do you have to try pulling together a rather scattered emotional response pattern, things come up which make you wonder if you actually feel anything at all. The extreme emotionalism of Pisces runs so contrary to your natal Gemini that you may find yourself fluctuating between extremes of non-thinking reactions and completely rational (and highly structured) intellectual responses. You want to develop more empathy with others, yet your thoughts (and your ability to reason) become scrambled whenever feelings get too strong. You may long for the days, only a year or so ago, when your progressed Moon was in Aquarius and you had it all together! Forgive your confused responses and mixed up analyses for the mutable square usually indicates that there is too much input for reason to be much use right now.

Natal Gemini Moon Progressed to Aries: You enter the Aries progression with considerable relief, for now you are back to the familiar initiation of response patterns. You can let go of the Pisces person who drove you nuts for the past two years (you won't worry about it as much, anyway). The combination of Gemini the thinker and Aries the doer allows you to form new emotional contacts. If you've been really upset by the Pisces square, you can change some of your habit patterns after the progressed Moon enters Aries. You don't have any problem with altering nonproductive habits, but you need some peace and quiet to be able to actually do this. While your progressed Moon is in Aries, you'll get the relief you need, for the solid relationship between your natal and progressed positions indicates that you won't find many emotional pitfalls.

Natal Gemini Moon Progressed to Taurus: The sign behind your natal positon is always difficult and the Moon is exalted in Taurus, so you get a double dose of the guilties. While your progressed Moon is in

Taurus, you'll be reminded of all the insufficiencies of your natal Gemini habit patterns. You'll want to settle down and be able to know how you feel about any single thing without those darned second thoughts you always have. You'll want to stop changing (or trying to change) your basic response nature. You'll want to "be yourself" even though you may not be positive how that Gemini Moon self really feels.

If what really happens during this time involves somebody with strong Taurus traits, you'll need to withstand a lot of implied (or openly stated) criticism of your own response nature. Don't let it get you down. If you can use this energy constructively, you'll approach the conjunction with a clearer sense that it's all right to have a Gemini Moon nature, regardless of how that nature changes.

NATAL MERCURY IN GEMINI

Mercury in rulership in Gemini
Mercury keywords: conscious mind, thought, action, manual dexterity

Natal Gemini Mercury Progressed to Cancer: Mercury rules Gemini and is powerful in your natal position. When your Mercury enters Cancer, if it is angular or heavily aspected, you will add a certain sensitivity and emotional weight to your thought patterns. However, as soon as the aspects have passed, you will revert to your much stronger natal Gemini wit and humor.

Natal Gemini Mercury Progressed to Leo: The progression of Mercury to Leo won't make any more difference in the way you think and act than the Cancer progression did. While your progressed Mercury is heavily aspected or angular, you'll project more confidence, or a more flamboyant manner of speech. You could become a little more stubborn about your point of view during these times. Most of the time you'll continue with the extremely successful Gemini mode of thought.

Natal Gemini Mercury Progressed to Virgo: In contrast to the other positions of progressed Mercury, Mercury rules Virgo and is as strong in the progressed position as it is in your natal position. (It will not reach this position if Mercury is in the first half of Gemini natally or moving slowly due to a retrograde motion just before birth or at any time during your life—Mercury progresses only 80-90° by age sixty-five.) Virgo adds fine discrimination and an ability to sort through mental input quickly. When your natal and progressed Mercury are both in signs that they rule, Mercury becomes one of the powerful planets in your chart, regardless of aspects. You will be known for your mental or verbal ability. If you've not chosen to develop the finer side of your personality you may be known as the worst gossip anyone has ever met. If you have worked on a spiritual as well as a mundane understanding of your life, you may be recognized for your intellect.

Natal Gemini Mercury Retrograde by Progression to Taurus: Unless your progressed Mercury is angular or heavily aspected, its progression into Taurus will be very subtle, felt on an internal level if at all. While Mercury is aspected, you may explore the concepts you actually hold dearest, the few ideas about which you can be stubborn and fixed. This progression is particularly good for study and introspection, for the hidden Taurus can steady and direct your thoughts.

NATAL VENUS IN GEMINI

Venus keywords: loving, being loved, pleasure, self-indulgence

Natal Gemini Venus Progressed to Cancer: When your Venus progresses to Cancer, you could become more possessive of loved ones or more sensitive to criticism of your flirtatious behavior. Since neither natal position nor progressed position is more powerful by sign, you may blend the two expressions into a projection of a loving, sensitive, changeable personality.

Natal Gemini Venus Progressed to Leo: When your Venus progresses into Leo, you develop pride in loved ones or possessions, or a desire to have a good time regardless of the circumstances. If you have developed depth in relationships, the progression to Leo can bring you considerable pleasure through your loved ones. If you have never formed strong ties to others, this progression can symbolize your attempt to find greater enjoyment in the things and people presently in your life.

Natal Gemini Venus Progressed to Virgo: Venus is in its fall in Virgo. This position will have very little influence on your concept of how you give and receive love. If Venus is angular or heavily aspected after it enters Virgo, you may become extremely self-critical. Fortunately, these feelings only last as long as the aspects are exact. When both progressed and natal Venus are in Mercury-ruled signs, you may worry about your love nature, criticizing yourself for real or imagined faults of shallowness or self-indulgence. Those of you who are the most self-critical probably are the least shallow or self-indulgent.

Natal Gemini Venus Retrograde by Progression to Taurus: In spite of the fact that the retrograde motion implies an internalization of the symbolism of Venus, your ability to give and receive love increases when Venus enters a sign that it rules. Until Venus turns direct in Taurus, you may not express the symbolism openly. Nonetheless, you'll discover that you do appreciate the physical pleasure of soft clothing and fine food more now, and you are more likely to recognize beauty in the things around you. Once Venus turns direct, you'll be able to demonstrate your loyalty and depth in love and romantic relationships. The combination of Gemini natal and Taurus progressed Venus really gives you a rather unique ability to express the warmth and softness of Taurus while retaining the flexibility of your natal position. You can, of course, choose to develop the stubborness and possessive, materialistic side of the Taurus while keeping the shallow and fickle side of the Gemini, but most of us simply can't be bothered putting much effort into developing a negative symbolism which brings so few rewards.

NATAL MARS IN GEMINI

Mars keywords: energy, initiative, aggression, anger

Natal Gemini Mars Progressed to Cancer: When Mars progresses into Cancer, sign of its fall, you may not notice any change at first. After Mars enters the Scorpio decanate (10 to 20 degrees of Cancer), you may find yourself cleaning furiously when you are upset about something. On the occasions that you really can't talk about what's bothering you (you may be the only one home), the addition of the Cancer influence (emotion) to your Mars energy can be useful, as it directs your energy in a slightly more focussed manner. Most often, however, the Cancer influence is just not strong enough to be noticeable.

Natal Gemini Mars Progressed to Leo: This progression of Mars will be either terrific or terrible, depending on how you grew while Mars was in Cancer. If you used the Cancer time to turn your energy inward rather than to focus your energy, you may have developed an impressive ability to sulk while Mars was in Cancer. When you add the fire strength of Leo to this style of Mars, you can get to the point that you actually have temper tantrums whenever you are crossed. Not very many people can get away with that on a regular basis and hope to keep any friendships. On the other hand, if you used the Cancer years to develop an ability to recognize and direct your own drives, you will find that the Leo progression allows open use of your energy. If this case, you will be very productive and quite happy in the freedom the fire sign symbolizes.

Natal Gemini Mars Retrograde by Progression to Taurus: Although Mars is weak in Taurus, the sign opposite its traditional rulership, Scorpio, the last ten degrees of Taurus are the Capricorn decanate, in which Mars is exalted. The energy of a retrograde planet is usually internalized, so other people won't see any immediate effects from this position. You may notice an initially positive change and unless your progressed Mars is heavily afflicted, you'll be able to focus your energy on one task at a time. If your Mars is making difficult aspects while it is retrograde in Taurus, you may try to repress your anger or you may be in a situation which demands that you be quiet about the things that annoy you. Fortunately, your natal Gemini position insures that you will find some way to tell someone about the daily irritations, thereby discharging the difficulties.

NATAL JUPITER IN GEMINI

Jupiter in detriment in Gemini
Jupiter keywords: expansion, growth, faith, optimism

Natal Gemini Jupiter Progressed to Cancer: Since Jupiter progresses only 14' per year (about 15° maximum in sixty-five years), unless your natal Jupiter is in the last fifteen degrees of Gemini, it will not progress to Cancer. It is in detriment in Gemini and exalted in Cancer, which means that the progressed position is quite a bit stronger than the natal. Once your Jupiter has progressed to Cancer, you gain a sensitivity which helps you recognize the effect your words have on others. The great mental expansion characteristic of your natal position gains focus and direction in this cardinal sign. Now you can implement some of the plans you've talked or thought about. The most noticable area of growth after Jupiter enters Cancer usually involves some type of parenting or nurturing of other people. You may decide to volunteer in a home for children or the elderly, you may become more involved in community outreach organizations, or you may actually parent kids, but the urge to help another grow enhances your own spiritual development. If you have absolutely no desire to help anyone outside of yourself, you may find that this progression results in an acquisitive type of materialism.

Natal Gemini Jupiter Retrograde by Progression to Taurus: When Jupiter is retrograde, it only moves about 6° in sixty-five years. Unless your natal Jupiter is in the first five or six degrees of Gemini, it will not retrograde to Taurus during your life. When Jupiter progresses to Taurus, the retrograde motion implies an internalization of the symbolism. In this case, internalizing the energy is the best possible way to use it for you can gain considerable practicality in your expansion and growth patterns without appearing to change at all in the eyes of other people. Some of you may choose to use the Taurus expression of Jupiter to pursue materialistic or sensual pleasures.

NATAL SATURN IN GEMINI

Saturn keywords: duty, responsibility, reality, restraint

Natal Gemini Saturn Progressed to Cancer: Saturn progresses a maximum of 7' per year, or about 8° in sixty-five years. In order for Saturn to progress into Cancer, its natal position must be between 24° and 30° of Gemini. The progression of Saturn to Cancer, its detriment, does little to alter your deliberate, intellectual approach to duty. If Saturn is angular or heavily aspected, you may restrict your responses to emotional issues while the aspects are exact.

Natal Gemini Saturn Retrograde by Progression to Taurus: When Saturn is retrograde, it only progresses about 3° in sixty-five years. Unless your natal Saturn is in the first three degrees of Gemini and retrograde, it will not progress into Taurus. The last ten degrees of Taurus are the Capricorn decanate where Saturn is strong. Although the retrograde motion implies an internalization of the energy of the planet, this progression symbolizes your growing attunement to practical realities. You may be able to gain a perspective on your own personal responsibilities after Saturn enters Taurus.

NATAL URANUS IN GEMINI

Uranus keywords: self-will, change, creativity, inventiveness

Natal Gemini Uranus Progressed to Cancer: If you were born in July or August 1948, or May or June 1949, you may have Uranus progress from Gemini to Cancer during your life. Uranus has a quite different influence in these two signs, for your Gemini natal position indicates erratic, sometimes brilliant flashes or ideas, while your progressed Cancer Uranus tends towards mood swings and upheavals in family relationships. The time that Uranus changes sign is likely to be the most troublesome, for you'll be between two expressions for about six months (Uranus was moving 2' per year at the 1948 sign change, and 4' per year at the 1949 change). Other aspects between your progressed and natal positions, or from transits, will provide insight into the facets of your life most likely to be affected by the changes indicated by this progression.

Natal Gemini Uranus Retrograde by Progression to Taurus: If you were born in September or October 1941, you may have Uranus progress from Gemini to Taurus. The retrograde motion implies an internalization of the effect of the sign change. This particular change does very well when experienced at this level, for the stubbornness associated with the Taurus position helps steady the fluctuation common with your natal position. You're more likely to turn your inventiveness and your creativity towards practical ends once Uranus is in Taurus.

NATAL NEPTUNE IN GEMINI

Neptune keywords: imagination, spirituality, unreality, deception, music, art

Natal Gemini Neptune Progressed to Cancer: Neptune progresses between 1′ and 2′ per year when direct. In sixty-five years, it may only move 2°. If you were born in March, April, or May of 1902, your Neptune progressed from Gemini to Cancer during you life. The sign position of Neptune indicates a generational rather than a personal effect, unless your natal position is heavily aspected by inner planets or angles. Neptune in Gemini symbolized a generation growing in intuition and receptivity to new ideas. When Neptune progressed to Cancer, the idealistic and intuitive insights were focussed on home and family life. If you have this Neptune spanning the generation change, you were brought up to idealize thought and ideas, watching the effects of the suffragettes who gained the vote for women. Then as you matured, you watched the idealism shift from the great thinkers to "Mom and apple pie," and may have noticed that, somehow during the shift, women's rights got buried again.

NATAL PLUTO IN GEMINI

Pluto keywords: force, dominance, permanent changes, power

Natal Gemini Pluto Progressed to Cancer: Pluto only progresses 2° in sixty-five years. Unless you were born in July, August, or September of 1912, you will not have Pluto progress from Gemini to Cancer. Like Neptune, the sign position of Pluto is generational, not personal, in effect unless your natal position is heavily aspected by inner planets or angles. Even then, any personal effect of the sign change seems to be minimal. Pluto in Gemini symbolized major changes in verbal expression, while Pluto in Cancer indicated major changes in the structure of the family.

PROGRESSIONS FOR CANCER NATAL POSITIONS

CANCER: YIN—CARDINAL—WATER

NATAL SUN IN CANCER

Sun keywords: basic life force, the physical body, internal "I"

Natal Cancer Sun Progressed to Leo: The progressed Sun enters Leo between age one week (natal ☉ 29° ♋ 59′) and age thirty (natal ☉ 0°♋ 00′). When your Sun progresses into Leo, the sign that it rules, your sense of self is strengthened. The progression into Leo marks a turning point in your life, for the underlying insecurity of your natal Sun can now change. If your natal Sun is in the third decanate, the change will occur during childhood and may not be experienced as a different approach to life, for it will have been with you from at least age ten. Leo adds pride in accomplishment, a desire to be noticed, and a desire to please (or to be better than) Daddy. Since your Cancer Sun tends to be mother-oriented, the progression to Leo can add some balance between parental influences. Most of your life will be colored by the thirty years that your progressed Sun is in Leo. In spite of the well-known drawbacks of the Leo position (vanity, dominance, a need for recognition), ego expression is easiest for you when your progressed Sun is in the sign that it rules. You can assimilate whichever Leo traits help you increase your self-expression.

Natal Cancer Sun Progressed to Virgo: The progressed Sun enters Virgo between age thirty (natal ☉ 29° ♋ 59′) and age sixty (natal ☉ 0° ♋ 00′). Because of the strength of the Leo progression, you will only notice the Virgo progression in terms of overt behavior changes when your progressed Sun is aspected or angular. During the times that your progressed Sun is aspected, the Virgo energy will add a discriminatory ability and perhaps a practical or critical sharpness to your self-expression. When your progressed Virgo Sun is not aspected, you will retain the Cancer-Leo combination of expression.

Natal Cancer Sun Progressed to Libra: The progressed Sun enters Libra between age sixty (natal ☉ 29° ♋ 59′) and age ninety (natal ☉ 0° ♋ 00′). Should your Sun progress to Libra, sign of its fall, you will find even less change than the Virgo progression occasioned. While your progressed Sun is aspected or angular, Libra will amplify your natal cardinal, initiatory side. You'll start new things a little more readily and perhaps be more willing to consider the other person's point of view. Libra, an air sign, is very social, so you may seek friendships or companionship more readily after your Sun progresses into Libra.

NATAL MOON IN CANCER

Moon in rulership in Cancer
Moon keywords: emotions, responses to life, habit patterns

Natal Cancer Moon Progressed to Cancer: The Moon rules Cancer. This powerful natal position dominates your progressed Moon cycle. Every twenty-eight years, your progressed Moon returns to its natal sign. When your Moon returns to Cancer, you again experience and must deal with the joys and difficulties inherent in the Cancer natal position. Problems of oversensitivity, overreaction, fluctuation of feelings, are among the drawbacks of the Moon in Cancer. You can learn to use the tremendous yin strength symbolized by Moon in Cancer. Each conjunction gives you the opportunity to tap this power. You may need to take a look at your tendency to identify with the emotions of others. You may take everything so personally that when anyone is upset about anything, you assume they are upset with you. Not all the difficulty in the world was caused by people with the Moon in Cancer.

Natal Cancer Moon Progressed to Leo: There is a yin-yang conflict between your progressed and natal Moon. Because of the strength of the natal Moon in Cancer, the progression may symbolize a mild frustration with your tendency to react or respond to all emotional input. Unless your progressed Moon is making major aspects while in Leo, you won't pick up any of the Leo Moon brashness or display tendencies because your progressed Moon is not strong enough to mute or alter your natal Cancer expression.

Natal Cancer Moon Progressed to Virgo: The yin nature of the Virgo position reinforces your natal yin Cancer position. You'll find that dealing with emotional issues and the flow of emotional response are quite easy while your progressed Moon is in Virgo. This position will soften any difficult transits occurring during the two and a half years that your progressed Moon is in Virgo. Attributes of the Virgo position that others may find difficult, such as the tendency to distance from emotional issues and look for practical ways to handle them, are useful to you, for you often become overinvolved in feelings. Virgo also helps your Cancer natal position discriminate between different issues and notice the little things contributing to your overall response. You'll be more flexible and more practical during this time.

Natal Cancer Moon Progressed to Libra: This position is an important part of your emotional growth cycle. (See Chapter 1, "You Can't Blame Your Mother," page 13, for further discussion of this cycle.) The yin-yang conflict here underscores your need to at least consider taking an active role in emotional responses. The cardinal conflict indicates that you need to work on problems associated with initiating action or making new beginnings. You may seek peace and harmony during this progression, but you will do this in a uniquely Cancerian manner, emphasizing the concessions you feel you are making in order that peace be accomplished. Libra also brings up the air element, i.e., thinking about how you feel. With a Cancer natal position, you know deep in your soul that intellect and emotion are quite separate parts of your personality. You may be confronted with situations demanding some analysis of your response nature during this square. Since you dislike the intellectual approach to emotion, finding it cold and unresponsive, you may have quite a bit of difficulty coping with these situations.

Natal Cancer Moon Progressed to Scorpio: Whenever the Moon is in the same triplicity as your natal Moon, emotions flow easily. Thus, in spite of the fact that the Moon is in its fall in Scorpio, this is a smooth period. Difficult transits or progressions will be softened by the strength of your emotional response nature while your progressed Moon is in Scorpio. You may hang onto grudges, become deeply entrenched in habitual response patterns, stubbornly refuse to acknowledge that change could be beneficial, yet you will be able to deal effectively and quickly with any emotional crises.

Natal Cancer Moon Progressed to Sagittarius: This sign is basically incompatible with your natal sign. The yin-yang difference indicates a need to develop some yang response patterns. Yet when you attempt to use the yang energy, the Sagittarius mutability scatters your responses, diluting their effectiveness. However, your natal Moon is so strong in Cancer that you immediately revert to your natal emotional expression in any except the most trivial situations.

Natal Cancer Moon Progressed to Capricorn: This is the halfway point of the emotional growth cycle of your progressed Moon. The Moon is in its fall in Capricorn, so the lessons that you assimilate during this two and a half year period have much more to do with the lessons of a Cancer Moon than the traits of a Capricorn Moon. Any problems you have with cardinality, hasty response, or overdependence will come up while your progressed Moon is in Capricorn. You may attempt to mask these problems by withdrawing emotionally. This withdrawal is really an attempt to manipulate and control both your responses and the reactions of others.

Natal Cancer Moon Progressed to Aquarius: This sign is basically incompatible with your natal position. The yin-yang difference now underscores any problems with your yin response nature that you did not completely resolve during the Capricorn opposition. Aquarius symbolizes a strong intellectualization of emotion, a concept nearly incomprehensible to any but the most evolved Cancerian Moon natives. However, you can and do feel a sense of frustration (and probably guilt) over your lack of interest in thinking about feeling. Alternately, you may be somewhat irritated at your tendency to absorb and reflect the feelings of those around you. Many Cancer Moon people develop relationships with air peaple during this inconjunct. These air people will probably analyze you to death, possibly increasing your feeling of inadequacy. If you really are fairly secure in your response nature, the inconjunct will bring out any itchy areas in your concept of sexuality and role acceptance.

Natal Cancer Moon Progressed to Pisces: Whenever the progressed Moon is in the same triplicity as your natal Moon, you find that emotions flow easily. Pisces may scatter your responses, or it may mean that you are including more people in your emotional circle. Your sympathies are easily aroused while your progressed Moon is in Pisces. More than any other position, this increases your ability to sense the emotions of the people around you. Other progressed or transiting aspects are eased while the progressed Moon is in Pisces.

Natal Cancer Moon Progressed to Aries: This is another quarter of your progressed Moon's emotional growth cycle. The Aries position accents any yin-yang imbalance, prompting you to notice the problems inherent in pursuing any one response pattern. The Aries energy may make you want to throw out old habits. You can use the tension of the square to make a new beginning. But when your natal Moon is in Cancer it's hard to throw out anything, be it a possession or a habit. Most of you will compromise, by temporarily placing your less useful habit patterns on a closet shelf. You'll find out whether or not you really threw them out in about seven years when your progressed Moon conjuncts your natal Moon.

Natal Cancer Moon Progressed to Taurus: Not only is the Moon exalted in Taurus, the Taurus energy is extremely compatible with your natal Cancer Moon. You may become even more nurturing, seeking steadiness in your response patterns. You may take the habit patterns shelved during the Aries progression off the shelf, dust them off, and again employ them. Although the Taurus progression may add some practicality, the combination of a strong progressed position and a strong natal position emphasizes your responsive nature. Be careful, for you are in your super-mothering phase right now, and, you may get involved in some dependent relationships. It's fine if you have a child, but not so fine if the dependent one is a spouse or partner. Other people may complain that you are smothering them. If you use the combination to increases already powerful protective, possessive tendencies, you may drive away loved ones by your oversolicitous behavior.

Natal Cancer Moon Progressed to Gemini: The sign behind your natal sign always uncovers your Achilles heel or the parts of your own response nature that you don't like. Gemini indicates that one of the difficulties of your natal Cancer response nature is your inability to analyze, objectify, or distance yourself from your feelings. Although you may become aware of this as a problem during the years that your progressed Moon is in Gemini, the strength of your natal position indicates that you are not likely to do much about it until your progressed Moon enters Cancer. Then you may feel much more intensely and may be able to use this very intensity to help you analyze why you feel the way you do.

NATAL MERCURY IN CANCER

Mercury keywords: conscious mind, thought, action, manual dexterity

Natal Cancer Mercury Progressed to Leo: Mercury is stronger in your natal position, Cancer, than in the progressed Leo position, sign of its fall. Unless your progressed Mercury is strong by house position or aspect, your outward expression of thought and your thinking process remain essentially Cancerian throughout the Leo progression. While your progressed Mercury is making aspects, or if your natal Sun is in Leo, you may incorporate the more showy and stubborn parts of Leo into your conscious expression. You will probably still combine thought and feeling in all of your conscious activities.

Natal Cancer Mercury Progressed to Virgo: In contrast to the Leo progression, once Mercury progresses into Virgo, a sign that it rules, you will feel and express the energy of Virgo in all your conscious thinking. Your discriminatory ability can improve dramatically, and you'll be able to think more logically. Whether you choose to manifest Cancerian sympathy or Cancerian manipulation, you have the opportunity to analyze both your own thoughts and your motivations. The only thing you have to watch here is the ability to nag endlessly, for if you choose to develop the difficult parts of both signs, you can use the Virgo to find little imperfections and then use the Cancer to remember them forever.

Natal Cancer Mercury Progressed to Libra: Because of the ease of expression symbolized by the Virgo progression, most of those thought patterns were incorporated rather fully into your daily life. Consequently, the progression of Mercury into Libra may appear to have little or no effect on your chosen methods of thought or speech. (Mercury will not even reach Libra if it is in the first half of Cancer natally or moving slowly due to a retrograde position just before birth or at any time during your life. It only moves a maximum of 80-90° in sixty-five years.) The return to cardinality may prompt you to mentally investigate new areas.

Natal Cancer Mercury Retrograde by Progression to Gemini: Although retrograde motion symbolizes an internalization of the energy of the planet and sign involved, the progression of Mercury into a sign of its rulership indicates a dramatic increase in your ability to communicate your feelings or thoughts. If you can use this to get at the roots of your emotions (a critical issue if your natal Mercury is in Cancer), you can gain tremendous insight into the causes and cures of your tendencies toward hypersensitivity. If you really do not want to investigate why you react emotionally to most things, the progression to Gemini may merely indicate a greater ability to let everyone know exactly why you are not happy with the current state of affairs.

NATAL VENUS IN CANCER

Venus keywords: loving, being loved, pleasure, self-indulgence

Natal Cancer Venus Progressed to Leo: When Venus progresses to Leo, you become oriented towards the display of beauty or the expression of pride in loved ones. You may push loved ones forward with the words "Make me proud of you!" You may give lavish gifts, or, alternately, demand that loved ones give you things, particularly things which show up well. If you've really worked at developing the martyr side of your natal Cancer position, you may give expensive gifts then refuse to allow loved ones to spend any money on you. Then you've got them right in that old Cancer guilt trap. If you give a lot more than you get, think about how you accept things. This may explain why you never seem to be on the receiving end of generosity.

Natal Cancer Venus Progressed to Virgo: When your Venus progresses to Virgo, sign of its fall, you won't notice the change right away. You may develop a bit more sensuality (earth) in the expression of love, or you may become a bit more discriminating in your choice of possessions. At best, you may put away the cherished but ugly "antiques" from your family. At worst, you may hound loved ones when they are not perfect.

Natal Cancer Venus Progressed to Libra: Your Venus love nature comes into its own when Venus progresses to Libra, the sign that it rules. Now you may accomplish a wholesale housecleaning, getting rid of disharmonious items. Of course, if your natal chart has more than just Venus in Cancer, or if your natal Venus is heavily aspected, you may give all the ugly old things to your relatives, especially if you can attach enough emotional charge to these things to guarantee that your relatives won't dare throw them out. Your progressed Venus will also influence your relationships in that you'll seek to promote harmony and balance in your interactions with others. You'll probably try compromise first, but if that does not work pretty quickly, you'll resort to manipulation to make those friends get along with each other.

Natal Cancer Venus Retrograde by Progression to Gemini: Since Venus is equally strong in both natal and progressed signs, and since the retrograde motion implies an internalization of the planetary symbolism, you may quietly blend the qualities of both natal and progressed positions into your nature. This particular progression may be quite difficult, for your natal Cancer position is not usually indicative of great self-confidence, and the progressed position indicates changing perceptions. The result may be wide swings in your ideas about your ability to give and receive love. You may try to tie others to you by being indispensable when you are feeling unlovable, then turn around and complain about their dependency needs when you are feeling a little more confident.

NATAL MARS IN CANCER

Mars in fall in Cancer
Mars keywords: energy, initiative, aggression, anger

Natal Cancer Mars Progressed to Leo: Although the expression of your energy is stronger when Mars progresses into Leo, you may still have difficulty channeling your aggressive instincts. Leo allows your energy to surface as pride or in creative endeavors. The inherent touchiness of your Cancer natal position is often increased by the addition of Leo energy. This means that you may be even more given to temper tantrums after your Mars progresses into Leo, unless you develop creative outlets for your aggressive drives.

Natal Cancer Mars Progressed to Virgo: The further progression of Mars into Virgo does not dramatically change your ability to express energy, initiative, and aggressive drive. You may develop a more practical means of distributing your energies, but the problem of handling anger is not directly addressed during the Virgo progression. You may feel that, except for a few emotionally sensitive areas, you have no difficulty with anger. Frequently this feeling is a reflection of complicated repression techniques rather than a true assessment of your ability to cope with your own aggressive tendencies.

Natal Cancer Mars Retrograde by Progression to Gemini: Since Mars is in its fall in Cancer, the progression to Gemini increases its energy even though the retrograde motion implies an internalization of this energy. Now you can choose to develop some insight into your methods of expressing your energy. Or you can develop a rather acid tongue, using intellect and sarcasm to discharge anger. You won't be as likely to brood about irritating things or people after Mars enters Gemini.

NATAL JUPITER IN CANCER

Jupiter in exaltation in Cancer
Jupiter keywords: expansion, growth, faith, optimism

Natal Cancer Jupiter Progressed to Leo: Since Jupiter only progresses 14' per year, or about 15° in sixty-five years, your Jupiter will not progress into Leo unless it is is in the last half of Cancer natally and in direct motion. Jupiter is exalted in Cancer; thus your natal expression is very strong. The progression of Jupiter to Leo adds a certain high-mindedness to your attempts at growth and expansion, but it will not change the sensitive, generous qualities inherent in your natal position. If Jupiter has hard aspects (squares or oppositions) while it is in Leo, others may notice a tendency to brag or show off. Usually this does not last longer than the aspects, because your natal expression is more comfortable for you.

Natal Cancer Jupiter Retrograde by Progression to Gemini: Since Jupiter is in its detriment in Gemini, and since the symbolism of retrograde motion implies internalization of the energy, unless Jupiter is angular or heavily aspected you won't notice this progression at all. While Jupiter is being aspected, you may indulge in optimistic intellectual pursuits, or you may develop an expansive oratorical style of speech.

NATAL SATURN IN CANCER

Saturn in detriment in Cancer
Saturn keywords: duty, responsiblity, reality, restraint

Natal Cancer Saturn Progressed to Leo: Saturn progresses about 7' per year or a total of 8° in sixty-five years when in direct motion. Unless your Natal Saturn is between 22° and 30° Cancer, it probably will not progress into Leo. Saturn is in its detriment in Cancer and in its traditional detriment in Leo. When Saturn progresses to Leo, you may limit your activities to things which you know will succeed. You may choose to express this energy in an entirely different manner by becoming quite hidebound and stubborn about your reality constructs and your definition of responsibility and duty. This response to Saturn in Leo restricts you, but really gets in your way if you try to apply your rules to others who may not appreciate what they see as a critical parent person in you.

Natal Cancer Saturn Retrograde by Progression to Gemini: Saturn only goes aobut 3° in sixty-five years when it is in retrograde motion. Unless your natal Saturn is in the first few degrees of Cancer and retrograde, it will not progress into Gemini. When Saturn progresses from Cancer to the third decanate (the Aquarius decanate) of Gemini, even though the retrograde motion implies energy internalization, Saturn gains strength. You may find that you can recognize, think about, and possibly release the restriction of emotion symbolized by your natal Saturn in Cancer. You may choose the rationalization implied by this position to escape responsibility, or you may use it more positively to define the limits of your own personal responsibility.

NATAL URANUS IN CANCER

Uranus keywords: self-will, change, creativity, inventiveness

Natal Cancer Uranus Progressed to Leo: If you were born in April, May, or June of 1956, you may have Uranus progress from Cancer to Leo during your life. Uranus in Cancer symbolizes your hatred of being tied down emotionally. When Uranus progresses to Leo, sign of its detriment, you may become increasingly stubborn about your dislike of emotional ties. You may also solidify your unusual beliefs about family life, refusing to listen to anyone else's opinion. Because your natal position is stronger, you aren't likely to show any of this Leo influence unless the position is triggered by other aspects.

Natal Cancer Uranus Retrograde by Progression to Gemini: If you were born during September, October, or November of 1948, you may have Uranus retrograde from Cancer to Gemini during your life. Since the influence of Uranus is quite different in these two signs, you are likely to notice upheavals or changes in your life during the six month period that Uranus changes sign. (Uranus was moving 2' per year at this point) Uranus in Cancer indicates unusual or rapid mood changes and a variable view of family life. The shift to Gemini incorporates sudden illuminations and a creative way of thinking. This mutable air sign increases the volatility of an already changeable planet. If there are any other aspects to natal and progressed Uranus (they are only 2° apart at the maximum), this volatility is quite likely to be triggered. You may find it a great adventure; those around you may find it completely confusing.

NATAL NEPTUNE IN CANCER

Neptune in exaltation in Cancer
Neptune keywords: imagination, spirituality, unreality, deception, music, art

Natal Cancer Neptune Progressed to Leo: If you were born during 1914, 1915, or 1916, you may have Neptune progress from Cancer to Leo, or from Leo to Cancer, for Neptune retorgraded twice during these years, crossing 0° Leo in both retrogradations. The sign position of Neptune is generational rather than personal unless Neptune is angular or closely aspected by your inner planets. Even then it is difficult to separate the progressed from the natal, for the planet only moved about a degree in your life. You were born between two generations of thought. The Neptune in Cancer position involves a romantic, idealistic, and unrealistic view of family and home life, while Neptune in Leo indicates an idealistic view of the governing abilities of various forms of leadership, or an unrealistic view of the self.

NATAL PLUTO IN CANCER

Pluto keywords: force, dominiance, permanent change, power

Natal Cancer Pluto Progressed to Leo: If you were born from September through December 1937, or May through August of 1938, you have Pluto progressing from Cancer to Leo, or from Leo to Cancer in retrograde motion. Pluto is generational in effect. The sign postion symbolizes a change in world thought or action rather than personal change unless your natal position is angular or closely aspected by the inner planets. Pluto in Cancer symbolized dramatic changes in the home and family, while Pluto in Leo indicated changes in forms of governement and leadership. Those of you born as Pluto changed signs may have experienced disruption or total change on both levels during your lives.

PROGRESSIONS FOR LEO NATAL POSITIONS

LEO: YANG—FIXED—FIRE

NATAL SUN IN LEO

Sun in rulership in Leo
Sun keywords: basic life force, the physical body, internal "I"

Natal Leo Sun Progressed to Virgo: The progressed Sun enters Virgo between age one week (natal ☉ 29° ♌ 59') and age thirty (natal ☉ 0° ♌ 00'). The symbolism of your natal Leo position will overshadow all of the progressions of your Sun, because the Sun rules Leo and is stronger in your natal position than it will be in any progression. Therefore, you will feel the differences of the progressions only while the Sun is active by angularity or aspect. All of the descriptions of the Leo personality—the pride, the leadership, the generosity—will be major forces in your basic nature all your life. When your Sun progresses to Virgo, unless your natal Mercury is in Virgo, you will hardly notice the small increase in critical ability. The yin-yang conflict between the sign Leo and the sign Virgo may cause you to pause slightly and consider the possiblitiy of using a yin approach to the world occasionally. Usually this simply occurs as a bit of worry about coming on too strong.

Natal Leo Sun Progressed to Libra: The progressed Sun enters Libra between age thirty (natal ☉ 29° ♌ 59') and age sixty (natal ☉ 0° ♌ 00'). You'll have even more difficulty detecting any change in basic self-expression when your Sun progresses to Libra, where it is in its fall. During times that your Sun is heavily aspected or angular, you may be more inclined towards taking the other person's point of view seriously, or even playing the devil's advocate occasionally.

Natal Leo Sun Progressed to Scorpio: The progressed Sun enters Scorpio between age sixty (natal ☉ 29° ♌ 59′) and age ninety (natal ☉ 0° ♌ 00′). Scorpio reinforces all of the fixity inherent in your natal Leo position. Although this position may bring out some yin-yang conflict, you will be at least sixty-one years old by this time and will most likely not worry about this projection of yourself. You can, however, become the most stubborn senior citizen in the city if you don't try to maintain some flexibility.

NATAL MOON IN LEO

Moon keywords: emotions, responses to life, habit patterns

Natal Leo Moon Progressed to Leo: Every twenty-eight years your progressed Moon conjuncts its natal position. This is the time that you must deal with the problems and joys inherent in your natal Moon's symbolism. The Moon in Leo indicates problems with habit formation, your tendency to express emotion in a yang fashion, and your eagerness to act on emotional input so quickly that you avoid recognition of the feelings involved. Yet you are quite vulnerable to criticism when your natal Moon is in Leo, fearing that your responses may somehow be inadequate. This underlying fear that you somehow don't "measure up" may lead you to be compulsively generous. If so, you need to look at why you feel so insecure in emotional situations. Are you demanding too much perfection from yourself?

Natal Leo Moon Progressed to Virgo: Your yin-yang conflict in the expression of emotion is quite obvious while your progressed Moon is in Virgo. You may attempt to both act and respond at the same time. The practical side of the Virgo projection conflicts with your natal desire to display emotion. You may resolve this dilemma by utilizing emotion to manipulate others, or you may yourself be manipulated as you expend emotional energy on a host of little things, leaving little energy to cope with larger issues. If you get stuck in a cycle of self-criticism while your progressed Moon is in Virgo, try to remember the good and positive parts of your response nature. Don't dismiss your loyalty, generosity or sincerity so quickly.

Natal Leo Moon Progressed to Libra: The yang nature of the Libra energy blends well with your natal Leo emotional response nature. You may now start to intellectualize and separate a bit from your emotions, analyzing different approaches and their effectiveness. You may seek the role of peacemaker in emotional situations, particularly if this effort results in other people admiring you.

Natal Leo Moon Progressed to Scorpio: This is the first quarter of the emotional growth cycle symbolized by the progression of the Moon. (See Chapter 1, "You Can't Blame Your Mother," page 13, for further discussion of this cycle.) Although the Moon is in its fall in Scorpio, the square position of this sign to your natal position insures that the Scorpio progression will be influential in your life. The yin-yang conflict between Leo and Scorpio highlights your need to incorporate both masculine and feminine qualities in your response patterns. Scorpio amplifies any problems you have with fixity, indicates a tendency to hold onto hurts or slights and to become vengeful or jealous. When it becomes obsessive, jealousy reflects your emotional insecurity. During the time that your progressed Moon is in Scorpio, difficulties in these areas will become too big to ignore. You'll have to do something about them.

Natal Leo Moon Progressed to Sagittarius: Whenever the progressed Moon is in the same triplicity as your natal Moon, your emotional energy flows more freely. Sagittarius may help loosen up some of your natal fixity and is a welcome relief after the intensity of Scorpio. While you may idealize the concept of emotion, you can feel much more secure in your yang projection. If you don't like what is happening in your emotional life, you may be able to initiate some changes during this progression.

Natal Leo Moon Progressed to Capricorn: The Moon is in its detriment in Capricorn and this sign is basically incompatible with your natal position. You may choose to completely ignore the Capricorn energy, feeling only frustration with your inability to control either your own emotions or the responses of others. While your progressed Moon is actually inconjunct your natal position, the underlying tension will increase the emotional effects of any other progressed or transiting aspects. Then you may have to cope with your fears of emotional inadequacy, for the Capricorn energy will amplify this part of your natal response until you cannot avoid noticing it. Most Leo Moon people blend two coping mechanisms when dealing with the Capricornian issues of emotional control. First, you form friendships with people who have prominent earth response patterns. Such folks may not actually criticize you, but you may compare yourself quite unfavorably with them. Then you attempt to use your natal fire to dominate emotional situations. Unfortunately, dominance and control are two very different patterns. When dominance does not work well, you may put yourself in the position of serving others. Any transits or other aspects which occur while your progressed Moon is in Capricorn will accent dominance/submission or control issues in your life.

Natal Leo Moon Progressed to Aquarius: This is the halfway point of your progressed Moon's emotional growth cycle. With both polarity and quadruplicity the same as your natal Leo, you encounter again natal problems of fixity and yang projection of emotion. Since Aquarius is an air sign, you will tend to seek intellectual solutions to emotional problems. Insofar as this leads you to analyze what you're doing and why, it can be a valuable aid to your growth. Unfortunately, you may merely become glib at describing how you feel without understanding how to change the way you respond.

Natal Leo Moon Progressed to Pisces: This sign is basically incompatible with your natal Leo position. Your yin-yang conflict may again become an issue, and you may try to act and react all at the same time. The strongly emotional, intuitive influence of Pisces may stretch your generosity to the breaking point, as you may try to resolve emotional conflicts by giving more and more of your time and your possessions. The sexual overtones of the eighth house inconjunct may bring to light habitual roles you've incorporated into your response patterns. Now is the time to change the responses which make you unhappy.

Natal Leo Moon Progressed to Aries: Whenever your progressed Moon is in the same triplicity as your natal Moon, your emotional responses flow more easily. Aries is comfortable with initiating emotional response and is willing to try new patterns of response. The cardinal impetus may relieve some of the stubbornness of your natal position. Furthermore, you won't feel as guilty about your habitual patterns while your progressed Moon is in Aries. All other transits or progressions will be eased by the presence of the progressed Moon in Aries.

Natal Leo Moon Progressed to Taurus: In the third quarter of your emotional growth cycle your progressed Moon is in the sign of its exaltation. This may be the most difficult of the four stages of emotional growth for you. Now you really have to acknowledge the yin side of your emotional nature. You will have to cope with situations in which the only appropriate response is a yin, nurturing, supportive one. If you won't let go of your natal yang projection, you'll have great difficulty getting through the mood swings which accompany this square. Since you won't be able to buy or bluff your way out of the situations that occur now, you'll have to adapt and change, dirty words to both natal and progressed fixed positions.

Natal Leo Moon Progressed to Gemini: After the trouble in Taurus, you'll really need the relative calm of Gemini, a sign quite compatible with your natal Leo position. You will be able to retreat from the intense emotional involvement of the two and a half years that your progressed Moon was in Taurus. During the Gemini years, you will be able to use the air sign's energy to either distance yourself from deep involvement, scattering your feelings somewhat, or analyze what happened to you during the square from your progressed Moon to your natal Moon. If you choose the second expression of Gemini, you'll be able to alter distressing habit patterns. Whichever approach you take, you won't really feel difficult transits or progressions as stressful emotional upheavals while your progressed Moon is in Gemini.

Natal Leo Moon Progressed to Cancer: The sign behind your natal Moon sign often uncovers hidden weaknesses or difficulties in responses. Since the Moon rules Cancer, an aspect that for most people is a minor aspect assumes significantly more importance for you. During this time you may find yourself floundering between the progressed yin expression of emotion and your natal yang habits. The strong input of water indicates that you need to learn how to respond rather than rush into action. This progression emphasizes your need to feel on a gut level. Whatever smugness you have about your ability to analyze your feelings (gained during the Gemini progression) will be washed away during the two and a half years that your progressed Moon is in Cancer. The Cancer years will show you the difference between feeling, thinking, and acting. For you, these two and a half years before your progressed Moon returns to its natal position will probably be more difficult than the actual conjunction. Unless other aspects are very strong, no major events are likely during this period. Nonetheless, your inner emotional turmoil is likely to peak while your progressed Moon is in Cancer.

NATAL MERCURY IN LEO

Mercury keywords: conscious mind, thought, actions, manual dexterity

Natal Leo Mercury Progressed to Virgo: When your Mercury progresses to Virgo, which it rules, your ability to express your ideas improves rapidly. The Virgo energy adds practicality, discrimination, and flexibility to your natal Leo position. The greater freedom of expression indicated by progressed Mercury in Virgo often enhances your Leo sense of humor. You have a particularly astute grasp of the ridiculous in daily life. During this progression you may be a little more adept at recognizing flattery, but if your natal Sun is also in Leo, you'll always fall for a sweet line.

Natal Leo Mercury Progressed to Libra: When Mercury progresses into Libra, you have spent a number of years incorporating the more useful Virgo traits into your conscious thought. Mercury isn't as strong in Libra as it is in Virgo, so you won't notice a major shift with this progression. The return to yang polarity usually seems to encourage a better blending of Virgo and Leo characteristics rather than indicating a clear Libran influence. Your Leo playfulness, joviality and good humor, and desire to look good in all situations can combine with your acquired Virgo ability to reason quickly and accurately and make you a delightful, sought after conversationalist. Yet, if you don't develop the pleasant traits of these signs, the Libran energy can indicate that you now choose the easiest way through any mental exercise, becoming obstinate about your own ideas while using any flaw in another person's argument to destroy any opposing point of view.

Natal Leo Mercury Progressed to Scorpio: If your Mercury progresses to Scorpio, you will solidify your thinking into fixed patterns. Whether this influence indicates depth of thought or stubborn vindictiveness really depends on how you've already chosen to develop your inner self. You'll be at least forty-five before Mercury can reach Scorpio. (Mercury moves a maximum of 80-90° in sixty-five years. If it's in the first half of Leo natally or moving slowly due to a retrograde motion just before birth or at any time during your life, it will not progress to Scorpio.) If you've worked towards your spiritual development, the addition of the Scorpio energy can lead you to sorting out what you really believe. The Scorpio energy may encourage you to discard unproductive reasoning. On the other hand, you may have spent your time criticizing yourself and others, refusing to see much good in anything. Then the Scorpio traits most in evidence are negative— jealousy, suspicion, secrecy and vengefulness.

Natal Leo Mercury Retrograde by Progression to Cancer: The retrograde motion implies an internalization of the effect of this progression. You may become rather upset by the thoughtless or hurtful things you or others say; if you concentrate on yourself, you'll wind up searching for hidden meanings in whatever others say. If you can turn your vision outward, you'll gradually become more aware of the impact your own words have on the people around you.

NATAL VENUS IN LEO

Venus keywords: loving, being loved, pleasure, self-indulgence

Natal Leo Venus Progressed to Virgo: When your Venus progresses to Virgo, sign of its fall, you won't notice any change unless Venus is heavily aspected or angular. While your progressed Venus is aspected, you'll notice a slightly more sensual love response and perhaps a tendency to criticize or find fault with loved ones or possessions. You may become much harder to please during these times.

Natal Leo Venus Progressed to Libra: In contrast, when your Venus progresses to Libra, a sign it rules, you begin to seek beauty and harmony in your surroundings. The combination of Libran balance and beauty with Leo pride usually indicates that you will set up pleasant (and pretty) love relationships at this time. This is one of the easiest combinations of natal and progressed Venus because you will seek and find pleasure and beauty in your surroundings. The yang energy of natal and progressed positions impels you to change unpleasant or dirty conditions.

Natal Leo Venus Progressed to Scorpio: Venus is so strong in Libra, which it rules, that it will be difficult to notice the Scorpio influence at first. In fact, you may never really see the intensity or the jealousy typical of Scorpio directly, for when Venus is in its detriment, the effects are quite subtle. What this really means is that the folks around you will probably notice that you are a little more touchy about love situations, a little less likely to tolerate someone flirting with your lover or spouse. Of course, with natal Venus in Leo, you never could stand it when anyone made a move on your lover. If you can retain some of the peaceful Libran influence, you won't go off in a rage to sulk (Scorpio) or make a scene (Leo), but you will very sweetly put yourself between the seducer and your lover.

Natal Leo Venus Retrograde by Progression to Cancer: When Venus progresses from Leo to Cancer, you often become much more sentimental about loved ones. Because the retrograde motion implies internalization, you may not show this romantic softness until Venus turns direct. You'll have an awfully hard time letting go of any kind of emotional attachment. If this extends to broken rocking chairs and old magazines, you may be in trouble.

NATAL MARS IN LEO

Mars keywords: energy, initiative, aggression, anger

Natal Leo Mars Progressed to Virgo: The progression to Virgo will not immediately alter your projection of energy. By the time Mars gets to the second decanate (ten to twenty degrees) of Virgo, you may start to spread out your energy, seeking the most practical manner of applying your drive and aggression. The Virgo influence can help lessen some of your intensity, which may be a very useful change because your Leo inclination to throw yourself entirely into a project often overwhelms others.

Natal Leo Mars Progressed to Libra: Mars is in its fall in Libra, so unless it is angular or heavily aspected, you won't notice this influence. While your progressed Mars is aspected, you need to remember that anger is one way you can choose to react to the actions of others, and no one but you can change your reactions.

Natal Leo Mars Retrograde by Progression to Cancer: Mars is stronger in Leo than in Cancer (its fall) and the energy of a retrograde planet is usually turned inward. Thus, except for the times that progressed Mars is aspected or angular, you won't notice this change. While Mars makes aspects, you may find that you are more emotional about the application of your energy, or you may find that emotional situations arouse anger.

NATAL JUPITER IN LEO

Jupiter keywords: expansion, growth, faith, optimism

Natal Leo Jupiter Progressed to Virgo: Jupiter only progresses 14' per year, or about 15° in sixty-five years when direct. Your Jupiter will not progress into Virgo unless it is in the last fifteen degrees of Leo. When Jupiter progresses to Virgo, it's traditional detriment, you'll only notice Virgo influence while Jupiter is aspected or angular. During those times you may become more self-conscious (and very self-critical) about some of your flashy mannerisms.

Natal Leo Jupiter Retrograde by Progression to Cancer: When Jupiter is retrograde, it only progresses about 6° in sixty-five years. Unless your natal Jupiter is in the first decanate of Leo, it cannot progress into Cancer. Jupiter is exalted in Cancer and is the traditional ruler of the last ten degrees of Cancer (the Pisces decanate). Thus, it is stronger in Cancer than in Leo. Therefore, even though the retrograde motion implies an inward turning of the energy, you will notice the transition whether or not anyone else does. You will become much more sensitive to your feelings and the feelings of others. You may develop a desire to nurture or care for the people in your life.

NATAL SATURN IN LEO

Saturn keywords: duty, responsibility, reality, restraint

Natal Leo Saturn Progressed to Virgo: Saturn progresses 7' per year, or about 8° in sixty-five years when direct. Your Saturn won't progress from Leo to Virgo unless it is in the last decanate of Leo natally. When Saturn progresses to Virgo, you may try to overcome whatever orgainizational problems you feel you have by structuring everything in your life. This may make life neater, but you can become fanatical about all this order. You need to back off and look at the whole picture if you find yourself constantly frustrated by the simple fact that no one can control every facet of life. Remember, Murphy's Law (the maximization of perversity) will win in the end.

Natal Leo Saturn Retrograde by Progression to Cancer: When Saturn is retrograde, it progresses about 3° in sixty-five years. Unless your natal Saturn is in the first few degrees of Leo and retrograde, it won't progress into Cancer. In your natal Leo position, the blend of caution and restriction characteristic of Saturn focussed on your own creative self-expression. The retrograde motion of Saturn to Cancer, where it is also in its detriment, implies an inward extension of this caution to your expression of emotion. You may assume more responsibility for family members, you may worry a lot more about their welfare, or you may retreat from interaction with family members out of a fear of rejection.

NATAL URANUS IN LEO

Uranus in detriment in Leo
Uranus keywords: self-will, change, creativity, inventiveness

Natal Leo Uranus Progressed to Virgo: If you were born in June, July, or August of 1962, you may have Uranus progress from Leo to Virgo during your life. When Uranus progresses to Virgo, some of your stubbornness will lessen and you may well move onto inventive problem-solving. If you can learn to work with others, this may indicate that you can apply your originality to practical matters.

Natal Leo Uranus Retrograde by Progression to Cancer: If you were born in Novemeber or December 1955 or January 1956, you may have Uranus progress from Leo to Cancer during your life. Although Uranus gains some strength by moving out of its detriment (Leo), the strength is an inward expression of creativity or desire for change. You may become disillusioned about family or home matters, seeking change but unsure of the ways to create that change. As long as you don't turn the restlessness of this planet agianst yourself emotionally, you can develop an ability to seek creative alternatives to difficult family relationships.

NATAL NEPTUNE IN LEO

Neptune keywords: imagination, spirituality, unreality, deception, music, art

Natal Leo Neptune Progressed to Virgo: If you were born in May, June, or July of 1929, you may have Neptune progress from Leo to Virgo in your lifetime. The sign position of Neptune is generational in effect rather than personal unless Neptune is angular or conjunct your inner planets. Neptune in Leo symbolizes an idealization of leadership or government authorities. The change to Virgo indicates a shift towards idealization of work or service to others.[21]

NATAL PLUTO IN LEO

Pluto in exaltation in Leo
Pluto keywords: force, dominance, permanent changes, power

Natal Leo Pluto Progressed to Virgo: If you were born in June, July, or August of 1957, or in the spring of 1958, you will have Pluto progress from Leo to Virgo or from Virgo to Leo during your life. Unless Pluto is angular or heavily aspected by your inner planets, the sign position is not personal but generational. Pluto in Leo symbolized major changes in attitude towards goverment. Pluto in Virgo symbolized changed attitudes towards work and service to others. You are between these two generations, the Leo demanding change in governments and in the view of the individual, the Virgo demanding change in the valuation of individual service.[22]

PROGRESSIONS FOR VIRGO NATAL POSITIONS

VIRGO: YIN—MUTABLE—EARTH

NATAL SUN IN VIRGO

Sun keywords: basic life force, the physical body, internal "I"

Natal Virgo Sun Progressed to Libra: The progressed Sun enters Libra between age one week (natal ☉ 29° ♍ 59′) and age thirty (natal ☉ 0° ♍ 00′) When your Sun progresses to Libra, sign of its fall, you will only notice the Libran energy as an ability to criticize every action you take which does not add to the harmony and balance of the world around you. In spite of the bad press that Virgoans get concerning their critical natures, you are harder on yourselves than you are on

---

[21] For natal Neptune in Leo retrograde to Cancer (for those born October, November, and December 1914 as well as January, February, and March 1916), see page 190, Neptune in Cancer.

[22] For natal Pluto in Leo retrograde to Cancer (for those born August, September, and October 1937 as well as December 1938, January and February 1939), see page 190, Pluto in Cancer.

others. This self-criticism can peak while your progressed Sun is in Libra because you may blame yourself for causing the disharmony around you. If you can develop the cardinal ability to work towards changing the things you don't find pleasing rather than merely noticing them, you can blend these two influences for the benefit of yourself and all those around you.

Natal Virgo Sun Progressed to Scorpio: The progressed Sun enters Scorpio between age thirty (natal ☉ 29° ♍ 59′) and age sixty (natal ☉ 0° ♍ 00′). The symbolism of Scorpio adds depth and persistence to your self-expression. You may use this energy to increase your self-esteem by actually sticking to your guns when challenged instead of going off to worry about whether the criticism was accurate. You may get stuck in repetitious behavior. On the other hand, you may notice jealousy creeping into your interactions with others. If this is happening, take a look at how you feel about yourself. The negative side of Scorpio will surface if you are stuck in the self-critical side of Virgo. If all you ever notice are the things others do better than you can, you are shortchanging yourself.

Natal Virgo Sun Progressed to Sagittarius: The progressed Sun enters Sagittarius between age sixty (natal ☉ 29° ♍ 59′) and age ninety (natal ☉ 0° ♍ 00′). If your Sun progresses to Sagittarius, you'll gleefully sweep away all of the Scorpio ruts in a magnificent return to mutability. Now you want to travel, to think about philosophy and the bigger things in life, and if you are stuck in one spot, you become increasingly restless. If you simply cannot globe-trot, get down to the local library, join a discussion group, investigate some of the senior citizen tours.

NATAL MOON IN VIRGO

Moon keywords: emotions, responses to life, habit patterns

Natal Virgo Moon Progressed to Virgo: Your progressed Moon conjuncts its natal position every twenty-eight years in your emotional growth cycle. During the two and a half years that your progressed Moon is in the same sign as your natal Moon, you experience the problems and the joys inherent in yor natal sign. Your Virgo Moon inclines you toward a rather cool emotional response, a response at once detailed and quietly grounded. You may fuss too much over little things, scattering the strength of your emotional response. You may analyze your feelings until you are not at all sure of what you felt in the first place. This is an excellent time for emotional housecleaning. You are flexible enough to release negative response patterns if you give yourself permission to do so. When you find yourself worrying about little things, stop and ask yourself "How important is it?"

Natal Virgo Moon Progressed to Libra: When your Moon progresses to Libra, you have to deal with a conflict in polarities, i.e., a desire to respond as well as act on emotional input. The air sign influence increases your desire to analyze actions and think about feelings. Since your natal position also signifies thinking about how you feel, the tension of the semi-sextile may be due to too much head involvement in your response patterns. The Libran energy may prompt you to consider the needs of others, the responses of others, the impact you have on others, while your natal influence suggests you want to get specific in every analysis of emotion. You probably won't have enough time to worry about all the things that go on in the emotional world of those around you, but you may try.

Natal Virgo Moon Progressed to Scorpio: The Moon is in its fall in Scorpio, but this sign is quite compatible with your natal Virgo position. You may hang onto your feelings longer while your progressed Moon is in Scorpio. If you have had a problem with scattered emotional response, you will welcome the intensity symbolized by Scorpio, which demands that you experience one feeling at a time. If you are insecure about your own response nature, the Scorpio influence may manifest as jealousy. You will be able to handle easily the events occurring in your life during the time that your progressed Moon is in Scorpio, for your emotional response nature is quite stable.

Natal Virgo Moon Progressed to Sagittarius: This is the first quarter of your progressed Moon cycle. (See Chapter 1, "You Can't Blame Your Mother," page 13, for further discussion of this cycle.) Problems of mutability become acute as you try to cope with responses to every single thing in the environment. Sagittarius confuses your natal discriminatory ability, so that it becomes much harder to tell the important emotional issues from the minor upheavals. Everything seems larger than life in the area of emotion while your progressed Moon is in Sagittarius.

Natal Virgo Moon Progressed to Capricorn: In spite of the fact that the Moon is in its detriment in Capricorn, this sign is the same triplicity as your natal Moon, so your emotions flow much more easily while your progressed Moon is in Capricorn. You relax with the addition of controlled, directed, and particularly grounded emotional energy. This progressed position will ease or mute difficult aspects from transits or other progressions. Other people may not find your progressed Capricorn Moon so wonderful if you use your progressed and natal combination to control their responses.

Natal Virgo Moon Progressed to Aquarius: This sign is basically incompatible with your natal Virgo position. The way you prefer to analyze or think about your feelings is practical and directed towards a concrete answer. However, you may feel the Aquarius energy directs this intellectualization towards separation from the feeling itself. You get very impatient with this approach to analysis, wanting results rather than the abstraction of the bigger picture. You may find yourself dealing with air people who refuse to be grounded or practical. As long as you avoid internalizing their criticism, you can avoid major problems during this inconjunct.

Natal Virgo Moon Progressed to Pisces: This is the halfway point of your progressed Moon's emotional growth cycle. Now you must deal with your difficulties in terms of both yin projection and mutability. While your progressed Moon is in Pisces, you may become more overtly emotional in your responses. Alternately, you may take on all the problems of the world. Occasionally this can lead to a martyr-like assumption of all kinds of emotional burdens. When you do this, you may be masking your own inability to sort out your feelings by supporting others around you.

Natal Virgo Moon Progressed to Aries: This sign is basically incompatible with your natal Virgo Moon position. The yin-yang conflict leads you to attempt action and reaction at the same time. The initiating energy of Aries simply aggravates your Virgo tendency to scatter response. You may become quite irritable while your progressed Moon is in Aries, for the Aries energy demands action while your natal Virgo Moon sees thousands of areas which could use emotional attention. If you are questioning your own approach to sex or sexuality you may form relationships with extremely aggressive fire sign people, and in the process may clean up their emotional or physical messes. Right now you can establish dependent relationships in which the other person appears to dominate while you provide emotional support.

Natal Virgo Moon Progressed to Taurus: Whenever your progressed Moon is in the same element as your natal Moon, the flow of emotions is easier. Furthermore, the Moon is exalted in Taurus so this is likely to be a wonderful period. Any difficult progressions or transits occuring during this two and a half year period will be much easier to manage. This combination brings out the best of your practical earth symbolism, as the fixity of Taurus helps you to focus your response nature. You'll stay with your feelings longer, you'll probably develop your "mothering" traits, but your natal Virgo flexibility should prevent the possessive, smothering possibilities of the Taurus from becoming dominant.

Natal Virgo Moon Progressed to Gemini: This is the third quarter of your progressed lunar cycle. You may try to analyze all your emotions, seeking to understand the causes of your internal conflict between initiation and reaction. If you have difficulty with scattered response patterns, it may become acute during this period. Inconsistency of response is probably the most important issue that you need to address now. Because Mercury rules both natal and progressed signs, the most obvious influence of the progressed position may be an ability to worry constantly about everything from the dinner menu to global disasters!

Natal Virgo Moon Progressed to Cancer: Your progressed Moon, in the sign that it rules, will be quite influential during this two and a half year period. Because Cancer energy blends well with your natal Virgo emotional nature, you will be able to sail through problems, working out any difficulties. You will experience an added depth and increased fluctuation of feelings, although this should not be uncomfortable. You won't be able to maintain your natal coolness or detachment, for the force of the Cancer symbolism demands gut level response to events.

Natal Virgo Moon Progressed to Leo: The sign behind your natal sign often uncovers secret or hidden weaknesses in your natal emotional patterns. The Leo progression suggests that you will experience a need to develop more fixity of response. Leo is very demonstrative, in contrast to your Virgo tendency to avoid the messy business of showing how you feel. You may start to realize that when you hide your emotions you sometimes deny your own ability to feel.

NATAL MERCURY IN VIRGO

Mercury in rulership in Virgo
Mercury keywords: conscious mind, thought, actions, manual dexterity

Natal Virgo Mercury Progressed to Libra: Because your natal Mercury is in a sign that it rules, you are not likely to notice the progression to any other sign much at all. While your progressed Mercury is aspected or angular, you may become the verbal peacemaker, promoting harmony in all your interactions. You may find it more difficult to make decisions, as you add consideration of the other point of view to your detailed natal thought pattern. You will form friendships more readily during this period if you let go of your more critical side.

Natal Virgo Mercury Progressed to Scorpio: Depending on the aspects that bring out the Scorpio symbolism, you may become rather rigid in your self-criticism or in your criticism of others. You may hang onto habits or ideas longer, exploring them in more depth. Sometimes all that seems to happen with the Scorpio progression is a turn towards keeping your thoughts to yourself. If that means that you stop criticizing others out loud, it could be good, but if it means that you are not talking about the petty annoyances but seething inside, it may backfire.

Natal Virgo Mercury Progressed to Sagittarius: Mercury moves a maximum of 80-90° in sixty-five years; if it's placed in the first half of Virgo natally or is moving slowly due to a retrograde position just before birth or at any time during your life, it won't progress to Sagittarius. If it does progress to this position, where Mercury is in its detriment, it will be a particularly subtle influence (which means you probably won't notice it at all). If anything, it will increase your natal mutable tendencies, making it difficult for you to decide what to do.

Natal Virgo Mercury Retrograde by Progression to Leo: The retrograde motion implies inwardization of the energy symbolized by the sign position of the planet. The only one who will be able to detect any Leo influence in your life will be you. Unfortunately, this particular progression seems to increase your ability to criticize yourself for your natal yin thought and speech patterns. The Leo adds a desire to be more outgoing, more yang, while the stronger yin natal position maintains your outward yin expression. You will become wonderfully adept at thinking about what you should have said after the opportunity for saying it has passed.

NATAL VENUS IN VIRGO

Venus in fall in Virgo
Venus keywords: loving, being loved, pleasure, self-indulgence

Natal Virgo Venus Progressed to Libra: After your Venus progresses to Libra, your love nature blossoms. Venus rules Libra, and this progressed position will influence your feelings about how you give love as well as enhance your belief that other people can love you. You'll start to seek beauty and harmony in the things around you; you will find that you finally believe you deserve some nice, comfortable, and beautiful things.

Natal Virgo Venus Progressed to Scorpio: After the impact of Venus in its rulership, the progression to its detriment shouldn't be very obvious. If your progressed Venus is heavily aspected during this time, you may become quite jealous, for depending on the aspects, the Scorpio position can reawaken your natal Virgo insecurities about whether or not you are a lovable person.

Natal Virgo Venus Progressed to Sagittarius: If your Venus progresses to Sagittarius, you may desire a bit more freedom in love relationships. You may start to consider an ideal of non-demanding love. The nicest part of this progression is an increased sense of humor, as you can poke fun at some of the silly situations love gets you into (and rescues you from!).

Natal Virgo Venus Retrograde by Progression to Leo: While Venus is in retrograde motion, you will absorb the Leo influence on an internal level. Until Venus turns direct you won't actually start to demonstrate the open, affectionate, warm and funny nature of Venus in Leo. Once your Venus is direct, you can get those things you've wanted, and better still, you can enjoy having and using them. You'll enjoy leisure time activities much more when you can use the Leo energy to dispel leftover Virgo worries about inadequacy in love situations.

NATAL MARS IN VIRGO

Mars keywords: energy, initiative, aggression, anger

Natal Virgo Mars Progressed to Libra: Mars is in its detriment in Libra, so this progression is not a great help in directing your efforts. Other people can irritate you more easily while Mars is in Libra, and you need to be careful that you don't start to project your own irritation onto the other people in your life. The yin-yang difference between Virgo and Libra indicates that you will sometimes express energy in an aggressive, forthright manner, and at other times you will refuse to acknowledge any angry feelings or aggressive impulses at all.

Natal Virgo Mars Progressed to Scorpio: When Mars progresses to Scorpio, its traditional rulership, you will find that it is much easier to focus your energy. Now you look for results from action. You are much more determined to get your own way, regardless of obstacles. If you have spent the years that your Mars was in Virgo and in Libra denying your own anger, you may be quite unpleasantly suprised to discover the depth of rage that has built up. If your reality absolutely cannot include anger or aggression as an expression of your energy, you may form relationships with thoroughly horrible, angry, vengeful people so that they express this part of you while you keep your passive self-image.

Natal Virgo Mars Retrograde by Progression to Leo: When Mars progresses from Virgo to Leo, the influence is internalized as a result of the retrograde motion. Once progressed Mars turns direct, you can openly express the Leo drive that you've quietly developed while it was retrograde. You will focus your energy and ambition more clearly after Mars turns direct. Sports can become an excellent outlet for you, as they enable you to use your competitive and aggressive energy in more productive ways.

NATAL JUPITER IN VIRGO

Jupiter in detriment in Virgo
Jupiter keywords: expansion, growth, faith, optimism

Natal Virgo Jupiter Progressed to Libra: Jupiter only progresses about 14' per year, or 15° in sixty-five years. Your Jupiter won't progress into Libra unless it is in the last half of Virgo natally. After your Jupiter enters Libra, you may recognize that you really need the approval of others to expand and grow. If you have not become mired in a negative expression of wit (sometimes called sarcasm) you can develop new friendships and grow through new relationships. Aspects to your natal or progressed chart occurring as Jupiter enters Libra are likely to indicate recognition or reward for past effort.

Natal Virgo Jupiter Retrograde by Progression to Leo: Jupiter only moves about 6° in sixty-five years when retrograde. Unless your natal Jupiter is in the first decanate of Virgo and retrograde, it won't progress to Leo. Even though the retrograde motion implies an inward manifestation of the planet's energy, the progression of Jupiter from Virgo to Leo usually indicates that you will become more optimistic, developing and expanding through creative endeavors. Often this expansion involves hobbies, games, or entertaining, for these creative outlets display the Leo influence as well as your natal Virgo symbolism.

NATAL SATURN IN VIRGO

Saturn keywords: duty, responsibility, reality, restraint

Natal Virgo Saturn Progressed to Libra: Saturn progresses about 7' per year, or 8° in sixty-five years. Unless your natal Saturn is in the last decanate of Virgo and direct, it will not progress to Libra. The progression of Saturn to Libra, where it is exalted, may bring you relief from your constant worry over details. When your progressed Saturn is in Libra, you seek balance and harmony in the ordering of your universe. You may be quite serious about the role of peacemaker, seeking to bring all of your friends into harmony with each other. You may get quite depressed if others don't like you or won't get along without bickering.

Natal Virgo Saturn Retrograde by Progression to Leo: Saturn progresses only 3° in sixty-five years when it is retrograde. Unless your natal Saturn is in the first few degrees of Virgo, it won't retrograde to Leo. Since Saturn is in its traditional detriment in Leo, and since the retrograde motion implies an internal manifestation, you won't notice too much difference in your opinion about duty and responsibility after Saturn enters Leo. If Saturn is heavily aspected or angular, you may restrict your own creativity or try to completely control the spontaneous Leo expression in your life.

NATAL URANUS IN VIRGO

Uranus keywords: self-will, change, creativity, inventiveness

Natal Virgo Uranus Progressed to Libra: If you were born in July, August, or September of 1968, or from March to June of 1969, you may have Uranus progress from Virgo to Libra during your life. When Uranus progresses into Libra, you want more freedom in relationships. You may seek out people who are unusual or unconventional. The two different expressions of Uranus creativity, Virgo with things and Libra with people, makes an uncomfortable mix. Thus the six month period during which Uranus changes sign may be full of changes with both people and things in your life. If there are any other major aspects during this time, they may involve much more change than usually is associated with them.

Natal Virgo Uranus Retrograde by Progression to Leo: If you were born in November or December 1961, or January 1962, you may have Uranus progress from Virgo to Leo during your life. Not only does the retrograde motion imply an inward direction of the planet's energy, Uranus is in its detriment in Leo. You are not very likely to notice this progression. If Uranus is aspected or angular, you may be more willing to try new things, particularly in any leisure or fun activities. You may change the way you approach hobbies and decide to take up something quite unusual.

NATAL NEPTUNE IN VIRGO

Neptune in detriment in Virgo
Neptune keywords: imagination, spirituality, unreality, deception, music, art

Natal Virgo Neptune Progressed to Libra: If you were born in May, June, or July of 1943, you may have Neptune progress from Virgo to Libra during your life. Neptune's sign position is generational in influence unless it is angular or heavily aspected by the inner planets. Neptune in Virgo symbolizes a tendency to idealize work and service to others. When Neptune enters Libra, it symbolizes a tendency to idealize other people and relationships.[23]

NATAL PLUTO IN VIRGO

Pluto keywords: force, dominance, permanent changes, power

Natal Virgo Pluto Progressed to Libra: If you were born in July, August, or September of 1971, or between February and August of 1972, you may have Pluto progress from Virgo to Libra or from Libra to Virgo during your life. The sign position of Pluto is generational rather than personal unless Pluto is angular or heavily aspected by inner planets in your natal chart. Pluto in Virgo symbolizes major social changes in attitude towards work and service to others. Pluto in Libra symbolizes changes in attitude towards marriage, partnerships, and relationships.[24]

PROGRESSIONS FOR LIBRA NATAL POSITIONS

LIBRA: YANG—CARDINAL—AIR

NATAL SUN IN LIBRA

Sun in fall in Libra
Sun keywords: basic life force, physical body, internal "I"

Natal Libra Sun Progressed to Scorpio: The progressed Sun enters Scorpio between age one week (natal ☉ 29° ♎ 59′) and age thirty (natal ☉ 0° ♎ 00′). When your Sun progresses into Scorpio, you become more intense, desiring more room for self-expression. You are less likely to excuse the behavior of other people after your Sun enters Scorpio. Although you are not likely to develop a confrontational style of self-expression, the Scorpio influence indicates that you grumble more about the bad behavior of others. It will be easier to make decisions and stick with them after your Sun enters Scorpio.

---

[23] Neptune did not retrograde from Virgo to Leo during this century.

[24] For natal Pluto in Virgo retrograde to Leo (for those born October, November, and December 1956 as well as January 1957), see page 200, Pluto in Leo.

Natal Libra Sun Progressed to Sagittarius: The progressed Sun enters Sagittarius between age thirty (natal ☉ 29° ♎ 59′) and age sixty (natal ☉ 0° ♎ 00′). Once your Sun progresses to Sagittarius, you will expand your self-expression. You may become more flexible, more idealistic, and much more optimistic about your own abilities. Your natal desire for peace and your progressed optimism can combine into a wonderfully open sense of humor. You want to know about new ideas and new places. Travel appeals to you, and so do intellectual pursuits.

Natal Libra Sun Progressed to Capricorn: The progressed Sun enters Capricorn between age sixty (natal ☉ 29° ♎ 59′) and age ninety (natal ☉ 0° ♎ 00′). If your Sun progresses into Capricorn, you may become much more serious about yourself and how you express yourself. Depending on the choices you have made during your life, you may become quite worried about future security, or you may simply become considerably more practical in your outlook. While your natal Libran social instincts may be enhanced by the practical side of Capricorn, you may develop into a bit of a snob if you are still looking for social achievement through your associations.

NATAL MOON IN LIBRA

Moon keywords: emotions, responses to life, habit patterns

Natal Libra Moon Progressed to Libra: Every twenty-eight years your progressed Moon conjuncts its natal position in the emotional growth cycle of the progressed Moon. While your progressed Moon is in the same sign as your natal Moon, you must deal with the problems and the joys inherent in your natal Moon's position. The Libran Moon symbolizes the need to think about and equalize your emotional responses. Your constant attempts to balance your feelings may lead to a fear of (and avoidance of) emotional depth. Your moods appear to be at the mercy of others because you always try to understand both sides of every issue. During the conjunction, you can assess your need for approval, for this is really what your peacemaking is all about. You can be popular and more secure in your expression of emotion if you can trust your own inner response nature.

Natal Libra Moon Progressed to Scorpio: The Moon is in its fall in Scorpio, so except while your progressed Moon is aspecting other planets, you will not express the retentive, secretive, and highly emotional Scorpio influence. You are not very comfortable with the depth and intensity of Scorpio, for you want to know the "why" of your responses. Scorpio may also bring out a bit of jealousy, a trait you personally abhor. You may find that you have to deal with other people who exhibit the Scorpio Moon traits rather than experiencing any of them internally.

Natal Libra Moon Progressed to Sagittarius: The sign Sagittarius is quite compatible with your natal Libra, and you will express your feelings quite easily during this two and a half year period. Any difficult aspects made by other transits or progressions will be eased by your emotional stability. You may tend to gloss over any unpleasantness, preferring an idealistic combination of intellectual analysis and action. You will be quite comfortable with your own response nature during this period.

Natal Libra Moon Progressed to Capricorn: This is the first quarter of your progressed Moon's emotional growth cycle. (See Chapter 1, "You Can't Blame Your Mother," page 13, for further discussion of this cycle.) The Moon is in its detriment in Capricorn, indicating that you not only need to deal with problems of cardinality, you must actually determine the importance of emotion in your life. Another effect of the Moon's detriment concerns noticing only the difficult parts of your own response nature. You may need to take stock of the positive parts of your response nature (the helpfulness, the consideration of others) in order to avoid a rather depressing self-evaluation. Capricorn can also indicate a desire to control emotion, or use it for practical purposes. You may seem quite cold while your progressed Moon is in Capricorn, for the tension between your natal and progressed positions highlights your need to integrete emotion into your daily life.

Natal Libra Moon Progressed to Aquarius: Whenever your progressed Moon is in the same triplicity as your natal Moon, your emotional responses flow more easily. You can now be more comfortable with your tendency to separate yourself from emotional response and with your desire to think about the reasons for your emotional responses. The Aquarius progression may allow you to separate enough from your feelings to recognize how and why you respond the way you do. You're likely to succeed when you use reason to cope with the emotional impact of events during this time.

Natal Libra Moon Progressed to Pisces: This sign is basically incompatible with your natal position. The increased fluctuation of emotional response symbolized by Pisces is difficult for you to reconcile with your lunar nature. You are by nature sympathetic and understanding (Libran Moons spend a lot of time thinking about and reflecting how others feel), but you dislike intensely the type of personal involvement symbolized by Pisces. Your natal cardinality wants to do something about problems; your progressed Pisces wants to sit and cry about them.

Natal Libra Moon Progressed to Aries: This is the halfway point in your progressed Moon's cycle. You need to recognize the problems of cardinality and the problems of a yang projection of emotion, i.e., your desire to do something about difficulties. The Aries position increases your impulse to get busy working on emotional input before you've had a chance to completely understand that input. You may seek to alleviate some problems through immediate action or through initiating totally new response patterns, but others will not be resolved in this manner. You may try to postpone dealing with old habits by becoming involved in supporting other people through their emotional crises.

Natal Libra Moon Progressed to Taurus: This sign is basically incompatible with your natal position, and the Moon is exalted in Taurus. Although the inconjunct does not usually indicate events, this two and a half year period may be more difficult for you than the actual opposition of your progressed Moon to your natal Moon. If there are hard aspects from other progressed positions or the outer planet transits, they will be more difficult to contend with while your progressed Moon is in Taurus. You will want to respond to emotion, rather than react to emotion, but your natal habit patterns get in your way. You can't do both at the same time, but you will probably try. The waning inconjunct also brings out questions of sexuality and sex roles. You may get swept into comparing your responses to whatever is the currently popular psychological view. No matter how useful or reasonable your own nature acutally is, you will be able to find fault with it. You want to nurture the whole world while remaining detached. It doesn't usually work out that way.

Natal Libra Moon Progressed to Gemini: You'll enter, with considerable relief, the period of easy emotional response present whenever the progressed Moon is in the same triplicity as your natal Moon. You can once again feel confident of your ability to analyze your emotional responses and the responses of those around you. Even though the mutability of Gemini may scatter and dilute your responses, most of us would rather have less depth and less pain, given a choice. If the Taurus inconjunct brought out an inner conflict concerning your ability to give and receive nurture, you now have the opportunity to understand the reasons behind that insecurity.

Natal Libra Moon Progressed to Cancer: Not only is this the third quarter of your progressed Moon's emotional growth cycle, the Moon rules Cancer. This will be the most difficult part of your growth cycle. You will discover a depth and intensity within yourself that you have probably tried to ignore. Now you'll find that commitment, fluctuation, and gut level feelings overwhelm your response patterns. Your habitual detachment will fall apart under the onslaught of cardinal water. Part of you will be screaming "NO! This is too much to bear!"

while another part of you will be saying "Wonderful! This is exactly how I feel! I don't need to think about it, I know I feel it!"

Natal Libra Moon Progressed to Leo: Once your progressed Moon has moved on into Leo, you can look back on the emotional storms that occurred during the Cancer years and begin to truly evaluate the importance of emotion in your continued growth and development. You may be better able to display emotion and release some of the intensity you felt during the Cancer years. This position will mute any difficult aspects, for you have a very stable emotional response while your progressed Moon is in Leo.

Natal Libra Moon Progressed to Virgo: The sign behind your natal position often reveals the hidden weaknesses of your natal Moon. While your progressed Moon is in Virgo, you may notice that you are not terribly practical. You may become fairly self-critical in your pursuit of some type of appropriate yin response to emotion. You may worry that others can manipulate you because of your tendency to react to emotional cues.

NATAL MERCURY IN LIBRA

Mercury keywords: conscious mind, thought, actions, manual dexterity

Natal Libra Mercury Progressed to Scorpio: When your Mercury progresses into Scorpio, you may establish more intense speech patterns, developing your ideas more fully before you allow the opinions of others to get in your way. You may also be able to see through the ruses of others. Whether or not the Scorpio progression encourages you to recognize your own mind games depends on the choices about self-development and honesty you have made while your Mercury was in Libra.

Natal Libra Mercury Progressed to Sagittarius: Depending on the direction of mental growth you chose while progressed Mercury was in Scorpio, the influence of Sagittarius, where Mercury is in its detriment, will vary considerably. On the one hand, Sagittarius can symbolize a scattering of your thoughts, with dreams of success and a tendency to exaggerate successes which may seem like conceit or snobbery. On the other hand, the progression can symbolize a growing interest in philosophy, a better sense of humor, and a desire to see the other side of the fence, both literally, through travel and figuratively, through study of other philosophies or social orders.

Natal Libra Mercury Progressed to Capricorn: If your Mercury progresses into Capricorn (it won't if it's in the first half of Libra natally or moving slowly due to a retrograde position before birth or at any time during your life as Mercury only moves 80-90° by age sixty-five), you may develop a more serious view of the world and of yourself within the world. In a positive expression of this position, you may become more practical and logical. Alternately you may become bitter or resentful of unfulfilled ambitions. A Capricorn key word is control, and you may try to develop complete control of your thinking process. As long as you don't extend this to include controlling your fantasies and imagination, it should not be a problem.

Natal Libra Mercury Retrograde by Progression to Virgo: Mercury is much stronger in the sign that it rules, so even though the retrograde motion implies an inward manifestaion of the energy, you will notice a change in your conscious thought patterns after Mercury enters Virgo. Once Mercury turns direct, you will express the logic, clarity, and detailed precision of thought that you developed during the retrograde phase.

NATAL VENUS IN LIBRA

Venus in rulership in Libra
Venus keywords: loving, being loved, pleasure, self-indulgence

Natal Libra Venus Progressed to Scorpio: When your Venus progresses into Scorpio, it is progressing from its rulership to its detriment, so you will only change your perception of how you give and receive love while Venus is making aspects to other planets or is angular. During those times you may become more jealous or more sensual. You may gain some understanding of the passion or jealousy of other people or you may find people with strong Scorpio traits attractive while your progressed Venus is in Scorpio, but your natal Libran expression of harmony, love, and beauty will be the strongest influence on your behavior.

Natal Libra Venus Progressed to Sagittarius: The progression of Venus into Sagittarius will be extremely difficult to see as a change in your love nature, for even while aspecting other positions or angular, the symbolism of Sagittarius only amplifies your natal love of a good time and increases your sense of humor. The Sagittarius influence seems to let you show your natal Libran nature (your love for art and music, your appreciation of beauty, your ability to smooth out differences between others, your ability to manipulate others) more fully.

Natal Libra Venus Progressed to Capricorn: If your Venus should progress into Capricorn, you may feel the loss of friends rather keenly.

You may hate the restrictions age places on your ability to enjoy art, music, and dance. But this is also a time for quiet reflection and memory of the wonderful Venus in Libra things and people you have experienced during your life.

Natal Libra Venus Retrograde by Progression to Virgo: Because of the strength of your natal position, and because the influence of retrograde motion is internal, you won't notice much change from this progression. However, it does symbolize a discriminating ability and practical application of art appreciation which can be quite useful should you choose to pursue a career in the arts. Venus is in its fall in Virgo, so you probably won't change your attitude towards love at all.

NATAL MARS IN LIBRA

Mars in detriment in Libra
Mars keywords: energy, initiative, aggression, anger

Natal Libra Mars Progressed to Scorpio: When Mars progresses into Scorpio, sign of its traditional rulership, directing your energy, initiative and drive becomes much easier. If someone else aggravates you enough, you will find that you would rather end the relationship right then than continue to accept the aftermath of their bad temper. You will be more willing to accept your own energy and use it as Mars progresses through Scorpio. Your intensity may surprise you when your progressed Mars aspects other planets or angles (either progressed or natal).

Natal Libra Mars Progressed to Sagittarius: The progression of Mars into Sagittarius may lighten some of the intensity of the Scorpio years, but won't be strong enough to change the habits you developed while Mars was in Scorpio. Mars in Sagittarius does, however, symbolize a clear and open expression of energy. You may be able to release some of the secretive or retentive traits you developed while Mars was in Scorpio. You may be able to have more fun by indulging in competitive sports after Mars gets into Sagittarius.

Natal Libra Mars Retrograde by Progression to Virgo: The retrograde motion implies an internal rather than external manifestation of the energy of Mars. This combination requires complete honesty about your motivations in order to achieve a positive expression of your inner drives. It is very easy to fall into a trap of rationalization in which you blame other people for all of your problems. You may completely deny that you are ever angry. Unless you can recognize your less wonderful side, you will not see how your hidden resentment can cause others to respond to you in a negative manner.

NATAL JUPITER IN LIBRA

Jupiter keywords: expansion, growth, faith, optimism

Natal Libra Jupiter Progressed to Scorpio: Jupiter progresses about 14′ per year, or 15° in sixty-five years. If your natal Jupiter is in the last half of Libra and direct, it may progess into Scorpio. When your Jupiter progresses into Scorpio, you usually develop a sense of privacy, depth and persistence concerning growth. If you have chosen to emphasize spiritual growth, you may find that this progression heightens your self-awareness. If you have no interest in your spiritual development, you may combine the secrecy of Scorpio with the interest in others indicated by your natal position to try to find out everything about everyone you know.

Natal Libra Jupiter Retrograde by Progression to Virgo: Jupiter only moves about 6° in sixty-five years when retrograde. Unless your natal Jupiter is in the first six degrees of Libra and retrograde, it will not progress to Virgo. Since Jupiter is in its traditional detriment in Virgo and the retrograde motion implies an inward expression of energy, you are not too likely to discover any major changes in your manner of growth and expansion after Jupiter enters Virgo. While your progressed Jupiter is aspected or angular, you may become more practical about your own expansion and growth.

NATAL SATURN IN LIBRA

Saturn in exaltation in Libra
Saturn keywords: duty, responsibility, reality, restraint

Natal Libra Saturn Progressed to Scorpio: Saturn progresses about 7′ per year, or 8° in sixty-five years. Unless your natal Saturn is in the last decanate of Libra and direct, it will not progress to Scorpio. Saturn is exalted in Libra, so unless the progressed position is heavily aspected or angular, the progression of your Saturn to Scorpio won't symbolize any major shift in your view of personal responsibility. While Saturn is aspected, you may become more rigid about the "right" way (your way) to assume duty or responsibility. You may become fanatical about expressing your natal Saturn desire for justice and fairness. On th other hand, you may develop the ability to operate to the letter of the law while ignoring the spirit of the law.

Natal Libra Saturn Retrograde by Progression to Virgo: Saturn only moves about 3° in sixty-five years when retrograde. Unless you have natal Saturn in the first few degrees of Libra and retrograde, it will not progress into Virgo. Saturn is stronger in your natal position of Libra than it is in Virgo. Except for the times that your progressed Saturn is angular or heavily aspected, you won't notice any change in the way you accept responsibility after Saturn enters Virgo. While it is being aspected you may be quite willing to tell everyone else how to do anything and everything. You may have difficulty recognizing this as a problem, for in your heart you know that you are right.

NATAL URANUS IN LIBRA

Uranus keywords: self-will, change, creativity, inventiveness

Natal Libra Uranus Progressed to Scorpio: If you were born in September, October, or November of 1974 or between March and September of 1975 you may have Uranus progress from Libra to Scorpio during your life. When Uranus progresses into Scorpio, where Uranus is exalted, you may become extremely obstinate about your desires for unusually structured relationships. You may choose to break up all of your old relationship patterns in order to build new ones.

Natal Libra Uranus Retrograde by Progression to Virgo: If you were born in March, April, or May 1969, you may have Uranus progress from Libra to Virgo during your life. The influence of Virgo is radically different from the influence of Libra on the expression of Uranus, with Libra seeking change and freedom through people, while Virgo seeks practical inventiveness with things as a primary means of change. Consequently, the six month period during which Uranus actually enters Virgo will probably involve abrupt changes in many areas of your life. Every transit to any natal position will involve some kind of alteration in your life. The best way to handle this transition is to stay flexible, for if you get angry or try to force things to remain constant, you'll be quite frustrated.

NATAL NEPTUNE IN LIBRA

Neptune keywords: imagination, spirituality, unreality, deception, music, art

Natal Libra Neptune Progressed to Scorpio: If you were born from October 1955 to October 1956, you may have Neptune progress from Libra to Scorpio or the reverse during your life. The sign position of Neptune is generational unless Neptune is angular or heavily aspected by inner planets. Neptune in Libra symbolizes the idealization of relationships, while Neptune in Scorpio symbolizes the idealization of sexuality or concepts of death and rebirth.[25]

---

[25] For natal Neptune in Libra retrograde to Virgo (for those born February, March, and April 1943), see page 208, Neptune in Virgo.

NATAL PLUTO IN LIBRA

Pluto keywords: force, dominance, permanent changes, power

Natal Libra Pluto Progressed to Scorpio: Those who are born in late 1983 or 1984 may have Pluto progress from Libra to Scorpio during their lives. The effect of Pluto is not personal, unless angular or aspected by the inner planets. Since none of us has yet experienced the symbolism of Pluto in Scorpio, we can only speculate about what it really will mean. Pluto in Libra seemed to be associated with changes in society's view of relationships. Pluto in Scorpio may symbolize the need for regeneration on all levels of human life.[26]

PROGRESSIONS FOR SCORPIO NATAL POSITIONS

SCORPIO: YIN—FIXED—WATER

NATAL SUN IN SCORPIO

Sun keywords: basic life force, the physical body, the internal "I"

Natal Scorpio Sun Progressed to Sagittarius: The sun enters Sagittarius between ages one week (natal $\odot$ 29° ♏ 59') and age thirty (natal $\odot$ 0° ♏ 00'). When your Sun progresses to Sagittarius, you can become a bit more flexible in attitude. You'll start to develop a sense of humor, and as your idealism and ability to see the whole picture increases, you may try alternate methods of self-expression. Sagittarius enlarges all your self-expression, both positive and negative. You can choose which Scorpio traits you want to retain and which Sagittarius traits you want to develop.

Natal Scorpio Sun Progressed to Capricorn: The sun enters Capricorn between age thirty (natal $\odot$ 29° ♏ 59') and age sixty (natal $\odot$ 0° ♏ 00'). When your Sun progresses to Capricorn, you seem to return to (or intensify) many of your natal Scorpio traits. Among other things, Capricorn symbolizes ambition, practicality, and goal orientation, all of which are very compatible with your natal Scorpio nature. Cardinal signs initiate change, but dislike any type of change they did not start. That trait fits well with your internal self, for you really don't like doing things which were not your idea.

---

[26] For natal Pluto in Libra retrograde to Virgo (for those born February, March, and April 1972), see page 209, Pluto in Virgo.

Natal Scorpio Sun Progressed to Aquarius: The progressed Sun enters Aquarius between age sixty (natal ☉ 29° ♏ 00′) and age ninety (natal ☉ 0° ♏ 00′). If your Sun should progress into Aquarius, you may find that this final progression solidifies all of the fixity in your nature. If you haven't paid much attention to the development of your spiritual side, you may become a truly stubborn, cantankerous senior citizen. However, both Aquarius and Scorpio have the potential for soaring spiritual insight. If you can avoid the pitfall of righteousness, you can discover serenity in your last progression.

NATAL MOON IN SCORPIO

Moon in fall in Scorpio
Moon keywords: emotions, responses to life, habit patterns

Natal Scorpio Moon Progressed to Scorpio: Your progressed Moon conjuncts its natal position every twenty-eight years, in the emotional growth cycle of human life. The conjunction brings out both the joys and difficulties inherent in your natal Scorpio Moon's symbolism. The Moon is in its fall in Scorpio. You experience an intensity of emotional response which is unmatched by any other sign placement of the Moon. It may be very difficult for you to analyze or understand your own emotions, for few can probe their psyche to that depth. You have an underlying insecurity about the emotional habits which you nonetheless stubbornly maintain. This insecurity can lead to extremes of jealousy sometimes associated with the natal Moon in Scorpio.

Natal Scorpio Moon Progressed to Sagittarius: When your Moon progresses into Sagittarius, you may try to project emotion in both a yin and a yang manner. Your natal position indicates that you prefer to keep feelings hidden under a cloak of secrecy. It may be quite difficult for you to cope with the Sagittarius impetus to open up to others with a frank display of emotion.

Natal Scorpio Moon Progressed to Capricorn: Although the Moon is in its detriment in Capricorn, this sign is quite compatible with your natal Scorpio position. The desire to control emotion symbolic of Capricorn supports your natal urge to hide emotion. You may become more manipulative, using emotion to control others while your progressed Moon is in Capricorn.

Natal Scorpio Moon Progressed to Aquarius: This is the first quarter of your progressed Moon's emotional growth cycle. (See Chapter 1, "You Can't Blame Your Mother," page 13, for further discussion of this cycle.) If you have problems with fixity or strong habit formation, they will surface now. You may feel torn between thinking about your feelings and experiencing your strong responses. While you do not want to change your habitual responses, you need to be able to separate enough from them to understand them better.

Natal Scorpio Moon Progressed to Pisces: Whenever the progressed Moon is in the same triplicity as your natal Moon, you find that your emotional responses flow more easily. While your progressed Moon is in Pisces, you have an extremely empathetic response, tuning into other people and their feelings instantly. Any difficult transits or progressions will be eased by the emotional stability symbolized by the trine between your natal and progressed Moon.

Natal Scorpio Moon Progressed to Aries: This position is basically incompatible with your natal position. Your natal Scorpio Moon does not take chances on new emotional responses, or initiate response patterns. You may try to ignore the Aries influence completely, or you may behave in a yang fashion at inappropriate times, appearing quite despotic because of your underlying rigidity. The tension symbolized by the combination of natal and progressed positions can exacerbate any hard aspects made by transits or other progressions during this period.

Natal Scorpio Moon Progressed to Taurus: Not only is Taurus the halfway point in your progressed Moon's growth cycle, the Moon is exalted in Taurus. Because of this increased influence of the progressed Moon, you may overreact to input. This may take the form of suspicion of anyone not in your immediate family. Sometimes your suspicion includes family members. If you will not recognize the part your own stubborn habit patterns play in your emotional upheavals, you may become an emotional isolationist, nurturing and clinging to immediate family members. This position is the most difficult part of your progressed Moon's cycle for you must face the strongest and weakest areas of your feelings.

Natal Scorpio Moon Progressed to Gemini: This sign is basically incompatible with your natal Scorpio position. You prefer to feel, while the Gemini influence encourages analysis of your emotional responses. The mutable air sign indicates a tendency to scatter emotional responses, while your natal tendency is to hoarde emotion, lavishing it on immediate family and close friends. While Gemini Moon people nibble at the edges of emotional response, Scorpio Moon people dive instantly for the center of feeling. It is often difficult for you, with your natal Scorpio position, to conceive of any valid pattern of response other than total commitment.

Natal Scorpio Moon Progressed to Cancer: The Moon rules Cancer, and the sign is trine your natal position. Whenever the progressed Moon is in the same triplicity as your natal Moon, your emotions flow easily. With this combination, the flow may become a torrent, drowning family members in extremely possessive protection. You may develop quite a martyr complex, unable or unwilling to acknowledge that others need to function on their own. On the positive side, this combination will never neglect any family member, and even though you may hold a grudge for the entire two and a half years of this progression, you will forgive anyone who appeals sufficiently to your desire to nurture or mother them. Any harsh aspects made by other progressions or transits will be eased by the stability of your emotional patterns now.

Natal Scorpio Moon Progressed to Leo: This is the third quarter of your progressed Moon's growth cycle. Again you must deal with problems of fixed habit patterns. You may explore the yang side of emotion, acting instead of responding in some situations. However, the primary problem indicated during this period stems from the conflict between secrecy (Scorpio) and display (Leo). You really do want to be appreciated for the depth of your loyalty, but unless you tell others how you feel, they may not recognize your strong emotional attachments. You may feel very isolated during this time, positive that no one else understands the tremendous sacrifices you make in order to support those you care about.

Natal Scorpio Moon Progressed to Virgo: This mutable earth symbolism may indicate that you are now willing to release some of your less positive emotional patterns, particularly any involving possessiveness, rigidity, or retention of negative emotion. The combination of Virgo and Scorpio usually works very easily, smoothing out difficulties as you respond in a more practical, cool manner. Virgo allows some separation from emotional intensity while supporting the strong yin response nature which your natal position indicates.

Natal Scorpio Moon Progressed to Libra: The sign behind your natal sign often uncovers hidden weaknesses or difficulties in your natal responses. While your progressed Moon is in Libra, you may notice (or others may inform you) that you are so secretive about emotions that others cannot understand your responses. Alternately, you may find that your intensity drives others away. Any problems with an overly yin projection will be more obvious during this two and a half year period, for Libra symbolizes balance, and what you need to balance is the yin and yang modes of emotional response.

NATAL MERCURY IN SCORPIO

Mercury keywords: conscious mind, thought, action, manual dexterity

Natal Scorpio Mercury Progressed to Sagittarius: Mercury is in its detriment in Sagittarius, so unless your progressed Mercury is aspected or angular, you won't notice any changes in thought patterns during this progression. During the times that your progressed Mercury is aspected, you may seek a more open means of expression. You may expand cognitively, or be more willing to listen to other people's ideas.

Natal Scorpio Mercury Progressed to Capricorn: The progression of Mercury into Capricorn may be difficult to discern for quite another reason. The influence of Capricorn on your Mercury seems to intensify many of your natal Scorpio traits. Capricorn, too, indicates taciturn speech patterns and emphasizes a serious approach in conscious thought. Both signs indicate persistence, Scorpio from stubbornness, Capricorn from goal orientation. Both signs manipulate others, Scorpio from an intense willfullness and urge to dominate, Capricorn from a desire to control both yourself and your environment. This combination can indicate success in almost any area, for you have the ability to formulate a goal and apply all of your resources to attaining it.

Natal Scorpio Mercury Progressed to Aquarius: If your Mercury progresses to Aquarius, where it is exalted, you will express your thoughts and philosophies much more readily. (Mercury moves 80-90° by age sixty-five. If it's in the first half of Scorpio natally or moving slowly due to a retrograde position before birth or at any time during your life, it will not progress to Aquarius.) You will not be one bit less stubborn, or less righteous about your philosophies, but you may begin to apply them to larger, more humanitarian issues. Whether or not you have chosen to develop the higher side of your spirit during your life, you are sure that your way of thinking is the only realistic approach to life.

Natal Scorpio Mercury Retrograde by Progression to Libra: The retrograde motion of Mercury implies that the symbolism of Libra will manifest on an inner level until Mercury turns direct. While Mercury is retrograde, you may think about the other person's point of view, but until Mercury is in direct motion you are not too likely to allow the opinions of others to influence your conscious thought.

NATAL VENUS IN SCORPIO

Venus in detriment in Scorpio
Venus keywords: loving, being loved, pleasure self-indulgence

Natal Scorpio Venus Progressed to Sagittarius: When Venus progresses to Sagittarius, you may develop a demand for personal freedom within a relationship while refusing to allow the same freedom to your partner. In the process of idealizing the expression of love, you may prefer to ignore your own possessiveness, and you always ignore your own wandering ways when faced with the real or suspected wandering of your partner.

Natal Scorpio Venus Progressed to Capricorn: If you have not maintained strong relationships while Venus progressed through Sagittarius, the progression to Capricorn may symbolize a growing coldness. You may be afraid that you are really not lovable and may turn to manipulation in order to gain some type of material success through love. On the other hand, if you have established a reasonably stable relationship while Venus was in Sagittarius, you are likely to settle down in that relationship once Venus enters Capricorn.

Natal Scorpio Venus Progressed to Aquarius: Should your progressed Venus reach Aquarius, all of the fixity symbolized by your natal position returns unabated. No one can be more jealous than you. It does not matter that both you and your partner are probably senior citizens; unless you have developed some confidence in your own intrinsic ability to love and be loved, you will still worry that your partner is likely to stray. For those of you who have developed your higher spiritual side, this progression can indicate a willingness to extend love to all of humanity.

Natal Scorpio Venus Retrograde by Progression to Libra: In spite of the fact that the retrograde motion of Venus implies an inner rather than outer manifestation of the symbolism involved, Venus rules Libra. Thus, you can put love and relating in better perspective. You are not as likely to take everything personally after Venus enters Libra. You will be able to develop a sense of beauty and a sense of the intrinsic harmony of life. After Venus turns direct, you will appreciate your love nature and then be able to accept the love of others with much less anxiety.

NATAL MARS IN SCORPIO

Mars is traditional ruler of Scorpio
Mars keywords: energy, initiative, aggression, anger

Natal Scorpio Mars Progressed to Sagittarius: Mars is not weak in Sagittarius, but is not as strong as your natal Scorpio position. Thus the influence of the progression mutes but does not transform your basic method of displaying aggression and drive. After your Mars enters Sagittarius, you may find that you no longer concentrate on the complete destruction of things (or people) who irritate you.

Natal Scorpio Mars Progressed to Capricorn: Mars, exalted in Capricorn, is as strong in this progression as it is in your natal chart. You can channel energy very well now, setting goals and applying the energy needed to reach them. You are much more likely to consider the outcome of your action as well as the effect you wish to have on others before you actually get moving in any area. You are able to defer short term gains for long term success.

Natal Scorpio Mars Retrograde by Progression to Libra: Unless Mars is angular or heavily aspected while in Libra, there will be little apparent effect from the progression of Mars from its traditional rulership to its detriment. The retrograde motion implies a turning of the energy inward, and this may result in a tendency to transfer aggression. You may choose to be the victim of aggression rather than express your own anger directly. Choosing an abusive partner or choosing to associate with violent people often accompanies this particular progression. If you find yourself in these positions, you need to examine your own expression of energy.

NATAL JUPITER IN SCORPIO

Jupiter keywords: expansion, growth, faith, optimism

Natal Scorpio Jupiter Progressed to Sagittarius: Jupiter progresses about 14′ per year (15° in sixty-five years) when direct. Unless your natal Jupiter is in the last half of Scorpio and direct, it won't progress into Sagittarius. Jupiter rules Sagittarius, and once your Jupiter progresses into its own sign, growth and change usually proceed at a rather rapid rate. At worst, you may exaggerate your own importance, while at best you may become a gifted philosopher. You can now discover a heretofore hidden sense of humor as well as an interest in justice, law, and diplomacy.

Natal Scorpio Jupiter Retrograde by Progression to Libra: When Jupiter is retrograde, it moves at most 6° in sixty-five years. Unless your natal Jupiter is in the first decanate of Scorpio and retrograde, it will not progress into Libra. The combination of these natal and progressed positions adds an inner potential for growth and development through partners, friends, or other people. The secrecy of your natal position may gradually lighten as the expansive potential of the Libran position (through partners or through other people) grows into external manifestation. If your Jupiter never turns direct, it may be difficult for you to admit the influence others have on your growth.

NATAL SATURN IN SCORPIO

Saturn keywords: duty, responsibility, reality, restraint

Natal Scorpio Saturn Progressed to Sagittarius: Saturn progresses at most 7' per year when direct. Unless your natal Saturn is in the last seven degrees of Scorpio, it probably won't progress into Sagittarius. When Saturn progresses into Sagittarius, you may choose to embark on serious studies of religion or philosophy. Although this may well lead to mastery of these subjects, you really need to develop a sense of humor along with your studies, for you can become quite dogmatic about your belief systems. The Sagittarius-Scorpio combination can symbolize that particular blend of idealism and practicality known as pragmatism.

Natal Scorpio Saturn Retrograde by Progression to Libra: Saturn only moves about 3° in sixty-five years when retrograde. Unless your natal Saturn is in the first few degrees of Scorpio, it will not progress into Libra. Since Saturn is exalted in Libra, this position can be quite influential in your life in spite of the fact that the retrograde motion implies an inner rather than outer manifestation of your sense of duty and responsibility. After your Saturn has progressed into Libra, you may become involved in providing balance, order, and law in all your interactions with others. This combination is almost the stereotype of the "law and order" person, for the fixity of your natal position remains as a self-righteous belief in your own definition of duty and responsibility, while the progressed position indicates that you share those concepts with others.

NATAL URANUS IN SCORPIO

Uranus in exaltation in Scorpio
Uranus keywords: self-will, change, creativity, inventiveness

Natal Scorpio Uranus Progressed to Sagittarius: If you were born between 1896 and 1898, or through 1980 and most of 1981 you may have Uranus progress form Scorpio to Sagittarius during your life. When Uranus progresses to Sagittarius, your desire to change things shifts to the areas of religion and philosophy where many original concepts are likely to surface.

Natal Scorpio Uranus Retrograde by Progression to Libra: If you were born in March or April of 1975, you may have Uranus retrograde from Scorpio to Libra during your life. Your desires for freedom or change may now shift to the relationships you establish. The tenacity of your natal Scorpio position will still be obvious, for you will either cling steadfastly to a relationship, all the while demanding that your partner change, or you may completely destroy a relationship in order to accomplish the change you're undergoing in your attitude towards relationships. If you can allow others the same freedom you need during this time, the progression won't be difficult.

NATAL NEPTUNE IN SCORPIO

Neptune keywords: imagination, spirituality, unreality, deception, music, art

Natal Scorpio Neptune Progressed to Sagittarius: If you were born at the end of 1969 or during 1970, you may have Neptune progress from Scorpio to Sagittarius (or the reverse) during your life. The influence of the sign position of Neptune is generational rather than personal unless Neptune is angular or heavily aspected by your inner planets. Neptune in Scorpio symbolizes the idealization of sex, or the idealization of concepts of death and rebirth, while Neptune in Sagittarius symbolizes the idealization of philosophy and religion, higher education, and mass ocmmunications.[27]

NATAL PLUTO IN SCORPIO

Pluto in rulership in Scorpio
Pluto keywords: force, dominance, permanent changes, power

Natal Scorpio Pluto Progressed to Sagittarius: Those who will be born in 1995 may have Pluto progress from Scorpio to Sagittarius during their lives. Not only is Pluto generational rather than personal in effect, we don't really know exactly what Pluto in Scorpio will mean. (At the time of this writing, Pluto is about to enter the sign of its rulership.) We can speculate that Pluto in its rulership will symbolize changing world concepts about sex, death, and rebirth, perhaps bringing a new world order. Pluto in Sagittarius might indicate major changes in world concepts of religion and philosophy.[28]

PROGRESSIONS FOR SAGITTARIUS NATAL POSITIONS

SAGITTARIUS: YANG—MUTABLE—FIRE

SUN IN SAGITTARIUS

Sun keywords: basic life force, the physical body, internal "I"

---

[27] For natal Neptune in Scorpio retrograde to Libra (for those born October 1955 to October 1956), see page 217, Neptune in Libra.

[28] For natal Pluto in Scorpio retrograde to Libra (for those born March, April, May, 1984) see page 218, Pluto in Libra.

Natal Sagittarius Sun Progressed to Capricorn. The progressed Sun enters Capricorn between age one week (natal ☉ 29° ♐ 59′) and age thirty (natal ☉ 0° ♐ 00′). When your Sun progresses to Capricorn, you will tend to add a little more realism to your view of yourself and the world. Most Sagittarians do not adopt the sober view of the world common the the Capricorn Sun, although those of you with your natal Mercury in Capricorn may find that this progression sparks your ambition and goal orientation. You will develop a bit more sensitivity to what other people think about you, but you aren't too likely to become as conservative or worried about this as someone with a natal Capricorn Sun.

Natal Sagittarius Sun Progressed to Aquarius: The progressed Sun enters Aquarius between age thirty (natal ☉ 29° ♐ 59′) and age sixty (natal ☉ 0° ♐ 00′). The Sun is in its detriment in Aquarius so this progression is not as strong an influence on your self-image as the Capricorn progression was. You may become a bit more fixed in your idealism or a bit less secure in your desire to jump from one involvement to another.

Natal Sagittarius Sun Progressed to Pisces: The progressed Sun enters Pisces between age sixty (natal ☉ 29° ♐ 59′) and age ninety (natal ☉ 0° ♐ 00′). If your Sun progresses into Pisces, you can develop a more emotional view of yourself. Whether this emotion manifests as sympathy for the other people in your life or maudlin self-pity depends on what you have done to develop your own spiritual potential during your life. You can combine your natal Sagittarius optimism and humor with the Piscean empathy to form close personal relationships, or you can use the less positive sides of both signs to manipulate (or con) everyone around you.

NATAL MOON IN SAGITTARIUS

Moon keywords: emotions, responses to life, habit patterns

Natal Sagittarius Moon Progressed to Sagittarius: Every twenty-eight years, your progressed Moon conjuncts its natal positon in the Moon's growth cycle. During the conjunction, the problems and joys of your natal symbolism are emphasized. You tend to initiate emotional responses. You may be restless, moving from one feeling to another quickly and easily. Your buoyant sense of optimism usually prevents your changes of feelings from becoming unmanageable mood swings. Problems arise when you react before you fully assimilate the emotional impact of an event. You may scatter your emotional responses, thus diluting their effectiveness, or ignore the smaller issues which ultimately prove to be the emotional troublemakers—like dirty socks under the bed and burned dinners. Don't neglect the little things just because your problems are not as big as those of a beggar in Calcutta.

Natal Sagittarius Moon Progressed to Capricorn: The Moon is in its detriment in this sign, and the sign conflicts with your natal position in both polarity and quadruplicity. While your Sagittarius Moon encourages freedom in emotional response, Capricorn indicates restriction or control of response patterns. During this progression you may acknowledge that you need to gain more control over your feelings, but since the progressed Moon is not strong by sign, you may keep planning to control your feelings tomorrow. On the other hand, you may become much more aware of the ways that other people mess up their lives through their inability to control their emotional outbursts without ever making the connection that you may have the same difficulty.

Natal Sagittarius Moon Progressed to Aquarius: This yang air sign signifies the intellectual understanding of emotion, which you, with the fire natal position, really admire. You have lofty ideals anyway, and the addition of the idealism of Aquarius simply makes all of your emotional exchanges flow easily. Any difficult aspects from other progressions or transits will be much easier to handle while your progressed Moon is in Aquarius.

Natal Sagittarius Moon Progressed to Pisces: This is the first quarter of your progressed Moon's emotional cycle. (See Chapter 1, "You Can't Blame Your Mother," page 13, for further discussion of this cycle.) This quarter emphasizes your need to develop and use the yin, or response, side of your emotional nature. Any difficulties that you have with scattered emotional response will be heightened while your progressed Moon is in Pisces. Your mood changes may well turn into moodiness, as it will be more difficult to separate yourself from your feelings. You may be a sucker for a sob story now, particularly if you won't confront your own internal issues. It's a lot easier to worry about, try to help, and in general focus on someone else's problem than to clean up your own emotional act.

Natal Sagittarius Moon Progressed to Aries: Whenever your progressed Moon is in the same triplicity as your natal Moon, your emotional responses flow more easily. Aries lends the initiating energy of cardinality to your normal fire desire to start things. You will react to emotional issues quickly and enthusiastically, the dragonslayer in person. The wonderfully buoyant "I can change it" feeling of this combination should carry you through any problems indicated by transits or other progressions.

Natal Sagittarius Moon Progressed to Taurus: This sign is basically incompatible with your natal position. Because of the strength of the progressed Moon in this sign, where it is exalted, you won't be able to ignore the tension of the inconjunct. The inconjunct itself rarely symbolizes events, but with this as background, all of the transits and other progressions take on added emotional significance. You will have to pay attention to your needs to nurture and be nurtured during this two and a half year period. You may begin to question the depth of your own emotional response.

Natal Sagittarius Moon Progressed to Gemini: This is the halfway point of your progressed lunar cycle. While your progressed Moon is in Gemini, problems arising from both yang initiation of response and mutable scattering of emotions become more obvious. The combination of fire and air indicates that you may spend hours trying to analyze exactly how you feel about nearly everything, but the mutable quadruplicity insures that just about the time that you think you know why you respond in a certain way, you will change your responses entirely.

Natal Sagittarius Moon Progressed to Cancer: This sign is basically incompatible with your natal position. Since the Moon rules Cancer, you will find this more than simply tense or irritating. All of the intellectual understandings that you painfully acquired during the opposition years may be swept away by a tide of emotionalism. The more you try to separate yourself from your feelings, the harder it will be to control or understand those feelings. For you, both inconjunct signs may be more of a problem than the opposition of your progressed Moon to its natal position, particularly if there are difficult transits or progressions occurring during the years that your progressed Moon is inconjunct its natal position.

Natal Sagittarius Moon Progressed to Leo: Whenever your progressed Moon is in the same triplicity as your natal Moon, emotional responses flow more easily. This position is a tremendous relief after the tension of the inconjunct. Now you can be comfortable with initiating emotional responses, and you can forge ahead with renewed fire enthusiasm into new areas of experience. For many of you, the Leo progression feels like emerging from a dark tunnel into the welcome sunlight of a beautiful spring day.

Natal Sagittarius Moon Progressed to Virgo: This is the third quarter of your progressed Moon's emotional growth cycle. You will feel the need to be more practical, more detached, and probably a little cooler in response. You may hop from one emotional involvement to another as the mutable quadruplicity is amplified. If you try to respond (yin) and act (yang) at the same time, you may become rather emotionally inconsistent and may have difficulty deciding how you feel about anything.

Natal Sagittarius Moon Progressed to Libra: While your progressed Moon is in this cardinal air sign, you want to balance your emotional responses, particularly in your relationships. You may attempt to explain away (or rationalize) the inconsistencies of the Virgo years by placing the blame squarely on the shoulders of those involved with you during that time. Nonetheless, this sign indicates an easy integration of emotion in daily life and mutes difficult transits.

Natal Sagittarius Moon Progressed to Scorpio: The sign behind your natal Moon's position often uncovers secret or hidden weaknesses of your natal symbolism. Because the Moon is in its detriment in Scorpio, you may be able to gloss over or ignore many of the lessons of this position. This is unfortunate, for you could learn about your need for yin response patterns and your need for more fixity (or consistency) in emotional response. The most difficult problem that the Scorpio progression could uncover is your dependency needs. You don't like to consider yourself dependent, because that conflicts with your desire for freedom. If the progression of your Moon through Scorpio is strengthened by angularity or major aspects, you may be able to recognize some of these issues. If you do, you have a head start on the changes that could occur during the conjunction of your progressed and natal Moon.

NATAL MERCURY IN SAGITTARIUS

Mercury in detriment in Sagittarius
Mercury keywords: conscious mind, thoughts, actions, manual dexterity

Natal Sagittarius Mercury Progressed to Capricorn: You may gain some realism and practicality in speech patterns and/or in the way your conscious mind works after Mercury enters Capricorn. Because you find Capricorn a bit restrictive, you usually vacillate between the natal and the progressed expression of thought. Sometimes you astound everyone (yourself included) by your patience and forethought, while at other times you use your natal position to blurt out what you really think.

Natal Sagittarius Mercury Progressed to Aquarius: Since Mercury is exalted in Aquarius, the progression to this sign symbolizes an opportunity to put your Sagittarius idealism to use in intellectual and humanitarian pursuits. The addition of fixed air enables you to think through issues, partiuclarly if they involve philosophy. You are more likely to pursue particular goals and less likely to talk before thinking.

Natal Sagittarius Mercury Progressed to Pisces: The progression of Mercury from its exaltation to its detriment won't bring much outward change in your thought patterns. (Mercury won't progress to

Pisces if it's placed natally in the first half of Sagittarius or moving slowly due to retrograde motion before birth or at any time during your life; Mercury moves a maximum of 80-90° by age sixty-five.) If you have chosen to develop the spiritual side of your mind, this progression can indicate a growing empathy and understanding of others. On the other hand, if you have not chosen to develop yourself spiritually, this progression may only symbolize the perfection of your ability to "pass the buck" and avoid responsibility for your own words or deeds.

Natal Sagittarius Mercury Retrograde by Progression to Scorpio: The retrograde motion of Mercury indicates that until Mercury turns direct, you will not make any changes on an external level. Thus as long as the motion is retrograde, you will keep on opening your mouth to stick your foot in it. Nonetheless, you are becoming much more aware of the effect that your words have on other people. Once Mercury turns direct, you will seem to gain mastery over your mouth for you will have learned when to be quiet.

NATAL VENUS IN SAGITTARIUS

Venus keywords: loving, being loved, pleasure, self-indulgence

Natal Sagittarius Venus Progressed to Capricorn: When your Venus progresses to Capricorn, you tend to become more serious about affairs of the heart. As you assume more responsibility within relationships, you may begin to let go of some of your more impractical ideas about life with a loved one. A tree house may be wonderfully romantic, but just does not do as a residence during a snowstorm.

Natal Sagittarius Venus Progressed to Aquarius: The progression of Venus to Aquarius usually indicates that you are becoming more fixed in your expression of love. If you have not established a stable long term relationship before Venus reaches Aquarius, it may be difficult to begin one, for this sign often brings a compassion for the welfare of the masses at the same time that it makes it difficult to be intimate on a one-to-one basis.

Natal Sagittarius Venus Progressed to Pisces: If your Venus progresses to Pisces, where it is exalted, you may be able to combine the influences of the three previous sign positions in a deeper, romantic softness which you can share with those around you. The sympathy and compassion of Venus in Pisces is a gentle influence which tends to deepen all of your relationships. There is an extremely spiritual quality in this placement. If you have developed any of your potential for spiritual growth, the progression of Venus to Pisces may signal a mystical ability to transcend the harsher parts of life in order to recognize the beauty around you.

Natal Sagittarius Venus Retrograde by Progression to Scorpio: The retrograde motion of a planet often implies an inner rather than outer manifestation of the energy of the planet. When Venus progresses to its detriment, Scorpio, you will not recognize a major change in your understanding of your ability to give or receive love except while Venus is angular or heavily aspected. If Venus is aspected strongly after it turns direct, you may discover your jealousy although jealousy is an emotion quite uncharacteristic of natal Venus in Sagittarius. Since your natal position is considerably stronger, you should not get stuck in the obsessive Scorpio expression for any length of time.

NATAL MARS IN SAGITTARIUS

Mars keywords: energy, initiative, aggression, anger

Natal Sagittarius Mars Progressed to Capricorn: Mars is exalted in Capricorn, and once your Mars progresses to Capricorn, you should find it easier to channel your energy and initiative into practical, goal-oriented activities. You should retain enough of your natal humor to avoid the Capricorn pitfalls of unbounded ambition. Once you are able to recognize the absurdity of extreme singlemindedness, you need not worry about your own ambitious use of your energy.

Natal Sagittarius Mars Progressed to Aquarius: Because of the strength of your natal Mars and the direction indicated by the progression of Mars thorugh Capricorn, you should find Mars in Aquarius easy. You will never repress your anger or aggressive drive, so the biggest problem of the fixed sign is not an issue for you. Aquarius may bring an increase in idealism or an increased belief that the way you express energy is the only sane way to do so. You may be right.

Natal Sagittarius Mars Retrograde by Progression to Scorpio: Since Mars is the traditional ruler of Scorpio, this progression is strong in spite of the fact that the retrograde motion indicates that the first expression of energy will be on an inner rather than outer plane. You will begin to direct your initiative, drive, and aggression in a manner designed to bring about results. If Mars turns direct, the combination of natal and progressed symbolism indicates an intensity and an ability to cope with energy that is almost unstoppable.

NATAL JUPITER IN SAGITTARIUS

Jupiter in rulership in Sagittarius
Jupiter keywords: expansion, growth, faith, optimism

Natal Sagittarius Jupiter Progressed to Capricorn: Jupiter progresses about 14' per year, or 15° in sixty-five years. Unless your natal Jupiter is in the last half of Sagittarius, it won't progress into Capricorn. Furthermore, your natal Jupiter is in the sign it rules and progressing into the sign of its fall. It will take extraordinarily strong aspects to ever bring out any Capricorn traits in your expansion or growth potential. While Jupiter actually crosses into Capricorn, you may experience some public award or distinction. Most of you will never notice the dash of practicality that Capricorn can add to your capacity for growth and expansion.

Natal Sagittarius Jupiter Retrograde by Progression to Scorpio: Jupiter progresses at most 6° in sixty-five years when retrograde. Unless your natal Jupiter is in the first six degrees of Sagittarius, it will not retrograde into Scorpio during your life. Your natal Sagittarius position is so powerful that even while Jupiter is aspected or angular, it will be very difficult to see any Scorpio influence on your capacity for faith, your means for growth, or your personal expansion. Not only is your natal position stronger, the retrograde motion implies that the change in energy is not on an outer level but rather on an inner or mental plane. You may become a little more stubborn about your concepts of freedom and justice while your progressed Jupiter is being aspected, or you may become a bit pointed in your sarcasm.

NATAL SATURN IN SAGITTARIUS

Saturn keywords: duty, responsibility, reality, restraint

Natal Sagittarius Saturn Progressed to Capricorn: Saturn only progresses 7' per year, or 8° in sixty-five years. Unless your natal Saturn is in the last seven degrees of Sagittarius, it will not progress into Capricorn. Saturn rules Capricorn and gains considerable strength by this progression. You may become extremely conscious of your own duties and responsibilities. You may also become very hard on yourself, accepting only perfection in the performance of whatever you have decided is your duty. Because of your inner standards of perfection, you may drive your body to the limit of endurance in order to live up to your own internally imposed concept of the upright life. If you can accept a reasonable compromise between the ideal and the reality, you can avoid the life of the workaholic.

Natal Sagittarius Saturn Retrograde by Progression to Scorpio: Saturn progresses about 3° in sixty-five years when retrograde. Unless your natal Saturn is in the first few degrees of Sagittarius and retrograde, it will not progress to Scorpio. The progression of Saturn from Sagittarius to Scorpio symbolizes a narrowing of the areas of life which you choose to accept as your personal responsibility. At the same time, you may increase the amount of responsibility that you assume within these areas. Because the retrograde motion symbolizes a change on an internal, mental level, no one but you is really aware of just how seriously you take your personal responsibility.

NATAL URANUS IN SAGITTARIUS

Uranus keywords: self-will, change, creativity, inventiveness

Natal Sagittarius Uranus Progressed to Capricorn: Those who were born in October, November, or December of 1904, or will be born in early 1988 may have Uranus progress from Sagittarius to Capricorn during their lives. The change to Capricorn indicates that your new ideas now involve authority, government, and business. You may try to institute changes in any of these areas, but more often you simply grumble loudly about these things.

Natal Sagittarius Uranus Retrograde by Progression to Scorpio: Those who were born in February or March of 1981 may have Uranus progress from Sagittarius to Scorpio during their lives. This progression can work in a very positive fashion if you use the fixity of Scorpio to bring the far-ranging ideas of Sagittarius into focus. In this case, the difference between the influences will be the difference between thinking up wonderful ideas and implementing them. In a less positive progression, the Scorpio influence may indicate a growing stubbornness about having your own way when it comes to any changes in your life.

NATAL NEPTUNE IN SAGITTARIUS

Neptune keywords: imagination, spirituality, unreality, deception, music, art

Natal Sagittarius Neptune Progressed to Capricorn: Those who are born in September, October, and November of 1984 will have Neptune progress from Sagittarius to Capricorn during their lives. The sign position of Neptune is generational rather than personal in effect unless Neptune is angular or heavily aspected by the inner planets. Neptune in Sagittarius seems to symbolize an idealism or mysticism in religion and philosophy. Neptune has not entered Capricorn at the time of this writing. Neptune in Capricorn could indicate an idealistic approach to government, business, or authority figures.[29]

NATAL PLUTO IN SAGITTARIUS

This position will not occur during this century.

---

[29] For natal Neptune in Sagittarius retrograde to Scorpio (for those born March or April 1970), see page 226, Neptune in Scorpio.

PROGRESSIONS FOR CAPRICORN NATAL POSITIONS

CAPRICORN: YIN—CARDINAL—EARTH

NATAL SUN IN CAPRICORN

Sun keywords: basic life force, the physical body, internal "I"

Natal Capricorn Sun Progressed to Aquarius: The progressed Sun enters Aquarius between age one week (natal ☉ 29° ♑ 00') and age thirty (natal ☉ 0° ♑ 00'). The Sun is in its detriment in Aquarius, so this progression will not help you to develop your self-image. Although Aquarius symbolizes personal freedom, your natal fears of rejection will probably keep you from any action which could bring loss of status within the community. If you can let go of some of your Capricornian inhibitions about how other people see you, you can use the Aquarius unconventionality to add spice to your fairly orderly life.

Natal Capricorn Sun Progressed to Pisces: The progressed Sun enters Pisces between age thirty (natal ☉ 29° ♑ 59') and age sixty (natal ☉ 0° ♑ 00'). The effect of the Pisces symbolism on your self-image depends to a large extend on your choices about personal and spiritual development. If you have attempted to develop the higher side of yourself, then Pisces can symbolize a growing understanding of how everyone needs emotion, sympathy, and strokes. If you are really not interested in spiritual development, the Pisces progression may indicate a growing desire and ability to manipulate others through emotion, or a desire to escape the consequences of your own actions.

Natal Capricorn Sun Progressed to Aries: The progressed Sun enters Aries between age sixty (natal ☉ 29° ♑ 59') and age ninety (natal ☉ 0° ♑ 00'). If your Sun progresses to Aries, where it is exalted, you will develop a much stronger self-image. This increased strength of expression does not of itself indicate a positive or negative outcome. Whether you can enjoy this as self-esteem or you find that this increases your dissatisfaction with the status quo depends on the choices about self-development you have made up to now in your life.

NATAL MOON IN CAPRICORN

Moon in detriment in Capricorn
Moon keywords: emotions, responses to life, habit patterns

Natal Capricorn Moon Progressed to Capricorn: Your progressed Moon conjuncts its natal position every twenty-eight years in the progressed Moon's growth cycle. When it returns to your natal sign, you must deal with the problems and joys inherent in your natal Moon's symbolism. You need to confront your desire to control both your own expression of emotion and the emotional expression of others. You often find it difficult to let your emotions show, for you are desperately afraid of rejection. You classify your feelings as "bad" or "good," regardless of whether psychologists tell you that this is unrealistic. You assume full responsibility for your negative feelings, using them as a kind of internal proof that you are not a good person. Your stern and righteous attitude towards yourself can leave you with an emotional insecurity which appears as coldness to other people. You have to forgive yourself for being a human being and therefore imperfect before you can free yourself from the fear of losing emotional control. Even if you lose control of your emotions, it is unlikely that you will immediately run amok.

Natal Capricorn Moon Progressed to Aquarius: When your Moon progresses into Aquarius, you try to analyze your response patterns. Because of the yin-yang difference between natal and progressed symbolism, you may try to respond and act at the same time, which gives rise to emotional ambivalence. You may become even more goal-oriented as you rationalize your desire to control your emotional responses. When the Aquarian energy prompts you to examine why you feel the way you do, you become very tense because you're afraid that your reasons are "bad" or materialistic or (worst of all) silly. If you're externalizing this position by associating with someone who has a great many Aquarian traits, you'll find that the Aquarian person is going to keep trying to get you to talk about how you feel, creating even more strain.

Natal Capricorn Moon Progressed to Pisces: When your progressed Moon is in Pisces, you gain some sensitivity, flexibility, and a more instinctual responsiveness. This is a good working combination, although you may manipulate others through emotion. Any hard aspects from transits or other progressions will be eased while your progressed Moon is in the sign sextile your natal Moon.

Natal Capricorn Moon Progressed to Aries: This is the first quarter of your progressed Moon's emotional growth cycle. (See Chapter 1, "You Can't Blame Your Mother," page 13, for further discussion of this cycle.) Your natal yin Moon indicates that you prefer to absorb fully the impact of emotional events before responding, but the yang progressed symbolism prompts you to react immediately. This conflict can result in rather erratic swings between the two extremes of emotional behavior. Aries often symbolizes the very lack of control that you fear the most.

Natal Capricorn Moon Progressed to Taurus: Whenever your progressed Moon is in the same triplicity as your natal Moon, your emotional response flows more easily. The Moon is exalted in Taurus, so you feel a positive strengthening of your response patterns. Taurus increases your desire to nurture and protect, and at the same time reinforces your emotional practicality. No matter how hard the other transit or progressed symbolism may be, you are not likely to question your emotional base while the progressed Moon is in Taurus.

Natal Capricorn Moon Progressed to Gemini: This sign is basically incompatible with your natal position. The Gemini symbolism indicates strongly mental response patterns as well as a yang reactive pattern. Your basic nature shies away from scattering emotion. You want to be in control of what you are feeling. When you try to analyze your feelings, you uncover your fear that you are not a good person, so you would rather stay away from that shaky ground. The result is an internal tension which, although not indicative of events, adds to the emotional impact of any other difficulties encountered while your progressed Moon is in Gemini.

Natal Capricorn Moon Progressed to Cancer: This is the halfway point of your progressed lunar cycle. Since the Moon rules Cancer, the combination of the opposition to your natal position and the strength of your progressed Moon here can pose certain problems. The high level of emotional response and extreme fluctuation of that response symbolized by the progressed Moon in Cancer shake up the careful controls you have set up regarding emotion. You may struggle with issues directly connected to parenting (either being a child or being a parent or both) during this opposition. Your real problem concerns who will control emotional expression. Will you control your children or will you allow them to control themselves? Will you control your own expression of emotion or will your parents control your expression? This last question is not limited to the first opposition, which occurs in adolescence, for many people, stuck in adolescent patterns of response with their parents at age forty-two, find that Mom or Dad can still churn them into an emotional frenzy.

Natal Capricorn Moon Progressed to Leo: This sign is basically incompatible with your natal Capricorn feeling nature. The tension between regulating your responses and showing them won't come out directly, for the inconjunct rarely indicates outer events. Nonetheless, any other aspects from transits or progressions will be played out against a background of tension. Many people with a Capricorn natal Moon deal with this by simply becoming involved with a person who has strong Leo traits. Then the overreacting isn't yours, nor is the show-and-tell emotional display. If you can control the relationship and get that Leo to tell you how it feels to be a Leo, you don't have to risk anything.

Natal Capricorn Moon Progressed to Virgo: Whenever your progressed Moon is in the same triplicity as your natal Moon, your emotional response flows more easily. Virgo reinforces your natal symbolism of practicality and adds a tendency to separate from your response patterns. Although the mutability may indicate a tendency to scatter your responses, diluting their effectiveness, you are in general much more comfortable with your emotions during this two and a half year period.

Natal Capricorn Moon Progessed to Libra: This is the third quarter of your emotional growth cycle. You again have to deal with a yin-yang difference between your natal and your progressed Moon positions, and any problems of cardinality will become more obvious. The Libra tendency to mentally balance emotion conflicts with your natal Capricorn fear of discovery. You need to let go of your guilt. You may be able to do so during this progression, as the Libran energy can allow you to see that your feelings are not so very different from those of the people around you.

Natal Capricorn Moon Progressed to Scorpio: Although the Moon is in its fall in Scorpio, this position is quite compatible with your natal sign. You are more likely than ever to hide your emotions. You also feel things more intensely while your progressed Moon is in Scorpio, and may hang onto feelings longer. This position eases the influence of difficult transit or other progressed aspects, for you have an underlying strength in your response patterns.

Natal Capricorn Moon Progressed to Sagittarius: The sign behind your natal sign often uncovers hidden weaknesses in your natal position. Sagittarius symbolizes ideas and the idealization of emotion. The freedom-loving qualities of this sign underscore the tremendous effort all that Capricorn self-control demands of you. If you can start to question your need to completely control your feelings, you will have a wonderful base from which you can grow during the conjunction.

NATAL MERCURY IN CAPRICORN

Mercury keywords: conscious mind, thoughts, actions, manual dexterity

Natal Capricorn Mercury Progressed to Aquarius: When your Mercury progresses to Aquarius, its exaltaion, this indicates a widening of your areas of interest. If you are working towards your own spiritual growth, the Aquarian idealism may help free you from worry about what other people think. If you are not too interested in spiritual pursuits, you may find the progression indicates a growing stubbornness concerning your own ideas and goals. In this case, you may stick to your own ideas without paying any attention to the ideas of others.

Natal Capricorn Mercury Progressed to Pisces: Mercury is in its detriment in Pisces. Thus this progression will not have the impact that the progression into Aquarius had. You may discover an added flexibility of thought or an increased ability to rationalize your own thoughts and actions.

Natal Capricorn Mercury Progressed to Aries: Mercury moves a maximum of 80–90° by age sixty-five. If it's in the first half of Capricorn natally or moving slowly due to a retrograde position just before birth or at any time during your life, it won't progress to Aries. If Mercury does progress into Aries, you may find that you are much more willing to express your ideas openly and rather forcefully. You've spent a lot of time developing a unique style of thought; now you want to express this to other people. Unless you have developed an ability to pay attention to the ideas of others, you may find that nobody else wants to listen to you.

Natal Capricorn Mercury Retrograde by Progression to Sagittarius: Because Mercury is in its detriment in Sagittarius, and because the effect of retrograde motion is expessed internally rather than externally, you won't notice this progression unless Mercury is heavily aspected or angular, or unless your natal Sun is in Sagittarius. While Mercury is being aspected, you will find that you can express yourself more easily, as the symbolism of Sagittarius loosens some of the controlling tendencies indicated by your natal Capricorn position. You may find a growing optimism (or sense of humor) in your speech, although you'll probably retain the dry wit associated with Capricorn. You'll be able to dream bigger dreams, although actually implementing them will probably wait until Mercury goes direct.

NATAL VENUS IN CAPRICORN

Venus keywords: loving, being loved, pleasure, self-indulgence

Natal Capricorn Venus Progressed to Aquarius: When your Venus progressed to Aquarius, you may find a way to escape your Capricornian fears of rejection by relating to groups of people rather than to one other person. Now you can rally behind a wonderful humanitarian cause, allowing yourself to love the masses (particularly if the masses you love live very far away) without risking loss on a personal level.

Natal Capricorn Venus Progressed to Pisces: Even though Venus is exalted in Pisces, this may not be an easy transition for you if you got involved in intellectual mind games about love and your own lovableness while Venus was in Aquarius. The idea of love is no longer sufficient. You discover a romantic, shy, sympathetic self under your coolness and your practicality. If you have become extremely fearful of love and were sure during your Capricorn and Aquarius years that you were completely unlovable, you may release the Pisces energy through daydreams and fantasies about perfect love. If you can understand that you don't have to be perfect to be loved, you can form a close relationship now.

Natal Capricorn Venus Progressed to Aries: If Venus should progress to Aries, you won't really notice it as a change, for Venus is progressing from a sign of exaltation to a sign of detriment. At most, the yang energy of Aries may prompt you to take a chance on initiating a relationship. However, if the relationship isn't wonderful instantly, you are likely to return to your Pisces dreams of gossamer and moonbeams.

Natal Capricorn Venus Retrograde by Progression to Sagittarius: Even though the retrograde motion implies an inward expression of the energy of Venus, this change can be quite dramatic because Venus is expressed so differently in Sagittarius. As Venus changes sign you may find that the things and people you love, or your concept of your own lovableness, is somehow public knowledge. Your new needs for freedom (Venus in Sagittarius) will be hard to control (natal Venus in Capricorn). You may vacillate between open expression of love and fear of rejection (or loss).

NATAL MARS IN CAPRICORN

Mars in exaltation in Capricorn
Mars keywords: energy, initiative, aggression, anger

Natal Capricorn Mars Progressed to Aquarius: Because of the strength of your natal position, the progression of Mars into Aquarius does not usually alter your manifestation or expression of energy. While Mars in angular or heavily aspected, you are likely to ignore the opinions of others, stubbornly hanging onto your own concepts.

Natal Capricorn Mars Progressed to Pisces: Mars is not any stronger in Pisces than it was in Aquarius, so this progression won't add any more to the expression of your energy than the Aquarius did. You may scatter your energy or misdirect some of your aggressive drives if Mars is heavily aspected or angular while in Pisces.

Natal Capricorn Mars Retrograde by Progression to Sagittarius: Not only is Mars stronger in your natal position of Capricorn, the retrograde motion implies an internalization of the energy expression. Thus you won't see a change in your initiative, drive or competitive instincts after Mars enters Sagittarius unless Mars is angular or heavily aspected. In this case, you will find that an increased involvement in outdoor sports can act as a release for your excess energy.

NATAL JUPITER IN CAPRICORN

Jupiter in fall in Capricorn
Jupiter keywords: expansion, growth, faith, optimism

Natal Capricorn Jupiter Progressed to Aquarius: Jupiter only moves about 14' per year, or 15° at most in sixty-five years. Unless your natal Jupiter is in the last half of Capricorn, it won't progress into Aquarius. The nonconformity of this fixed air sign may encourage you to loosen up a bit in order to grow in new ways. Whether or not you will be able to develop the freedom to grow in the many directions indicated by this progression depends largely on your own choices. If you can recognize and discard your self-defeating patterns, you may find a new world opening up with Jupiter in Aquarius. On the other hand, you may choose to ignore the fact that your own fears block your possibilities for positive growth. In this case, the progression may merely symbolize your discontent with the status quo, with no real indication that you can change your old habits.

Natal Capricorn Jupiter Retrograde by Progression to Sagittarius: When Jupiter is retrograde, it only progresses 6° in sixty-five years. Unless your natal Jupiter is in the first six degrees of Capricorn, it will not progress into Sagittarius. With Jupiter progressing from its fall to its rulership, the inward symbolism of the retrograde motion is somewhat muted. You will probably feel the change strongly enough to show it on an outer as well as inner level. While you may never be quite as expansive as your friend with Jupiter in Sagittarius natally, you will reach for the growth and expansion symbolized by this position. If there are any other transiting or progressed aspects to either your natal or progressed Jupiter when your Jupiter crosses into Sagittarius, you may be recognized by other people or receive some sort of award.

NATAL SATURN IN CAPRICORN

Saturn in rulership in Capricorn
Saturn keywords: duty, responsibility, reality, restraint

Natal Capricorn Saturn Progressed to Aquarius: Saturn progresses about 7' per year, or 8° maximum in sixty-five years. Unless your natal Saturn is in the last decanate of Capricorn, it will not progress into Aquarius. Since Saturn is the traditional ruler of Aquarius, this position reinforces the strength of Saturn in your chart. The only problem with all this Saturn strength is rigidity, for you may get firmly entrenched and believe that your way is the only possible way to approach anything. Since you usually succeed with your approach, it is very difficult for you to pay attention to other people who differ from you in method. As long as you refrain from trying to control how everyone in the world does things, your strong Saturn should bring considerable success.

Natal Capricorn Saturn Retrograde by Progression to Sagittarius: When Saturn is retrograde, it progresses at most 3° in sixty-five years. Unless your natal Saturn is in the first three degrees of Capricorn and retrograde, it will not enter Sagittarius. The retrograde motion implies an inward rather than outward manifestation of change, and your natal Saturn is in its rulership, so there will not be a major change accompanying this progression. You may turn your attention to religion, philosophy, or law, but you will work in these areas as if Saturn were still in Capricorn. Do watch the year that Saturn crosses from Capricorn to Sagittarius, for if there are any other transits or progressions to your natal or progressed Saturn, you will be in the public eye. Since Saturn brings exactly what you deserve, use the years before Saturn crosses into Sagittarius to insure that you'll like what you deserve.

NATAL URANUS IN CAPRICORN

Uranus keywords: self-will, change, creativity inventiveness

Natal Capricorn Uranus Progressed to Aquarius: Those who were born in November or December of 1911, January 1912, or will be born in November and December 1995 and January 1996 may have Uranus progress from Capricorn to Aquarius during their lives. When Uranus progresses into Aquarius, which it rules, you may become more aware of your desire for intellectual freedom. You may want to change things because of humanitarian interests or from a simple desire to alter the existing environment. Occasionally you may become quite stubborn about the inherent justice or rightness of your own ideas and insist that all changes take place in exactly the manner you have decreed.

Natal Capricorn Uranus Retrograde by Progression to Sagittarius: Those who will be born between March and May, 1988 will have Uranus retrograde from Capricorn to Sagittarius during their lives. These people will be changing from an unconventional approach to career, profession or authority to unusual concepts of religion, philosophy or mass communications. In 1904, when Uranus entered Capricorn last, it did not retrograde into Sagittarius. It will be interesting to watch our children respond to this progressed change.

NATAL NEPTUNE IN CAPRICORN:

Although Neptune will enter Capricorn in January 1984, it will not enter Aquarius until January 1998. At the time of this writing, Neptune has been in neither Capricorn nor Aquarius, so any analysis of this progression would be completely speculative.

NATAL PLUTO IN CAPRICORN

This position will not occur during this century.

PROGRESSIONS FOR AQUARIUS NATAL POSITIONS

AQUARIUS: YANG—FIXED—AIR

NATAL SUN IN AQUARIUS

Sun keywords: basic life force, the physical body, internal "I"

Natal Aquarius Sun Progressed to Pisces: The progressed Sun enters Pisces between age one week (natal ☉29°♒59′) and age thirty (natal ☉0°♒00′). When your Sun progresses into Pisces, you will find that whichever spiritual path you have chosen in your life will be amplified. For the humanistic reformer, the Pisces influence brings some flexibility and concern for other people. Pisces brings the rebellious hermit confusion about goals. Occasionally, Pisces can stimulate your ability to convince yourself that the end justifies the means.

Natal Aquarius Sun Progressed to Aries: The progressed Sun enters Aries between age thirty (natal ☉29°♒59′) and age sixty (natal ☉0°♒00′). Since the Sun is exalted in Aries, this progression symbolizes a greater ability to express yourself openly. You will find that you are quicker to choose a path and better able to aggressively pursue your objectives. You won't take advice or criticism any better, but you can change your mind with a little less pain.

Natal Aquarius Sun Progressed to Taurus: The progressed Sun enters Taurus between age sixty (natal ☉29°♒59′) and age ninety (natal ☉0°♒00′). If your Sun progresses into Taurus, you will solidify all the growth you've attained through the other progression. The strength of the Aries progression now appears as habit within you as Taurus reinforces your natal Aquarian fixity. You will be a bit more practical about when you choose to climb up on your soapbox, although in spite of the Taurus influence, you won't abandon your pet reforms.

NATAL MOON IN AQUARIUS

Moon keywords: emotions, responses to life, habit patterns

Natal Aquarius Moon Progressed to Aquarius: Your progressed Moon conjuncts its natal position every twenty-eight years in the progressed Moon's emotional growth cycle. The conjunction brings out both the joys and the liabilities inherent in your natal Moon position. When your natal Moon is in Aquarius, you have an unconventional or unusual emotional response pattern. You seek emotional freedom, tend to be rebellious, and constantly analyze emotion. During the conjunction years, you must deal with problems stemming from your belief that your feelings are not the same as the feelings of others. Whether or not there is any objective reality to this belief, it brings considerable loneliness as you worry about emotional sterility. If this worry becomes a central part of your life, you may find it difficult to express any emotion at all.

Natal Aquarius Moon Progressed to Pisces: No sign of the Zodiac is more antithetical to emotional sterility than Pisces. When your Moon has progressed to this sign, you experience a conflict between thinking and feeling. You may attempt to use the flexibility of Pisces to manipulate others for your own ends. Even if you recognize your internal yin-yang conflict, this intensifies your own insecurity concerning appropriate emotional responses. You're likely to go back and forth between emotional outbursts and stubborn adherence to your fixed methods of coping.

Natal Aquarius Moon Progressed to Aries: This position reinforces your natal yang method of initiating responses. While your progressed Moon is in Aries, you may prefer to react before assimilating the complete impact of emotional situations. The combination of "do" and "think" may preclude "feel" as part of your emotional repertoire. Nonetheless, the excellent working relationship between natal and progressed positions indicates that any difficult aspects from transits or progressions happening at this time will be eased by the emotional stability symbolized by your progressed Moon.

Natal Aquarius Moon Progressed to Taurus: This is the first quarter of your progressed Moon's growth cycle. (See Chapter 1, "You Can't Blame Your Mother," page 13, for further discussion of this cycle.) The Moon is exalted in Taurus, so your internal conflict between acting and responding will be intensified. The earth symbolism of Taurus demands that you recognize and respond to your feelings. Although both natal and progressed Moon are in fixed signs, the habit patterns that you have formed may have to be broken while your progressed Moon squares your natal Moon.

Natal Aquarius Moon Progressed to Gemini: Whenever your progressed Moon is in the same triplicity as your natal Moon, your emotions flow more easily. The analytical bent of mutable air encourages your desire to separate from emotion in order to gain an intellectual understanding of your feelings. You can talk about feelings, explain feelings, and start to grasp some of the reasons you feel the way you feel. You are always more comfortable when you have good reasons for your responses.

Natal Aquarius Moon Progressed to Cancer: Not only is this sign basically incompatible with your natal position, the Moon rules Cancer. Thus, the tensions inherent in the inconjunct position are intensified. When the Moon is in its rulership it is impossible to ignore your need for some yin patterns of emotional response. You won't be able to rationalize the mood swings which accompany this progression. Cancer demands that you acknowledge your own irrational patterns of emotional response. While the inconjunct does not usually indicate events, this sets up a background of tension that intensifies any other difficult aspects from transits or progressions.

Natal Aquarius Moon Progressed to Leo: This is the halfway point in your lunar growth cycle. After the tension of the two and a half years of Cancerian influence, the opposition may seem to be a reaction against irrational emotional moodiness. You may try to avoid yin responses at all costs, separating yourself from your feelings as much as possible. This avenue often backfires, because in order to cope with the events accompanying the opposition, you usually need to use both yin and yang within your nature. Your growth at this opposition point depends on your ability to integrate your responsive and reactive nature.

Natal Aquarius Moon Progressed to Virgo: This sign is basically incompatible with your natal Moon's position. This inconjunct is not as difficult as the Cancer inconjunct for the Moon is not as strong in Virgo. You can identify with the Virgo tendency to withdraw from open expression of emotion, but the yin symbolism of waiting until all the factors are assembled before responding in an emotional situation is more difficult to assimilate.

Natal Aquarius Moon Progressed to Libra: Whenever your progressed Moon is in the same triplicity as your natal moon, the flow of emotion is eased. During this two and a half year period you can achieve a balanced emotional calm. Now you can develop intellectual under-standing of why you do what you do. As long as the waters appear unruffled, you will be content with the smooth surface of your response nature. You will be able to cope with any kind of problem in an evenhanded, reasonable manner.

Natal Aquarius Moon Progressed to Scorpio: This is the third quarter of your progressed Moon's emotional growth cycle, and the Moon is in its fall. Consequently, the difficulties of the square to your natal position are increased by the possibility of a negative expression of emotional energy. You may become quite suspicious of the motives of others and jealous of the responses of those close to you. Scorpio stirs up the depths of your feeling nature, bringing out your completely irrational habits and responses. Although you really hate change, the power of your internal emotional conflicts may push you towards choosing which patterns you wish to eliminate.

Natal Aquarius Moon Progressed to Sagittarius: This fire sign, compatible with your natal air Moon, is a relief after the Scorpio years. Although this position tends to scatter your response patterns, diluting their effectiveness, it lessens the painful intensity of feeling uncovered during the Scorpio square. Now you can idealize the realm of emotion, seeking larger (and less personal) issues to catalyze your response patterns.

Natal Aquarius Moon Progressed to Capricorn: The sign behind your natal sign often uncovers hidden weaknesses of your natal position. Because the Moon is in its detriment in Capricorn, you are more likely to come across the drawbacks of your Aquarius Moon after the fact, when you can't do much but think about them. Your unconventional response patterns are often impractical. Furthermore, your desire for emotional freedom yields little control of either your own emotional response or the responses of others. Consistent yang reaction to events precludes forethought. A yin response allows you to judge and control both your personal response and the response of others to you. If you can use the input of the Capricorn progression to begin a process of change within yourself, the conjunction years will be much easier.

NATAL MERCURY IN AQUARIUS

Mercury in exaltation in Aquarius
Mercury keywords: conscious mind, thoughts, actions, manual dexterity

Natal Aquarius Mercury Progressed to Pisces: When Mercury pro-gresses from its exaltation to its detriment, you may not notice any immediate change in your speech or thought patterns. Eventually the Pisces influence may soften some of your stubbornness. If you have followed a path of spiritual growth, you may discover that you are paying more attention to individual people and their needs as well as the needs of the greater society. On the other hand, you may find that the Pisces influence only increases your confusion and lessens your practicality.

Natal Aquarius Mercury Progressed to Aries: There is slightly more influence from the Aries progression of Mercury than the Pisces position primarily because the fire sign is more compatible with your natal air sign. Now you can express your Aquarian opinions directly. Although Aries does not add to the practicality of those opinions, it does encourage you to take action concerning your thoughts. The cardinal influence seems to encourage you to instigate action along your natal fixed lines.

Natal Aquarius Mercury Progressed to Taurus: If your Mercury progresses into Taurus, you may finally become more practical in your manner of speech. (It will not progress to Taurus if natally Mercury is placed in the first half of Aquarius or is moving slowly due to a retrograde position just before birth or at any time during your life; Mercury moves a maximum of 80-90° by age sixty-five.) At the very least, you may figure out when to be quiet so that you don't antagonize others. However, the double fixity (natal and progressed positions) may indicate that you are even more stubborn and single-minded about the correctness of your belief systems.

Natal Aquarius Mercury Retrograde by Progression to Capricorn: Mercury is exalted in Aquarius, and the retrograde motion implies an inward rather than outward manifestation of the energy of the position. You won't notice the addition of practicality and forethought in a conscious manner until after Mercury turns direct. Once Mercury is direct, the influence of the third (Virgo) decanate of Capricorn, which Mercury rules, may be strong enough to add persistent consideration of the outcome of your actions. This can be a strong indication of eventual success, for the combination of unconventionality and practicality can result in an ability to change things from within the existing structure.

NATAL VENUS IN AQUARIUS

Venus keywords: loving, being loved, pleasure, self-indulgence

Natal Aquarius Venus Progressed to Pisces: When your Venus progresses into Pisces, where it is exalted, you will start to express a softer, more romantic kind of love. If you have staunchly defended or verbalized your Aquarian conception of love, you may have a bit of difficulty reconciling yourself to the romantic idealism which now affects the way in which you give and receive love. You are more vulnerable in love situations, but this very vulnerability allows you to set up rewarding intimate relationships. Since Venus is strong in Pisces, you will probably incorporate much of the Piscean symbolism into your attitude towards love.

Natal Aquarius Venus Progressed to Aries: Venus is in its detriment in Aries, and except for the time that Venus actually crosses over into Aries or while it is aspected or angular, you won't notice a major change. The time that Venus enters Aries is an event-oriented period, particularly if there are any other aspects from progressed or transiting planets to trigger this position. Marriage is always a possibility when progressed Venus is involved in any aspect position, but crossing into this cardinal sign can indicate any event which brings your personal relationships to the public eye.

Natal Aquarius Venus Progressed to Taurus: Venus rules Taurus. After your Venus progresses to this sign, the truly affectionate, warm, comfortable side of your love nature will blossom. If you have been able to develop your self-image as a loving, responsive person, you will find ease in relationships and peace with your surroundings. If you have retained your natal fear that your love responses are unlike anyone else's, the Taurus symbolism may merely signify a possessive, self-indulgent materialism.

Natal Aquarius Venus Retrograde by Progression to Capricorn: The retrograde motion of Venus implies an inward rather than outward manifestation of the changing symbolism. You may try to control your responses in love situations. Venus in Capricorn symbolizes a fear of rejection in love situations, and Venus in Aquarius symbolizes an intellectual approach to intimate relationships. The combination can indicate a tendency to analyze all your relationships, thus distancing yourself from true intimacy. You need to let go of the "shoulds" and "oughts" that you attach to relating, one set from your natal Aquarian ideal of the perfect relationship and the other set from the progressed Capricorn implication that duty and responsibility are always part of love.

NATAL MARS IN AQUARIUS

Mars keywords: energy, initiative, aggression, anger

Natal Aquarius Mars Progressed to Pisces: When your Mars progresses into Pisces, you may find that it is more difficult to define your aggressive tendencies, as your own motives become confused. Sometimes this confusion can lead you to transfer your anger to people who really had nothing to do with the irritation in the first place. Because your natal Mars is in a fixed sign, you may have difficulty believing that you could be the cause of the anger you perceive around you.

Natal Aquarius Mars Progressed to Aries: Once your Mars progresses to Aries, its rulership, any confusion from the Pisces progression will be relieved. You can now develop a strong, open expression of your own initiative and drive. In fact, when Mars crosses into Aries, there may be an event which requires immediate, decisive action. Because of the strength of Mars in its rulership, you won't have a problem with immediate action. Although you may develop a tendency to act before thinking, this progression is almost always positive. You don't have to bottle up your energy anymore; you can use it to achieve whatever goals you set for yourself.

Natal Aquarius Mars Retrograde by Progression to Capricorn: Mars is stronger in Capricorn, where it is exalted, than it is in Aquarius. Thus, although the energy of a planet in retrograde motion is usually manifested on an inner rather than outer level, you will find that you can control and direct your expression of energy, drive, ambition and aggression more easily once Mars is in Capricorn. Once Mars turns direct, you will show the self-control symbolized by Capricorn in an ability to work tirelessly towards defined goals.

NATAL JUPITER IN AQUARIUS

Jupiter keywords: expansion, growth, faith, optimism

Natal Aquarius Jupiter Progressed to Pisces: Jupiter progresses a maximum 14' per year, or 15° in sixty-five years. Unless your natal Jupiter is in the last half of Aquarius, it won't progress into Pisces. When your Jupiter progresses to Pisces, its traditional rulership, imagination, service to others, and a kind of mystical idealism become more important to you as avenues of expansion. The higher or more spiritual meaning of Jupiter in Pisces involves kindness, sympathy, and a strong desire to help others. If you do not choose to develop the higher side of your personality during this life, you may find that the progression symbolizes the growth of impracticality in your life. You may spend time dreaming and planning great castles in the air without actually bringing any of these schemes into reality. Or you may use the versatility of this position to become a fairly accomplished con artist.

Natal Aquarius Jupiter Retrograde by Progression to Capricorn: Jupiter moves about 6° in sixty-five years when retrograde. Unless your natal Jupiter is in the first decanate of Aquarius, it won't retrograde into Capricorn. Since Jupiter is in its fall in Capricorn, and retrograde motion implies an inner rather than outer effect, the influence of this progression may be very subtle except while Jupiter is angular or being aspected. This really means that you aren't likely to notice any change in your means and methods of growth or expansion, or in your expression of optimism or humor except when Jupiter is aspected or angular. During those times you may develop a practical circumspection about your own growth patterns.

NATAL SATURN IN AQUARIUS

Saturn in traditional rulership in Aquarius
Saturn keywords: duty, responsibility, reality, restraint

Natal Aquarius Saturn Progressed to Pisces: Saturn progresses at most 7' per year, or 8° in sixty-five years. Unless your natal Saturn is in the last decanate of Aquarius, it won't progress into Pisces. When your Saturn progresses from Aquarius to Pisces, the change brings little outward alteration of your behavior concerning duty or responsibility, unless Saturn is angular or heavily aspected since Saturn, the traditional ruler of Aquarius, is more powerfully expressed through your natal sign. You may choose to view the needs of others in terms of duty or responsibility, or you may become quite rigid about your belief that others must help themselves out of their own predicaments.

Natal Aquarius Saturn Retrograde by Progression to Capricorn: When Saturn is retrograde, it only moves about 3° in sixty-five years. Unless your natal Saturn is in the first few degrees of Aquarius and retrograde, it will not progress to Capricorn. Your Saturn is progressing from its traditional rulership to its rulership. You have excellent self-control, are ambitious, and have a strong determination to succeed. You accept responsibility well and in fact have great difficulty delegating responsibility. You may have considerable doubt about your own self-worth. If Saturn turns direct, you will find that your self-image improves. Even if Saturn never turns direct, you are likely to achieve your goals, probably because you have spent so many years working towards them.

NATAL URANUS IN AQUARIUS

Uranus in rulership in Aquarius
Uranus keywords: self-will, change, creativity, inventiveness

Natal Aquarius Uranus Progressed to Pisces: If you were born in 1919 or January 1920, you may have Uranus progress from Aquarius to Pisces during your life. Uranus is in its rulership in Aquarius; thus this progression may not influence your behavior patterns much at all. When your Uranus progresses into Pisces, if you see any difference, it may involve seeking release from unconscious motivations. This position often confuses practical change with impractical dreams, making it difficult for you to actually implement the changes you think about.

Natal Aquarius Uranus Retrograde by Progression to Capricorn: Those who were born between June and September 1912, as well as those who will be born in April or May 1995, may have Uranus retrograde from Aquarius to Capricorn during their lives. Uranus is much stronger in its rulership than in the sign Capricorn, so there is little likelihood that the retrograde motion (which implies an internalization of the energy) of Uranus to Capricorn will bring any overt behavior change. While you may develop some unconventional attitudes towards authorities, you probably won't actually say or do too much about this.

NATAL NEPTUNE IN AQUARIUS

This position will not occur during this century.

NATAL PLUTO IN AQUARIUS

This position will not occur during this century.

PROGRESSIONS FOR PISCES NATAL POSITIONS

PISCES: YIN—MUTABLE—WATER

NATAL SUN IN PISCES

Sun keywords: basic life force, the physical body, internal "I"

Natal Pisces Sun Progressed to Aries: The progressed Sun enters Aries between age one week (natal ☉29°♓59') and age thirty (natal ☉0°♓00'). When your Sun progresses to Aries, where it is exalted, you gain strength and courage in self-expression. You will be able to assert yourself more easily. If you do not choose to look at why you need to assert yourself, you may find that this new courage is based on a foundation of sand. Depending on the path you choose to follow in this life, the Aries progressed Sun can symbolize either a more positive feeling about yourself or a tendency to become more self-centered.

Natal Pisces Sun Progressed to Taurus: The progressed Sun enters Taurus between ages thirty (natal ☉29°♓59′) and age sixty (natal ☉0°♓00′). After your Sun progresses into Taurus, the changes which occurred during the thirty years that your progressed Sun was in Aries become solidified into your personality. If you became more self-centered, you will become more stubbornly so as your Sun progresses through Taurus. If, however, you used the Aries years to develop a positive sense of self-worth, you can become more relaxed with this projection while your progressed Sun is in Taurus.

Natal Pisces Sun Progressed to Gemini: The progressed Sun enters Gemini between age sixty (natal ☉29°♓59′) and age ninety (natal ☉0°♓00′). If your Sun progresses into Gemini, you will find that you are quite open to new and different experiences as a senior citizen. You will adapt well to changing circumstances and changing surroundings and may choose to initiate changes within your life. The flexibility indicated by both natal and progressed Sun in mutable signs means that you will be comfortable no matter what your surroundings. You may choose to develop your intellectual curiosity through new studies, or through gossip, but it will be hard for you to ignore this part of your self-expression.

NATAL MOON IN PISCES

Moon keywords: emotions, responses to life, habit patterns

Natal Pisces Moon Progressed to Pisces: Your progressed Moon conjuncts its natal position every twenty-eight years in its emotional growth cycle. The conjunction brings out the joys and the difficulties inherent in your natal Pisces position. You are extremely emotional; you sense the emotions of others and respond to them. You may have difficulty separating your own emotions from the emotions of those around you. You may cry easily and may willingly sacrifice yourself for others. Because of the strength of your response nature, you may not be able to understand or define the causes of your mood swings.

Natal Pisces Moon Progressed to Aries: The conflict between the yang expression indicated by this progressed position and your natal yin response nature often leads to frustration if you try to act on emotional input while you are responding to it. Most of you will simply ignore the Aries symbolism except during the time that your progressed Moon aspects other planets. Then you will find that you really want to do something about the things that are happening during this period.

Natal Pisces Moon Progressed to Taurus: Not only is the Moon exalted in Taurus, this position is quite compatible with your natal position. You will be able to cope with anything that arises during this two and a half year period with little emotional turmoil. You will nurture, protect and support the other people in your life and will find that others respond with support for you. Any difficult aspects from progressions or transits are eased by the position of your progressed Moon.

Natal Pisces Moon Progressed to Gemini: This is the first quarter of your progressed Moon's emotional growth cycle. (See Chapter 1, "You Can't Blame Your Mother," page 13, for further discussion of this cycle.) You will be dealing with problems of scattered responses. When you respond to every emotional nuance around you, it is difficult to sort out the important issues from the trivial. Gemini brings out your need to act on as well as repond to emotion. Furthermore, Gemini encourages you to think about why you feel the way you do. Intellectual analysis of feeling is difficult for you; you may try almost anything to avoid this. You may actually get around this part of the symbolism by forming a friendship with someone who analyzes feeling constantly. Then all the irritation of an intellectual approach to feeling can be manifested through this friend.

Natal Pisces Moon Progressed to Cancer: Whenever your progressed Moon is in the same triplicity as your natal Moon, your emotions flow more easily. Since the Moon rules Cancer, you may wallow in a flood of emotion, for Cancer reinforces the sensitive, caring potential of your natal position. This may be a case of too much of a good thing; you may have some difficulty during this progression if you allow your emotions to completely dominate your life. In this case, you may respond so strongly to your feelings that you cannot react logically at all. Nonetheless, you should not have much difficulty with other transits or progressions during this two and a half year period.

Natal Pisces Moon Progressed to Leo: This position is basically incompatible with your natal sign position. The yin-yang difference indicates tension whenever you try to act and respond at the same time. Leo often involves not only acting on emotional input, but openly displaying your feelings, while your natal mutability indicates sudden shifts in feelings. Then the Leo display can backfire as your emotions change in the middle of an event!

Natal Pisces Moon Progressed to Virgo: This is the halfway point in the emotional growth cycle of your progressed Moon. Problems connected with yin responses and with mutability are underscored during this two year period. You may try to separate your response patterns into neat little areas in order to put these responses into some practical order. You may recognize that fluctuation of response is a problem. You may be spending so much time dealing with the emotional problems of others that you effectively avoid looking at your own problems.

Natal Pisces Moon Progressed to Libra: This sign is basically incompatible with your natal position. Pisces symbolizes a total commitment to emotional response, while Libra symbolizes consideration for both the social consequences of emotion and a sensitivity to social appearances in the demonstration of emotion. The yang nature of Libra tends towards initiation of response, while your natal desire is to avoid this. Since your Moon's energy is expressed more easily through your natal position, you may develop magnificent hindsight about what you should have done in social situations while your progressed Moon is in Libra.

Natal Pisces Moon Progressed to Scorpio: Although the Moon is in its fall in Scorpio, this position is the same triplicity as your natal Pisces so the flow of emotion is easier. Scorpio may signify problems of jealousy or suspicion about another's motives. Nonetheless, the fixity of the water sign should help direct your emotional energy and cut down the enormous mood swings. Other aspects from transits or progressions will be eased by this progressed Moon sign position.

Natal Pisces Moon Progressed to Sagittarius: This is the third quarter of your progressed Moon's emotional growth cycle. While your Moon is in Sagittarius, you may have problems with scattered responses. You need to use some of your new yang initiative to extricate yourself from some of the extremes of feeling inherent in your natal Pisces symbolism. Since Sagittarius symbolizes the idealization of emotion, it may be very difficult for you to achieve much self-control while your progressed Moon is in this sign.

Natal Pisces Moon Progressed to Capricorn: The Moon is in its detriment in Capricorn, but this sign is quite compatible with your natal position, and Capricornian control of emotion is usually very positive for you. You need some restriction in areas of response, and the coolness of Capricorn can help you achieve this. Unless you use the energy of this progression to control and manipulate others, this can be the most positive position of your progressed Moon's cycle.

Natal Pisces Moon Progressed to Aquarius: The sign behind your natal sign often uncovers hidden weaknesses of your natal position. While your progressed Moon is in Aquarius, you may become much more aware of the drawbacks inherent in complete surrender to emotional input. The yang nature of Aquarius symbolizes acting on emotional input rather than passively accepting whatever comes. Furthermore, the fixity of Aquarius may emphasize your need for focus and stability in emotional situations. You may develop a belief that freedom in emotional response can only be obtained when you have some control over and intellectual understanding of your own responses. On the other hand, you may simply become hysterically stubborn about your feelings.

NATAL MERCURY IN PISCES

Mercury in detriment in Pisces
Mercury keywords: conscious mind, thoughts, actions, manual dexterity

Natal Pisces Mercury Progressed to Aries: When your Mercury progresses into Aries, you can start to assert your own brand of thinking more loudly. If you are one of the Pisces Mercury people who combine the left and right brain into logical sequences, you may be quite intolerant of people who do not agree with your opinions or with people who are not as brilliant as you are. If you are predominantly intuitive, you may develop the courage to actually sell your art or to promote your own creativity.

Natal Pisces Mercury Progressed to Taurus: When your Mercury progresses into Taurus, you gain strength from the double yin placement of natal and progressed Mercury. Now you can fully develop the strength of the yin, responsive side of your conscious mind. You can collect your scattered thought processes into a more coherent package. Be careful, though, for you can easily slip into mental habits or ruts. Since your natal Pisces Mercury doesn't need reasons for beliefs, you may become prone to prejudging situations after your Mercury enters Taurus.

Natal Pisces Mercury Progressed to Gemini: If your Mercury progresses into Gemini, which it rules, you will become both more flexible and more articulate. (Mercury moves a maximum of 80-90° by age sixty-five. If it's in the first half of Pisces natally or moving slowly due to a retrograde position just before birth or at any time during your life, Mercury will not progress to Gemini.) Sometimes this flexibility only means that you rationalize all kinds of behavior. If you choose this means of expression, you can be really rude and then rationalize this as "telling it like it is." Fortunately, most of you don't get involved in this kind of verbal bullying. For many, the progression roughly coincides with retirement and indicates that you can finally investigate all the things you've been curious about for years.

Natal Pisces Mercury Retrograde by Progression to Aquarius: Mercury is stronger in the sign of its exaltation than in the sign of its detriment. Thus, although the retrograde motion implies that you'll internalize the symbolism of Mercury in Aquarius, you will find it easier to direct your train of thought. You are better able to concentrate on the matters at hand. Once your Mercury turns direct, this is one of the stronger combinations possible in the progressed chart. Aquarius is the symbol of the left brain (logical) idealist, and Pisces is the symbol of the right brain (intuitive) romantic. With this combination you are the only one who can limit the spiritual growth you can achieve.

NATAL VENUS IN PISCES

Venus in exaltation in Pisces
Venus keywords: loving, being loved, pleasure, self-indulgence

Natal Pisces Venus Progressed to Aries: After your Venus progresses into Aries, you may start to wonder why you have been hiding the romantic side of your persona. Venus is stronger in your natal position of Pisces, where it is exalted, than it is in Aries, which is its detriment. The only overt effect of this progression will be the growing desire to express your Pisces natal traits. When Venus crosses into Aries, there may be an event (such as a marriage or engagement announcement, or a gossip column about you) which brings your love relationships into the public eye.

Natal Pisces Venus Progressed to Taurus: When your Venus progresses into Taurus, the combination of natal exaltation and progressed rulership indicates that Venus is likely to be one of the important symbols of your chart. There are two sides to this Venus energy, one that is soft and loving, the other, self-indulgent and rather lazy. None of us can escape some influence from both symbolisms. Venus alone will not indicate which of these manifestations you choose to embrace. At one end is the indolent bonbon muncher, surrounded with lush fabrics, pillows and poodles. At the other extreme is Grandma and Grandpa surrounded by adoring, loving offspring, radiating love and kindness. Both of these are exaggerations which only occur in the natal Venus in Pisces daydreams. However, once your Venus enters Taurus, you will try to have parts of either or both of these fantasies materialize in your daily life.

Natal Pisces Venus Progressed to Gemini: The strength of Venus in both Taurus and Pisces means that even if your Venus reaches Gemini, you won't notice any change in your feelings about the things and people you love. You may flirt some or change your mind a bit more while Venus is being aspected in Gemini, but either of these responses could be as easily attributed to your natal Pisces position as to your progressed Gemini placement.

Natal Pisces Venus Retrograde by Progression to Aquarius: Since your natal Venus is exalted in Pisces, and since the retrograde motion implies an inner manifestation of the changing energy, you are not likely to notice a major change in your attitude towards the things and people you love after Venus enters Aquarius. Once your progressed Venus turns direct, you may add some humanistic ideals to your romanticism. You may become quite upset about social injustice, or you may become involved in neighborhood beautification projects. If you have a tendency to hide your romantic nature, you may use the Aquarius position to intellectualize your need for beauty and harmony in daily life, neatly circumventing the problem of admitting romanticism while allowing yourself some outlets for it.

NATAL MARS IN PISCES

Mars keywords: energy, initiative, aggression, anger

Natal Pisces Mars Progessed to Aries: When your Mars progresses into the sign that it rules, you can shed a lot of your natal indecision. The mere presence of Mars in Aries does not mean that you will suddenly make all of the right or best choices about the application of your energies, but it does mean that you will make choices. If you prefer to ignore the underlying causes of aggression, you may continue to misdirect your energy. However you choose to use your internal drive, you will do so with much more force. You may confound those who know you by blowing up over trivial matters. If you can't or won't acknowledge the causes for your anger, or if you refuse to recognize that you are angry at all, the Aries influence can symbolize some rather startling outbursts of temper. On the other hand, you may choose to associate with someone who has a violent temper in order to allow the expression of aggression without acknowledging your own anger.

Natal Pisces Mars Progressed to Taurus: There are two very different effects possible from this progression. The one you manifest seems to be directly connected to the way you incorporated the energy of progressed Mars in Aries. If you took the Pisces position and insisted that you are never angry, the Taurus progression may indicate that you are now trying to repress all expressions of aggression. If you are doing this, you will find that the same things bother you over and over again. If it seems that people are doing certain things only to annoy you, you may need to look at why you are annoyed by these things in the first place. Are you setting yourself up so that someone else will display Mars energy for you? On the other hand, you may have chosen to develop a fairly open and clear means of expressing aggression while your progressed Mars was in Aries. If your reality includes the possibility that you can be angry, very, very angry and not destroy things, then you probably won't notice the change of Mars from Aries to Taurus.

Natal Pisces Mars Retrograde by Progression to Aquarius: The combination of natal Pisces and progressed Aquarius symbolizes a blending of personal and humanitarian idealism. The retrograde motion of Mars indicates that the change of expression will not occur in an outward fashion until Mars turns direct. Thus you may still have a problem expressing aggression. Although the fixity of Aquarius encourages you to focus your energy, you will not be more open in your expression of irritation. You may be more structured in your display of energy, or you may choose to transfer this energy to a soapbox type of idealism. Throwing darts at a poster of a current political figure may not directly address the causes of your anger, but the ability to throw darts at all allows you to release aggression in a nondestructive manner.

NATAL JUPITER IN PISCES

Jupiter in traditional rulership in Pisces
Jupiter keywords: expansion, growth, faith, optimism

Natal Pisces Jupiter Progressed to Aries: Jupiter only progresses 14' per year, or about 15° in sixty-five years. Unless your natal Jupiter is in the last half of Pisces, it won't progress to Aries. Jupiter is the traditional ruler of Pisces, so your natal expression of energy will probably remain the predominant influence on your patterns of growth throughout your life. While Jupiter is being aspected or is angular, you will expand through personal expression. You may gain public recognition or acclaim, particularly during the year that your Jupiter enters Aries.

Natal Pisces Jupiter Retrograde by Progression to Aquarius: Jupiter progresses about 6° in sixty-five years when it is retrograde. Unless your natal Jupiter is in the first six degrees of Pisces and retrograde, it won't enter Aquarius. Most people don't notice this change at all, for Jupiter is much stronger in Pisces (its traditional rulership) and the retrograde motion implies an internal change. If your Jupiter is heavily aspected, the Aquarian symbolism may indicate that you are directing your natal Piscean idealism towards bringing about change in the world at large.

NATAL SATURN IN PISCES

Saturn keywords: duty, responsibility, reality, restraint

Natal Pisces Saturn Progressed to Aries: Saturn progresses at most 7' per year, or 8° in sixty-five years. Unless your natal Saturn is in the last decanate of Pisces, it won't progress to Aries. Saturn is in its fall in Aries, where it symbolizes either a limitation of your self-expression or difficulty in defining the limits of your personal responsibility. During the year that Saturn enters Aries, you may receive public recognition. The events of this year depend on what you've done before Saturn reaches Aries, for Saturn never brings you anything you don't deserve.

Natal Pisces Saturn Retrograde by Progression to Aquarius: When Saturn is retrograde, it progresses about 3° in sixty-five years. Unless your natal Saturn is in the first three degrees of Pisces and retrograde, it won't enter Aquarius. Saturn is stronger in Aquarius, its traditional rulership, than in Pisces. Thus, this progression usually indicates that you can change your attitude towards duty, responsibility, and restriction in spite of the fact that the motion is retrograde. You can start to work with the belief that personal responsibility leads to personal freedom. Your concern for others, indicated by your natal position, now can center on developing the means to achieve freedom through hard work and persistence.

NATAL URANUS IN PISCES

Uranus keywords: self-will, change, creativity, inventiveness

Natal Pisces Uranus Progressed to Aries: Those of you born in January, February, March or December of 1927, or January 1928, will have Uranus progress from Pisces to Aries during your life. Uranus in Pisces symbolizes a desire to change hidden or unconscious motivations, while Uranus in Aries indicates a desire to reform yourself. You will find that you turn from trying to elevate all of humanity to trying to elevate yourself. You accomplish this through radical changes in how you control your temper or desire nature.

Natal Pisces Uranus Retrograde by Progression to Aquarius: If you were born in June, July, or August of 1919, you may have Uranus progress from Pisces to Aquarius during your life. In spite of the fact that the retrograde motion usually implies an inner manifestation of energy, Uranus is moving into its rulership. Therefore, you are very likely to show this progression through a stronger desire to use your creative, inventive side. You may vacillate between worrying about appearing unconventional and doing outrageously unusual things.

NATAL NEPTUNE IN PISCES

This position will not occur during this century.

NATAL PLUTO IN PISCES

This position will not occur during this century.

WHAT CAN WE RELEASE?

PROGRESSING THE NODES OF THE MOON

Nodes are the points where the orbit of the Moon or any other planet crosses the plane of the earth's orbit. Although all the planets have nodes (except the Sun, because the planets' orbits are around the Sun) the nodes of the Moon seem to have the greatest influence in the analysis of the astrological chart.[30]

If you imagine the Moon's nodes as a dragon, the North Node is the head of the dragon, and the South Node is its tail. When the dragon moves forward, she drags her tail along with her but does not spend her time looking at her tail, or even thinking about it too much. If she gets too interested in her tail, she will either go around in circles or simply sit down and go nowhere.

The North Node symbolizes the area of life you need to use or expand in order to grow and move forward. The South Node symbolizes the area of life that you need to release in order to accomplish that growth. It's easy to sit down and contemplate your South Node. Whenever you are stuck with matters indicated by the South Node position, you are probably sitting still or going in circles rather than growing. Your North Node is not necessarily harder to pursue than your South Node, but you do have to get up and start moving.

---

[30] Recently there has been some controversy over the use of the so-called "true" node instead of the "average" node. The choice of names for the two positions is unfortunate, for it implies erroneously that the "true" node is more precise than the "average" node. This impression is further complicated by the fact that the "average" node moves at a regular rate, or three minutes per day in retrograde motion, while the "true" node varies from this rate. The difference between the two nodes is a difference in the means of calculation.

I used both positions for a number of years, and I found the "average" node more frequently aspected exactly (orb of 10' or less) by conjunction, square or opposition at the time of events. I've talked to other astrologers who insist they have done similar studies with the opposite results. Even though the separation between the two positions is not usually more than a degree or so, when you are using secondary progressions, you need aspects more exact than that. You may want to try both positions in your charts before making a decision.

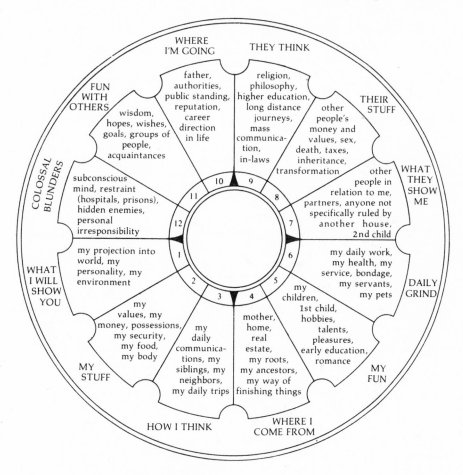

Figure 4.1 Basic house meanings.

Each chart has this symbolic dragon wending her way across a particular house axis. The sign placements of the nodes indicate the ways that the energy of growth or stagnation will manifest. The houses indicate the areas of life most heavily involved.

Nodes, like interceptions, emphasize the fact that opposite houses involve similar principles. Houses one through six, the northern hemisphere houses, are inner-directed, concerned with you on a personal level, while houses seven through twelve are external, or concerned with your relationship to the outer world.

Figure 4.1 provides keywords for the houses. The connections between opposite houses are not always clear, for when we learn house meanings, we usually don't learn them in terms of pairs of opposites. Not to mention that astrologers don't agree on the meaning of each house. These house descriptions are what I use in my practice.

The first house—"what I show you"—is the persona you exhibit in the world, or your personality. It's also your environment and your interaction with the world right around you. Some astrologers also include early childhood experiences in the first house. The experiences of childhood which remain in your conscious mind, like the kind of house and the part of the country you lived in, are first house matters. However, the things about growing up that you incorporated into your subconscious mind (all those tapes from Mom, Dad, Aunt Ethyl, and your first grade teacher) are not first, but twelfth house matters.

The seventh house—"what you show me"—is the "not-me," or everyone and everything that isn't you, with the exception of the specific other people (usually relatives) who are indicated by the third, fourth, fifth, ninth and tenth houses. When I refer to "others" I mean people outside your family. The seventh house tells how you relate to others in the world, and how they relate to you. It is the house of partnerships and marriage, the most intimate relationship you can set up, as well as the house of more distant relationships in that it indicates how you deal with unfriendly people (those who don't like you, or in older terms "open enemies").

The second house—"my stuff"—indicates your personal value system. All the things you value are related to the second house. Your money, your possessions, your food, your personal security needs (Linus's blanket, the twelve cans of soup in the cabinet, the ten dollar bill in your underwear drawer), and your body are second house matters.

The eighth house signifies "their stuff" and how you relate to "their stuff." So it's other people's values, money, and possessions. It is inheritance (when you get something that belonged to someone else) and taxes (when you have something that belongs to someone else, i.e., the government). It is sex, or relating your body to someone else's body. The eighth house is also death, which changes or transforms you into another.

The third house—"how I think"—involves your daily communications. Third house communications are the kind you don't really prepare in advance, for this part of your conscious mind works without much effort. You don't usually rehearse most conversations or spend time thinking about what you'll say if your friend Sally calls on the telephone. These are third house communications, third house thinking. The third house includes your brothers and sisters, and your neighbors. Most of us relate to these specific people in pretty automatic ways. We see (or have seen) a great deal of them and don't regard communication with them as extraordinary. The third house includes your daily commute or trips to the store, and thus usually includes your car. The third house traditionally involves short letters, but most of us have replaced short notes with telephone conversations.

The ninth house—"how they think"—brings communication to a higher plane. Religion, philosophy, higher education, all the "biggies" concerning how other people think and how you relate to those ideas, are ninth house matters. Mass communication (books, television, radio) are all connected to the ninth house. Long distance journeys (which put you in touch with foreign or different ways of thinking) are in the ninth house.

The fourth house—"where I come from"—involves your roots, the home you grew up in and the home you set up for yourself. In this connection, the fourth house indicates your real estate holdings, although if you own quite a bit of property the second house is also involved. The fourth house includes your mother, for she is a large part of your concept of where you come from. How you finish your daily tasks is a fourth house matter. Everyone finishes cooking dinner or getting dressed somehow, and the fourth house indicates how you do it.

The tenth house—"where I'm going"—arises from the fourth of where I come from, taking this out into the world. Your career and your direction in life are tenth house matters. The tenth house also includes your reputation or public standing, for this is the result of your choices about where you want to go. Authority figures and your father are indicated by the tenth house.

The fifth house—"my fun"—involves all the things you do or can do in your leisure time. It includes children, the first child specifically. For women, the fifth house is the first pregnancy. Your talents or hobbies are fifth house matters, as are your romances and your early education.

The eleventh house—"fun with others"—relates your talents and your interests to the interests of other people. The groups you choose to join, the acquaintances you make through these interests are eleventh house matters. The eleventh house includes your long range goals in areas other than career, and your hopes and wishes. An old definition of the eleventh house includes wisdom, which is really a measure of whether or not you are satisfied with your goals.

The sixth house—"my daily grind"—involves your daily responsibilities and work, both at home and on the job. It's the parts of your routine which don't require lots of thought or preplanning. Most sixth house work eventually becomes nearly automatic, e.g., we don't usually spend hours planning how to wash the clothes. The sixth house also includes your health, in that it signifies how you take out the stress on your body. When you are under pressure, do you get headaches, stomach aches, stiff muscles? These are sixth house health matters. The sixth house is traditionally the house of slavery. We don't talk too much about that today, but it is relevant, for the sixth house shows how you put yourself in bondage to others. It's the kind of automatic service you perform that you probably don't notice, but it's like the grain of sand in the oyster. If the grain of sand isn't too big, it can turn into a pearl. If it becomes a major issue, resentment builds and that piece of sand can make the oyster's life quite difficult. The sixth house is also the way you treat people who work for you, like the tv repair man, and the kind of people you hire. Your pets are also shown in the sixth house.

The twelfth house—"colossal blunders or personal irresponsibility"—involves all the things about yourself you'd rather not show to other people. It is your subconscious mind, and all the things the "grown-ups" told you not to do while you were little. Although you may do them anyway, you're sure to feel guilt about them and usually don't like to admit that you do (or avoid doing) the things indicated by the sign on the twelfth house. The twelfth house is both how you restrict yourself through these subconscious beliefs and how others restrain you, either through prison or hospitalization. The service part of the twelfth house almost always involves working with people who are in one way or another restrained or restricted. Through twelfth house service you can help yourself and others release the mental or physical bonds which impede growth. In this context, the twelfth house symbolizes spiritual enlightenment.

Although the sign position of the nodes indicates the manner in which you grow and the manner in which you release your excess baggage, the average node moves 4°43′ in ninety days (equal to ninety years of life in a secondary progression). Thus, the nodes will only change sign during your life if they are in the first four degrees of a sign. The nodes will not form any new aspects to natal positions during your life. The progression of the secondary cusps will carry the nodes to different houses in the secondary chart, although they won't do more than progress from one side of a natal cusp to the other side of the same cusp.

Because of these facts, your natal nodal axis exerts the most influence in your life. The progressed house positions of the progressed nodes work as adjuncts to the basic behavior patterns indicated by your natal positions. The following section delineates the possible house changes of the nodes as your chart progresses. To use this section, look up the house position of your natal North Node. The first delineation, your natal potential, is followed by the meaning of each progressed house position.

NATAL NORTH NODE IN THE FIRST HOUSE, SOUTH NODE IN THE SEVENTH

You must forge ahead on the strength of your own ego-projection. When you get overly involved in the needs or demands of partners or other people, your progress in life is impeded. You tend to allow other people to dominate your life, all the while resenting this domination. You must let go of others if you are ever to be able to help either yourself or them.

First House North Node—Seventh House South Node Progressed to Twelfth—Sixth Houses: When your nodes progress to the twelfth and sixth houses, you may try to get around your South Node dependence on other people by becoming much more involved with daily responsibility or work. If you can retain the direction of your first house North Node, you can use the twelfth house position to uncover your own subconscious motivations. When you can understand why (or how) you restrict your own progress, you won't need to place yourself in bondage or service to others through your sixth house South Node.

First House North Node—Seventh House South Node Progressed to Eleventh—Fifth Houses: When the progression carries your nodes to the eleventh and fifth houses in your progressed chart, you can realize your leadership abilities if you have been following your North Node. If you are still mired in the South Node, you will find that the other people who are demanding your time and attention are the children (literally or figuratively) of seventh house partnerships. If you don't have any children, you can rest in your South Node through involvement in hobbies or leisure activities rather than following your North Node into leadership of groups.

First House North Node—Seventh House South Node Progressed to Tenth—Fourth Houses: After your Nodes are carried to the tenth and fourth houses by progression, you may receive the recognition due you for all of your North Node work, or you can attribute the lack of growth in your life to your home situation. Often those who consistently refused to grow along their North Node path become rather reclusive, staying at home (fourth house) after the South Node reaches this house in the progressed chart.

NORTH NODE IN THE TWELFTH HOUSE, SOUTH NODE IN THE SIXTH

When you have this natal position, you must not allow work and routine to dominate your life. You can easily get lost in the details of day-to-day life, losing your ability to move foward towards understanding your own subconscious input. Unless you investigate the ways you restrict yourself, you may allow others to demand constant service from you. This sixth house service doesn't encourage your growth, it just keeps you busy fixing this and fetching that. If you feel like the maid, butler, chauffeur, cook and handyman rolled up into one, you're probably in your South Node. If your service is uplifting you and others, you're probably working through your North Node.

Twelfth House North Node—Sixth House South Node Progressed to Eleventh—Fifth Houses: When the progression of the chart brings your North Node to the eleventh house and your South Node to the fifth, you may turn from a workaholic into a hobby-a-holic! If you can release the pull of the South Node, you can offer your spiritual (or psychological) understanding selflessly to a wider community or group of people.

Twelfth House North Node—Sixth House South Node Progressed to Tenth—Fourth Houses: If you have chosen to pursue your North Node, the progression of the chart that brings the North Node to your tenth house and the South Node to your fourth symbolizes your ability to combine your spiritual or psychological understandings with your career. If you have chosen to live from your South Node, the progression brings a concentration on home or finishing day-to-day matters. This can be rather isolating and sometimes leave you bitter, for it will seem that you did everything you were supposed to do, you worked hard, you paid attention to details, and now you are all alone.

Twelfth House North Node—Sixth House South Node Progressed to Ninth—Third Houses: If the progression of the chart brings your nodes to the ninth and third houses, you have a lifetime of choices to review and communicate. If you have forged ahead with your North Node, working on personal and spiritual development to the best of your ability, the ninth house symbolism suggests a focus on philosophy, religion, and a larger world view. Those of you who have followed the line of least resistance (South Node) may find that the progression brings a trivialization of whatever successes you have achieved.

NORTH NODE IN THE ELEVENTH HOUSE, SOUTH NODE IN THE FIFTH

You may become extremely involved in either romantic interludes or time-consuming hobbies, so involved that you lose sight of your life's goals. You also lose the ability to relate to groups of people outside of the narrow confines of romance or hobbies. If you remain stuck in your fifth house expression, you may experience quite a bit of frustration because your growth depends on formulating clear goals as well as sharing your abilities and talents with the rest of the world through involvement with groups.

Eleventh House North Node—Fifth House South Node Progressed to Tenth—Fourth Houses: When the progression of your chart brings your nodes to the tenth and fourth houses, those of you who have chosen to stay with your South Node expression now have a specific group, the family, to blame for your lack of progress. Those of you who chose to move in the direction of your North Node find that your career can be separated from your family and may become the vehicle for the realization of your eleventh house goals.

Eleventh House North Node—Fifth House South Node Progressed to Ninth—Third Houses: When the nodes progress to the ninth and third houses, you may become preoccupied with shallow communications or daily trivia if you are sitting in your South Node. You know all of the latest gossip, go to all the cocktail parties, and trip lightly through tinsel town. Others with this same nodal position who have chosen to develop their North Node become involved with philosophy or higher learning. You may travel to increase your knowledge or at least read extensively.

Eleventh House North Node—Fifth House South Node Progressed to Eighth-Second Houses: If you are following your North Node, the progressed eighth house brings the impetus to question or investigate society's values relative to your natal eleventh house goals. The transformation of the eighth house indicates that you are likely to bring about change in either your goals or in your view of society's values. You may inherit money which forces you to choose between the materialistic second house South Node and the other-directed eighth house North Node. If you've coasted through life with your South Node, you are measuring your worth by how much you've acquired. Even if you've amassed a fortune, you can't really be satisfied, for life is more than silver spoons or large bank accounts.

NORTH NODE IN THE TENTH HOUSE, SOUTH NODE IN THE FOURTH

You often find that the demands of your home are such that your home constantly interferes with your career. If you do not strive to separate the needs of your home and family from your own career needs, you may go nowhere, either at home or in a career. You resent mightily the family which impedes your progress. Those of you who choose to follow the South Node rarely recognize this as a choice, feeling that you had to devote your life to home and family.

Tenth House North Node—Fourth House South Node Progressed to Ninth—Third Houses: When your progression carries your nodes to the ninth and third houses, you may join in shallow communication, filling your days with gossip and neighborhood gatherings, complaining about what you could have done if it weren't for your family situation. If, however, you have managed to work out a compromise between home and career which allows you to follow your North Node without abandoning your family, you can embrace the ninth house areas of philosophy or higher learning as the next logical extension of your life direction.

Tenth House North Node—Fourth House South Node Progressed to Eighth—Second Houses: When the progression of the chart brings the

North Node to the eighth house and the South Node to the second, you may find that family connections have now saddled you with a load of possessions which must be guarded. It's hard to enjoy life while you are adjusting the burglar alarm and positioning the fourteenth lock on the door. On the other hand, if you have decided to develop the North Node side of yourself, this progression will bring an eighth house transformation to your concepts of success. You may change the philosophies adopted while your North Node was in the ninth house or question and change the values of those around you.

Tenth House North Node—Fourth House South Node Progressed to Seventh—First Houses: If the progression of your chart brings your North Node to your seventh house, you find that your senior citizen years bring either recognition for accomplishment or alienation from other people. Those of you who pursued your North Node can receive through others in the seventh house the recognition symbolized by the natal tenth house position. Those who chose to relate through the South Node find that when the South Node is in the first house, they have only themselves left, along with all of their possessions.

NORTH NODE IN THE NINTH HOUSE, SOUTH NODE IN THE THIRD

Your South Node position symbolizes preoccupation with trivia, talkativeness, and endless curiosity, while your North Node indicates a desire to forge ahead through higher learning, travel, religion or philosophy. If you allow yourself to become preoccupied with learning a little bit about everything, you may never learn much about anything. You are the college student who is tempted to listen to all of the problems of your roommates or neighbors rather than study. You are the homemakers who allow neighbors or siblings to usurp all of your spare time, making higher education an impossibility. In order to follow the North Node in the ninth house, you have to learn to say "no" to shallow chit-chat and idle gossip. If you learn to extend and focus your curiosity you can develop the North Node side of yourself.

Ninth House North Node—Third House South Node Progressed to Eighth—Second Houses: When the progression of your chart brings your North Node to your eighth house and your South Node to your second, inquisitiveness may turn to acquisitiveness if you are living from the South Node. In doing this, you abandon the philosophical ideals of the North Node in the ninth as you concentrate on material or worldly success. If success is measured in fur coats and fancy cars, you will probably be quite successful. Those who choose to follow the North Node now have to deal directly with the values of others. You will find that your own values have to go through a period of transformation in order for you to grow any further.

Ninth House North Node—Third House South Node Progressed to Seventh—First Houses: As the progression of your chart brings your North Node to your seventh house and your South Node to your first house, those who have worked to develop a cogent life philosophy find that this results in an ability to form true and lasting relationships. In contrast, those who have chosen to follow the easier path of the South Node find that the self-involvement symbolized by the South Node in the first effectively bars you from deep relationships. Looking out for Number One may yield material success but often does not result in psychological peace.

Ninth House North Node—Third House South Node Progressed to Sixth—Twelfth Houses: If you have followed your ninth house natal North Node by studying a larger philosophy of life and expressed the eighth house progression by examining other value systems, then transferred this involvement to the others in your life during the seventh house progression, you'll find considerable pleasure and peace in your daily routine as a senior citizen. If you always followed the path of least resistance in the South Node, you have accumulated a great store of surface knowledge, a pile of possessions, have spent a while wondering why others don't want you to tell them what to do, and are left with twelfth house dreams of what might have been.

NORTH NODE IN THE EIGHTH HOUSE, SOUTH NODE IN THE SECOND

This nodal axis is a particularly difficult position, for at the South Node you are constantly aware of the material world and your position relative to it. The North Node in the eighth house symbolizes your need to give up societal values in order to be reborn into a higher value system. The death and rebirth symbolism of the eighth house suggests the need for complete release of material possessions before you can move ahead in this life. However, if you don't do anything towards your North Node, you'll still get a lot of things or material possessions through your South Node.

Eighth House North Node—Second House South Node Progressed to Seventh—First Houses: Frequently you will not recognize your choices concerning these two natal paths until the chart progression has carried your nodes to the seventh and first houses. The second house is your own possessions and your own value system, while the eighth house is the values of society and the possessions of the other people in your life. While it isn't too hard to tell which is which with possessions, it is often difficult to separate your own value system from the values of the society you are in. After the nodes are in the seventh and first of your progressed chart, you must choose between the South Node self-absorption and accumulation of wealth (natal second house, progressed first house) and the North Node direction of reaching out to the others in your life and understanding their values.

Eighth House North Node—Second House South Node Progressed to Sixth—Twelfth Houses: This progression (North Node in the sixth, South Node in the twelfth) adds to the difficulties of the natal North Node in the eighth, South Node in the second. We're supposed to look at our subconscious motivations in order to gain spiritual enlightenment. At least a lot of people have made a lot of money telling us this, through books on psychology, self-analysis, and spiritual growth. You, however, can get lost wandering through psychoanalysis or various spiritual studies without gaining more than confusion and a stock of buzz words. Your North Node path isn't self-analysis. You have to buck the values of society to follow your North Node and pay attention to the nitty-gritty details of the daily grind. Spiritual enlightenment comes to you when you stop hunting for it.

Eighth House North Node—Second House South Node Progressed to Fifth—Eleventh Houses: If you've consistently followed your South Node, you can pass out "instant analysis" or "spiritual enlightenment" when your South node is in your progressed eleventh house. You have, after all, learned all the appropriate words. You are not likely to value these words too much, because that's not the path of your growth. At best, you'll confuse the people you preach to, at worst you'll impede their growth, because you'll be laying your natal second house South Node (materialism) through the first house (self-absorption) then the twelfth house (self-analysis) trip on everyone else. If you've managed to avoid the trap of your South Node and have really taken a look at society's values (natal eighth house North Node), then taken these ideas to the other people in your life (seventh house) and paid attention to your daily responsibilities (sixth house) you'll reach the fifth house North Node able to develop your own talents and abilities. Besides that, you'll be able to have a good time in your leisure activities, for you won't be preaching empty wisdom to everyone around you.

NORTH NODE IN THE SEVENTH HOUSE, SOUTH NODE IN THE FIRST

You need to reach out to other people and pursue relationships which have stability and continuity. Unfortunately, the South Node in the first house indicates that you often have difficulty seeing things from any point of view other than your own. Since your own personality constantly impinges on your view of other people, you often find that it is easier to function from your South Node position, the position which puts you first. If you succeed in forming close personal relationships with this nodal axis, you have probably learned to function with and grow through your North Node. Self-interest is your worst problem.

Seventh House North Node—First House South Node Progressed to Sixth—Twelfth Houses: When the progression of your chart carries your nodes to the sixth and twelfth houses, you may carry the South Node's "me first" into the cloudy world of solitary thoughts and subconscious or hidden motivations. The more you become involved in examining your own subconscious mind, the more isolated you can become. This is not a particularly easy progression for "everybody knows" that we grow through examining our own subconscious motivations, either through psychology or the study of spiritual development, both twelfth house concerns. You are not one of those "everybodys." Your growth involves paying attention to your daily responsibilities and your daily routine. If you have chosen to balance your self-interest with involvement with others, the progression can indicate that you are able to proceed with your daily grind in a purposeful way and mindful of others.

Seventh House North Node—First House South Node Progressed to Fifth—Eleventh Houses: When your nodes progress to the fifth and eleventh houses, you either recognize your personal talents and abilities, sharing these abilities with the others in your life (back to the natal North Node in the seventh house), or you come to believe that all of the goals you have attained have been reached solely through your own efforts. If the second belief is the strongest, you have chosen to follow the South Node path in your life. You may have little feeling of companionship or kinship with other people.

Seventh House North Node—First House South Node Progressed to Fourth—Tenth Houses: If the progression of your chart brings your North Node to the fourth house of your progressed chart, you will reap the results of a life directed towards others or a life directed towards yourself. Those who have chosen to follow the North node find that the final progression brings self-recognition and family security. If you have chosen to follow the South Node, you now find that although you have career success and recognition, you constantly seek security and sorely miss a family structure.

NORTH NODE IN THE SIXTH HOUSE, SOUTH NODE IN THE TWELFTH

You need to pay attention to the details of day-to-day life if you are to progress and grow in this life. The South Node in the twelfth house indicates that it is very easy for you to get lost in dreams and schemes, escaping everyday realities through an evasive introspection. You may go to great lengths to avoid picky realities. You may spend a great deal of time with different kinds of therapy, formal or informal, trying to find out who you are and in the process sidestep being responsible for your daily activities. If you can develop a sense of value in work and routine, you can transcend the personal irresponsibility symbolized by the South Node in the twelfth house and form a solid base for personal growth.

Sixth House North Node—Twelfth House South Node Progressed to Fifth—Eleventh Houses: When your chart progression brings your nodes to the fifth and eleventh houses, you may need to readjust your goals. If you've stayed with your natal South Node in the twelfth house and meditated on your dragon's tail, you have probably picked up a wonderful vocabulary to cover your avoidance of personal responsibility. You can describe all your fears, worries and neuroses, but you still don't cope with doing the wash regularly. Now you can tell everyone in your groups (eleventh house) why you (and they) can't seem to go to work regularly. On the other hand, if you decided that your natal sixth house *is* your growth area, you aren't too worried about your subconscious motivations. You've set up your daily routine efficiently enough that you can now develop your creative talents and enjoy your leisure time.

Sixth House North Node—Twelfth House South Node Progressed to Fourth—Tenth Houses: When the progression brings the North Node to the fourth house of the progressed chart and the South Node to the tenth, those of you who forged ahead in life along the North Node path find that you finish things well and that you enjoy the stability of close family ties. Those who have chosen to pursue the easier South Node often find your careers, while successful enough, do not really satisfy you. Unless you can discover your essential worth as it is indicated by the position of your natal North Node, you are constantly unsure of your efforts and always aware of your neuroses (twelfth house natal South Node). This position could be the successful psychologist or therapist whose personal life is complete chaos.

Sixth House North Node—Twelfth House South Node Progressed to Third—Ninth Houses: If the progession of your chart brings your North Node to the third house and the South Node to the ninth house, your experience in communicating will indicate which side of your personality you have chosen to develop. If you can find and communicate your sense of self-worth and the worth of the other people you meet, you have followed your North Node. If you are extremely adept at psychological jargon, but not very good at conversations with other people, you are still stuck with your natal twelfth house South Node. It's really time to let go of those psychological shadows and move into the sunshine. You are probably no more or less neurotic than anyone else.

NORTH NODE IN THE FIFTH HOUSE, SOUTH NODE IN THE ELEVENTH

Anyone without this particular nodal axis in their charts probably feels that this is the easiest natal postion for the nodes. Even if you never choose to exert any effort towards following your North Node, you seem to reach your goals with little interference. This particular axis usually indicates that you are fun to be with, for you do not demand much of yourself or of others. If you choose to follow your North Node and develop all of the talents and abilities that you have, you can grow into a strong sense of self-worth. Even if you don't choose to develop your talents completely, you may still attain your goals, but with little sense of achievement. While accepting the success of your halfhearted efforts, you may feel

> Life's but a walking shadow, a poor player
> That struts and frets his hour upon the stage,
> And then is heard no more; it is a tale
> Told by an idiot, full of sound and fury,
> Signifying nothing.
>
> Shakespeare, *Macbeth*

Fifth House North Node—Eleventh House South Node Progressed to Fourth—Tenth Houses: When the progression of your chart brings your nodes to the fourth and tenth houses, you realize that gaining recognition and attaining your goals are not enough. If you have chosen to develop your fifth house North Node through your talents, you don't need other people to tell you that you are talented. You know it. If you have never worked to perfect your abilities, you feel that the praise is offered by fools, for you know that you've never really tried to do any of these things well. You may be able to cover your talents with the label "hobby," thus allowing yourself to drift about without fully developing your abilities. This then makes it possible for you to blame your career for your decision to ignore your talents.

Fifth House North Node—Eleventh House South Node Progressed to Third—Ninth Houses: When your progressed chart has the North Node in the third and the South Node in the ninth house, those who have chosen to slide along with your South Node often find your philosophy of life (ninth house) colored by the talents you never chose to develop. Whether you decide to blame this on the demands of your career or on the necessity for "getting ahead" in life, you find it difficult to accept or justify any success or praise for your poorly developed talents. In contrast, those who have chosen to work with the North Node side of your personality now discover that it is easy to communicate your talents to others. You can enjoy the success of your efforts through recognition by close associates.

Fifth House North Node—Eleventh House South Node Progressed to Second—Eighth Houses: If the progression of your chart brings the North Node to the second house and the South Node to the eighth house, your growth now involves values systems, either your own (second house) or society's (eighth house). If you have pursued your North Node, you find that your personal values are oriented towards creative self-development. You admire and identify with self-realized personalities, rejecting the values of a society geared towards material success. But if you have followed your natal South Node in the eleventh house, you find it difficult to separate your own values from the values of those around you. You may feel tugged back and forth as the fashions change concerning what is really important.

NORTH NODE IN THE FOURTH HOUSE, SOUTH NODE IN THE TENTH

Although you may have relatively easy success in a career, you cannot recognize your own self-worth unless you consciously seek to develop it through the fourth house. If you can balance your career and your home, bringing to your family the success and peace which you seek, you will be able to satisfy yourself in the long run. If you choose to ignore your North Node in the fourth house and allow your home to disintegrate while you seek career success, you will be pursued by a demon of your own making, a demon that insists that your success is never enough. You may be seeking a "Daddy" figure through your South Node, a figure who will tell you that you are all right. Until you realize that you are the only one who can approve or disapprove of your life, you can never achieve enough to satisfy your need for approval.

Fourth House North Node—Tenth House South Node Progressed to Third—Ninth Houses: When the progression of your chart brings your North Node to your third house and your South Node to your eleventh house, you who have followed the South Node may try to hide your insecurities by learning more, travelling more, or embracing a new philosophy or religion. If you have chosen to develop the North Node side of yourself, you now begin to sharpen your ability to communicate with the people around you.

Fourth House North Node—Tenth House South Node Progressed to Second—Eighth Houses: When your chart progression brings your nodes to the second and eighth houses, you have begun to define your self-worth either in terms of personal values (North Node in the progressed second house) or in terms of other people's values (eighth house South Node). The North Node path leads to strong values and personal rewards, while the South Node path always brings you to someone else who does any task better than you can. An alternate expression of the eighth house South Node may involve marrying or depending on someone who has more (fill in the blank, money, power, prestige) which then forces you to conform to that person's value system.

Fourth House North Node—Tenth House South Node Progressed to First—Seventh Houses: If your chart progression brings your nodes to the first and seventh houses, this indicates the completion of either the undirected life (dominated by others, South Node in the seventh) or the self-directed life (leading others, North Node in the first). If you have developed a sense of personal worth through your natal North Node in the fourth house, you find that leadership positions come rather easily later in life. Those who have never followed the North Node may complain about the dictates of others, but usually follow these demands because it is the easier way out.

NORTH NODE IN THE THIRD HOUSE, SOUTH NODE IN THE NINTH

You need to learn how to communicate effectively. Your South Node in the ninth house indicates that philosophy and higher learning are easy for you. This very ease can set up barriers in interpersonal communication, for you often inject jargon into conversations, making it difficult for others to understand you. In truth, you may not understand these high-flown phrases either, but the use of them points out your erudition. If you will take the time and effort to communicate with other people instead of with ideas and ideals, you can reap the best of the world of philosophy and the world of people.

Third House North Node—Ninth House South Node Progressed to Second—Eighth Houses: If you've stayed in your natal ninth house South node and turned every conversation into a philosophical discourse, you may now find that you have not formed any personal value system. You may try to adopt society's values or the values of a partner or spouse, but when these values conflict, you'll have a problem because you don't know what you think is important. You may find that you establish communication through sex, which tends to limit your relationships. If you've worked on your communication skills (natal North Node in the third), you'll find the transition easier, for you will have a better grasp on what you think. In this case you won't have much confusion about the relative importance of security, possessions, money or sex in your life.

Third House North Node—Ninth House South Node Progressed to First—Seventh Houses: When the progression of your chart carries your nodes to the first and seventh houses, you may completely abandon any attempts to communicate with others or you may develop the ability to lead others. Those who have developed your North Node ability to communicate find that this has brought you to a position of leadership. If you have not developed your North Node, you may find that after your South Node reaches the seventh house in your progressed chart, other people demand your attention and your help without giving you any recognition or even any thanks for your efforts.

Third House North Node—Ninth House South Node Progressed to Twelfth—Sixth Houses: If you chose to follow your South Node, preferring ideas to people, you now find that it is necessary to fuss with these ideas and philosophies constantly, adjusting and readjusting them to catch a glimpse of the spirituality you so desperately seek. In constrast, if you chose to learn how to communicate with those around you, you now find a path to spiritual enlightenment, although you would probably not presume to call your philosophy of life "spiritual."

NORTH NODE IN THE SECOND HOUSE, SOUTH NODE IN THE EIGHTH

You can achieve material success and an enduring sense of values only if you are willing to let go of the values of others. This is not easy, for when you have your South Node in the eighth house, other people are usually willing to support you, particularly in a material sense. However, accepting this support requires accepting the values of the person or people giving the support. Alternately, you may become involved in many sexual affairs, shifting your values along with your partners. When this is the path of your South Node, you may have great difficulty establishing any sort of personal value system, for the ease of sexual conquest degrades both your sense of self-worth and your perception of the worth of others.

Second House North Node—Eighth House South Node Progressed to First—Seventh Houses: If you've followed your natal eighth house South Node and have never developed a personal value system (second house), you'll find that your dependence on others increases as the South Node enters your seventh house. Unless you go back to your natal North Node in your second house to clarify your priorities, you won't be able to use your first house North Node to lead others. As long as you are content to be supported by others, you will find that they dominate your life.

Second House North Node—Eighth House South Node Progressed to Twelfth—Sixth Houses: When the progression of your chart brings your North Node to the twelfth house and the South Node to the sixth house, you can justify or at least ignore a weak value system by immersing yourself in the details of day-to-day life. If you have followed your natal South Node in the eighth house and accepted the values of others, you may now be stuck in the position of servant to the people (or person) who support(s) you. If you have chosen to pursue your natal North Node in the second house, you find justification of your value system unnecessary, for you have established your own internal values. In this case, the progression of the North Node to the twelfth house can indicate a growing spiritual awareness and/or a growing desire to help other people out of their own unconscious traps.

Second House North Node—Eighth House South Node Progressed to Eleventh—Fifth Houses: If the progression of your chart brings your nodes to the eleventh and fifth houses, you may find that this position seems to return you to your natal dilemma. If you have relied on your South Node expression, the fifth house position of the South Node may indicate an intensification of your search for a perfect romance or may indicate that you are looking for fun and games in all of your activities. Meanwhile, you may abandon any pretext of goal orientation as you take on the role of social butterfly. If you have developed your North Node in the second house, you find that your sense of value and self-worth is enhanced by your realization of eleventh house goals. You may be the people who attain the wisdom that ancient astrologers assigned to the eleventh house.

5

PROOF
OF THE PUDDING:

LOOKING AT AN EXAMPLE

READING PROGRESSIONS

BEGIN WITH THE NATAL CHART

This chapter really *is* the proof of the pudding! Reading progressions for other people, or for yourself, requires practice. Before looking at the progressed charts, we need to look at the natal chart to get some background information about the natal characteristics. We won't do an indepth analysis of the natal,[31] but you have to start with it when you read progressions. It is also important that you understand how I analyze a chart, so you can follow me later when we discuss the progressed aspects.

I'm using the chart of a client I know quite well, for it's easy to provide accurate information about her background, life experience, and example progressions we shall discuss. Her natal chart, as well as progressed charts for her marriage and subsequent separation, are included. The event charts were not calculated ahead of time by an astrologer.

Before we begin to discuss the natal chart, I would like to share some information about Marjorie Singer's background. She is a white Anglo-Saxon Protestant, born into an upper middle class family in New England. She has a B.S. in nursing, although she doesn't always choose to work as a nurse, and attended Harvard Divinity School for two years. She sometimes sings in nightclubs with a band, and sometimes sings and plays the piano. She had a nervous breakdown, described on page 51. She married in 1974, separated in 1982, and has two children.

---

[31] In-depth delineations of natal sign placements can be found in: Hone, Margaret, *Modern Textbook of Astrology*, L. N. Fowler & Co., London, England, 1970; Sakoian, Frances, and Acker, Louis, *The Astrologer's Handbook*, Harper & Row, New York, 1973.

BRIEF ANALYSIS OF THE NATAL CHART

The first thing I noticed about Marjorie's chart (Chart 33) is the Sun—all alone in Capricorn. Whenever someone has a singleton Sun (the only planet in the sign) it signifies a difficulty reconciling the inner self with the self seen by the world. The Sun symbolizes the true essence of any life on earth, hence the inner self of each person. Marjorie, with Mercury in Aquarius, won't let others know her well, nor will she know herself very easily. Mercury is exalted in Aquarius, so Marjorie will be able to express her thoughts clearly, but this very clarity obscures her very real problem of accepting her underlying Capricorn self. Both Capricorn and Aquarius have Saturn overtones (Saturn is the traditional ruler of Aquarius) which could help Marjorie form an identity system. However, she'll have to watch out for rigidity of thought, a by-product of Saturn.

Marjorie has the majority of her planets in cardinal fire (Aries signature) which supports the cardinality of her Sun sign. Her Moon and Ascendant are in Sagittarius, supported by the fire symbolism of the signature, yet not the same as the signature. Marjorie wants to be more aggressive, quick, decisive. She'll try to overcome both the inherent conservatism of the Capricorn Sun and the indecision of the Sagittarius influence. The Aries ideal self allows her plenty of room to dislike or distrust the manner in which she expresses herself in the world by providing an idealized self who does not vacillate or fear failure.

Marjorie's Sun is in a yin sign, her Moon and Ascendant yang. She will behave in an outgoing, yang manner, since the yang polarity predominates. She can express her emotions clearly, for not only is the Moon the same polarity as the Ascendant, it is in the same sign and in the first house. The difference in polarity between the Sun and the Ascendant increases her problems in determining (or showing) exactly who she is.

Since her natal Moon is in the first house, she tends to absorb the emotions of the people around her. She greets the world in a yang fashion, acting on, rather than reacting to, environmental stimuli.

There are five planets above the horizon, and five below, symbolizing a balance between extroversion and introversion. There are six planets in the eastern hemisphere and four in the western. The numbers alone suggest a pretty even balance between self-direction and sensitivity to the needs of others, but both Sun and Moon are in the east. This plus the slight numerical advantage tips the balance towards action based upon her own wants and needs rather than the needs of the others in her life.

This chart is a locomotive shape (110° between Mars and Jupiter are close enough to a trine for chart shaping). A locomotive chart yields energy along a single track, the track determined by the leading planet in a clockwise direction. Jupiter exalted in Cancer in the eighth

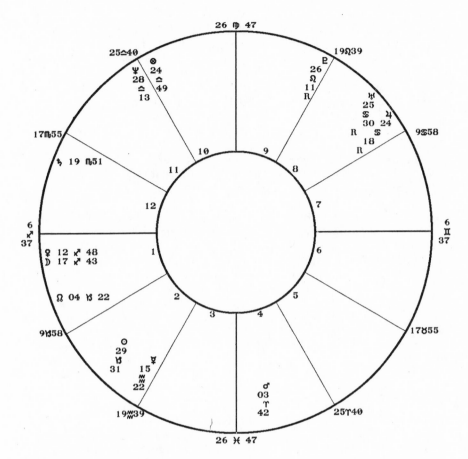

Chart 33. Marjorie Singer: January 20, 1955, 3:45 AM EST, 44N01, 73W10; data from hospital records; Placidus houses.

house leads this chart. Idealism, optimism, faith, concern with religion (the eighth house is death and afterlife) are the positive manifestations of this position. Overt sexuality, living off the money of others, self-indulgence or religious fanaticism are the most negative manifestations. Marjorie's life usually falls between these extremes, occasionally swinging towards one or the other.

Pluto is the planet closest to the Midheaven. Marjorie will dominate and manipulate to achieve her own direction in life. She has undergone transformation several times during her life. The combination of Jupiter leading the locomotive and Pluto accidentally dignified in the ninth house adds to the possibility of fanatical religious views.

The only planet Marjorie has in the sign that it rules is Mars, alone in Aries. This indicates an ability to act impulsively giving little consideration to cause and effect or logic. We have to look at the aspects of Mars to see how it is integrated in her life. Fortunately, the closest aspect is a sextile to Marjorie's Sun. Thus her energy, drive, and ambition hook into her sense of self (no matter how confused or isolated that sense of self may be). The square between Mars and her North Node shows that she often thwarts her own progress towards the growth symbolized by the nodal axis. She may find it difficult to work with others as the nodal axis also shows connections with other people.

Jupiter and the Moon are in mutual reception, (i.e., each is in the sign the other rules) and are biquintile. A mutual reception works a bit like a conjunction, in that anything affecting one of the planets brings in overtones of the other. The biquintile aspect (a minor fifth harmonic aspect) signifies creativity but can mean stubborn adherence to an unusual manifestation of the energies of the two planets involved. Jupiter exalted in Cancer is slightly more powerful in both mutual reception and the aspect. Thus Jupiter enlarges every emotional exchange, adds idealism, faith and optimism to emotion. Marjorie has never had (and probably never will) a small emotional involvement! The Moon in Sagittarius tends to seek larger than life solutions to emotional problems by nature, and the mutual reception heightens this inclination.

Next, we'll look at the tightest major aspect pattern in the natal chart, a T-square. The Sun squares Neptune and opposes the Jupiter-Uranus conjunction, which also squares Neptune. Within this pattern, the closest aspect is the Uranus—Jupiter conjunction (1°12') but the Sun-Neptune square at 1°18' from exact is stronger because it involves a "light." The Sun-Neptune square tends to obscure Marjorie's ability to see herself realistically, which further increases the identity problems arising from Marjorie's singleton Sun, Sun-signature difference, and polarity difference between the Sun and the Ascendant. Neptune, placed higher in the chart (closer to the MC), is slightly stronger than the Sun. This means that Marjorie would like to see herself as someone with many Neptunian traits (specifically as a musician or as a spiritual leader or both). However, this very desire causes internal tension, for the aspect linking these two planets is a square.

Because Jupiter is exalted in Cancer, it dominates the Jupiter-Uranus conjunction in the eighth house. The conjunction indicates a willingness to rebel against (eighth house) values of other people or society. Jupiter's influence adds the possibility of enlarging this rebelliousness (or justifying it) through idealism or religion. Jupiter in the eighth house often indicates an inheritance, and in this chart Jupiter trines Saturn, ruler of the second house, making an inheritance very likely. (Although Saturn may restrict the terms of the inheritance, it isn't likely to deny it for the aspect is a trine.)

The square between the Jupiter-Uranus conjunction and Neptune indicates confusion between the areas of personal growth, creativity and spiritual development. Expanding into music (which is Marjorie's creative outlet) all too often involves expanding into heavy use of alchohol and marijuana.

The opposition of Marjorie's Sun to the Jupiter-Uranus conjunction further strains her ability to trust and believe in herself. This is evidenced in the sudden breaks with the values of other people (or society) which she's experienced in her life. She may ignore her own best interests when she is actively opposing or supporting something. This Uranus self-will opposing the Sun seems to work in Marjorie's life whenever she is thwarted in a desire or direction. Under these circumstances, Marjorie is likely to behave in a particularly outrageous (and potentially self-destructive) manner. This behavior includes such things as writing to the IRS declaring her intention to stop paying income taxes because she opposes military build-up (and she did stop paying taxes, but they haven't done anything yet), and offering to help at her church by getting the church newsletter printed, then including a letter in the newsletter urging all the parishioners to stop paying their taxes. These things made plenty of people angry with her, particularly her husband with whom she was filing a joint tax return. It may not be entirely clear to Marjorie that a large part of the reason she stopped paying taxes was not because of the military build-up but because she wanted to irritate her husband. She sometimes acts out the opposition in a more dangerous fashion by taking off for the closest city and getting drunk and/or stoned (here the negative side of Neptune, focus of the T-square, is also active). Whenever Marjorie rebels against the values of others (or society), this rebellion usually surprises everyone. The square between Marjorie's natal Saturn and natal Mercury inhibits her just enough to mask the Uranian side of Mercury in Aquarius. In addition, the sextiles from Mercury to her Venus-Moon conjunction result in such a pleasant manner than others either don't take her seriously or simply assume she will not act on her complaints.

Now that I've finished a cursory analysis of this chart, I'll move into a more line-by-line analysis, starting at the Ascendant and covering the planets and aspects as they come up house-by-house.

A HOUSE-BY-HOUSE LOOK
AT THE NATAL CHART

The Ascendant symbolizes your interface with your environment, your projected personality. Marjorie has Sagittarius rising, with Venus in Sagittarius conjunct both her Ascendant and her Moon. Venus conjunct the Ascendant usually indicates someone who projects warmth, love, friendliness and harmony. Venus isn't particularly strong in Sagittarius nor is the Moon strong in this sign. Sagittarius scatters much of the affection of Venus and may ever signify a rather idealistic and/or fickle love nature. In a similar fasion, Sagittarius symbolizes scattered emotional responses, diluting the impact of the emotions, as well as idealizing response patterns. Because these two planets are conjunct the Ascendant, they gain a considerable amount of strength, more than making up for the sign weakness. Marjorie forms strong, loving, emotional bonds with all the people around her. She is totally charming and persuasive. Her self-indulgence (Venus conjunct the Ascendant) seems excusable and feminine, when in fact it is often used as a device to get her own way. The Venus conjunct the Ascendant means she will have a pleasant enough manner, regardless of environmental circumstance, to assure some success. The Venus-Moon conjunction sextiles Marjorie's Mercury. She talks easily about love and feelings. The signs involved would indicate an intellectualization of emotion if the Venus-Moon conjunction was not also conjunct the Ascendant. As it stands, Marjorie is not likely to forego feeling in favor of analyzing that feeling.

Marjorie has the North Node in the first house, South Node in the seventh. This indicates that she needs to pay attention to enlarging her own personal impact on the environment. If she follows the easier South Node path, and spends her time backing up a partner or spouse, she will lose her own potential for growth in this life. Notice that the South Node here corresponds to the traditional wife-mother role in American society and the role that Marjorie's own mother played. Here is another wedge between Marjorie's growth imperatives and her essentially conservative Capricorn Sun sign.

The second house has Capricorn on the cusp, indicating a need for a strong, stable value system. Since Marjorie's Sun is in the second, she may value herself according to the amount of money she earns or how well she manifests her personal value system in the world. Mercury in the second means that she thinks a lot about material possessions and/or her underlying values. The combination alone does not tell which will concern Marjorie most. However, tendencies towards materialism will be countered by 1) Jupiter, ruler of the Ascendant, in the eighth house (other people's values) and leader of the locomotive chart; 2) Mercury, exalted in Aquarius, where her conscious mind is strongly inclined towards humanistic ideals; and 3) the ruler of the second house (Saturn) is placed in the twelfth house of subconscious or unrecognized areas of life. When the ruler of the second is in the twelfth, a materialistic approach to life is unlikely. This subconscious and subtle modification of second house values and/or materialism is further indicated by the tight square between Marjorie's Sun and Neptune, discussed above.

Mercury is close enough to the third house cusp (4°) to have an influence on the third as well as the second house. Aquarius on the third brings a sense of difference or unconventional thought. People with Aquarius here frequently believe that they do not think like other people. Often they isolate themselves because of this perceived difference. Marjorie, with Mercury close to the cusp of the third, talks about (and thinks about) this difference. Even though she sometimes has to strain to find the points of difference between her way of thinking and the way that other people think, she will do so. She has an intellectual rapport with neighbors and siblings, all the while thinking that she's quite different from them. She vacillates between believing that the difference indicates superiority or inferiority.

With Pisces on the fourth house, Marjorie doesn't have a traditional view of home to counter the third house tendency towards mental isolation from others. Her concepts of home, mother, and finishing things are vague. Her Mars in the fourth house occasionally appears as abrasive behavior at home, but usually manifests in her difficult relationship with her mother. Marjorie sees her mother as a person who escapes reality whenever possible, sliding through life armed with social niceties, which in Marjorie's opinion amount to essentially fradulent relationships. Neptune, ruler of Marjorie's fourth, focusses the T-square discussed above. This adds to the problems she has in her relationship with her mother, because she doesn't see any fourth house matters clearly or realistically. Yet at the same time, the square from Neptune to Marjorie's Sun can surface as an identification with her mother. So Marjorie tries to root out any evidence of her mother's influence upon her. This is yet another part of her identity problem.

The trine from Mars to the Ascendant and the sextile to her Sun show that the expression of energy outside of her home is usually easy. She does have a sesquiquadrate between Mars and Saturn which shows up as erratic timing. She often does not use her energy productively.

Marjorie's fifth house of romance, children, talents and hobbies has Aries on the cusp. She does rush into romantic adventures. She's in a hurry with her hobbies, too. Although the influence of Venus and the Moon conjunct the Ascendant led her to try the traditionally "feminine" hobbies such as knitting and crocheting, the result of these excursions usually is a sweater with no arms.

Marjorie's relationship with her children will be more a product of her Moon-Venus-Ascendant conjunction than her fifth house. She has a need to project a feminine, nurturing, almost "earth mother" image. This image isn't connected to the fifth house or its ruler. Thus, she'll either be the totally devoted super-mom or seem completely unconcerned with the children.

Taurus, on Marjorie's sixth house, is part of the earth triplicity convering second, sixth and tenth houses. Marjorie's BS in nursing fits an earth triplicity as well as the Moon-Venus-Ascendant combination. It does not, however, satisfy the T-square, or the symbolism of Jupiter leading the locomotive, or Pluto accidentally dignified. Marjorie's need to rebel against the values of others (Jupiter-Uranus conjunction opposing the Sun) and her need for creative expression (Neptune focusing this opposition) cannot be satisfied in the socially approved, safe field of nursing. Pluto accidentally dignified shows that Marjorie really does not like to follow orders. She'd much rather be her own boss. Marjorie only works as a nurse occasionally.

Marjorie plays the piano and sings at small bars or with small rock groups. This helps fill out the need for creative self-expression. I'll talk more about this when we get to the eleventh house and Neptune.

Marjorie has Gemini on the seventh. While there is an old belief that Gemini or Pisces on the seventh house symbolized two marriages, I can't corroborate this. Many of my clients are divorced people with other signs on the seventh. This chart would tend to support that belief, but there are many which don't.

Versatility, flexibility and intelligence in a partner are important and evident in Marjorie's life. Because Mercury, the ruler of the seventh, is in the second, Marjorie would also look for security and stability in a person she considered marrying.

Marjorie has Cancer on the cusp of the eighth house and Jupiter conjunct Uranus in the eighth. We've already talked about some of the symbolism of this combination. When I discussed the sexual symbolism of this with Marjorie, she characterized herself as very active sexually (she called herself the "town pump") during her high school years. Not only does she have the Jupiter-Uranus conjunction in the eighth house, but the ruler of the eighth, the Moon, is predominent in her first house. Marjorie projects an easy sensuality.

The ninth house of religion, philosophy, higher education and travel has Leo on the cusp and Pluto in the house. Marjorie's father is a commercial airline pilot. She has travelled extensively. Her religious views are of major importance in her life and transform her approach to many things.

Marjorie has Virgo on the MC. The Midheaven indicates direction in life, both spiritual and material (or career). The tenth house further symbolizes the father, other authority figures, and one's reputation. The father symbolism of the tenth house is shared with Saturn, just as the mother symbolism involves both the fourth house and the Moon. Marjorie's Saturn is in the twelfth, indicating separations from her father. Indeed, Dad was not available much of the time since his career as an airline pilot meant periods of absence alternated with periods of presence in the household. The Virgo symbolism shows up in what Marjorie perceives as a critical nature. Her father's dominance in the home is shown by the yang polarity of Marjorie's Moon and Ascendant. The aspects to Marjorie's Midheaven enlarge the understanding of her relationship with her father. Saturn sextiles the Midheaven, the Sun trines the Midheaven, Jupiter and Uranus sextile the Midheaven. The only difficult aspects to the Midheaven are a wide square from the Moon and a wide opposition from Mars.

Marjorie knows that she can persuade or manipulate Daddy into giving her whatever she wants. No matter how outrageously she acts out her oppositions, Daddy will still come to the rescue. Marjorie will pull this con with other authority figures when necessary. Interestingly, the results are usually positive. When she falls into the Moon square (emotional outbursts) or the Mars opposition (uncontrolled anger) she does not fare as well.

The other major influence on Marjorie's Midheaven comes from the semi-sextiles from Neptune and Pluto. Normally, semi-sextiles are relatively minor aspects which I wouldn't mention in a brief analysis of a chart. In this instance, the Midheaven is almost exactly at the midpoint of the two planets. (The midpoint is 22' of arc from the Midheaven. Not only is the position of Pluto usually only exact to at best 10' of arc, a forty second change in the birth time would place the MC directly on this midpoint.) This pattern personalizes the sextile between Pluto and Neptune, a sextile which almost all of us share. Since Pluto and Neptune have been in sextile position for most of the twentieth century, most astrologers assign this particular sextile a generational meaning dealing with the transformation of spiritual ideals. We are not all the movers or makers of the transformation, but we all share in the effects of the transformation.

In Marjorie's case, the effects of the Pluto-Neptune sextile are not simply those of being alive during this century. Rather, she will face these changes as part of her own choices in life direction. The negative part of this midpoint structure is the possibility of deception (self-deception or deception of others). Sorting reality from fantasy can also be problematical, particularly since Saturn, planet of reality, is tucked away in the twelfth house.

Marjorie's eleventh house of goals, hopes and wishes and groups of people has Libra on the cusp and Neptune, focus of the T-square, in it. Marjorie sets up grand spiritual goals or unrealistic artistic goals for herself. She's comfortable with groups who are either spiritual/psychic/religious or musical/artistic. The artist/musician group includes fairly regular escape (Neptune) through the use of alchohol, grass, or other vehicles.

Marjorie's twelfth house, with Scorpio on the cusp and Saturn in it, does not increase her ability to recognize reality or to accept personal responsibility. She does not acknowledge her own efforts to control the behavior of others. She rationalizes any abdication of responsibility as necessary for spiritual growth. Since the ruler of the twelfth house is in the ninth, she may be entirely correct in these explanations.

Despite all of the difficulties of this chart, Marjorie offers her love and emotions so openly and with such trust that other people love her. She has a charisma which extends beyond the things she does or does not do. People who are extremely critical of her actions melt when actually in her presence—a most remarkable presence.

GOING TO THE ALTAR:

THE SECONDARY CHART ON THE WEDDING DAY

This secondary chart (Chart 34) is for the day Marjorie got married. The wedding was not planned astrologically as Marjorie did not become my client until 1979.[32]

The first thing that I noticed in this secondary chart was progressed Mars 1' of arc from the progressed IC. A change of less than a minute of birth time would put that Mars exactly on the IC. This isn't a wonderful marriage indicator. It's not an aspect that I'd recommend. The IC concerns home, mother, roots and family, and because it opposes the MC, involves career, father, life direction, authority. Mars symbolizes personal energy, aggression, precipitate action, and anger. The combination of Mars and the IC suggests the marriage was, at least in part, a rebellion against parents. The man Marjorie married is ten years older than she. He was one of her teachers in high school.

Marjorie's progressed Venus was 28' of arc from conjunction with her progressed North Node on her marriage day. They conjuncted each other during the first year of marriage. This aspect is lovely for a wedding, for it soothes some of the potential irritation indicated by progressed Mars. The growth symbolism of the North Node can now occur by combining love, harmony and North Node connections to other people, quite appropriate for a marriage. On a mundane level, the conjunction can mean other people give you things (like wedding presents?). Misuse or too much stress on this conjunction can mean self-indulgence and/or manipulation of others.

Of the other aspects within the progressed chart, the closest is the progressed Moon semi-square progressed Uranus, which occurred five days before the marriage day. This aspect adds rebellion to the emotional background, intensifying the Mars-IC symbolism. The semi-square (45°) indicates tension of a hidden sort. Dorothea Lynde calls the semi-square a "stab in the back" aspect because it often surfaces when you least expect it.

Progressed Mercury, in retrograde motion, has passed the trine to progressed Neptune (by 41' or arc) so the extreme of intellectual idealism should have passed. The progressed Sun will not square progressed Saturn for roughly twenty-one months, because the square is 1°38' of arc apart, and the progressed Sun moves about 5' per month. The sobering reality of Saturn won't really intrude on this chart for almost two years.

---

[32] I chose a chart that was not an astrological election for this example, because if the wedding date had been chosen by an astrologer, the example would demonstrate the competence (or, in this case, lack of competence) of the astrologer. Had she been a client at the time, I hope I would have been ethical enough to refuse to do the election for reasons demonstrated by the analysis of the transits.

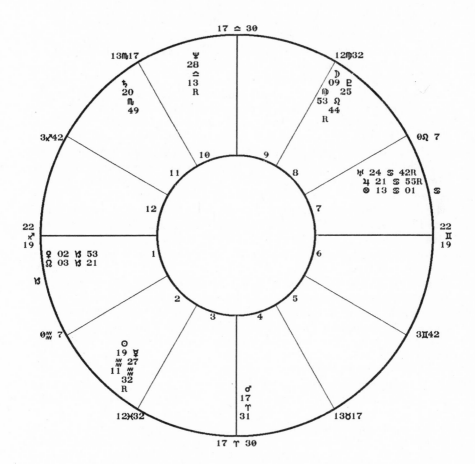

Chart 34. Marjorie Singer: wedding, Chart 33 progressed to June 1, 1974 using the Sun's mean motion in RA for the MC.

Before we compare the aspects between the progressed chart and the natal chart, where the actual marriage indicators will be found, let's look at the changes in Marjorie's progressed chart. Marjorie's progressed Sun has joined natal and progressed Mercury in Aquarius. Marjorie's natal Capricorn Sun, isolated in her birth chart, remains unsupported. Progressed Venus in Capricorn will not reinforce her inner ego structure until it gets much closer to the natal Sun position of 29° Capricorn. Marjorie's decision to marry may be based on what she thinks she "should" do rather than on what she really wants for herself.

Marjorie's progressed Sun in Aquarius actually has much more support than her natal position, for the Uranus-ruled sign calls for action, thought, and steadfast views, all of which harmonize with her natal Mercury in Aquarius. Her progressed internal "I" (her present concept of her inner self) agrees with the way she thinks. Even the natal Sun-Uranus opposition may be easier to rationalize, for her abrupt changes fit better with an Aquarius Sun which encourages new adventures (at least on an intellectual level) than with an essentially conservative Capricorn Sun. She may have a problem with stubborn adherence to the unusual with this combination of natal opposition and progressed sign position. The major difficulty, though, is that Marjorie may now try to obliterate (or ignore) her Capricorn self.

The polarities of Sun, Moon, and Ascendant are still yang-yang-yin, but now her progressed Moon is in a yin sign and Sun and Ascendant are yang. Although the balance is the same as the natal, Marjorie will try to alternate between yin and yang expression of emotion (Moon) and inner self (Sun). This should be positive, for it gives Marjorie an opportunity to utilize both yin and yang modes of action in her life. Since her marriage partner is ten years older than she, it is quite possible that she was transferring her yang masculine side to him, rather than recognizing and owning her own yang projection.

Although Marjorie has no signature in her progressed chart, she has a clear cardinal emphasis with five planets in cardinal signs. Thus, she wants to initiate action, but with three planets in air, three in water, two in earth and two in fire, she can't quite decide between thinking (air) and feeling (water). Most people simply revert to their natal signature when there is none in the secondary. So Marjorie would continue with the Aries dilemma outlined in the natal analysis.

Neptune in the tenth house is accidentally dignified in this progressed chart. Spiritual ideals, music, art, service to others, escape from reality all go along with Neptune closest to the MC. However, the Mars opposition to the MC far outweighs the symbolism of Neptune right now. Until Neptune is closer to the MC than Mars is to the IC, the accidental dignity of Neptune won't really mean much.

The chart shape has changed from locomotive to splash, as there are now only 95° between Mars and Jupiter. Marjorie will have more difficulty focussing herself on any one path now since she scatters her energies. She'll shift back and forth between the symbolism of the natal and progressed charts, questioning some of her goals, becoming disillusioned with others.

With progressed Venus in Capricorn, love is now connected to duty and responsibility, a mixed advantage. The marriage itself could be a manifestation of Venus in Capricorn accepting responsibility in love.

In summary, the background of the progressed chart on Marjorie's wedding day shows that several basic dilemmas of the natal chart have changed, some have become easier, while others have intensified. First, her natal Sun in Capricorn remains unsupported, i.e., she has not resolved her identity as a Capricorn. Second, the cardinal majority (with no clear signature) in the secondary chart means that Marjorie will still see the idealized Aries natal signature as the person she would like to be. Third, the planet accidentally dignified happens to be outweighed by Mars opposing the MC. This can undermine efforts towards both spiritual growth and career direction. The fourth area, the chart shape, scatters rather than consolidates energy use.

COMPARING THE SECONDARY PROGRESSED CHART TO THE NATAL CHART

When we compare the progressed chart to the natal chart, we see three strong marriage indicators. First, Marjorie's progressed Moon is 3° past a square to her natal Ascendant and 3° from squaring her natal Venus. It is 10' of arc from exactly square the midpoint of Ascendant-Venus, which means that the effect of each square (to Venus and to the Ascendant) is maximized while the two squares are connected to each other. Since the progressed Moon moves about 2' per day, it's about five days from exactly square the midpoint. A tiny change in birth data would eliminate the 10' of arc. I consider this the major indicator on this day.

The next two aspects, in order of importance as marriage indicators, are the progressed Midheaven 13' of arc approaching sextile to natal Moon, and progressed Mars 12' of arc approaching trine to natal Moon. The sextile-trine relationship between the MC-Mars opposition and the natal Moon alleviates the outer expression of Mars in that it becomes a major (and apparently favorable) emotional event. The symbolism of rebellion and anger associated with the Mars-MC opposition will not be manifested clearly, as the trine-sextile to the natal Moon allows an acceptable outlet for the energy.

Marjorie's progressed Venus will square her natal Mars in nine months. It's close enough (within a year) to have some effect on her behavior at this time. The square from progressed Venus to Natal Mars isn't a very difficult aspect, for it usually indicates sexual attraction with a possibility of aggressive display with a loved one.[33]

Thus far, the aspects between the progressed and natal charts show emotion (Moon), love (Venus), and sexual energy (Mars). The missing ingredient is Saturn. Without the Saturnian influence of

---

[33] With secondary charts, the orb of influence of an aspect can't be used in the way a natal orb is stated. Translate orbs into time in order to determine the extent of influence. Any aspect more than a year away from exact won't be very prominent in timing events except as background. When you look at aspects with this in mind, you see that the progressed North Node square to natal Mars actually occurred on Feb. 2, 1955, equal to five years before the wedding. Even though the square is 20' of arc apart, it doesn't affect the events of 1974. Likewise, progressed Uranus will not conjunct Marjorie's natal Jupiter until Feb. 20, 1986. So in spite of the fact that this aspect is only 20' of arc away, it does not affect the events of the marriage day.

reality, duty, and responsibility, marriage becomes an adventure rather than a commitment, and the aspects so far delineated equal moving in with someone rather than marrying that person.

Marjorie's progressed Sun will square her natal Saturn in eight months. In five months her progressed Sun will be within 15' of arc of the square. Since the Sun is 30' of arc wide, I consider any aspect to or from the Sun exact from the time it is within 15' of arc before to 15' of arc after it is exact. Any aspect made by the progressed Sun is therefore exact for six months. This square symbolizes personal acceptance of responsibility, quite appropriate for marriage. It also indicates a certain restriction of self-expression and could be interpreted as further rebellion against Daddy.

The aspects between the secondary positions and the natal positions indicate a high probability of marriage. In order of relevance, the major aspects are: progressed Moon square natal Ascendant-Venus midpoint, progressed MC sextile natal Moon, progressed Mars trine natal Moon, progressed Sun square natal Saturn, progressed Venus square natal Mars, progressed Moon semi-square natal Uranus (and natal Uranus/Jupiter midpoint).

The next step in analysis (particularly if you're working on prediction rather than hindsight) involves integrating the transits into the picture created by the combination of natal and secondary analyses.

INTEGRATING THE TRANSITS

PROGRESSIONS AND TRANSITS TOGETHER

If I were working on this chart for a client, I'd now have a good idea that she had a high probability of marriage in late May or early June. When I looked at these transits (Chart 35) I'd have a fit. A quiet fit, all by myself, before the client arrived. Then I'd go fix myself a cup of herbal tea and meditate on why people get married. Then I'd pray a lot. When she arrived, I'd try to discourage the marriage as positively as possible. She'd probably get married anyhow, but at least I'd try to outline some of the possible psychology behind the marriage.

The transits for June 1, 1974, event-oriented as they are, really suggest something major, but I'd expect an accident more than a marriage if I didn't have the secondary chart as background. Since I've got the secondary, and since the secondary points to a marriage during this month, the transits will time it and tell me more about Marjorie's reasoning right now.

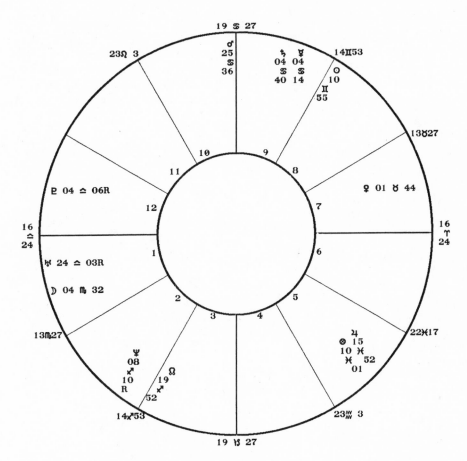

Chart 35. *Marjorie Singer: wedding day transits, June 1, 1974, 3:30 PM EDT, 42N28, 71W21 (approximate time of wedding).*

Marjorie, with her wonderful Ascendant-Venus-Moon conjunction natally would probably convince me that the marriage was created in heaven, the idea was marvelous, my fears were purely negative astrology. I'm glad she wasn't a client. In 1982, when the marriage broke up, she admitted that others had said all these things before she got married. One more person saying this would not have changed a thing. But I'm getting ahead of myself.

If you look at the transits for June 1, 1974, you'll see there are twenty-six major aspects: thirteen difficult, seven easy, and six conjunctions (conjunctions are variable aspects, so I've not included them in either the positive or negative count). The closest transiting aspect is transiting Mars conjunct natal Uranus (6' orb). Mars-Uranus

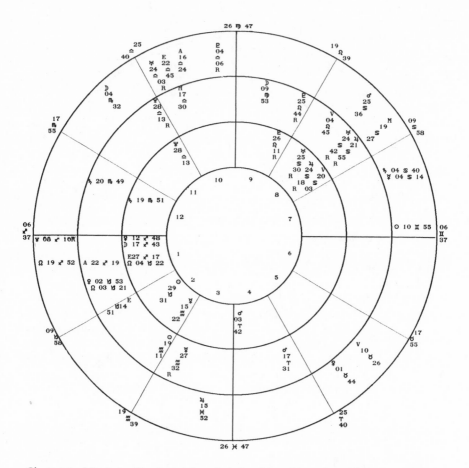

Chart 36. Marjorie Singer: triple wheel for the wedding day. The inner wheel is Marjorie's natal chart. Her progressions are in the middle wheel and her transits on the outer wheel. I find these triple wheels very difficult to read, and the student might find them difficult as well. The information here appears in Charts 33, 34, and 35.

aspects (even the conjunction) tend to be associated with abrupt breaks or changes (or accidents) in your life. This conjunction triggers Marjorie's T-square, activating the opposition to the Sun, the conjunction to Jupiter, the square to Neptune.

Transiting Uranus at 24°♎03′ squares Marjorie's Jupiter (14′ of arc) activating the T-square from the Neptune end. Although Uranus retrograde is moving away from both the square to Marjorie's Sun and the conjunction to her Neptune, it's actively aspecting both through the natal T-square. As if those two were not enough pressure on the T-square, transiting Venus (admittedly, usually a benign influence) is opposing natal Neptune, square the Sun and the Uranus-Jupiter conjunction, forming a grand square. With transiting Venus here, Marjorie really expects the fairytale happily-ever-after romance. She'll do her best to pretend that this marriage provides complete bliss.

Remember that progressed Mars conjuncts the progressed IC and progressed Sun squares natal Saturn. These transits amplify the possibility that marriage provides Marjorie with a form of rebellion or escape from parental restrictions. (For the student's convenience, Marjorie's natal chart, progressions, and transits are shown together in Chart 36.)

The nicest transiting aspect to Marjorie's natal Mars comes from Neptune, a trine. A spiritual interpretation would yield easy motion towards a spiritual end. Another equally valid interpretation indicates easy action with no real understanding of the motivations for that action.

Three other transiting planets aspect Marjorie's natal Mars. Transiting Pluto opposing natal Mars outweighs by a whisker transiting Saturn squaring natal Mars. Transiting Mercury conjunct transiting Saturn (square natal Mars) is like a horsefly at a picnic. Transiting Saturn is the rain at the picnic and transiting Pluto the earthquake. Since Marjorie's natal North Node is at 4°ⱽ22', she has another grand square formed by the combination of transits and natal positions. If you add her progressed Venus at 2°ⱽ53', you see quite a full grand square. The Pluto-Mars-Node configuration indicates that she'll do whatever she darn well pleases, whether it alters any or all of her connections with other people, whether it interferes with her personal growth, whether it annoys or angers anyone. The Saturn-Mercury conjunction, opposing the North Node and square the Mars, shows that she'll talk a lot about accepting responsibility, about sacrificing her own goals for the good of the relationship, but the sesquiquadrate (135°) between her transiting and natal Saturn suggests that there is a question of how much of this duty she'll *really* accept.

It would be hard to imagine more difficult transits for the beginning of a marriage. We are not quite done with the transits, for there are still more. Even though transiting Jupiter trined Marjorie's natal Saturn (which is usually an indication of success, for it signifies patient work towards a goal or clarification of intention), it squared her natal Venus (indicating the possibility of obsessive behavior in love situations) and squared her natal Moon (intensifying or enlarging all emotional responses, as if Marjorie, with her prominant natal Moon symbolism needed any more emotional responses). The only transiting planet that didn't make major difficult aspects to the natal chart was Neptune, planet of unreality. Marjorie's progressed Moon squared that Neptune, clouding present response patterns. Between transiting Jupiter square the natal Moon, progressed Moon square natal Ascendant and Venus and in the sign square natal Moon, and progressed Moon square transiting Neptune, Marjorie's feelings are on automatic pilot, flying through a fog of exaggerated and misunderstood emotion.

EIGHT YEARS LATER:

HOW DID IT WORK?

The marriage survived until 1982. When Marjorie's progressed Moon conjuncted her natal Venus (December 26, 1981), she rekindled an affair with a musician. Although he didn't want to become involved at that time, Marjorie concocted an elaborate fantasy around him. Marjorie separated from her husband on June 28, 1982 (Chart 37). A separation is not easy to time even after the fact, for when exactly does the marriage die? The date on which the physical separation of the two people occurs merely confirms that the marriage is over. As Marjorie's progressed Moon moved from conjunct her natal

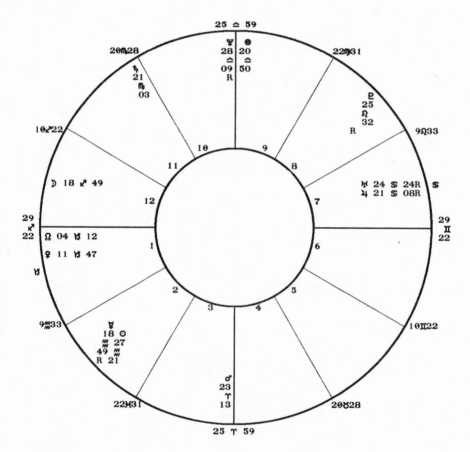

Chart 37. Marjorie Singer: separation, Chart 33 progressed to June 28, 1982 using the Sun's mean motion in RA for the MC.

Ascendant to conjunct her natal Venus (the position it squared when she got married), she became more and more restless with the marriage. Her progressed Moon conjuncted its natal position about a month before the actual separation. Marjorie certainly did make a new beginning in emotional response nature.

Although the progressed Moon is the clearest indicator of timing within this marriage, the progressed Moon aspects alone don't indicate a breakup, for progressed Moon conjunctions (particularly to Venus) are not usually negative. About six months before the separation (30' of arc earlier) her progressed MC squared her natal Uranus. If her birth time were changed by about forty seconds, this square would be exact at the time of separation. The addition of the MC axis to her natal T-square draws her career, direction in life, reputation and

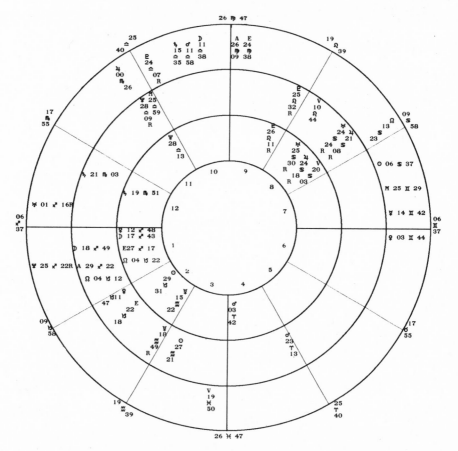

Chart 38. Marjorie Singer: triple wheel including transits and progressions for June 28, 1982 (inner wheel is natal chart).

relationship to authority figures (Daddy figures) into her natal conflict between who she is, how she expands, where she applies her will, and her spiritual beliefs. Progressed Mars is coming closer to squaring her natal Uranus (it's only progressing at 43' a year, so the 1°5' orb means a year and a half before the aspect is exact). When that square is exact, Marjorie's natal T-square will be a grand square, and she'll have to deal with her aggressive behavior patterns. Chart 38 on page 299 shows transiting Pluto at 24°♎07' which pulls in her progressed Mars through an opposition and squares her natal Jupiter (11' arc). The aspects from transiting Pluto to natal Jupiter and progressed Mars indicate the pressure Marjorie felt during the period leading up to the separation. The opposition created a climate of explosive anger, the square implies possible destruction of her own apparent best interest. Pluto also has the property of rebirth, but the changes occurring during Pluto transits are permanent.

HOW TO DO THE MATH:

PROGRESSIONS MADE EASY

HOW TO DO THE MATH

PROGRESSIONS MADE EASY

If there were a standard method of erecting a natal chart, the instructions for erecting a secondary chart would be extremely simple. Unfortunately, in our Uranian independence, we astrologers do astrological math with logs, with calculators, with plain old arithmetic, and all too often by using a formula we neither understand nor follow accurately. Many of us have abandoned math completely, relying on a computer (either through a computer service or our very own micro, programmed by someone else).

As if by diabolical intent, to further complicate what should be simple, there are five different Midheavens which can be calculated for the secondary progressed chart. Four of the five Midheaven calculations will arrive at a Midheaven within a degree or two of each other.

QUOTIDIAN PROGRESSION OF MIDHEAVEN

The fifth method, the Quotidian, moves the MC approximately 361° per year, reasoning that if a day equals a year, then the MC should move as it does in a day or about 361°. This last method is complicated to use unless you have a computer and not terribly useful for prediction because of it's very cumbersome nature. It is, however, a fascinating tool for "hindsight" astrology. When you know the date of an event, you can put up the Quotidian angles and see wonderful correlations for whatever the event was. Mohan Koparkar in his book *Precise Progressed Charts*, uses a method similar to Quotidian angles. Carl

Stahl in *Introduction to Sidereal Astrology* and Fagin and Firebrace in *Primer of Sidereal Astrology* both give the math behind this method.[34] If you want to play with these angles, try these books.

A DEGREE FOR A YEAR

The four other methods of reaching a MC follow. The easiest of the four (and one which only puts you in the ballpark, hardly ever aspected exactly at the time of events) is to add one degree to the natal MC for every year of life elapsed. If you only know the birth time to an approximate hour ("Oh, he was born between three and four A.M.") and you haven't rectified the chart, it's silly to do much more than this. This method is extremely useful for verifying a birth time, because you can add a degree to the MC for each year of life in your head. You can look at the year of a major event, figure out how old the person was, add degrees equal to the age to the natal MC, then see if the progressed MC is within a degree of a major aspect. If it is, you know you've got a pretty accurate birth time.

SOLAR ARC MIDHEAVEN

The next easiest method of determining the progressed MC, and the method usually used by the major computer services unless you specify otherwise, is the solar arc Midheaven. To calculate the solar arc MC, count one day per year from birth in the ephemeris, then subtract the midnight position of the Sun on the day of birth from the midnight position of the Sun on the progressed day. The resulting angle is the solar arc. Add this angle (degrees and minutes) to the natal Midheaven. The result is the solar arc Midheaven. (If you're still using a noon ephemeris, use the noon positions on the Sun.)

NAIBOD ARC
(SUN'S MEAN MOTION IN RIGHT ASCENSION)

The next method of getting the MC is called the Naibod arc, or the Sun's mean motion in right ascension. This method averages the Sun's motion along the equator, adding about 3'57" per day. This is the same as the change in sidereal time on successive midnights (or noons). This is a method available from most major astrological computing outfits. For two reasons, all of the charts in this book use the Sun's mean motion in right ascension to progress the MC. Not only can all of you

---

[34] See Koparker, Mohan, *Precise Progressed Charts*, Mohan Enterprises, Rochester, New York, 1976; Stahl, Carl, *Introduction to Sidereal Astrology*, Stahl, Bay City, Michigan, 1969; Fagin, Cyril, and Firebrace, R. C., *Primer of Sidereal Astrology*, Littlejohn Publications, Isabella, Missouri, 1973.

get this method of progression from most astrological computing services, it arrives at the same MC as the next method.

TRADITIONAL METHOD (MEAN SIDEREAL TIME)

This method gives the Midheaven for the person's birthday every year. Simply put up a natal chart for the time and place of birth on the progressed day. Do the houses exactly as you would for a natal chart, changing only the sidereal time from that of the birthday to that of the day as many days after birth as years old the person is at the time of the progression. For someone who is fifteen, count fifteen days after birth. For someone who is thirty, count thirty days, and so on. The only reason this method is more difficult is that you have to erect another chart. If you have a computer, you just tell the computer to put up a new natal chart for the progressed date. The computer will never know you just fooled it into doing a progression. The chart it gives you will be the progressed chart for the birthday. I've engaged in many a friendly argument (and a few not so friendly fights) with adherents of the solar arc method of progressing the MC. I've used both this MC and the mean sidereal time MC in ninety degree work since 1974. I found that the mean sidereal time MC was more likely to be directly aspected (within 5' of arc) when events occurred, although the solar arc MC was usually within a degree. Unless you're using the ninety degree dial with your secondaries, you probably won't care about the small discrepancy. Again, unless you're pretty sure of the accuracy of the birth time, there is not much reason to do the extra work to get the mean sidereal time MC.

There you have all of the ways that I know to cast the houses for the progressed chart. The next step involves figuring out where the planets are at any time during the progressed year.

THE ADJUSTED CALCULATION DATE

It's often useful to know on which day the ephemeris positions will be exact for any person. If each day equals a year, then at some point during the year the ephemeris positions will be right. So rather than do a lot of arithmetic to figure out where the planets are, say on the birthday, why not figure out what day equals the ephemeris positions? Then you won't have to do any arithmetic for that day. It's nice to know this even if you have a computer, because sometimes you just want to look up what's going on without the bother of going through a lot of charts. If you know what day during the progressed year equals the ephemeris positions, you can get a quick fix on timing the events of the year.

Just as in the MC calculations, there are several methods of arriving at the right day, which is usually called the adjusted calculation date or ACD. Some people call it the limiting date. I don't think there's anything special or magic about the day itself; it's just an astrological convenience.

The easiest method of finding the ACD is not, of course, the method I use. That has nothing to do with accuracy, but with the way I was taught. Since I used the method I was taught for about eight years before I learned the easier way, I can never remember the easier way. I hope you learn the easier method first and always forget the method I use. This method is given in Marcia Moore's book *Astrology, the Divine Science*[35], although Robert Hand first taught it to me.

CAUTION: Step one, the same in both methods, is the critical step. Over 90 percent of the calculating errors which occur in finding the ACD are due to either skipping this step or doing it incorrectly.

1. Change the birth time to GMT. First, change your birth time to 24 hour notation. This just means that if you have a P.M. birth, you add 12 hours. Sometimes this is called U.T., or universal time. If the birth was *west* of Greenwich, add the hours (equal to the time zone) to the birth time. If the birth was *east* of Greenwich, subtract the hours (equal to the time zone) to get GMT (Greenwich mean time).

2. Subtract the GMT of birth from the following midnight (or noon).

3. To this answer add the sidereal time for Greenwich (the time given in the ephemeris) on the birthday to get the sidereal time of the ACD.

4. For a midnight ephemeris look backwards to the day which has this sidereal time in it. That is the ACD. For a noon ephemeris, look forward in the ephemeris to the day which has this sidereal time in it. (The days should be six months apart for noon and midnight.)

That's all there is to it. Simple, isn't it? If you never learned a way to do the ACD before you read this, *stop here. Go straight to the example.* I'm only including the method I use so that those of you who learned it but forgot exactly how to do it can be refreshed and reassured that it, too, gets the right answer (or very close).

1. CHANGE THE BIRTH TIME TO GMT. First, change your birth time to 24 hour notation. This just means that if you have a P.M. birth, you add twelve hours. Sometimes this is called U.T., or universal time. If the birth was *west* of Greenwich, add the hours (equal to the time

---

35 See Moore, Marcia, *Astrology, the Divine Science*. Arcane Publications, York Harbor, Maine, 1978.

zone) to the birth time. If the birth was *east* of Greenwich, subtract the hours (equal to the time zone) to get GMT (Greenwich mean time).

2. Divide the hours by 2, the minutes by 4.

3. For a midnight ephemeris or a noon ephemeris and a birth *after* noon, subtract the hours ÷ 2 from the month of birth, and the minutes ÷ 4 from the day of birth. The resulting day is the ACD. For a noon ephemeris and a birth *before* noon, add the hours ÷ 2 to the month of birth and the minutes ÷ 4 to the day of birth. The resulting day is the ACD.

The only reason that this gets complicated is that it sometimes runs into the previous year. That's really obvious with the first method, but not always obvious with the second. Now I'll run through an example, using both methods, so that you can see how they work.

EXAMPLE

John Doe, May 5, 1955, 14:30 GMT

```
 24 hrs  00 min
-14 hrs  30 min
─────────────────
  9 hrs  30 min (is your answer)
```

```
 14 hrs 48 min 22 sec (= the sidereal time for midnight, 5/5/55.)
+ 9 hrs 30 min 00 sec
──────────────────────
 23 hrs 78  min 22 sec (is your answer)
```

However, 23 hrs 78 min 22 sec needs to be further converted.

```
60 min = 1 hr, so
78 min = 1 hr 18 min =
24 hrs 18 min 22 sec =
00 hrs 18 min 22 secs (final answer)
```

Whenever you go over 24, you start again at 0 because the days form a circle. When you go back up in the ephemeris to the day that has this sidereal time in it, you have to go all the way back to September 26, 1954 before you find it. So John Doe's ACD is September 26, the *year before.* Suppose you wanted to progress John Doe's chart to 1985. You would add 30 days (equal to thirty years) to the birthday. May 5 + 30 days = June 4.(May has 31 days.) The midnight ephemeris positions of the planets on June 4 equal the progressed positions for Sept. 26, 1984. The midnight positions for June 5, 1955 equal the progressed positions on Sept. 26, 1985.

If you were to use the other method, you would follow these steps:

1. 14:30 GMT of birth; 14 ÷ 2 = 7 and 30 ÷ 4 = 7

2. 1955 year   5 month 5 day
   – 7 month 7 day

Since you can't directly subtract 7 days from 5 days or 7 months from 5 months, you have to borrow. 1955 year, 5 month, 5 day = 1954 year, 17 month, 5 day = 1954 year, 16 month, 35 day.

   1954 year 16 month 35 day
   – 7 month   7 day
   _____
   1954 year   9 month 28 day

The ACD is September 28, the year before.

The reason the two answers are not precise (two days off) is that in the second method, months are rounded to thirty days each. Not only is the second method more cumbersome, it's not as accurate. So unless you are bound by habit, use the first method.

Now that you've found the ACD, you can *interpolate* to find where the planets are on specific days during the year. You'll want to do this primarily for the progressed Moon, which moves 12 to 15 degrees a year, depending on how close to the earth it is.

Make a list like this on your paper. I'm still using John Doe, so it starts September 26. Of course, your list will start on your ACD.

MOON: SEPT. 26, 1984   _____

OCT. 26, 1984   _____

NOV. 26, 1984   _____

DEC. 26, 1984   _____

JAN. 26, 1985   _____

FEB. 26, 1985   _____

MAR. 26, 1985   _____

APR. 26, 1985   _____

MAY 26, 1985   _____

JUN. 26, 1985   _____

JUL. 26, 1985   _____

AUG. 26, 1985   _____

SEPT. 26, 1985   _____

Write in the Moon's position on June 4, 1955 from the ephemeris next to Sept. 26, 1984. (The position is 25°♍22′8″). Write in the Moon's position on June 5, 1955 next to Sept. 26, 1985. (The Moon's position is 7°♐10′59″.) Now subtract the June 4 position from the June 5 position:

$$
\begin{array}{r}
7°\ ♐\ 10'59'' = 37°\ ♍\ 10'59'' \\
-\ 25°\ ♍\ 22'08'' \\
\hline
11°\ \ \ \ 48'51'' \\
\end{array}
$$

Divide this answer by 12 to get the monthly motion. To divide degrees, minutes and seconds, you need to change them to decimal parts of a degree. To do that, take your hand calculator and divide 51″ by 60 to get decimal parts of a minute. (51 ÷ 60 = .85) Now you have 11°48.85′. Next you divide 48.85 by 60 to get the decimal parts of a degree. (48.85 ÷ 60 = .8142) Now you know that the decimal motion of the Moon in the year is 11.8142°. Divide this by 12 months to get the monthly motion (11.8142 ÷ 12 = .9845°) We'd really be able to use this better if it was in minutes instead of decimal parts of a degree, so multiply this number by 60 to find out the minutes. (0.9845 × 60 = 59.071′) You could quit here, but let's be precise, just for this example. To find the seconds, multiply .071 by 60. (.071 × 60 = 4.25′) So now you know that you have to add 59′4″ per month to get the monthly motion of the moon. Now you can fill in that chart you made earlier.

Moon:				
SEPT. 26, 1984	25°	♍	22′	07″
OCT. 26, 1984	26°	♍	21′	12″
NOV. 26, 1984	27°	♍	20′	16″
DEC. 26, 1984	28°	♍	19′	20″
JAN. 26, 1985	29°	♍	18′	24″
FEB. 26, 1985	00°	♐	17′	28″
MAR. 26, 1985	01°	♐	16′	32″
APR. 26, 1985	02°	♐	15′	36″
MAY 26, 1985	03°	♐	14′	40″
JUN. 26, 1985	04°	♐	13′	44″
JUL. 26, 1985	05°	♐	12′	48″
AUG. 26, 1985	06°	♐	11′	52″
SEPT. 26, 1985	07°	♐	10′	58″ (Ephemeris = 7° ♐ 10′ 59″)

You can interpolate all of the rest of the planets just like this if you want to.

There is just one more thing which can help you utilize your tools with maximum effectiveness. Some ephemerides have an aspectarian at the bottom of each page. It's a shame not to use this aspectarian to get the day that progressed aspects are exact, since it isn't too hard.

If one year = 24 hours, then 12 months = 24 hours and 1 month = 2 hours, and 15 days = 1 hour = 60 minutes. 1 day = 4 minutes. Are you with me? According to the aspectarian for June 4, 1955, the Moon trined Jupiter at 6:02 A.M. Six hours equal three months. (1 month = 2 hours) Two minutes isn't even a day, so we forget it. Add three months to the ACD (Sept. 26, remember?) and you get Dec. 26, 1984. That's when John Doe's progressed Moon will trine his progressed Jupiter. Another major aspect that occurs on June 4 is Moon inconjunct Mars, which happens at 10:33 P.M. Change that to 24 hour notation by adding 12 hours, so you don't get all mixed up, that is, 22:33.

22 hours equals 11 months (22 ÷ 2).
33 minutes equals 8 days (33 ÷ 4).
Sept. 26, 1984 plus 11 months 8 days = Sept. 3, 1985.

That's when John Doe's progressed Moon will be inconjunct his progressed Mars and he'll pick a fight with some woman in his life.

BIBLIOGRAPHY

Bowlby, John, *Maternal Deprivation*. Basic Books, New York, 1969

DeLuce, Robert, *Complete Method of Prediction*. DeLuce Publishing, Los Angeles, California, 1935

Doane, Doris Chase, *Progressions in Action*. American Federation of Astrologers, Tempe, Arizona, 1977

Dobyns, Zipporah, *The Node Book*. TIA Publications, Los Angeles, California, 1973

———, *Progressions, Directions, and Rectification*. TIA Publications, Los Angeles, California, 1975

Dobyns, Zipporah, and Roof, Nancy, *The Astrologer's Casebook*. TIA Publications, Los Angeles, California, 1973

Fagin, Cyril, and Firebrace, R.C., *Primer of Sidereal Astrology*. Littlejohn Publications, Isabella, Missouri, 1973

Gauquelin, Michel, *Planetary Heredity*. Paris Planete, Paris, France, 1966

Hand, Robert, *Essays on Astrology*. Para Research, Gloucester, Massachusetts, 1982

———, *Horoscope Symbols*. Para Research, Gloucester, Massachusetts, 1981

———, *Planets in Composite*. Para Research, Gloucester, Massachusetts, 1975

———, *Planets in Transit*. Para Research, Gloucester, Massachusetts, 1976

Hone, Margaret, *Modern Textbook of Astrology*. L.N. Fowler & Co., London, England, 1970

Jones, Marc Edmund, *The Guide to Horoscopic Interpretation*. David McKay, Philadelphia, Pennsylvania, 1972

Koparker, Mohan, *Precise Progressed Charts*. Mohan Enterprises, Rochester, New York, 1976

Lundsted, Betty, *Astrological Insights into Personality*. Astro Computing Services, San Diego, California, 1980

———, *Transits—The Time of Your Life*. Samuel Weiser, Inc., York Beach, Maine, 1981

Milburn, Leigh Hope, *Progressed Horoscope Simplified*. American Federation of Astrologers, Tempe, Arizona, 1936

Moore, Marcia, *Astrology, the Divine Science*. Arcane Publications, York Harbor, Maine, 1978

Pelletier, Robert, *Planets in Aspect*. Para Research, Gloucester, Massachusetts, 1974

Rudhyar, Dane, *The Astrological Houses*. Doubleday, Garden City, New York, 1972

———, *The Astrology of Personality*. Doubleday, Garden City, New York, 1970

Sakoian, Frances, and Acker, Louis, *The Astrologer's Handbook*. Harper & Row, New York, 1973

_____, *Predictive Astrology*. Harper & Row, New York, 1977

Schulman, Martin, *Karmic Astrology, The Moon's Nodes and Reincarnation*. Samuel Weiser, Inc., York Beach, Maine, 1975

Stahl, Carl, *Introduction to Sidereal Astrology*. Stahl, Bay City, Michigan, 1969

Townley, John, *Planets in Love*. Para Research, Gloucester, Massachusetts, 1978

Watters, Barbara, *Sex and the Outer Planets*. Valhalla Paperbacks, Washington, D.C., 1971

INDEX

Page references which are italicized indicate where a reader may find a definition of the term. Definitions which appear in footnotes have been referenced to page and footnote number. Text references are indicated by roman numerals.

A

Accidental Dignity, *106*, 283, 288, 292
ACD (Adjusted Calculation Date), *205*
active, *6*
air, *9*, 25
angular houses, *105*
angular planet, *105*, 147
anima, *6*
animus, *6*
approaching aspect, 14n.4
Ascendant, *4*, *53*, *117*, 285
average node, 260n.30

B

benefic, 110n.17
biquintile, *284*
bowl chart, *78*
bucket chart, *79*
bundle chart, *79*

C

cadent, *19*
cadent houses, 105

cardinal, *9*, 18
conjunction, *52*

D

decanate, 10n.2
Descendant, *127*
detriment, *98*, 147
direct, 147

E

earth, *9*, 25
eastern hemisphere, *66*
element, 7, 9
exaltation, *98*, 149
exalted, 284

F

fall, *98*, 147
feminine, *5*
fire, *9*, 25
fixed, *9*, 19

G

GMT (Greenwich Mean Time), *306*

Nancy Anne Hastings was born January 18, 1945 at 11:20 P.M. EWT in Attleboro, Massachusetts. She was a well-known lecturer and taught astrology to anyone who would listen. She served as president of the New England Astrological Association, executive committee member on the national board for the National Council for Geocosmic Research, president of the Mass Bay Chapter of the NCGR, had a gold card from the American Federation of Astrologers, participated in many conferences held by various organizations in the United States, and served as the clerk at the NCGR until her untimely death in December of 1991. Nancy is—and always will be—even though she is not with us anymore—passionately involved in the subject of astrology. She loved her clients and her students, and wrote this book to help other people become better astrologers. She is also the author of *The Practice of Prediction: An Astrologer's Handbook of Techniques Used to Accurately Forecast the Future.*